THE NATIONAL
GEOGRAPHIC TRAVELER
THAILAND

THE NATIONAL
GEOGRAPHIC TRAVELER

THAILAND

Phil Macdonald & Carl Parkes

Contents

How to use this guide 6–7 About the authors 8
The regions 63–346 Travelwise 347–90
Index 391–97 Credits 398–99

Page 1: Temple
woodcarving detail
Pages 2–3: Procession of
monks with candles
Left: Umbrella painting,
Chiang Mai

How to use this guide

See back flap for keys to text and map symbols

The *National Geographic Traveler* brings you the best of Thailand in text, pictures, and maps. Divided into three main sections, the guide begins with an overview of history and culture. Following are eight regional chapters with featured sites selected by the authors for their particular interest. Each chapter opens with its own contents list.

The sites within the regions are arranged geographically. A map introduces each region, highlighting the featured sites. Several walks and a boat trip, plotted on their own maps, suggest routes for discovering an area. Features and sidebars give intriguing detail on history, culture, and contemporary life.

The final section, Travelwise, lists essential information for the traveler—pretrip planning, special events, getting around, and emergencies—plus offers a selection of hotels, restaurants, shops, activities, and entertainment. A language guide lists useful Thai words and phrases.

To the best of our knowledge, all information is accurate as of the press date. However, it's always advisable to call ahead when possible.

Metric measurements In this book metric equivalents are given in parentheses after imperial measurements.

212

Color coding
Each region is color coded for easy reference. Find the region you want on the map on the front flap, and look for the color flash at the top of the pages of the relevant chapter. Information in **Travelwise** is also color coded to each region.

National Museum
🅜 66 C4
✉ Na Phra That Rd.
☎ 02-215-8173
🕑 Closed Mon.–Tues.
🅢 $
🚌 Air-con bus 8 or 12
⛴ Chao Phraya River Express to Maharat Pier (Tha Maharat)

Visitor information
Practical information for most sites is given in the side column (see key to symbols on back flap). The map reference gives the page number of the map and grid reference. Other details are address, telephone number, days closed, entrance charge in a range from $ (under $4) to $$$$$ (over $25). Other sites have information in italics and parentheses in the text.

TRAVELWISE

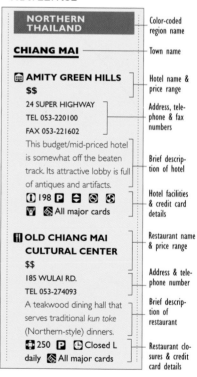

Color-coded region name — **NORTHERN THAILAND**

Town name — **CHIANG MAI**

Hotel name & price range — 🏨 **AMITY GREEN HILLS** **$$**

Address, telephone & fax numbers — 24 SUPER HIGHWAY TEL 053-220100 FAX 053-221602

Brief description of hotel — This budget/mid-priced hotel is somewhat off the beaten track. Its attractive lobby is full of antiques and artifacts.

Hotel facilities & credit card details — ① 198 🅿 🛗 🅢 🅑 📺 💳 All major cards

Restaurant name & price range — 🍴 **OLD CHIANG MAI CULTURAL CENTER** **$$**

Address & telephone number — 185 WULAI RD. TEL 053-274093

Brief description of restaurant — A teakwood dining hall that serves traditional *kun toke* (Northern-style) dinners.

Restaurant closures & credit card details — 🪑 250 🅿 🕑 Closed L daily 💳 All major cards

Hotel & restaurant prices
An explanation of the price ranges used in entries is given in the Hotels & Restaurants section (beginning on p. 356).

REGIONAL MAPS

Road number

Adjacent region

Point of interest

Important featured town

Map reference

- A locator map accompanies each regional map and shows the location of that region in the country.
- Adjacent regions are shown, each with a page reference.

WALKING TOURS

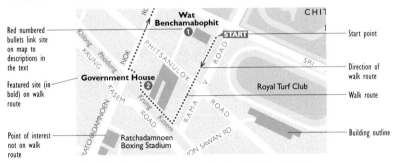

Red numbered bullets link site on map to descriptions in the text

Featured site (in bold) on walk route

Point of interest not on walk route

Start point

Direction of walk route

Walk route

Building outline

- An information box gives the starting and ending points, time and length of walk, and places not to be missed along the route.

TOWN PLANS

Bold in text

Map reference

District name

Canal

Building outline

- A grid facilitates the location of places of interest.

THE NATIONAL
GEOGRAPHIC TRAVELER

THAILAND

About the authors

Phil Macdonald moved to Hong Kong from Sydney, Australia, in 1989 to continue a career in journalism that had begun eight years earlier in the west-coast city of Perth. He worked for the *Hongkong Standard* and *South China Morning Post* for a number of years before settling—by way of Laos and Singapore—in Phuket, Thailand, in 1996. He now lives in Bangkok, working as a freelance journalist and publisher, and contributing to a number of regional publications. His interests include Southeast Asian politics and recent history, and the beaches of Southern Thailand.

Carl Parkes spent his childhood in the United States and Japan, where his love of Asia first began. He now lives in San Francisco. Parkes has written several guidebooks to Southeast Asia and has contributed to numerous magazines and newspapers.

Further contributions to the book were made by Tim and Oi McLachlan, who live in Chiang Mai, Thailand.

History & culture

Reclining Buddha at Bangkok's Wat Pho

Thailand today

THAILAND HAS THE DISTINCTION AMONG SOUTHEAST ASIAN COUNTRIES of never having been colonized. Neither has it suffered civil war nor the racial conflicts that have—at one time or another—plagued other countries in the region. This remarkable feat in an often-volatile part of the world is celebrated in its name: Thailand, or *Prathet Thai*. Translated it means "Land of the Free."

Thailand's escape from the domination of foreign powers for any extended period of time (it did suffer invasions of Burmese and Khmers, and was briefly occupied by the Japanese during World War II) is reflected in the nature of the Thai people. They are fiercely proud and independent. These traits rarely manifest themselves in arrogance or intolerance but rather in self-assuredness, confidence, and a generosity of spirit toward foreigners. Many visitors see Thais as easy-going and fun-loving (which, in the main, they are), but they are also a people who cherish their independence and tenaciously cling to the wonders of their past. Even as— for better or worse—the inevitable onslaught of Western cultural influence leaves its mark on the country, Thais fight to maintain their identity and their uniqueness.

Consequently, you must be prepared to encounter a paradox: an ancient culture juxtaposed against a vibrant and dynamic modern age. The result can be a mixture of exhilaration and confusion, as traditional culture stands its ground against the surge of modernity. Take a look at Bangkok, which, with 8 million people, is by far the country's largest city. Here East does more than meet West—it collides in a thunderous explosion. You'll find traffic jams, bustling crowds, high-rise office towers, a neon-pulsing nightlife, unashamed consumerism in gigantic shopping malls, a fashion-conscious people, and a fair share of street hustlers. Then take another look. Buddhist monks in saffron robes ride the city's modern skytrain. An elephant, being ridden by his handler, lumbers down busy Sukhumvit Road among the BMWs, smoke-spewing, overcrowded buses, and colorful three-wheeled *tuk tuks*. In quiet side streets people make daily food and incense offerings to spirits in doll-size temples set on pedestals. People still greet each other

with a traditional *wai* (hands joined in a prayerlike position in front of the chest and head bowed slightly—see p. 150). Standing next to the highrise office towers, huge, riotously ornate temples, full of gilded images, are constant reminders of the pervading influence of Buddhism in the country.

Thailand's past, represented in its art, architecture, and religion, is in itself reason enough to visit the country. But add to this a surfeit of natural beauty, an ease of traveling to all regions, safety, superb cuisine, and the traditional friendliness and hospitality of the Thai people and you end up with an exceptional country.

THE THAI PERSONALITY

Perhaps better known than "Land of the Free" is the sobriquet "Land of Smiles." Visitors to Thailand are struck by the ubiquity of smiles. But all is not always as it seems. Smiles can mean many things in Thailand. In fact, Thais have managed to label 13 types of smiles, running a gauntlet of emotions from sadness to gloating and despair. There is even a smile for not smiling—*yim mai awk* or "I'm-trying-to-smile-but-I-can't" smile. But generally smiles appear with an easygoing nature born out of a desire for *sanuk* (fun) and a quickly forgiving *mai pen rai* (never mind).

Anything worth doing in Thailand, even the most menial, laborious, and boring of tasks, must contain some element of sanuk, or it is not worth doing. This playful quality—cracking jokes, flirting, singing, playing practical jokes—does not imply that Thais do not work hard or strive to achieve their life's goals; it just means they have a bit

Two sights that will become familiar to all visitors to Bangkok—laughing children and a lavishly adorned *tuk tuk*

of fun along the way. Any activity described as *mai sanuk* (not fun) is anathema.

A shrug of the shoulders followed by the words mai pen rai is a gesture entwined with a Thai's determination to avoid conflict—to save face. The importance of face in Thai society (along with almost all Asian cultures) cannot be understated. Mai pen rai is a term used to cool conflict, to ease embarrassment, to lessen stress, and to play down other difficult situations. When a Thai smiles and laughs after you trip on an uneven pavement and fall down, it is an attempt to save face for all involved, including you.

The country's dominant religion, Buddhism, is a major shaper of this Thai personality, with its precepts of a detached view of life and lack of judgmental attitudes to most actions and human frailties. Buddhism traditionally values respect, quietude, and subtleness. Interpersonal relationships are complex—a legacy of a

complicated pyramid social system that ranks people according to certain values. Generally, social rank is determined by age, wealth (how the wealth is obtained is not always a factor), professional rank, religious merit, and personal and political power. (If you have all or most of these, then you are very near the top of the heap.) This may be not unlike other cultures in the world, but the difference lies in the rigid divide between the levels of social order and the set of obligations that links all

With a population of eight million, Bangkok is Thailand's largest city. Beneath its modern veneer lies an unmistakable Thainess.

members of society. Forget egalitarianism. It does not exist in Thailand. It is almost automatic to defer to someone of higher status and to accord a respect that, in some cases, Westerners would liken to fawning. But in patron–client relationships, in return for respect, those of higher social status are expected to show benevolence to those of lesser rank. For example, if an employee is loyal to a boss, then the boss will, at some stage, be obligated to grant a favor to the employee—perhaps a loan to help with his or her children's education. A Thai learns early in life where he or she stands in this social hierarchy. As a foreign visitor, you will find yourself automatically a good way up the social ladder simply because Thais are gracious and warm hosts. To stay there, you need to maintain the respect afforded you. It's easy enough to do: Simply show respect toward individuals, their beliefs, and their institutions. Voluntarily and freely compliment the country and its people, and you will find yourself even more admired.

The traditional and graceful *wai* with which Thais greet each other may appear to be simple, but this too is tied up in the complicated set of social rules touched on above. There is no need to return a wai: A simple smile and nod of the head will do fine. Often, a hand will be proffered in the Western handshake tradition. Thais address each other by their first names, so don't be surprised if they do the same to you. Your name will usually be preceded by the honorific *khun*—both for male and female. Learn a few words of Thai. The all-purpose greeting *sawadee krap* (used by males) and *sawadee ka* (females), accompanied by a warm smile, is the perfect icebreaker.

BEHAVIOR

Fist-thumping outrage, abuse, and contempt will never get you anywhere in tense situations. But there is another admirable Thai quality that will: *jai yen,* or cool heart. Remain calm in stressful situations. A smile will always get you a lot further than a snarl. What people in the West might regard as constructive criticism of a particular problem or person, when voiced in even a mildly aggressive way, labels you with *jai rorn,* or hot heart. Such direct criticism is often seen as a personal attack, which will mean extreme loss of face. Thais are easygoing, but if tempers fray and face is lost, a darker side of their personality can come to the fore.

The feet are spiritually the lowest part of the body, so it is insulting to point them directly at a Thai. Keep your feet on the ground when sitting, and never point them at anything—to do so is regarded as a grave insult. Always remove your shoes when entering a person's home. Conversely, the head is the most important part of the body; never touch a person (even a child) on the head.

THAIS & THE MONARCHY

Thais relish their nascent democracy and love to gossip and criticize the often outlandish and arrogant behavior of their politicians, and, to a certain extent, they tolerate criticism of their culture (many middle-class and educated Thais find the hierarchal social system anachronistic and stifling). However, they will not abide any criticism of the monarchy. Thais revere their royal

family—it is common to see photographs of the king in prominent positions in shops and homes. Not only is criticism of the institution not tolerated, it is against the law. People have been jailed for the mildest of jibes against the king and other members of the royal family. In honor of king and country, in towns and villages all over Thailand and in some areas of Bangkok, loudspeakers play the national anthem at 8 a.m. and 6 p.m. Thais stop whatever they are doing and stand still, and visitors are expected to do likewise.

LEISURE TIME

Thais are sociable and enjoy gatherings of family, friends, and workmates with relish. Even a work lunchbreak can turn into a mini-party, with plenty of food, laughter, and

Although steeped in gentle tradition, the Songkran festival, celebrated in April, has developed into a full-blown, nationwide water fight.

company. They frequently have get-togethers at the end of the workday, when the partying takes on a more boisterous aspect. If you happen to find yourself involved in a meal with a group of locals, accept their generosity with gratitude. When it comes to paying the bill, offer. If refused, do not insist. On weekends and public holidays, people head to the beaches and national parks for picnics, swimming, and walking. Thailand's national parks can get very crowded, especially those close to Bangkok, so it is best to avoid them during these times.

VISITORS' THAILAND

First stop for most visitors to Thailand is Bangkok, a clamorous, often maddening city that can inspire a gamut of emotions—loathing, despair, humor, and even affection—often all within minutes of each other. The country's political and commercial center, this steamy, chaotic place is hard

A detail from the lively ceramic work at Wat Pho, one of Bangkok's oldest and largest temples

work for the visitor, but its rewards are outstanding. Here you'll find magnificent temples and palaces, world-class restaurants, intriguing museums, and an unrivaled nightlife. The rising sun striking riverside temples along the Chao Phraya river—the city's main watercourse—is one of the great sights of Southeast Asia.

After Bangkok, head to the countryside, a place that both soothes and dazzles. In some cases, you'll find it an almost clichéd reckoning of one's notions of Southeast Asia: extraordinary temples done in wildly flamboyant architectural styles; centuries-old cities of powerful, long-gone empires; fruit-laden boats gently rowed down calm canals; caparisoned elephants heading parades in northern villages; multicolored kites fluttering below clear blue skies; lush paddy fields being worked by plow-pulling oxen; and expansive plantations of rubber trees,

coconut palms, and bananas. Thais turn to their rivers and waterways at the end of the rainy season and Buddhist Lent, celebrating successful harvests on the one hand with partying and raucous boat races and on the other with that most tender and beautiful festival, Loy Krathong (see p. 18), which draws you back to that calmness and graciousness that so often defines Thailand.

In the rich, fertile plains of Central Thailand (and easily reached either on a guided tour or independently—ask at your hotel) are the ancient cities of the Ayutthaya and Sukhothai, remnants of past dynasties whose links to modern-day Thailand remain strongly forged.

Just a few hours from Bangkok on the eastern gulf coast, visitors pour into the hedonistic beach resort of Pattaya. Head there with an open mind. Some travel farther along the coast to the rugged and beautiful island of Ko Chang, Thailand's second largest island and reckoned by some to be the kingdom's next tourist hot spot.

In the north of the country, mountains sweep down from the foothills of the Himalayas. Here hills, valleys, and forests present some of the most dramatic scenery in the country. On the porous borders with Myanmar (Burma), in the north and west, a rugged frontierism pervades. In the northeast, known as Issan, village and farming life remain entrenched, and life moves at a sedate pace. Here, too, lies evidence of a once great civilization—the Khmer. The masterly restored ruins at Phimai and Phanom Rung make a trip to this vast and rarely visited region well worthwhile.

South of Bangkok, the beaches and islands that string along and off the Malay Peninsula are peerless in Asia—sparkling and shimmering tropical gems that are extremely popular with foreign visitors.

FESTIVALS

Hardly a day goes by in Thailand without some town or village celebrating something. You may want to plan your trip to coincide with major festivals (see pp. 385–86). Thais

The simple pleasures of paradise await at Ko Phi Phi, in the far south.

love to party and festivals are mostly lively affairs, with plenty of food, music, dancing, and laughter, often capped off with a beauty contest. The Thai New Year, Songkran, celebrated in April, is perhaps the most famous, when the entire country erupts into a good-natured water fight. Others to look out for include Surin's elephant festival and Phuket's Vegetarian Festival—the country's most unusual, when young men pierce their cheeks with spears. Loy Krathong, held in November to celebrate the end of the rains, is always a delight. Candles are placed on tiny boats crafted from banana leaves and sent afloat by the hundreds of thousands down waterways all over the country. The effect is extraordinary.

TEMPLES

Wats, or temple complexes, especially in small towns or villages, are central to the community. They are places of worship and

gathering places for local people to chat and gossip. Monks have residences there, and they often contain community centers and schools. On some occasions, especially during festivals, they become retail outlets, with market stalls selling all manner of goods.

Such openness can often be misleading to the visitor. Remember, many buildings on temple grounds are sacred places. Always dress neatly—long trousers and shirtsleeves for men, modest dress for women—and take

An archetypal vision of Southeast Asia: Monks collect food from villagers in Northern Thailand at sunrise.

your shoes off when entering a temple. (You will find it best to wear slip-on shoes during your travels.) All Buddha images in Thailand are sacred. Never clamber on an image. If you pose for a photograph in front of one, do so with respect. Sitting in a temple, keep your feet pointed away from any Buddha image. ■

Food & drink

THAILAND IS TRULY BLESSED WHEN IT COMES TO FOOD. IT IS QUITE possible to eat for a month without having to order the same dish twice (indeed, it is highly recommended that you do just that)—though once you have discovered a special favorite you will probably find it becoming a regular choice for awhile.

Eating will be one of the highlights of your stay in Thailand. And, while different regions of Thailand claim certain foods and recipes for their own, you will be able to find amazing dishes from all parts of the kingdom, wherever you are.

Staying at a good class hotel gives reasonable (though not guaranteed) assurance that the restaurant food will be of a high quality, the service will be good, and the menu will be extensive. If you want to pepper your meal with a bit of extra culture, don't be afraid to try the cleaner restaurants frequented by the locals. All restaurants must abide by health regulations as laid down by the local council (this does not apply to street vendors or temporary roadside eateries, which must be approached with caution), and so eating hot stir-fried meals, curries, or soups in a clean restaurant can be regarded as safe.

Avoid dishes that are kept on display (ducks and chickens hanging in glass cabinets, for example), don't accept seafood upcountry, and forget about experimenting with locusts and grasshoppers as the chances are they met their fate by insecticide poisoning.

Thai-style dining is a very sociable affair. Unless the food is served *jarn deeyo* as an individual meal (fried rice or *pad thai*, for example), the main dishes will be placed in the center of the dining table (or, more traditionally, will be laid out on a mat placed on the floor), where everybody is free to ladle small portions onto their own plate of rice as they eat.

STAPLES

Rice *(kow)* is the staple diet, and most meals are served with boiled white rice *(kow suay)*. There are, however, many variations. Rice porridge *(jok)* and rice soup *(kow tom)* make good breakfast dishes, though they are often eaten late in the evening for supper as well. A popular form of rice eaten in the north and northeastern provinces is sticky rice *(kow neeyo)*, which is eaten with the hand and used for dipping into soups and pastes. Fried rice is also very popular and can be ordered in many styles, including chicken *(gai)*, pork *(mu)*, prawn *(gung)*, and vegetarian *(jay)*. Also worth trying is "*kow pud* American," a legacy of American soldiers stationed in Thailand during the Vietnam War. This is undoubtably the mother of all fried rice dishes, made with such special additions as sausages, vegetables, and pineapple—all mixed in with a bit of ketchup and nicely crowned with a fried egg.

Noodles *(phat)*, introduced to Thailand from China, also play a large role in the Thai diet and are served in many forms. One distinctly Thai variety is pad thai (literally, "fried Thai"), a favorite among Thais and travelers alike. Thin noodles are fried with a blend of sweet and bitter sauces, tofu, egg, and dried shrimp to produce a great meal—which will not be complete until you have added the complementary peanuts and a squeeze of lemon.

Another favorite dish is *pad see yoo*, often listed on menus in English as "Chinese-style noodles in soy sauce." Flat noodles are fried together with egg and *kanar* (a popular green vegetable) in soya sauce. Make use of the extra condiments that are usually provided (vinegar, sugar, dried chili powder, and the ever present fish sauce) to create a taste to suit yourself.

REGIONAL SPECIALTIES

The following are the dishes that visitors will come across most often, classified by region.

Central Thailand

Many of the dishes originating from this region use coconut cream *(gati)* and chili paste *(nam prik)* as a base to which vegetables,

Floating markets, like this one at Damnoen Saduak, still form an intrinsic part of community life in the canals near Bangkok.

herbs, and seasonings are added to produce a curry. Most curries include meat.

Gai pud med mamuang himapaan (fried chicken and cashew nuts) Cashews, chicken, and oyster sauce are the main ingredients—a bit exclusive because of the price of the cashew nuts. Complements most Thai dishes well.

Panang (Thai red curry) Usually made with

People from the Northeast enjoy fried cockroaches and other insects as a snack—best avoided by visitors for health reasons.

chicken (gai) or pork (mu). Other ingredients include garlic, red onion, lemon grass, chopped kaffir leaves, basil, and Thai spices.

Tom kar gai (sweet, sour, and spicy chicken soup) Plenty of mushrooms, basil, and galangal root (kar) are blended with other favorite sauces and seasonings to give a very distinctive Thai flavor.

Tom yum gung (sour and spicy prawn soup) In July 1999 a survey by the National Culture Commission of over 500 Thai restaurants worldwide concluded that tom yum gung was the favorite Thai dish—and most Thais would agree with the survey's result.

Yum woon sen (mixed jelly noodles) *Yum* means to mix together—jelly noodles (similar to vermicelli) are mixed with peppers, lemon juice, fish sauce, scallions, parsley, and onion and, usually, either minced pork (pre-boiled) or prawns.

Northern Thailand

Gang hunglay (pork and ginger stew) A combination of ginger, curry powder, and Thai sauces produce a sweet stew usually eaten on rice. Highly recommended.

Kow soi gai (spicy northern chicken curry) An interesting mixture of large pieces of chicken and both soft and crunchy noodles set in a smooth curry. This dish is always hot enough to tickle the back of the throat but has a nice flavor that is both sweet and spicy.

Nam prik ong (mild red chili paste with pork and tomato) You may have difficulty finding this in high-class restaurants, but it is a favorite among locals in the North as it is convenient to eat with sticky rice and makes for a very cheap meal.

There are a surprising number of chili paste styles available in the north (as well as the rest of the country), created by using different types of chili peppers with varying combinations of vegetables, meat, and seasoning. Nam prik ong tends to be one of the milder forms of these pastes—but is probably still best left to chili freaks.

The Northeast (Issan)

Larp (spicy ground meat) Larp is made from cooked ground chicken, pork, beef, or fish and relies on a blend of mint, basil, and other herbs and spices. It is also possible to find water buffalo-flavored larp *(larp kwai)* in rural areas. (For vampires, there is even *larp lueat*, which is raw meat, usually water buffalo, minced with fresh blood and spices.)

Som tam (papaya salad) This is sometimes known as papaya *bok-bok* because of the sound produced by the striking of the pestle against the mortar as the ingredients are pounded together. The primary ingredient is shredded green papaya, mixed in with tomatoes, beans, garlic, miniature dried shrimp, a dash of fish sauce, lemon juice, and honey. This produces a tangy taste, which is characteristic of other Thai dishes. Often a whole crab or two will be thrown in *(som tam pu)*, or, if you prefer something slightly less crunchy, you could order it with peanuts instead *(som tam thai)*. Thais tend to prefer their som tam quite spicy; it is probably a good idea to order som tam without chili peppers, as just one rebellious pepper is enough to ruin an otherwise enjoyable experience. Som tam is eaten with sticky rice and often complemented with grilled chicken *(gai yarng)*, fried pork *(mu yarng)*, and/or larp.

South Thailand

Kow yum This dish relies for its distinctive sweet, sour, and salty flavor on a specially prepared mix of fish sauce, roasted ground coconut, prawns, and a selection of fruit, vegetables, and herbs. It is presented with a bowl of rice, which you stir into the dish. Highly recommended.

Mussamein gai This is a spicy curry popular among Muslims, with chicken and potatoes in a thick *mussamein* sauce—a very satisfying meal, eaten with rice and/or *roti* (flat bread).

FRUIT

There is a vast array of delicious fruit on offer in Thailand, many of which you may never have seen before. Do try to visit at least one fresh fruit and produce market (they are most active in the mornings) during your stay. You'll get some great photo opportunities, and the tantalizing sights, sounds, tastes, and smells make it a truly memorable experience. Well-known fruits that grow year-round and are found in abundance here include bananas *(kluay)*, coconuts *(maphrao)*, watermelon *(taeng moh)*, and pineapples *(sap-parot)*. Other fruits, also available year-round, that are less familiar to visitors, include:

Cantaloop (cantaloupe) Tropical melon, very sweet and juicy when ripe.

Farlung (guava) Thais often eat guava (and mangoes) while they are still unripe, sprinkling them with a mixture of sugar, salt, and ground chili pepper.

Malakor (papaya) The unripe fruit is used in salad (see som tam, p. 22). When ripe, its orange flesh is slightly sweet and very juicy.

Mang-khut (mangosteen) Much prized, sweet white fruit that comes in a hard, purple shell.

Ngor (rambutan) Small, hairy, bright red fruit with sweet, litchi-like flesh.

Som-oh (pomelo) The largest of all citrus fruit, not unlike a large, sweet grapefruit.

Seasonal fruits

Lumyai (longan) A small, round, sweet fruit with a brown shell, grown in the North (predominantly in Chiang Mai) and most widely available during the northern rain season (June–September).

Ma muang (mango) There are many varieties of mango, most of them appearing from April on, through the hotter months. They are often eaten as dessert with sweet sticky rice and coconut milk syrup *(kow neeyo ma-muang)*.

Thais use red-hot chilies to spice up many dishes. Despite their tiny size, these *prik kee noo* are the hottest around.

Toorian (durian) This bizarre-looking fruit has the appearance of a spiky football and a smell that could lose you friends. People love it or hate it—try it for yourself to see what the fuss is about. Mostly available May–June.

DRINK

Some of the fruits available in Thailand are transformed in restaurants into deliciously refreshing juices. Try *naam farlung*, made with guava, or *naam lumyai*, made with longan.

Liquor drinking is traditionally a predominantly male pastime, though as cultural values change, it is becoming quite common to see young women drinking beer (usually Thai-produced Singha beer) or wine. The men generally prefer beer or Thai whiskey, such as Saeng Thip or Mekong—or more expensive, foreign imports if there is a need to uphold social status. ■

People & religion

THAILAND IS ONE OF THE MOST RACIALLY HOMOGENOUS NATIONS IN Southeast Asia. Of a total population of 60 million, about 80 percent are ethnic Thai. There are significant numbers of ethnic Chinese, with a smaller population of Malays found mainly in the south of the country. Cambodian, Burmese, and Vietnamese immigrants make up smaller groups, and numerous settlements of indigenous hill tribes are found in the north of Thailand.

Ethnic Thais speak four dialects, which correspond to the country's four geographic regions: Central, Northeastern, Northern, and Southern. The Central Thais of the Chao Phraya Basin compose about 36 percent of the ethnic Thai population and are the dominant social and political group. The Central Thai dialect is considered "standard" Thai language and is the medium for education. It is the language of television and radio and is used for communication between Thais from different regions. The Northeastern Thai (32 percent of ethnic Thais) of the Issan region are large in number but are perhaps the most politically and socially underrepresented in the country. Their dialect is a colorful mixture of the Thai and Laotian languages. The Northern Thais make up about eight percent of the ethnic Thai population, while the Thai Pak Tai of Southern Thailand—from Bangkok south to the Malaysian border—consider themselves a people apart, with distinctive forms of culture and a crisp and quick-talking native tongue. They also make up about eight percent of the ethnic Thai population. In addition, there are about ten interregional dialects spoken by Thais in certain pockets of the country.

BUDDHISM

While each regional group speaks its own language and, to an extent, practices customs unique to its area, Thai culture and social values entwine all Thais— including most of the ethnic minorities. General acceptance, albeit sometimes grudging, of ethnic minorities, and their inclusion in most aspects of Thai culture can, to a large degree, be attributed to the tolerant and nonjudgmental precepts that are essential to Buddhism.

About 95 percent of the population profess to be Theravada Buddhist, the official religion. It forms the core of modern Thai culture, dominating many aspects of daily life. Thailand's relatively harmonious society is to a large degree credited to Buddhism and its inherent traditional value systems, which place great emphasis on the sanctity of family, friends, and social harmony.

Buddhism's teachings eschew the notion of an omnipotent god or gods. There is no divine ruler who decides the fate of the individual. In Buddhism, life is not a series of free choices, but rather each person's life is controlled by the karma he or she accumulated in previous lives. It is solely the action of the individual that determines the course of his or her life, and no god can change the effects once humankind has created the causes. Evil conduct cannot be forgiven and must reap its own punishment, while righteous deeds will reap their due rewards.

Thais believe that the fortunate, rich, or powerful obtain their status from a position of superior karma, while the poor and suffering have been cursed with their fate as a result of indiscretions in a previous existence. This notion goes a long way toward explaining the intractable social hierarchy of Thai society. A person who is rich, powerful, or influential is obviously so because of a meritorious past life. His superior karma earns him the right and privilege of deference.

Fundamental to Buddhism is the belief in the Four Noble Truths, discovered by the Buddha at the moment of his enlightenment: All life is suffering; all suffering has a cause

The great majority of the Thai population are Buddhist. There are some 30,000 temples around the country.

in cravings or desire; the suffering can be overcome by eliminating the desire; and the desire can be overcome by following the Eightfold Path. This eight-step recipe for success includes right view, right intention, right speech, right action, right livelihood, right mindfulness, and right concentration. The first two principles of the Eightfold Path concern motivation, the next three address moral code, and the last three concern man's mind for right ends. Salvation occurs when the individual recognizes these eight truths and follows their guidelines to destroy desire, thereby breaking the train of reincarnation. The end result is enlightenment and entrance into a state of nirvana—the ultimate aim. This Eightfold Path is also known as the Middle Way, as it avoids extremes of behavior. An adherent does not have to live an austere life, nor should he or she move to the high-end scale of sensuality.

As a result of their belief in karma and reincarnation, Buddhists refuse to assign moral shame to the actions of an individual. Life is nonjudgmental, and Buddhists neither fear nor look forward to an eternity in heaven or hell. Thus most Thais feel free to behave without guilt, as judgment in their next life will be based on their actions and not on religious dogma.

Buddhism, unlike Christianity, refuses to answer many of the basic questions about the meaning of life, such as human origins or final disposition. Life is seen as an imperma-nent condition filled with contradictory forces that demand no explanation and which are experienced with little attempt at rationalization. Thai Buddhists are largely left alone to determine their own value systems and levels of morality.

To speed their path to nirvana by reducing their number of rebirths, Thais will make merit by feeding monks, giving donations to temples, and making regular appearances at temples for worship. Making merit is an intrinsic part of Thai social behavior. *Wats*, or temple complexes, are central to community life in many towns and villages. To be generous in your dona-tions to your local wat not only speeds your passage to nirvana, but can also increase your social standing in the community.

Buddhist images are cast in a limited number of poses, accorded by Buddhist scriptures.

Buddhists do not keep any particular day of the week for religious observation in the way that followers of Christianity, Islam, or Judaism do. Nor do they celebrate mass or any other type of liturgy presided over by a priest or other religious leader, although they attend discourses of Buddhism given by abbots and will often seek counsel with a monk or nun to discuss life's problems. They are free to visit a wat whenever they like, and they worship personally and individually rather than in groups. Favorite days for visiting their temples tend to be every full moon and new moon, but many Buddhists

will make a visit when good fortune befalls them (for example, on winning the lottery, being given a job promotion, or getting a pay rise) or on their birthday.

Monks

Lines of young monks clasping bowls and making their rounds from house to house collecting alms, donations, and food every morning is a common sight in towns, villages, and cities around the country.

Many visitors to Thailand are surprised at the large number of young men involved in monkhood. Every young man is expected to become a monk for a short period of time. Generally, this is between finishing school or university and finding a job or launching into a career and marrying. Most of these young

men are expected to spend about three months as monks, traditionally accepting their robes in July, at the start of the rainy season. But a majority will stay for only one or two weeks. The reason for this religious conscription is to enhance the young men's knowledge of the teachings of the Buddha and to improve their karma. It is also done to make merit for—and honor—their parents, who see even such a short tenure as an important part of their son's life. Some are ordained for a lifetime.

At any one time in Thailand's 32,000 monasteries there are 200,000 monks. Many of these men dedicate their lives to study and become Buddhist scholars and teachers. Life for a monk is frugal and disciplined; days are spent meditating, studying scriptures, and doing menial tasks around the temple grounds. Despite their austere lives, monks are generally friendly and welcoming to visitors. Some Buddhist monks have a tendency to stray from the path, boasting to gullible followers of supernatural powers assigned to them because of their position. It is common to find monks predicting lottery

Thai boys enter the monkhood to learn about Buddhism—often for only a few months or even weeks.

outcomes, practicing faith healing, selling magical charms, and charging lucrative fees in return for performing marriage and other ceremonies.

Spiritualism

Beyond the world of glittering temples and wandering monks is the underlying fact that Thai Buddhism has never completely superseded earlier beliefs enshrined in Hinduism (from which Buddhism was adapted and refined) and spiritualism. Hindu ceremonies—births, marriages, and funerals—still play an important role in Thai society. Some of the most powerful religious motives are connected with animist beliefs, including the propitiation of spirits, which are called *phi* (pronounced PEE).

Spirit worship in Thailand revolves around these wandering supernatural apparitions, who have the power to bring good fortune. Equally they can inflict great pain if not continually appeased with offerings of food, flowers, and incense. Among the most prevalent and powerful of all phi is the "spirit of the land," who must be provided with a doll-size spirit house (see p. 85) outside a property to compensate for the building of the house on land that belongs to the spirit.

Hinduism and spirit propitiation may not follow strictly in accordance with Buddhist teachings, yet few Thais feel any ideological conflicts between burning incense to honor the Buddha, then making food offerings to placate animist spirits.

Buddhist iconography

Buddhist statues festoon almost every temple in Thailand. A cursory examination gives the impression that they are similar in design, with few indications of original artistry. This uniformity was crafted by Buddhist sculptors, who for centuries followed the physical descriptions of the Buddha as related in ancient Buddhist texts. Bound by tradition, sculptors sought a standard lexicon of symbolism that could easily be understood by pilgrims.

Sculptors also wanted to create reproductions of earlier images that had achieved fame as magical talismans, or were believed capable of performing miracles or providing the pious with supernatural protection. This melding of Buddhist beliefs with the power of the occult served to popularize the religion and provided the mystical link that is so beloved by contemporary Thais.

But look closely and you will see that Buddhist images throughout Thailand share a number of common body positions and hand gestures, known as *mudras* (see pp. 78–79), which symbolically represent important events in the life of the Buddha and reinforce the compassionate nature of the religion.

Buddha images are generally shown as seated, standing, walking, or reclining. The walking position, rarely employed except by the school of Sukhothai (see pp. 202–203), depicts the Buddha descending from Heaven to Earth. The reclining position—also rare—is often employed in very large images, to show the Buddha at the exact moment of entering nirvana. Standing and seated positions are often determined by the mudra. For example, standing images can show the Buddha either granting blessings or subduing evil forces. Sitting Buddha images can represent almost any important event in the life of Buddha, again as indicated by the position of the hands.

THE CHINESE

Several Chinese groups have migrated to Thailand over the past 250 years. The Hokkiens were the first to arrive in significant numbers, in the late 18th century, and made themselves indispensable to the monarchy as tax collectors. They were followed by the Teochews, who arrived poor and dispossessed, but soon used their entrepenurial skills in Bangkok to build their wealth. Northern Thailand opened up to substantial numbers of Hui—Chinese Muslims—in the late 19th century as they escaped religious persecution during the Ch'ing dynasty.

Today, the Chinese, who make up about 11 percent of the population, dominate many sectors of business and commerce in Thailand. There is marginal resentment among ethnic Thais of the Chinese because of their success in business, but it has never resulted in any serious conflict. Nor have legal barriers been imposed—as they have in other countries in Southeast Asia—to hinder the success of ethnic Chinese.

The acceptance of the Chinese in Thai culture has as much to do with the Chinese wish to assimilate as with the traditional tolerance of Thais. Intermarriage has been common since the enlightened reign of King Mongkut (R.1851–1868), who promoted immigration and intermarriage as a means of instilling a strong work ethic—for which the Chinese are famed—into the general population of his country. Rich Chinese merchants

also endeared themselves to the monarchy by offering their daughters to the royal court as consorts! Not only did this please the court but it helped the Chinese develop royal contacts and added a Chinese bloodline that extends to the present king. People of mixed Thai-Chinese descent are also strongly represented in political life.

Thailand's Muslim minority is found mainly in the southern provinces, near the border with Malaysia.

HILL TRIBES OF THE NORTH

The remote hills of Northern Thailand are home to tens of thousands of hill-tribe people. Although they make up only about 2 percent of the population, hill tribes have attracted a huge amount of interest from visitors, thousands of whom make treks to tribal villages each year. Most hill tribes are immigrant groups who came to Thailand from Myanmar (Burma), Laos, and China over the last century. Most are dirt-poor farmers who receive little assistance from the central government. Public services that are available to the average Thai citizen—paved roads, portable water, electricity, sanitation, medical facilities, and education—very rarely find their way to hill-tribe villages.

Hill-tribe people are one group that tests the traditional and much celebrated Thai spirit of tolerance. Most Thais see them as foreign interlopers and as such afford them little respect. Many have lived in Thailand for generations and still have not been granted citizenship. Hill tribes are a marginalized people who are clinging to the very bottom rungs of the social and economic ladders.

The Thai government officially recognizes six major groups of hill tribes (there are about 20 groups in all), based on their languages, faith, social customs, dress, and historical lineage. The Karen, a tribe that numbers about 265,000, is by far Thailand's largest hill-tribe group. While most hill tribes live solely in the northern provinces of Chiang Mai, Chiang Rai, and Mae Hong Son, the Karen trickle south as far Kanchanaburi and Tak Provinces, to the west of Bangkok.

The second largest hill tribe is the Hmong (called Meo by Thais), who came from Laos in the 1950s and 1960s and number about 80,000. Many Hmong in Laos allied with the U.S. military during the Vietnam War. Hmong are much in evidence at Chiang Mai's sprawling night market, where they sell finely crafted silver jewelry and exquisitely embroidered costumes.

The 34,000 Akha have been the most obstinate group as far as assimilation is concerned. The group's villages are popular among foreign visitors chiefly because of the photo opportunities presented by the colorful and highly ornate headdresses worn by the women. These consist of an elaborate collection of old coins, beads, and feathers.

The majority of Lahu (numbering about 60,000) are, like the Karen, Christian, and this group has proved the most successful in adapting to the Thai mainstream. The color-fully costumed Lisu (about 25,000) have become adept at commerce and are accepted as keen businesspeople. Many Mien (also known as Yao) can trace their origins back to Yunnan Province in China. They clad them-selves in distinctive black turbans and red feather boas. Some maintain traditional

Lishu hill-tribe people harvest rice. Hill tribes are popular with visitors, but many of them live in poverty.

Chinese customs, including Taoism and the use of Chinese script.

Hill tribes, along with Vietnamese immigrants, make up the major part of Thailand's Christian community, which accounts for about 0.5 percent of the population. For more on the hill tribes of the north, see pages 234–35.

MUSLIMS OF THE SOUTH

Thailand has over three million Muslims, most clustered in the southern provinces of Satun, Pattani, Yala, and Narathiwat, on the border of predominantly Muslim Malaysia.

Significant populations can also be found in other southern provinces of Phuket, Krabi, Trang, and Songkhla. Most southern Muslims are of Malay descent. Relationships with the majority ethnic Thai have not always been smooth, with Muslims complaining of social and political discrimination over the years. In the past, radical Islamic elements have used these prejudices to garner support for autonomy or even for unification with Malaysia. But throughout the 1990s the Thai government has taken steps to quell dissent, recognizing Islamic laws that are used to resolve disputes over marriage, inheritance, and other family matters and allowing limited use of the Malay *yawi* language as a medium of education in schools.

WOMEN

Thailand's constitution enshrined equal rights for women, but in many aspects of daily life, women—as is the case in many countries—still face discrimination. But over the past few decades women have made giant strides in attaining equality. Half of all university students are female, and women often hold top executive positions in companies and high-ranking positions in the public service and the political arena. Less well-educated women make up a fair share of the urban workforce and are often seen laboring on building sites alongside men. You will also find women driving buses, cleaning buildings, and running roadside food stalls and small businesses such as laundries and hairdressing salons. ■

The land

THAIS LIKEN THE SHAPE OF THEIR COUNTRY TO THE HEAD OF AN elephant, the Malay Peninsula—extending south to the Malaysian border in the south—being the trunk. At 198,115 square miles (513,115 sq km), Thailand, roughly the size of Texas, lies at the heart of Southeast Asia. It borders Myanmar (Burma) to the west, Laos and Cambodia to the east, and Malaysia to the south. Hundreds of islands are sprinkled off its lengthy coastline, which runs along the Gulf of Thailand and the Andaman Sea.

Thailand is a varied and rich country of forested mountains, deep valleys sliced by fast-following rivers, patchworks of cultivated areas fed by extensive waterways, thick rain forests, and vast swaths of arid land cursed with weak soil and enigmatic weather conditions.

The lush central basin is Thailand's bread-basket. This densely populated area holds nearly one-third of the country's population. Through it flows the mighty Chao Phraya river or Mae Nam (Mother of Waters), which runs south from the confluence of the Ping, Yom, and Nan Rivers at the city of Nakhon Sawan to Bangkok and on to the Gulf of Thailand. Countless rice fields in these fertile central plains, cut by a maze of canals, produce up to three crops a year. Huge rice barges use these canals to ferry crops down to Bangkok for dis-tribution to other parts of the country and for export. These geographic conditions have made the region the center of Thai civilization for over 400 years, host to three successive capitals—Ayutthaya, Thon Buri, and Bangkok.

Above the central plains is the mountain-ous north. Here is the country's highest moun-tain, Doi Inthanon, at 8,400 feet (2,565 m). Rivers such as the Mekong, Nan, Yom, and Ping feed the spectacular tumbling waterfalls for which the region is noted. Caves, too, are plentiful—burrowed deep into limestone mountains. Varying rainfalls and rugged ter-rain preclude large rice crops here, but temper-ate fruits such as oranges, apples, and tomatoes thrive. The north was once heavily forested with teak and other handsome trees, but log-ging, agriculture, and slash-and-burn farming have destroyed vast areas. Logging has been banned since 1989, and many national parks have been created. But logging continues ille-gally—often with the compliance of corrupt officials in national parks—and remains one of Thailand's greatest environmental problems. It

is estimated that 50 years ago forests covered 70 percent of Thailand; today, the figure stands at just 15 percent.

The arid northeast region, also known as Issan, sprawls across 66,000 square miles (170,000 sq km). Its dominant feature, the 655-foot-high (200 m) Khorat Plateau, reaches north to the Mekong River, which forms most of the border with Laos, and south to the Dongrek Mountains, on the Cambodian bor-der. It is harsh land, often subject to drought and floods, suitable for hardy crops such as tapioca and cotton, and for mulberry trees, whose leaves are used to feed silk worms.

Down the Malay Peninsula, much of the tropical rain forest that once matted the region has been lost to rubber and coconut planta-tions and illegal logging, but pockets still exist, mainly in the mountainous national parks that form the spine of the peninsula. The most out-standing features of the south, however, are the gigantic limestone formations that explode from the Andaman Sea; these are best seen in the provinces of Phangna and Krabi. On the east coast, the scenery is more sedate, with wildlife-rich mangrove forests. Off both sides of the peninsula are many offshore islands, some popular tourists spots, others pristine gems of rain forest, coconut trees, sparkling white sand, and colorful coral and marine life.

FLORA & FAUNA

What forests remains—almost all within national parks—are the deciduous, tropical monsoon variety found in Central, Northern, and Northeastern Thailand, and the rain forests of Southern Thailand, where the seasons are less distinct and rainfall is heavier.

Patchworks of cultivated land and mountains predominate in much of Northern Thailand's landscape.

Relatively abundant mangrove forests exist along the coast near river mouths and among the limestone crags of Southern Thailand.

Thailand affords a wide variety of habitats for flora and fauna. Its most celebrated plant is the orchid (see pp. 246–47), with about 1,000 species. Tropical plants are abundant, including hibiscus, acacia, lotus, frangipani, and bougainvillea. In the cooler, northern regions, azaleas and rhododendrons thrive. In all, there are some 27,000 species of flowering plants.

As Thailand's forests disappear so does much of its wildlife. Tiger numbers have plummeted, mostly through poaching. Elephants, so admired and, at times, even revered by Thais, survive in dwindling numbers in national parks and elephant sanctuaries. Of the 5,000 or so that remain, about half are domesticated. Shy Asiatic brown bears, also victims of poachers, are found only in small numbers. Gibbons remain in relatively high numbers, along with other primates, such as macaque monkeys,

plus wild boar, various species of deer, and flying squirrels. Thailand is also home to the rare khun kitti bat, the world's smallest, and the tiny mouse deer. There are over 100 species of snake, including the poisonous king cobra. It grows up to 20 feet (6 m), but is small fry compared with the nonvenomous, reticulated python, which may grow to an incredible 50 feet (15 m). Also formidable, and sometimes tetchy, is the monitor lizard, found in the south, which can reach 7 feet (2 m).

Enormous karst formations typify Thailand's far south landscape.

Thailand is rich in birdlife, with over 1,000 resident and migratory species, including the great hornbill, the white-crested laughing thrush, and the swiftlet, with its edible nest (see p. 331). Bird-watchers should head for Khao Yai National Park, near Bangkok, Khao Sam Roi Yot, south of the capital, and Thaleh Noi Waterfowl Park, in the far south. ■

History of Thailand

FROM THE EARLY CENTURIES OF THE FIRST MILLENNIUM, A SUCCESSION OF dynasties conquered and ruled over various parts of Thailand. But it was not until the rise of the Sukhothai Kingdom in the mid-13th century that the country gained its true identity. While from the 12th to the mid-20th centuries foreigners used the name Siam, citizens called their country by the name of the ruling dynasty's capital city.

Archaeological evidence is sketchy, but it is thought that the Mekong River Valley and the Khorat Plateau in Northeast Thailand and parts of Laos and Cambodia were inhabited more than 10,000 years ago. Farming implements dating from about 3500 B.C. have been uncovered at Spirit Cave near Mae Hong Song and at Ban Kao in Kanchanaburi. But the most significant archaeological finds were made at Ban Chiang in the northeast. Here, bronze tools and other implements dating from 3000 B.C.—earlier than those discovered in the Middle East, which was thought to be the center of the Bronze Age—were found. So, too, was decorated pottery as well as evidence of agriculture, which indicate that the area once supported a thriving and sophisticated culture.

Thailand's early inhabitants were gradually displaced and absorbed by the Tai peoples moving down into Southeast Asia from China from about the first century A.D. A further, and much larger, wave of migration followed in the mid-13th century as people fled the forces of Chinese emperor Kublai Khan (R.1260–1294). They settled in the northern reaches of Myanmar (Burma), Thailand, Cambodia, and Vietnam.

There is also conjecture that early Tai peoples originated in Thailand and spread out through Southeast Asia and into China, establishing a center at Nanchao, in modern China's Yunnan Province. After the Mongol armies invaded Nanchao in 1253, these people moved south once more and resettled in Thailand.

SRIVIJAYA PERIOD (2ND–13TH CENTURIES)

The Srivijaya Kingdom spread from its southern capital in Sumatra in Indonesia, northward through Malaysia, gradually making its way up to Thailand's southern peninsula, and establishing centers in Nakhon Si Thammarat and Chaiya in Surat Thani Province around the 8th century. Some argue that the name Chaiya is a derivation of Srivijaya (or Srivichai, as Thais refer to it), which would point to the city's major role in the empire. Many of the artifacts that were found at Chaiya—one of Thailand's oldest cities—are Srivijayan. (They can be seen in the National Museum in Bangkok.)

DVARAVATI (MON) PERIOD (6TH–13TH CENTURIES)

Before the tidal wave of migration of Tai peoples from southern China in the mid-13th century, the Mon had forged a loose collection of city-states with the likely capital at Nakhon Pathom, west of Bangkok. Archaeological work in the area has uncovered evidence of the Mon, including coins bearing Sanskrit inscriptions of the name Dvaravati. But most of the historical and cultural evidence of this mysterious kingdom, save for a few temple ruins (Wat Kukut in Lamphun is the most significant), remain lost in time. The Dvaravati Kingdom is known to have included Hariphunchai, established in 661 A.D. near present-day Lamphun, as well as Nakhon Pathom. The much-traveled Chinese monk Xuan Zang mentions the area as Tuoluobodi in a description of a pilgrimage to India. It has been suggested that at its peak the kingdom extended from southern Myanmar (Burma), across Thailand's central plains, and into western Cambodia.

The Mon were originally a missionary tribe from India, sent to spread the word of Buddhism, who moved east through the mountain ranges of Myanmar. This theory

Once the main transport arteries of Bangkok, nearly all of the *khlongs*, or canals, have been filled in and replaced by roads.

Ancient murals in temples often relate tales of the Thai epic, the *Ramakien*.

is supported by Indian records, which note that the religion was promoted throughout Southeast Asia in the third century A.D. by Theravada Buddhist missionaries sent by Mogul King Ashoka in India.

The Mon presence at Nakhon Pathom and the lower Chao Phraya river basin, along with its eastern outposts, were swallowed up by the westward march of the Khmers from their capital at Angkor in Cambodia. The only Mon stronghold to survive Khmer territorial gains was Hariphunchai. It managed to hold out until 1281, when the armies of the Lanna Kingdom conquered it.

KHMER PERIOD (8TH–13TH CENTURIES)

At its height, the Khmer Empire had become the dominant power in Southeast Asia, having spread its influence from its magnificent capital at Angkor, in Cambodia, westward to the Myanmar border with Thailand, north to Laos, and southward as far as Nakhon Si Thammarat in Thailand. It set up centers in That Phanom and Sakhon Nakhon in the central Mekong Valley; Phimai and Phanom Rung in Khorat; and Lop Buri,

Nakhon Pathom, and Phetchaburi in the Chao Phraya Basin; and Sukhothai, Si Satchanalai, and Phitsanulok in the central plains.

The Khmers built grand temples and cities. Two of the best extant examples are the ruins at Prasat Hin Phimai and at Prasat Phanom Rung—both of which have been restored. Connecting these was a Royal Road, which was notable for its engineering and for the construction of rest houses, clinics, and places of worship for pilgrims along its route.

The Khmer Empire was ruled by a succession of god-kings and, up until the 12th century, worshiped the Brahmanic gods of Hinduism. At this point, the great King Jayavarman VII adopted Mahayana Buddhism as the official religion, although Brahmanic rituals and gods were maintained. By the mid-12th century Lop Buri had become the cultural center of the kingdom as leaders in the scattering of Khmer cities began to assert their independence from Angkor. The authority of Angkor soon diminished, and by the mid-13th century the Khmer Empire was in rapid decline.

LANNA KINGDOM
(1259–1558)

Before the rise of the Sukhothai Kingdom, several small fiefdoms claimed territory around the Mekong River and in Chiang Mai in Northern Thailand. These were gradually overshadowed by the Lanna Kingdom, which centered on Chiang Mai and held sway in the north for some three centuries.

The most outstanding Lanna king was its founder, Mengrai (R.1259–1317). As a young prince, Mengrai fought successful military campaigns to expand his empire and unify warring principalities. He transferred the capital from Chiang Saen to Chiang Rai and artfully aligned his kingdom with rulers from states to the south, many of whom were princes he befriended when studying at Lop Buri in his youth. Allies included Sukhothai and Phayao, as well as the Pegu in Burma.

Mengrai went on to conquer the Mon at Hariphunchai in 1281, and in 1292 he moved his capital again, this time to Chiang Mai. Here it would flourish for another 260 years. Mengrai later formed an alliance with the Pagan of upper Myanmar and successfully repulsed an attack of Mongols from the Chinese, who were resentful of his decision to set up his capital at Chiang Mai. Under Mengrai's guidance, Lanna became strong and prosperous, controlling the Shan to the west and Lao to the north and northeast. Mengrai adopted Sinhalese Buddhism.

After Mengrai's death in 1317, the Lanna Empire declined as successors to the throne fought over sovereignty. By 1328 stability had returned, and the kingdom began to reassert itself, especially under the rule of King Ku Na (R.1355–1385). Ku Na continued to promote Sinhalese Buddhism, which eventually became the preeminent cultural force and religion in the kingdom (until Theravada Buddhism became the dominant religion in the next century). King Tilok (R.1441–1487) was Lanna's last great king. He warded off attacks on Lamphun, extended the empire, and fought off the territorial designs of Ayutthaya. After his death, lengthy battles with Ayutthaya continued, and a succession of civil wars gradually weakened Lanna. It was finally overrun by the Burmese, who used it as a base for battles with Ayutthaya.

SUKHOTHAI PERIOD
(1238–1360)

Thai leaders of Khmer principalities in the Mekong Valley began to seize the initiative from their autocratic rulers in Angkor as the central rule of this once great city rapidly fell into decline. In 1238 a small battalion of soldiers led by Prince Indraditya routed the garrison at the relatively unimportant Khmer city of Sukhothai and took over. Eventually, other principalities joined Indraditya to smash Khmer control and establish the kingdom of Sukhothai (Rising of Happiness), with Indraditya declaring himself its first sovereign.

During Indraditya's 40-year rule, Sukhothai remained relatively small. But by the end of the reign of Indraditya's son Ramkamhaeng, Sukhothai's second king, in 1318, the kingdom had spread from Luang Prabang in Laos, through Thailand's central plains, and on to the Malay Peninsula in the south. Sukhothai is recognized as the first true Thai kingdom. Although the Sukhothai period was relatively short, its legacy of culture, politics, and religion shaped the foundations of a new Thai identity. Most of these achievements have been credited to the rule of Ramkamhaeng (R.1279–1298).

The legend of King Ramkamhaeng began early in his life. At 19, on a military campaign with his father, he challenged the leader of a neighboring state to a hand-to-hand combat on the back of an elephant. His victory earned him the title of Ramkamhaeng—Rama the Bold. But Ramkamhaeng didn't always use the power of the sword to expand his empire. Skillful diplomacy and political wisdom were the main weapons he used to unite the Thai peoples and keep potential enemies on his side (alliances with the northern kingdoms of Phayao and Lanna, and the establishment of diplomatic relations with China—a looming threat—are some examples). He also fostered marriages between ruling houses in his dominions to entrench loyalty and solidarity.

Golden era

Ramkamhaeng presided over what Thais like to call their golden era. He was a visionary and progressive monarch whose contribution to Thai culture, education, and art were enormous. He is credited with the invention of the Thai alphabet, borrowing elements of Khmer and Mon script and adding Thai tonal marks. One of the first examples of the new language was an inscribed stele, carved in 1292, which detailed the accounts of Sukhothai life and Ramkamhaeng's achievements. These included his above-mentioned meritorious victory on the back of elephant, as well as the riches and progressiveness of the kingdom (abundant food, free trade, the ending of slavery, the right to inheritance, and other hallmarks of prosperity).

Ramkamhaeng showed scant prejudices in borrowing the best from other cultures and refining this to the demands of a nascent Thai identity. The architecture of his temple complexes show influences of the Khmer and the Mon, but he added flourishes of some-times subliminal art to both the interiors and exteriors of temples and palaces. Sukhothai artists, artisans, and architects slowly developed their own styles under his patronage to create what is these days recognized as the most sophisticated of all Thai artistic styles.

During his reign, Ramkamhaeng revived Theravada Buddhism, using its precepts as a platform of governance. This enlightened approach earned Sukhothai a peace and prosperity that was unrivaled by any of the preceding kingdoms.

Decline of Sukhothai

After Ramkamhaeng's death, Sukhothai fell into terminal decline as subsequent kings were unable to maintain political and eco-nomic power. Ramkamhaeng's son, Lo Thai (R.1298–1347), largely neglected affairs of state and enveloped himself in religious pursuits and the construction of temples to enhance his personal merit. By the time of Lo Thai's death, Sukhothai was facing the ever increasing threat from one of its upstart dominions, Ayutthaya.

The last Sukhothai ruler of any signifi-cance was Ramkamhaeng's grandson, Li Thai (R.1347–1368). Li Thai continued to surrender power to Ayutthaya but remained a strong patron of the arts. It was during his reign that many of Sukhothai's great temples were created. Under Ayutthaya's eventual rule, Sukhothai became little more than a regional outpost. The town was abandoned in 1438 and was all but forgotten for four centuries, until its rediscovery in the mid-19th century. It is now a historical park at the modern city of Sukhothai and a popular tourist attraction.

AYUTTHAYA PERIOD (1350–1767)

Late in the 14th century, after the disintegration of the Khmer Empire and the sacking of the great Burmese Empire at Pagan by the Mongols, mainland Southeast Asia was experiencing something of a power vacuum. Lanna's power in Northern Thailand was enigmatic, while Sukhothai spluttered along under the leadership of Ramkamhaeng's descendants. The scene was set for a new power to hold together the Thai peoples.

The key turned out to be Suphan Buri, a relatively small Sukhothai suzerainty. The dominion had early claimed indepen-dence from Sukhothai on the death of Ramkamhaeng but lacked the leadership and strength to carry out its aim fully until the rise to power of U Thong (R.1350–1369). An outbreak of cholera in 1351 forced the new leader to move his population from the present-day area of U Thong to Ayutthaya, a site almost completely surrounded by rivers. Here he took the name Ramathibodi and declared himself king. He immediately applied himself to expanding his empire, proving his mettle as he set about a prolonged and bloody assault on declining Sukhothai and conducting military cam-paigns against smaller Thai dominions in the south.

The benevolent and accessible monarchy established by the kings of Sukhothai was brushed aside in favor of the Khmer notion of god-kings—an absolute monarchy whose power was mandated by divine forces.

Although this tradition was tempered to some extent by Ramathibodi's embracing of Theravada Buddhism as the major religion, he and subsequent Ayutthaya kings employed the Khmer rituals of royal court, carving a

Several Ayutthaya kings used Wat Phra Si Sanphet as the royal temple-palace.

rigid, unapproachable divide between royalty and subjects.

Other Ayutthaya kings

After Ramathibodi's death in 1369, his son Ramasuen (*R.*1369–1370, 1388–1395) became leader but was overthrown shortly afterward by Boromraja I. Boromraja held control for 18 years, continuing attacks on Sukhothai, capturing Nakhon Sawan, Phitsanulok, and Kamphaeng Phet, claiming suzerainty over Sukhothai, and waging war against Lanna. Ramasuen regained power in 1388, captured the Lanna capital of Chiang Mai in 1390, and successfully staved off the military designs of the Burmese to the west. In 1431 Ayutthaya's armies marched into Angkor, forcing the Khmer rulers to flee the ancient capital and set up in Phnom Penh. Fighting with the Lanna continued for over 100 years.

The reign of King Boroma Trailokanath, better known as Trailok (*R.*1448–1488), gathered together the kingdom's states under centralized rule, bringing military and administrative controls to Ayutthaya. He instituted the *sakdi naa* system of land ownership, which set up rules and rankings of social status and hierarchy that were to shape Thailand's social order for another four centuries and that still exist in a similar, but less emphatic, form today.

Trailok also introduced a form of conscription whereby men were required to contribute their labor for a certain period of time each year. Trade was brought under royal control, and the kingdom prospered—despite the fact that it remained perpetually in a state of war.

The Burmese sacked Ayutthaya in 1569, and most of the court and citizenry were captured and hauled back to Pegu and held as hostages. Prince Naresuen (*R.*1590–1605), who inherited the throne from his father, reversed this humiliating defeat a few years later, in 1584.

By now Ayutthaya was starting to receive a growing number of European visitors. Portugal had earlier set up an embassy in 1511. A century later, others began arriving—the Dutch (1605), the English (1612), the Danes (1621), and the French (1662). European influence peaked during the reign of King Narai (*R.*1656–1688). European traders and diplomats were in awe of the grandeur of

Ayutthaya, which had by now developed into the most magnificent city in Southeast Asia.

The kingdom's affair with Europe ended with the expulsion of a garrison of 600 French soldiers, which King Narai had earlier allowed to be based in the city (the Thai word for foreigner, *farang*, comes from the abbreviated name for the French, *farangset*) as fears grew about French intentions. The doors to foreigners were subsequently shut for 150 years.

The persistent Burmese continued their attacks on the kingdom. All-out war developed, and they laid siege to the capital, finally breaking through in 1767. Ayutthaya was overrun and destroyed.

FOUNDATIONS OF BANGKOK

The destruction of its great capital might have proved the end for the Thai nation had it not been for the military prowess of Praya Taksin (*R.*1767–1782), a half-Chinese, half-Thai general. Taksin organized an army, drove the Burmese from Ayutthaya, and regained control of the country. Aware of the threat the Burmese still held, Taksin abandoned Ayutthaya as the capital and moved it to a more defensible location at Thon Buri, then a small fishing village on the Chao Phraya river, opposite present-day Bangkok.

Despite his military success, Taksin was not an effective ruler. He neglected his administrative duties, became increasingly brutal, and slowly went insane. When he declared himself the reincarnation of the Buddha, his alarmed ministers removed him from office and had him executed in the fashion reserved for royalty—beaten to death in a velvet sack so that none of his blood would touch the ground.

CHAKRI DYNASTY (1872–PRESENT)

Another general, Chao Phraya Chakri, came to power and was crowned Ramathibodi (*R.*1782–1809). His original name is given to the Chakri dynasty, whose royal lineage continues to this day.

Ramathibodi moved the capital across the river to Rattanakosin island, in present-day Bangkok, in 1782 and set about securing

the city from the still restless Burmese. He then began restoring the grandeur of Thai art and architecture destroyed at Ayutthaya.

Successors—King Phutthalaetia, more officially known as Rama II (*R.*1809–1824), and his son King Nangklao, known as Rama III (*R.*1824–1851)—continued Ramathibodi's work of rebuilding Thai civilization. Rama II is remembered for the construction of Wat Arun and was famed as a great poet, developing the Thai version of the Indian Hindu epic, the *Ramayana*—known as the *Ramakien*—during his reign.

Following the tentative contacts with European powers that had been made by his predecessors, Rama III continued to open the doors to the West but remained suspicious of its motives. He was a deeply religious and

conservative ruler, and was not held in high regard by the Europeans and Americans intent on forcing more trade with Siam.

Rama III's elder half-brother, Prince Mongkut (R.1851–1868), who had forgone ascension to the throne in favor of his younger sibling in order to enter the monk-hood, became the next Chakri monarch as Rama IV. Mongkut had used his 27 years of monastic life well, learning Latin and English so that he could study Western culture. He had a keen interest in the sciences, history, geography, and astronomy—all put to good use during his reign.

Mongkut was in a sagacious and progressive leader. He was the first Thai king to realize that Siam's independence could be retained by moving his country into

Royal barges such as these are still seen on Bangkok's Chao Phraya river.

the modern era and encouraging contact and trade with the West. He also set about reforming the legal system, promoting social reforms and modeling Siam's education system along Western lines. Mongkut died of malaria in 1868, shortly after returning from a trip to Phetchaburi, south of Bangkok, with an entourage of European diplomats who had traveled there to observe a solar eclipse—which, legend holds, Mongkut had predicted.

MODERNIZATION OF SIAM
Mongkut's son, Chulalongkorn, or Rama V (R.1868–1910), continued his father's work

of reform and modernization. He opened Thailand's first hospital and its first post and telegraph office, and he set about linking the the various parts of the country with a network of roads and rail. He built up a civil service, introduced further improvements to the educational system, and ended the age-long practice of compulsory state labor.

In his battle to maintain Siam's independence—Britain had colonized Burma and Malaysia, and France had control of most of Indochina—he ceded parts of the then extended kingdom of Siam to Indochina and to Burma. The French occupied the provinces of Chanthaburi and Trat on the Cambodian border in 1893 and did not hand them back to Siam until 1905. (More land was later ceded to the French, whose colonization continued until 1941.)

British-educated King Vajiravudh, or Rama VI (R.1910–1925), is chiefly remembered for carrying on the work begun by his father of modernizing the country. He introduced compulsory education and made other educational reforms, and instituted Thailand's first university (Chulalongkorn, named after his father). His reign witnessed the first attempt to overthrow the absolute monarchy, made in 1912 by the Thai military. Military coups were a feature of the Thai political scene during the 20th century.

MODERN AGE (1925–PRESENT)

Prajadhiphok, Vajiravudh's brother and the 76th child and youngest son of Chulalongkorn, reigned as Rama VII (R.1925–1935)—the last absolute monarch of the Chakri dynasty. A group of democratically minded students, with the help of the military, overthrew the monarchy in 1932 in a bloodless coup d'etat. Prajadhiphok was playing golf at Hua Hin, south of Bangkok, when he learned of the coup.

A civilian/military government was set

up, and the absolute power of the monarchy was dissolved, being replaced by a constitutional monarchy. This left royalty with a largely ceremonial role in state affairs. A group of royalist sympathizers launched an unsuccessful attempt to reinstate absolute monarchy in another coup d'etat in 1933. In 1935 Prajadhiphok abdicated and went into self-imposed exile in Britain without declaring an heir. The government decided that his nephew, 10-year-old Prince Ananda Mahidol (R.1935–1946), would be king.

Ananda was born in Germany and studied in Switzerland before arriving in Thailand in December 1945. Meanwhile, the military leader Phibun (Pibul) Songkhram (1897–1964) bullied his way into leading the government in 1938. He renamed the country Thailand in 1939 and remained in power, on and off, until after World War II.

Ananda was shot dead in his palace bedroom in June 1946 under mysterious

King Mongkut began the modernization of Thailand and invited Western ideas.

circumstances. His younger brother, Bhumibol Adulyadej, became Rama IX and continues to rule as king today (see pp. 106–107). Although they were never convicted of the crime, two of Ananda's attendants—generally considered to be scapegoats—were arrested and later, in 1954, executed. The events behind Ananda's death have never been established, and speaking or writing of the event remains virtually taboo in Thailand.

Out of expediency, Thailand allowed the occupation of Japanese troops during World War II and declared war on the Allies—although the Thai ambassador to the United States of America, Seni Pramoj (1905–1997), refused to deliver the declaration to Washington. Pibul resigned in 1944 under pressure from Thailand's resistance movement, and ambassador Seni became premier.

However, he was unseated two years later in a general election as Pridi Phanomyong (1900–1983), a left-wing intellectual and one of the leaders of the 1932 coup d'etat, took control of a civilian government. But that was also short-lived. Pibul returned and led a successful coup in 1947, suspending the constitution. He took a strong anti-Communist stance, pandering to U.S. and French policies in Southeast Asia.

During the 1950s and 1960s, Thailand had a succession of military governments, which continued to rule with an iron fist. From the mid-1960s to the early 1970s, the U.S. was allowed to set up military bases in the country to support its campaign in Vietnam.

Continued military control of the government came to a head in 1973, when thousands of students gathered at Thammasat University in Bangkok and demanded an end to military rule and the setting up of a new constitution. The ruling generals, Thanom Kittikachorn (1912–) and Praphat Charusathien, called in troops and a blood-bath ensued. In one of his rare forays into politics, the highly respected King Bhumibol, with another moderate, General Krit Sivara, condemned the violence. Thanom and Praphat fled the country. Democratic elections followed, and left-leaning Kukrit Pramoj (1911–1995; brother of Seni) took charge of a multiparty coalition government.

But democracy was short-lived. When Thanom returned to Thailand in 1976 in the guise of a monk, students once again protested at Thammasat University. This time police and paramilitary right-wingers launched a bloodthirsty attack on the students, killing hundreds. Using the unrest as an excuse, the military pushed aside the government and took control. As a result, thousands of students, intellectuals, and other disillusioned people fled to the countryside, joining the left-wing People's Liberation Army of Thailand (PLAT). By the time the moderate, military-installed leader Prem Tinsulanonda (1920–) took power in 1980, PLAT and the Communist Party of Thailand had combined forces that numbered well over 10,000.

Prem ruled for the next eight years, gradually introducing political stability and

reform. He reduced the ranks of the PLAT and the Communist party of Thailand through military campaigns and by making offers of amnesty. In 1988, after general elections, Chatichai Choonhavan (1922–1998) became Thailand's prime minister. Chatichai oversaw the country's further democratization and its unprecedented economic growth, but did little to curb rampant corruption.

Using this corruption as its excuse, the military once again intervened. On February 23, 1991, a bloodless coup d'etat ended civilian rule, and power was handed to the National Peace-Keeping Council (NPKC), led by General Suchinda Kraprayoon (1933–). A well-respected civilian, Anand Panyarachun (1932–), was appointed caretaker prime minister while a

Royal Guards ride to the Grand Palace through the streets of Bangkok.

new constitution, which favored continued military participation in government, was drawn up and passed by parliament.

Elections were held in March 1992, heralding a five-party coalition as government. However, after military machinations, Suchinda took power, much to the outrage of many Thai citizens, who were sick of military involvement in politics. In May, people took to the streets in tens of thousands to make their protest.

The military opened fire on the demonstrators, killing at least 50 people. Suchinda and the leader of the protestors, Bangkok governor Chamlong Srimuang, were hauled before King Bhumibol, who told them to end the madness. Suchinda resigned, and new elections were held in September. These brought to power Chuan Leekpai (1938–), a man admired for his integrity.

The events of May 1992 were pivotal in the democratization of Thailand. Since then, a number of general elections have taken place without military meddling. In 1999 a new, liberal constitution was established, overhauling the electoral system and enshrining freedoms for the country's citizens.

Corruption, patronage, and vote-buying are still very much part of the political system in Thailand, but most sectors, including the military, seem committed to stability and democracy. ■

The arts

THAILAND'S ARTISTIC HERITAGE WAS FOUNDED ON AN AMALGAM OF ASIAN influences, but it has been crafted into a style that is distinctively its own. Architecture, visual art, drama, crafts, literature, and song and dance all reveal elements drawn, at different stages, from Indian, Khmer, Chinese, Malay, and European cultures. Be prepared for a rich and startling array of Thai arts throughout the country.

TEMPLE ART & ARCHITECTURE

Religion was the prime mover behind the early development of Thai art. Thai Buddhist architects of the Sukhothai Kingdom—a period that saw the first real attempts to unify the Thai people—borrowed from Khmer temple architecture, then added their own distinctive, soaring multitiered rooftops and golden spires. Later, in the Ayutthaya period, Chinese influence predominated, with ornate decoration—particularly the use of porcelain fragments to veneer many temple buildings. This richness of ornamentation reached its peak in the first half of 19th century, when glass mosaics highlighted gables and pillars, lacquerware and gold leaf adorned walls, and mother-of-pearl was inlaid into doors and shutters—the sum of which created a riot of color.

Wats

Wats—an estimated 30,000 are scattered throughout the country—are much more than places of worship. This is especially so in smaller towns and villages, where they form an intrinsic part of the community, containing clinics, funeral homes, schools, community centers, places of entertainment, markets, and monasteries. Some even act as drug rehabilitation centers.

Inside the wats are numerous buildings used for specific purposes. These include the *bot, wihan, chedi, prang, mondop, prasat,* and smaller structures such as the *sala* and *kutis.*

Wats often have names that reflect the history or religious significance of the compound. Many temples are prefixed with "Rat," "Raja," or "Racha" as a sign of respect to Thai royalty, members of whom were responsible for the construction or renovation of the buildings. Others make a more direct connection to the major benefactor by including the name of a specific king in the wat's title. Temples such as Wat Phra Kaeo in Bangkok are named after their central Buddha image, while those that are famed for their possession of a great *(maha)* and sacred *(that)* relic of the Buddha may include "Wat Mahathat" in their name.

Bots

The most important and sacred structure within the wat is the bot, often the most spectacular building inside the temple compound, replete with lavishly decorated shutters and doors and soaring roofs with gleaming towers. The bot is a meeting hall where religious ceremonies and monks' ordinations are held, and where novice monks meditate daily. Senior monks also use bots as a place to recite scriptures for Buddhist priesthood and to give sermons to supplicants.

These rectangular buildings are usually surrounded by eight sacred boundary stones known as *bai sema.* Resembling small tombstones and often enclosed within miniature tabernacles, these stones keep evil spirits outside the consecrated ground.

Intrinsic to a bot's design are *chofas,* curling up at roof extremities to represent *garudas* (mythical half-bird, half-human creatures).

Interior murals follow a standard form. For example, the main mural behind the central Buddha image shows the Buddhist cosmological order (see p. 140). Murals above the main entrance often show the enlightenment of the Buddha, or the devil divinity Mara, tempting the Buddha during his meditations. Murals on the side walls depict other stories from the life of the Buddha.

The workmanship of temple art is often exquisitely detailed, as seen in these superb door carvings.

Wihan

This structure is the secondary assembly hall, where devotees gather to honor a wat's primary Buddha images. While there will be only one bot in a wat, there may be several wihans. The wihan is also used as a sermon hall for monks and lay worshippers.

Wihans lack the consecrated boundary stones that define the bot, but the wealth of exterior and interior murals often rivals those of the more significant building. Wihans found within larger complexes such as Wat Pho in Bangkok (see pp. 75–76) are enclosed by rectangular cloisters filled with images of the Buddha and backed by resplendent murals depicting such classic Buddhist tales as the *Ramakien*. The images inside the wihan may be repositories of ashes of devotees.

Chedi

Chedis are Indian-derived stupas—dome-shaped monuments that were originally

designed to hold sacred Buddha relics such as texts, images, and bone fragments. (Many Thais believe that Buddha bone fragments have the power to reproduce themselves, so they can be distributed to thousands of other wats.) Later, chedis were built to cover and commemorate the remains of kings and saints. These days, they may hold the remains of anyone wealthy enough to afford the construction. In the hope that they will bring merit to the builder, many newer chedis are

Bangkok's Grand Palace and Wat Phra Kaeo exemplify Thai temple architecture.

designed to replicate historic ones that contain Buddha relics.

The chedi is generally a bell-shaped structure. Raised on square or round terraces of diminishing size, it often dominates the grounds of the wat. The world's largest chedi is found at Nakhon Pathom near Bangkok (see pp. 120-22).

WIHAN
Similar in structure to the bot, but not surrounded by boundary stones. There may be more than one wihan in the complex.

BOT
The bot is the most important, but not necessarily the largest, building in the complex.

Bai sema (sacred boundary stone) enclosed in tabernacle

PRANG
Wat Chai Wattanaram, Ayutthaya

LIBRARY
Wat Phra Sing, Chiang Mai

Prang
Prangs are soaring towers; Thai prangs are modeled on those found in Khmer temples. Although they partly reflect the basic outline of a chedi, prangs are much slimmer in profile and more elegant than chedis. They are also more decorative, with imaginative rows of carved or cast demons and angels ringing the lower

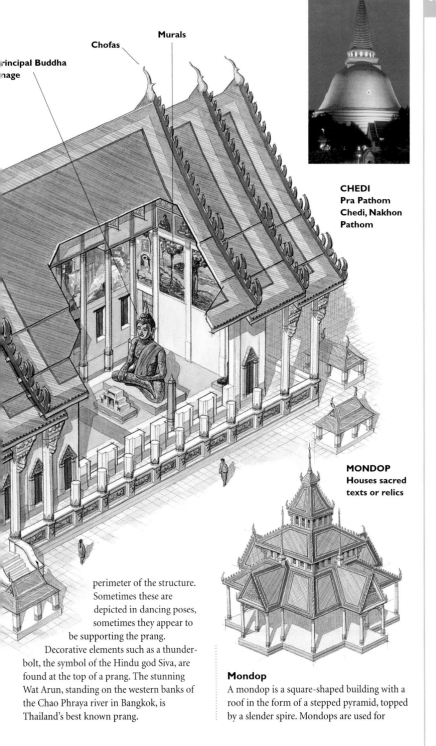

Principal Buddha
image

Chofas

Murals

CHEDI
Pra Pathom
Chedi, Nakhon
Pathom

MONDOP
Houses sacred
texts or relics

perimeter of the structure. Sometimes these are depicted in dancing poses, sometimes they appear to be supporting the prang. Decorative elements such as a thunderbolt, the symbol of the Hindu god Siva, are found at the top of a prang. The stunning Wat Arun, standing on the western banks of the Chao Phraya river in Bangkok, is Thailand's best known prang.

Mondop
A mondop is a square-shaped building with a roof in the form of a stepped pyramid, topped by a slender spire. Mondops are used for

storing sacred text and relics (often a Buddha footprint cast or carved in stone and much larger than life-size.). A good example is at Wat Phra Phutthabat, near Saraburi (see p. 143); highly venerated, it attracts tens of thousands of pilgrims each year.

Prasat

These sanctuary towers were adapted from those built during the Khmer era, when they were central features in a temple. The main tower of the prasat—the prang—and four smaller surrounding towers represent the peaks of Mount Meru, the center of the Hindu universe and home to the gods. In wats, prasats take on a less significant role, being used for secular functions, as well as religious ceremonies. Prasats designed for royal and secular ceremonies feature the sweeping, multileveled roofs seen on most buildings in the wat, while religious prasats take the Khmer form.

Sala

Salas are graciously styled, open-sided buildings used by pilgrims and monks to escape the heat of the day. They are also used as classrooms and community halls, and to provide overnight shelter for visitors during festivals.

Other structures

The *hor rakang* is a small, simply constructed structure that contains a drum or bell tower used to call monks to ordinations, meals, or meditation. Most temples also have a *hor trai*. This is an elaborately carved and decorated library. It is often raised on stilts to keep insects and other pests from invading the building and damaging the texts. *Kutis* are monks' quarters, usually built behind a wall, fence, or canal to separate them from the wat's religious buildings. They tend to consist mainly of dormitories, with individual cells for only a small number of monks.

Some larger wats may have cloisters—open galleries displaying rows of Buddha images or small chedis. In many towns or villages, wats have a crematorium—its needlelike chimney is easily identifiable.

DOMESTIC ARCHITECTURE

Thai domestic architecture evolved from that of temple architecture, although necessarily less grandiose. Builders used prefabricated panels of teakwood—the predominant material—attached to a framework of heavy pillars, with wooden pegs for joining. Various styles developed in different regions of the country. The style of the central plain probably best mirrors temple style, with steeply pitched roofs, ornate gables, decorative boardwalks separating different structures, and slightly inward-leaning walls. Ponds and gardens added to the sense of grace and elegance. Jim Thompson's House (see p. 94) is a fine example.

Traditional Thai architecture began to decline in the early 1900s as Western tastes took over from—and in some cases blended with—local styles. In recent years some hotels have employed traditional Thai architecture with impressive results. One striking example is the Sukhothai Hotel in Bangkok, with its expansive, shallow pond and, in its lobby area, row of small chedis built in naked brick.

HANDICRAFTS

Many crafts, such as woodcarving, mother-of-pearl inlay, ceramics, and lacquerware, have their origins as decorative forms in temple architecture. Some crafts have inevitably declined with the modernization of Thailand and the loss of skilled craftsmen, but others have thrived because of the increase in foreign tourism and the demand for high-quality souvenirs. Woodcarving and silverwork have maintained high standards, while woven silk manufactured in Northeast Thailand has become a major export item. Ceramics, such as celadon stoneware and finely wrought nielloware bowls, can sometimes be of exceptional quality.

Most of the artifacts described below can be purchased in Bangkok and, at lower prices, in Chiang Mai. Chiang Mai is recognized as the craft center of Thailand and is one of the premier places in Southeast Asia for handicrafts.

Ceramics

Thailand produces a number of different types of ceramics, including lustrous greenglazed celadon pottery. The most celebrated ceramic is the delicate and highly decorated

Classical Thai theater often employs masked dancers in scenes from the *Ramakien*.

Benjarong, the manufacture of which dates back to China's Ming dynasty (1368-1644). Benjarong follows traditional patterns of intricately woven floral designs with the use of five colors—red, green, yellow, blue, and white. Benjarong items range from pots and vases to entire dinner services.

Lacquerware

Lacquerware from Northern Thailand comes in two varieties: gold and black, and a matte red with black and/or green details. It is found on ornate containers and trays, wooden figurines, woven bamboo baskets, and Buddhist manuscripts. At least three coats of lacquer are applied to the object being decorated, giving it a lustrous surface. Craftsmen paint a design with a water-soluble resin and, in the case of gold and black lacquerware, the area to which the gold is to adhere is left unpainted. Gold leaf is then pressed over the entire surface. The object is later washed with water to remove the excess gold leaf.

Mother-of-pearl inlay

Mother-of-pearl inlays are used in presentation trays and in various containers, as well as on plaques bearing classical scenes. The style of decoration dates back to the Dvaravati period. Little else is known of its evolution between then and the late Ayutthaya and early Bangkok periods, when it was used extensively to decorate doors and windows in temples, as well as furniture and drinking vessels.

Nielloware

Portuguese traders to Southern Thailand probably introduced this exquisite craft to the kingdom. Nakhon Si Thammarat has been the center of nielloware production for several centuries, and the craft has recently undergone a revival in the province, as well as nationwide. A design is incised in silver and sometimes gold, and then the background is cut away and filled with an amalgam of darker metals. This creates a dark background against which the figures stand in relief. Nielloware items

include rings, necklaces, bracelets, bowls, pedestals, boxes, and trays.

Silk weaving

Shimmering, handwoven Thai silk is regarded as among the world's best and is much sought after by decorators and designers. Silk remnants discovered at Ban Chiang, in Northeast Thailand, suggest the craft was practiced there in ancient times. Thai-speaking migrants probably introduced other components of silk culture from Yunnan Province in China.

What is certain is that silk was woven in the first Thai capital of Sukhothai and, around that time, at several settlements in Southern Thailand, including Nakhon Si Thammarat and Songkhla. During the Bangkok period,

the silk industry became entrenched in the northeast of the country, where conditions are good for growing mulberry trees (essential food for silkworms). By growing mulberry trees, farmers can earn extra income between rice harvests.

Silk declined in importance in the early 20th century as factory-produced textiles became available but was revived after World War II by American entrepreneur Jim Thompson (see p. 94).

Silverwork

Legend holds that in the late 13th century 500 families of silversmiths fled to Chiang Mai from Myanmar (Burma) as refugees from the Mongol invaders. There they settled, and the area now produces some of the most refined

Evocative locations—such as ancient ruins—sometimes serve as backdrops for classical theater performances.

Woodcarving

Thailand's once extensive forests of teak and other hardwoods were a ready source of material for woodcarvers, whose skillful handiwork can be seen in the elaborately decorative gables, doors, and roof supports that grace almost every temple in Thailand.

A ban on logging was implemented in 1989, but woodcarving is still one of the most prominent Thai crafts. The timber used these days is mainly imported from Myanmar (Burma) or taken from existing supplies that have been confiscated from illegal loggers or salvaged from dilapidated buildings. Illegal logging is still rife in Thailand, so there is little doubt that some of the products you see for sale in markets have come from this source.

Craftsmen turn out an amazing range of woodcarvings, from intricately carved screens, bedsteads, furniture, and 6-foot-high (2 m) elephants to delicate figurines, elegant salad bowls, and novelties and games. Even moderatley priced woodcarvings sometimes display impressive craftsmanship.

DANCE & DRAMA

Traditional Thai theater has developed over several centuries under royal patronage into a rich variation of classical dance, elaborate theater, and sometimes bawdy, down-to-earth folk entertainment. There are six forms: the *khon*, which uses masks and formal dance to depict scenes from the *Ramakien*; *lakhon*, which employs both formal and less structured theater and carries various themes; *li-khe*, the country's most popular drama form, often employing comedic and melodramatic themes; *manhora*, the southern Thailand version of li-khe and based on Indian folklore; *nang*, or shadow puppetry, a dying art form also from the South; and *lakhon lek*, which uses marionettes dressed in costumes similar to khon performers.

Khon

This classical theater finds large numbers of exclusively male dancers. Traditionally, khon was played out by hundreds of dancers in front of royalty and their guests; today, because of the expense, numbers have been reduced. Khon relates tales from the Thai epic, the *Ramakien*, with performers adorned in a

silverwork in Asia. Among the best of the silverwork products to look out for are classically styled bowls used as water vessels and food containers, contemporary teapots and tableware, and filigree jewelry.

Umbrellas & fans

Handpainted umbrellas and folding fans are made from pounded bark (often mulberry), silk, or cotton. The bamboo frame is split by hand, and the holes are punched with a foot-powered bow drill. The items are handpainted with designs of birds, dragons, and village scenes, and are mostly used for ornamentation.

dazzling array of costumes, head dresses, and masks representing four types of characters—male humans, female humans, monkeys, and demons. Performers mime the dialogue provided by narrators and choruses, and the performance is backed by the Thai *pipat* orchestra. Truncated but still dazzling versions of khon can be seen at Bangkok's National Theater.

Lakhon

The lakhon bases its appeal on female grace and refined dexterity. Themes derived from the *Ramakien* are expanded with folk dances from the Northeast and ancient legends from the far south.

This style of theater is noted for its gilded costumes and profuse decorative elements, which greatly exceed those in other Thai performing arts. Its use of singing and dialogue make it much livelier than the khon, with its controlled strictures. In contrast to the muscular displays of the khon, the lakhon demonstrates the highly restrained and subtle use of the upper portion of the female body. The dancer employs a range of eye and hand movements to indicate emotion and the development of the storyline.

Li-khe

This is the most popular form of live theater, performed at temple fairs, village festivals, and other venues in towns and villages throughout Thailand. It is good-time theater, incorporating classical and folk music, wild costumes, slapstick comedy, melodrama, and sexual innuendo. Often it is used as political satire and cutting social commentary. Traveling troupes of entertainers put on the shows, and entire villages gather for a night of boisterous fun. Over the centuries li-khe has remained hugely popular and has translated well onto the television screen. Li-khe sitcoms are now a staple on daytime Thai television.

The southern version of li-khe is known as the *ma-norah*. It is loosely based on the *Ramakien*, where, in this case, Prince Suthon travels in search of the kidnapped Manhora, a half-woman, half-bird princess. Narrators relate the story of the prince's travails in comic rhyming prose.

Shadow puppetry

Although rarely performed these days, shadow puppetry, or nang (see p. 311), was once Southern Thailand's most popular form of entertainment. There are two forms of nang. *Nang yai* uses life-size puppets, which are manipulated by skilled puppet masters using two poles. They are moved behind an illuminated white screen that is positioned between the puppets and the audience. The illumination casts wavering shadow images of the puppets out into the crowd. Nang yai puppets are still crafted but are usually sold as interior decorations rather than for use in performances. *Nang thalung* uses smaller, more maneuverable puppets with articulated joints, similar to the *wayang kulit* of Indonesia. This form is still occasionally seen at temple fairs in Southern Thailand. Traditional nang performances typically act scenes from the *Ramakien* and can last for hours. These days, they are often given a contemporary theme by the puppet masters.

Lakhon lek

Lakhon lek, translated as "little theater," is no longer performed. It used marionettes up to 3 feet (90 cm) high and made from paper and wire. The puppets were dressed in elaborate costumes similar to those worn in khon, and the plays carried similar themes. Puppet masters used poles to move the marionettes' arms, legs, hands, and sometimes fingers and eyes. The Bangkok National Museum has a small collection of the puppets. Another puppet theater that uses three-dimensional figures is *hun krabok*. These are hand puppets, each about 12 inches (30 cm) high, carved from wood and viewed from the waist up.

Ram wong

Thailand's most popular traditional dance, performed at temple fairs and festivals, is the *ram wong* (dance circle). Movements appear simple and natural, with the dancers' emotions expressed with graceful arm and hand movements. Thais of all social classes enjoy dancing the ram wong, a very social affair.

Jim Thompson's famous Bangkok shop purveys an exquisite array of Thai silk. The American revived the country's silk industry.

MUSIC

Traditional music

Traditional classical Thai music, dating from the Sukhothai period, combines Chinese, Indonesian, and Indian influences. It may sound strange and discordant to unfamiliar ears, but the longer you listen, the more sense it makes. It is based on a five-tone diatonic scale, used long before the evolution of the contemporary Western scale. The music is performed by an orchestra that emphasizes percussion instruments—so you should expect the sounds of drums, gongs, and vibraphones, along with a range of string instruments drawn from Asian musical traditions.

These tunes have long backed up performances of the khon, lakhon, and li-khe; a reduced version of the Thai orchestra is used to introduce and play backing music for Thai boxing matches (see p. 62), adding an almost surreal touch to the mayhem of fight nights.

Modern music

Thai pop music contains the syrupy lyrics found in Western pop, but there are also some styles that have a distinct Thai flavor, using traditional instruments and biting lyrics that shed light on modern-day Thai culture. Popular music came of age in the 1980s with the crafting of a socially conscious form of song known as *pleng peur cheevit*. This gave lyrical importance to social and political issues rather than themes of young and unrequited

The restoration of Thailand's extraordinary heritage of temple art is a never-ending chore that requires patience and expertise.

love. The popular Bangkok-based group Carabao, which wrote and performed the 1980s hit "Made in Thailand," first forged the change. This song, and later ones from a growing number of bands, questioned the importance of Western materialism in Thai society and addressed issues of morality and poverty.

LITERATURE

The *Ramakien,* the Thai version of the Hindu epic, the *Ramayana,* is the most pervasive of Thai classical literature, also celebrated in visual art, drama, and song. It arrived in Thailand about 900 years ago with the Khmers, who carved scenes from the epic into stone at Prasat Hin Phimai (see p. 170), Prasat Phanom Rung (see p. 174), and other temples. The Thai version was put down on paper during the reign of Rama I and contains 60,000 verses. The *Ramakien* remains essentially the same as the *Ramayana,* but certain characters are embellished, while others are given less emphasis. The story is an odyssey of quest, love, betrayal, and war.

MARTIAL ARTS

Thai boxing

In most countries, boxing lies directly in the realm of sport, but in Thailand, *muay Thai,* or

Thai boxing, the country's most popular sport, blends ritual with excitement and violence.

Thai boxing, infuses elements of art and ritual. The sport is a mixture of conventional boxing and eastern martial arts such as karate and tae kwon do. Opponents can use their fists, elbows, knees, and feet to batter their opponent in just about any part of the body where the opportunity avails itself.

Watching the sport, you will find it hard to believe that it could ever be more violent— but it used to be. Up until the 1930s, the rules and regulations were few, and serious injuries were common among fighters, who also employed biting, scratching, strangling, and spitting in their repertoire. (The sport was banned in the 1920s and revived in the 1930s under new rules.)

Before the match begins, strident music erupts from a small orchestra in the stadium. The fighters enter the ring wearing a colored headband and an armband, which are regarded as sacred ornaments that offer blessing and protection. They kneel and perform a quick prayer, then—with the orchestra still playing—move into a mesmerizing boxing dance around the ring called the *rom muay.* The dance, performed with heavily exaggerated movements and in slow motion, is traditionally the participants' way of paying respect to the trainer and the boxing school to which they belong.

After the rom muay, the headband is removed, but the armband, which contains a small Buddha amulet, is worn throughout the fight. The orchestra keeps on playing throughout the five three-minute rounds, with often frenzied crescendos rising and falling in tune with the action in the ring.

There are an estimated 60,000 muay Thai fighters in Thailand. Fights are held regularly at Lumphini and Ratchadamneon Stadiums in Bangkok and in towns and villages around the country.

Krabi kabong

This traditional Thai martial art has its roots in Ayutthaya's Wat Phutthaisawan as far back as 400 years, when the king's bodyguards learned the skills that incorporate sword, quarterstaff, and club fighting, and hand-to-hand combat. Although the martial art is today an integral and exciting part of cultural shows for international visitors and festivals, it is nevertheless still taken seriously by its exponents, and contests continue to be held, with winners being judged on stamina and technical skills. Although sharpened swords and other weapons are used, krabi kabong fighters avoid striking their opponents. ■

Bangkok—the vast, sprawling City of Angels—is one of the most fascinating cities in Asia, with a well-deserved reputation for splendid restaurants, non-stop nightlife, superb shopping, and magnificent temples.

Bangkok

Mural detail, Wat Phra Kaeo

Bangkok

VISITORS TO THAILAND'S CAPITAL CANNOT HELP BEING OVERWHELMED BY it all. The city is daunting—a steamy, modern sprawl that seems to carry on endlessly. The traffic is maddening, the din endless, and the crowds irritating. Most can't wait to escape to the beaches of the South or the jungles and mountains in the North. That's a shame, because to get involved with Bangkok is to enjoy one of Asia's great cities.

Bangkok's full name is the longest city name in the world. It is Krungthepmahanakhon Amonratankosin Mahintharayutthaya Mahadilokphop Nophosin Ratchathaniburirom Udomrathaniwetmahasa Amonphiman Awatansathit Sakkathatiya Witsanukamprasit. This means: City of Angels, Great City of Immortals, Magnificent City of the Nine Gems, Seat of the King, City of Royal Palaces, Home of the Gods Incarnate, Erected by Visvakarman at Indra's Behest. Thais commonly call the city Krung Threp, or City of Angels.

Bangkok (*bang* means "riverside village"; *kok,* "a wild olive") became Thailand's capital when Rama I moved the city across the Chao Phraya river from Thon Buri in 1782 to ensure fortification against the Burmese, who had sacked the capital of Ayutthaya. Magnificent palaces, temples, and canals were built. The area, known as Rattanakosin island, or the old royal city, exists today, housing the Grand Palace, the National Museum, and some of the city's most celebrated *wats* (temple complexes).

From Rattanakosin the city spread. Chinese merchants, under royal orders, moved eastward to form a new settlement—today's vibrant Chinatown. King Chulalongkorn (Rama V), inspired by his European travels, built wide, tree-lined boulevards and erected neoclassic buildings that are still much in evidence in Dusit, north of Rattanakosin.

Unbridled development began in the late 1950s and has, more or less, continued since. Canals *(khlongs)*, which had earned the city the appellation of the Venice of the East by early European travelers, were mostly filled in and roads built. Rows of monotonous shophouses were constructed. Later came the mad rush of office towers, hotels, and condominiums with little, if any, thought to town planning.

Today, Bangkok hammers the senses of visitors with its controlled chaos. But scratch the surface of this metropolis—population about eight million—and you'll find pockets of surprising beauty and grace. A surfeit of grand, riotously ornate Thai architecture links the city to its past, while gleaming modern, at times fantastic, skyscrapers point to its future. Just off the frenetic, traffic-clogged streets are quiet, snaking *sois* (side streets) with rows of wooden houses and a community feel. A trip on the city's Skytrain unfolds rooftop views of parks, lush tropical gardens, and huge colonial mansions that have escaped development. The main

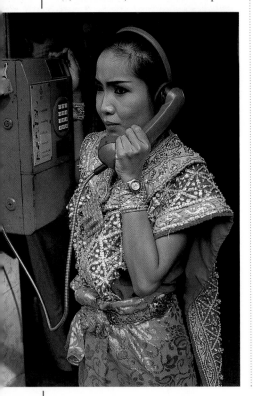

A dancer in traditional clothing talks on a phone at Erawan Shrine.

Bangkok has hundreds of markets full of cheap, but notoriously fake, goods.

waterway, the Chao Phraya river, reveals a tranquil side of the city; exploring it and the maze of khlongs either by public water transport or by charter is a highlight of a visit.

Indeed, it is the dichotomy of Bangkok that appeals. This is a place where the truly shocking, horrendous, and horrible exist alongside moments of pure beauty. Sukhumvit Road, a main avenue in the eastern part of the city, is a perfect example. Sukhumvit appears to be a creation of the devil, with absurdly packed sidewalks, broken chunks of concrete, the sky blackened by the concrete pillars and tracks of the skytrain, vendors crammed into every square inch, and a total sense of anarchy and mayhem. Yet, walk slowly and you see the magnificence of carved fruit among vendors selling copy watches, the smiling girl selling exquisite floral baskets next to an open sewer, a Buddhist shrine at a busy intersection, and perhaps an old Hindu astrologer predicting people's fortunes in the middle of all this madness.

At night the city explodes with the liveliest entertainment in Asia. Superb Thai restaurants are found in traditional houses.

International cuisine ranks with the world's best. Sophisticated nightclubs, along with raunchy bars and entertainment venues, are scattered through the city. About the only thing Bangkok doesn't offer the visitor is boredom.

World-class traffic jams are a constant frustration. Luckily, taxi fares are cheap. Trips around town will most times cost less than $2, even in heavy traffic. (Make sure the driver turns on the meter. If he refuses, get out and catch another taxi—they are plentiful.) Many locals, and the odd adventurous tourist, opt for the city's army of motorcycle taxis that weave expertly through traffic. It is a quick and hair-raising way to get around. *Tuk tuks*, colorful three-wheeled taxis—named because of the noise made by their small engines—are fun for short journeys but are often more expensive (and dangerous) than taxis. Always agree on a price beforehand. The modern Skytrain is the most efficient and agreeable way to get around.

Organized tours of Bangkok are easily arranged from your hotel tour desk. They are generally inexpensive and often the best way to see the city if time is limited. ■

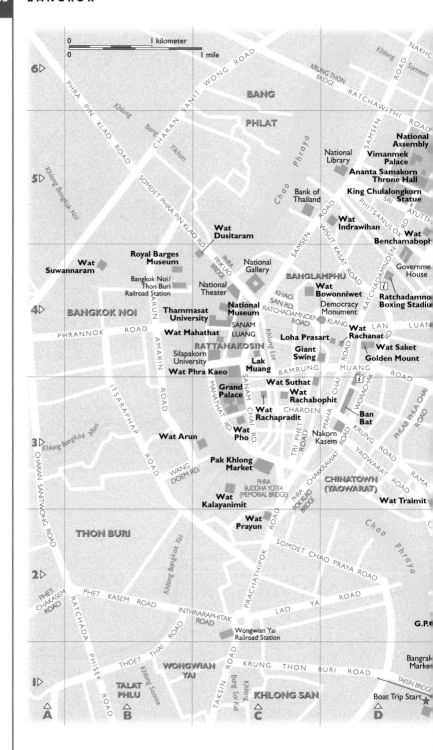

0 _____ 1 kilometer
0 _____ 1 mile

BANG PHLAT

KRUNG THON BRIDGE

RATCHAWITHI ROAD

PHRA PIN KLAO ROAD

CHARAN SANIT WONG ROAD

Khlong Bang Yikhan

SOMDET PHRA PIN KLAO RD.

Khlong Bangkok Noi

Chao Phraya

National Assembly

National Library

Vimanmek Palace

Ananta Samakorn Throne Hall

Bank of Thailand

King Chulalongkorn Statue

SAMSEN ROAD

PHITSANULOK ROAD

SRI AYUTTH

Wat Dusitaram

Wat Indrawihan

WISUT KASAT ROAD

Wat Benchamaboph

Royal Barges Museum

Wat Suwannaram

National Gallery

PHRA PIN KLAO BRIDGE

Bangkok Noi/ Thon Buri Railroad Station

National Theater

ARUN

BANGLAMPHU

Wat Bowonniwet

KHAO SAN RD.

Democracy Monument

RATCHADAMNOEN ROAD

Ratchadamno

Ratchadamno Boxing Stadiu

Governme House

BANGKOK NOI

PHRANNOK ROAD

AMARIN

Thammasat University

National Museum

SANAM LUANG

Khlong Lot

KLANG

Wat Lan Rachanat

LAN LUAN

Wat Mahathat

RATTANAKOSIN

Silapakorn University

Lak Muang

Loha Prasart

Giant Swing

BAMRUNG

MUANG

ROAD

Wat Saket

Golden Mount

ITSARAPHAP ROAD

Wat Phra Kaeo

Grand Palace

SANAM CHAI

MAHATHAT RD.

Wat Suthat

Wat Rachabophit

CHAI

WORACHAK

ROAD

Wat Arun

Khlong Bangkok Mon

CHARAN SANITWONG ROAD

WANG DOEM RD.

Wat Rachapradit

Wat Pho

CHAROEN

Ban Bat

Nakorn Kasem

MAHA CHAI

KRUNG ROAD

YAOWARAT

PHLAB PHLA CHAI

Pak Khlong Market

PHRA BUDDHA YOTFA (MEMORIAL BRIDGE)

CHAKKRAWAT

CHINATOWN (YAOWARAT)

YAOWARAT ROAD

RAMA

TRI PHET ROAD

Wat Kalayanimit

PHRA POK KLAO BRIDGE

Wat Traimit

THON BURI

Wat Prayun

SOMDET CHAO PRAYA ROAD

Chao Phraya

PRACHATHIPOK ROAD

PHET CHAKASEM ROAD

RATCHADA

PHET KASEM ROAD

Khlong Bangkok Yai

INTHRARAPHITAK ROAD

LAD YA ROAD

G.P.O

Wongwian Yai Railroad Station

THOET THAI ROAD

Khlong Samre

PHISEK ROAD

WONGWIAN YAI

TAKSIN ROAD

KRUNG THON BURI ROAD

Bangrak Market

TALAT PHLU

Bang Sai Kai

KHLONG SAN

TAKSIN BRIDGE

Boat Trip Start

6 ▷
5 ▷
4 ▷
3 ▷
2 ▷
1 ▷

△ A   △ B   △ C   △ D

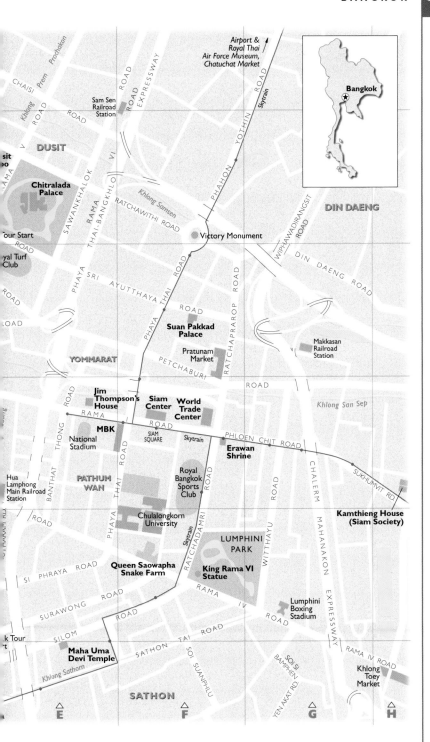

Airport &
Royal Thai
Air Force Museum,
Chatuchat Market

Bangkok

CHAISI

Khlong Prem Prachakon

Sam Sen
Railroad
Station

DUSIT

sit
o

Chitralada
Palace

Khlong Samsen

DIN DAENG

our Start

yal Turf
Club

Victory Monument

RATCHAWITHI ROAD

DIN DAENG ROAD

PHAYA SRI AYUTTHAYA ROAD

YOMMARAT

Suan Pakkad
Palace

Pratunam
Market

Makkasan
Railroad
Station

PETCHABURI

ROAD

Khlong San Sep

Jim
Thompson's
House

Siam
Center

World
Trade
Center

MBK

National
Stadium

SIAM
SQUARE

Skytrain

PHLOEN CHIT ROAD

RAMA ROAD

Erawan
Shrine

Hua
Lamphong
Main Railroad
Station

PATHUM
WAN

Royal
Bangkok
Sports
Club

SUKHUMVIT RD

Kamthieng House
(Siam Society)

Chulalongkorn
University

LUMPHINI
PARK

Queen Saowapha
Snake Farm

King Rama VI
Statue

RAMA IV

Lumphini
Boxing
Stadium

SI PHRAYA ROAD

SURAWONG ROAD

k Tour
t

SILOM

Maha Uma
Devi Temple

SATHON TAI ROAD

SOI SUANPHLU

RAMA IV ROAD

Khlong
Toey
Market

Khlong Sathorn

SATHON

E

F

G

H

Khon figures guard a stupa at the Grand Palace at Rattanakosin, the ancient heart of Bangkok

Rattanakosin

The historical and cultural heart of Bangkok is Rattanakosin island, site of the old royal city. Fronting a curve on the Chao Phraya river and backed by canals *(khlongs)*, Rattanakosin contains many of Bangkok's architectural and religious splendors. Here you will find the magnificent Grand Palace, the renowned temple complexes of Wat Mahathat, Wat Suthat, and Wat Phra Kaeo, the city's top universities, and the National Museum and National Gallery.

When Rama I moved the capital across the Chao Phraya from Thon Buri to Bangkok in 1782, he decided to model his country's new seat of power on the architectural magnificence of the former capital at Ayutthaya. Concentric canals were built to emulate the old capital, brick was salvaged from there to build palaces and temples, and Buddha images were collected from the ruined Ayutthaya and installed in the new temples at Rattanakosin.

Both the new Royal Palace and Wat Phra Kaeo were embellished by subsequent Chakri kings, who added their own royal temples within the confines of the Rattanakosin district, including Wat Saket and several structures near the Golden Mount. As the new capital became established, temples and government offices were constructed in outlying districts, and Bangkok spread in all directions.

Rattanakosin and Bangkok expanded further under the rule of King Mongkut. In 1862 he ordered the building of the city's first road, to connect his palace with the commercial enclave of Chinatown. Until the opening of this road, all transportation had been conducted on the Chao Phraya or on the canals that formed expanding circles from the centrally placed Royal Palace.

King Chulalongkorn continued to modernize the city, which developed into the bustling political and economic centerpiece of the kingdom. The historical quarter remained a royal enclave, housing the royal family's quarters, government offices, and royal temples, until the overthrow of the absolute monarchy in 1932. To a large degree, however, the flavor of the original old royal city remains intact in Rattanakosin. ∎

Wat Phra Kaeo & the Grand Palace

Wat Phra Kaeo & Grand Palace
🏛 66 C3 & C4
✉ Na Phralan Rd.
💲 $
🚌 Air-con bus: 8 or 12
⛴ Chao Phraya River Express to Chang Pier (Tha Chang)

THE MOST DAZZLING SIGHT IN ALL OF THAILAND AND ONE of the great wonders of Asia is Wat Phra Kaeo (the Temple of the Golden Buddha), with the adjoining Grand Palace. The temple and palace grounds are filled with a bewildering number of other buildings and sacred structures that, taken together, provide an architectural lexicon of the country and the single most comprehensive introduction to the physical and cultural charms of Thailand.

The entrance to the grounds of the royal temple leads through a narrow gateway and directly into a scene of incredible, dazzling brilliance, a world of shimmering golden spires and extravagantly ornate pavilions, all of which is guarded by a host of garish mythological creatures.

Rather than rushing directly to the *bot* that houses the famous Emerald Buddha, you should work up to this highlight by first slowly exploring the collection of buildings within the temple grounds, starting with the Ramakien Murals, and then the structures just outside the confines of the *wat*. The clockwise walk then proceeds through a narrow gate into the grounds of the Grand Palace, before leaving the grounds through the main gate just opposite Sanam Luang.

RAMAKIEN MURALS

The profuse and potentially confusing *Ramakien* Murals cover the entire walls of the interior cloister—a length of 2,080 yards (1,900 m). A professional guide is recommended to explain the story line, which begins by the north gate with the discovery of Sita, and then advances through the various adventures of her consort, Rama, and his assistant, the white monkey-god Hanuman. This legendary account of Rama is a Thai adaptation of the Hindu epic, the *Ramayana*, which dates from the early days of the Christian era and has been compared with the works of ancient Greek storytellers for its complexity and sheer breadth.

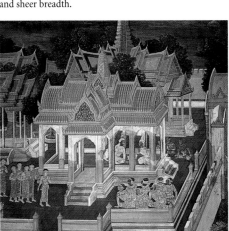

The murals date from the early 19th century, but the humid climate has taken its toll and they have been restored several times over the past 150 years. The quality of workmanship in the restoration varies, but the overall result maintains the basic integrity. Along with the story of Rama and Sita, the murals provide amusing insights into ordinary Thai life, from scenes of children at play and portraits of royal concubines, to depictions of grinning gamblers and souls lost to the wages of sin.

A mural depicting scenes of the Thai epic, the *Ramakien*, adorns the inside walls of Wat Phra Kaeo.

A gilded bell tower is a superb example of flamboyant temple decoration.

The Emerald Buddha, a symbol of power and enlightenment

Wat Phra Kaeo is a temple complex within the Royal Palace compound.

Prasat Phra Thep Bidon (Royal Pantheon)

Prang

Ramakien gallery

Ho Phra Monthien Tham (library)

Wihan Yot

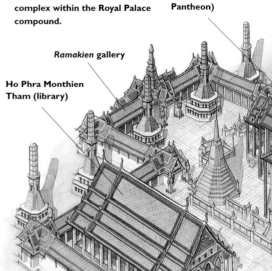

GOLDEN CHEDI

After inspecting the *Ramakien* Murals, stop by **Phra Sri Rattana** (Golden Chedi), built by King Mongkut to house a piece of the Buddha's breastbone and inspired by Phra Sri Rattana Chedi in Ayutthaya. Between the Golden Chedi and the bot is a richly carved **Phra Mondop**, which serves as a library, with a gleaming silver floor and a chest covered with mother-of-pearl inlay in which sacred Buddhist texts are held. This struc-ture is usually closed to the public.

Just below the mondop is a small reproduction of the Cambodian temple of Angkor Wat, which provides an overview of the famous Khmer structure. King Mongkut ordered this miniature to be placed here during a period when Cambodia belonged to the Thai Empire, as a public reminder of his vast territorial realm. The nearby gabled structure, known as

Wihan Yot, and covered with a profusion of ceramics and porcelains, is home to the Manangasila Stone, an ancient throne used by King Ramkamhaeng and worth a brief visit. **Ho Phra Nak,** in the north-west corner of the complex, is a royal mausoleum holding urns that contain the ashes of royal family members. It is closed to the public, though its magnificent exterior is well worth close inspection for its wealth of traditional detail.

The western facade of the **Ho Phra Monthien Tham,** the large secondary library of the temple complex, is considered the finest of its type in the country. The doors, inlaid with mother-of-pearl,

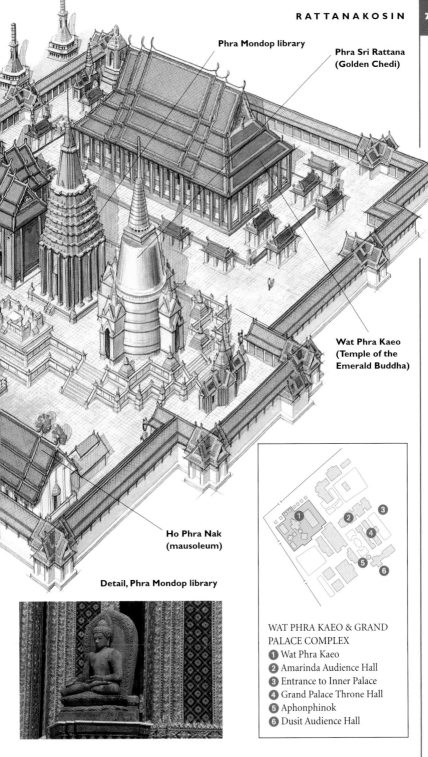

Phra Mondop library

Phra Sri Rattana
(Golden Chedi)

Wat Phra Kaeo
(Temple of the
Emerald Buddha)

Ho Phra Nak
(mausoleum)

Detail, Phra Mondop library

WAT PHRA KAEO & GRAND
PALACE COMPLEX
1 Wat Phra Kaeo
2 Amarinda Audience Hall
3 Entrance to Inner Palace
4 Grand Palace Throne Hall
5 Aphonphinok
6 Dusit Audience Hall

are particularly magnificent. The closed interior contains Buddhist texts and copies of the *Tripitaka*.

In an elevated position a few steps above the temple grounds stands the **Royal Pantheon** (Prasat Phra Thep Bidon), surmounted with an ocher-colored *prang*. Inside are life-size statues of the early rulers of the Chakri dynasty. Look for the strange mythological creatures that surround the Royal Pantheon, such as the *kinaree*, a divine part-human, part-bird creature of Himalayan origins, and ferocious lions, known as *norasinghs*, which guard the main entrance. Hindu-derived *garudas*, the sacred animal of Vishnu, are displayed on the friezes that flank the main entrance.

TEMPLE OF THE EMERALD BUDDHA

The bot, or chapel, is the largest building within the temple complex, and Thailand's most significant religious structure. Note that visitors must show great respect, be well dressed and covered, and remove their shoes before entering. Photography is prohibited. Bangkok's Royal Temple was constructed at the end of the 18th century by Rama I to house the **Emerald Buddha** (Phra Kaeo), a most holy and powerful statue, and a symbol to the Thai people of the power, divinity, and enlightenment of their country. The image is actually carved from green jasper. For its importance, it is also tiny—just 26 inches (66 cm) tall. Its origins are obscure, but the story goes that it was discovered by accident, hidden in a lump of plaster in Chiang Rai, northern Thailand, in 1434. Transported at one point to Laos, it was eventually restored to Thailand in 1778. It rested temporarily in Bangkok's Wat Arun while a new and suitably lavish

home was built. Although it is difficult to view, because of its remote and highly elevated position at the back of the temple, the Emerald Buddha draws a steady stream of pilgrims, who believe that the image represents the near mystical relationship between Thailand and its king. The king himself changes the sacred golden vestments on the statue three times yearly, as the seasons change.

The **interior frescoes** of the bot follow the classic arrangement: Those between the windows tell of the *Jataka* stories from the previous lives of the Buddha, while the Buddhist universe is shown on the rear wall, just behind the central altar. Of special note for its hellish imagery is the fresco above the temple entrance, which depicts the story of the Buddha resisting the temptations of Mara (see p. 79).

Just outside the Temple of the Emerald Buddha, the pair of glaring bronze lions ranks among the finest examples of Khmer art in the country.

GRAND PALACE

Rama VII was the last monarch to live here officially—he moved out in 1925 and now the Grand Palace fulfills a purely ceremonial function. While the palace lacks the exuberant exoticism of Wat Phra Kaeo, its curiously successful fusion of disparate Thai and Western styles makes it worth a quick inspection.

Built at the same time as the wat, the audience halls and former private royal residences adopted an unusual combination of formal Italian Renaissance styles in the main rooms and structures, with a familiar Thai roofline placed on top. Much has been altered over the centuries, and today only the Dusit and Amarinda Audience Halls are in regular ceremonial use.

A prime example of Buddhist architecture, Wat Phra Kaeo contains more exquisite carvings and decoration per square inch than any comparable site in the world.

Amarinda Audience Hall

Walking from the interior courtyard of Wat Phra Kaeo, you come first to the Amarinda Audience Hall, part of the original private residence of Rama I and later the national Hall of Justice. Inside, the walls are painted with murals, and there is a splendid boat-shaped throne. This was separated from the main hall by heavy brocade curtains, which hid the king from his audience until, with a great fanfare, they were parted.

Just outside the hall are several red and gold painted wooden posts; these were hitching posts for the royal elephants. A small pavilion decorated with glass mosaics was the king's dressing room, where he could change his robes before setting out on a ride.

The **Inner Palace** behind Amarinda Audience Hall was once the private home for the king's wives, children, and concubines. Cut off from the world, they ran their own community with their own laws. With the introduction of monogamy under Rama VI, such a place became obsolete, and today it serves only as the venue of the king's birthday party.

Throne Hall

The impressive Throne Hall (Chakri Maha Prasat) is a strange edifice, erected by King Chulalongkorn in 1882 to honor the 100th anniversary of the Chakri dynasty and heavily influenced by Western architecture. The *prasat* on the top helps it to blend in with its surroundings, but inside, the state

Grand Palace

- 66 C3
- Na Phralan Rd.
- 02-222-2208 or 02-255-0968
- $$$$$
- Air-con bus: 8 or 12
- Chao Phraya River Express to Chang Pier (Tha Chang)

SANAM LUANG

The immense grassy field situated between the Grand Palace and the National Museum is one of the best places to see kite fliers. It is also the scene of national celebrations such as the Hindu Brahmanic planting ceremonies, presided over by the king each spring.

rooms follow a Western neoclassic design, complete with marble pillars, gilded plasterwork, and heavy oil paintings of past kings.

Visitors are permitted only in the reception rooms that flank each side of the main entrance. Both are decorated with marble columns, portraits of Siamese princes and former kings, and marble busts of Western rulers. Beyond the reception rooms, another hall leads to the throne room, where foreign ambassadors once presented their letters of introduction to the king, and where state banquets were held. Several other reception rooms, lavishly decorated with marble urns and gilded objets d'art, are located upstairs. This was the official royal residence of King Ananda (Rama VIII) until his death in 1946.

Aphonphimok

Next stop is this small wooden pavilion, where in earlier days King Mongkut would step down from his royal elephant and show himself to members of the court below. The building was

constructed at such a height that the king could then continue directly to the royal buildings without the need to descend.

This lovely little building is considered the epitome of refined Thai architecture, to the extent that it has been copied twice—once for the king's summer retreat in Bang Pa-in (see pp. 141–42), and again in Brussels for the 1892 World's Fair.

Dusit Audience Hall (Dusit Maha Prasat)

With its magnificent decoration and gilded, nine-tiered spire, this undoubtedly ranks as Thailand's most splendid royal building. Constructed on a cross-shaped platform of white marble, the hall was built in 1789 at the instigation of Rama I. The interior has typical late 18th-century Siamese murals, and the doors and windows are heavily lacquered and gilded in abstract designs. The highlight is the original teak-wood throne of Rama I, beautifully inlaid with mother-of-pearl. ■

Temptations of the Buddha

It may not be a great artistic statement, but the small white pavilion, and its elevated female statue, opposite the Royal Hotel (corner of Ratchadamnoen and Atsadang Roads), is worth a brief visit as it relates an important story about the Buddha.

According to traditional folklore, Buddha once entered into a long period of meditation to discover the truths of life. During his arduous ordeal, he was subjected to a series of temptations by an evil goddess named Mara and her company of sensual dancing ladies. This story of 40 days of fasting and temptation by the devil (Mara) is, of

course, comparable to the biblical story of Christ in the desert.

Buddha refused to submit to the onslaught of hedonistic temptations and continued his meditations. His trials and tribulations were closely watched by an earth goddess known as Torani, who was so impressed with his moral fortitude that she decided to honor his courageous acts. Torani aided the Buddha by wringing out her long hair, which unleashed a tidal wave that destroyed Mara and her wicked cohorts. This extremely popular legend is retold endlessly in murals and statues throughout Thailand. ■

Wat Pho

Intricate mother-of-pearl inlays decorate the feet of Wat Pho's immense and highly revered Reclining Buddha.

CONVENIENTLY ADJACENT TO WAT PHRA KAEO, WAT PHO (also known as the Temple of the Reclining Buddha) is the oldest and largest temple complex in Bangkok. Established in the 16th century and bustling with life and interest, it contrasts starkly with its more formal, reserved neighbor. Officially called Wat Chetuphon, it has a wonderful collection of religious structures, rock gardens, unusual statuary, painted bell towers, several significant *chedis*, a magnificent central *bot*, and, its most famous inhabitant, the 150-foot-long (46 m) Reclining Buddha.

Wat Pho was established long before the rise of Bangkok as the national capital, and many of the buildings were restored in the late 18th and early 19th centuries. In 1832 the progressive Rama III opened the gates of the temple to public learning. Paintings, inscriptions, and sculptures throughout the temple deal with varied subjects, including warfare, literature, astronomy, and archaeology. The mounds of stone found throughout the grounds encouraged the study of geology. Statues of *rishis* (Indian hermits) wrapped in yoga positions guided students in the correct postures for meditation and other relaxation techniques, and murals demonstrated massage techniques. The early science of palmistry continues to be practiced at the *wat*.

The **College of Traditional Medicine** is still based here, in the eastern courtyard. This unassuming site was the first place in the country to teach Thai massage, and it still serves to some degree as the original home of this ancient skill, offering 10- or 15-day courses of professional instruction. At the eastern end of the compound, rows of benches are set aside for students to practice their massage

Wat Pho

- 66 C3
- Chetuphon Rd.
- $
- Air-con bus: 6, 8, or 12
- Chao Phraya River Express to Tien Pier (Tha Tien)

GUIDES

Guides, many of them univeristy students, can be hired at the entrance for a few dollars per person. Most are knowledgeable, but tend to linger too long at the Reclining Buddha. Politely suggest you would like to see more of the complex. ■

techniques on visitors. Getting a massage here is highly recommended: It's inexpensive and the colorful, bustling atmosphere of Wat Pho enlivens the experience. At the center of the complex, the souvenir shop is housed in the former Medicine Pavilion; look for the murals depicting massage points.

Guarding the monumental gates of the main entrance and at other parts of the inner courtyard are fearsome demons, huge stone figures bedecked with top hats. These statues were carved from stone ballast used in the rice barges that plied the Chao Phraya.

Four tall and brightly colored chedis stand to the left of the main bot, honoring the first four kings of Thailand. The most intriguing of these is the blue structure at the back, the Phra Si Sanphet Chedi, erected by King Mongkut in memory of his wife, Queen Suriyothai. According to legend, she gave her life in battle to save her husband, an act of piety that brings her special honor among queens. Hundreds of standing Buddha images in the double-blessing pose watch from the surrounding cloister.

EASTERN BOT

The eastern courtyard of Wat Pho is dominated by the immense bot, famed for its elegant proportions, soaring rooflines, and profuse decoration. It is enclosed by a rare double gallery, now glazed, and filled with almost 400 Buddhas cast in the classical Ayutthaya style. Khmer *prangs* of white marble stand at each corner, balanced by four *wihans,* each with its own Buddha statue.

Eight stairways, each guarded by a pair of finely cast bronze lions and with bas-reliefs underneath showing scenes from the *Ramakien,* lead up to the temple walkway. If all this carving and relief isn't enough

to overload your senses, the superb doorways are set with mother-of-pearl inlays depicting scenes of Moorish traders, Chinese landscapes, and Western visitors riding horses.

Entrance to the bot is finally made through the eastern doorway. The interior is dominated by a magnificent bronze Buddha, mounted on a high, gilded pedestal at the back. Murals on the walls and above the entrance are highly decorative, including scenes from everyday Thai life such as women bathing and children playing.

THE RECLINING BUDDHA

The western courtyard is home to Wat Pho's biggest attraction, the huge, gilded Buddha that reclines on its elbow. The Reclining Buddha—150 feet (46 m) long and 50 feet (15 m) high—is the largest of its type in Thailand. Although mere brick and plaster underneath, on the outside it gleams with shiny gold leaf. The statue virtually fills the vihara that Rama III built to house it. It is a shame the *vihara* is not bigger, as the size makes it difficult to grasp the dimensions of this immense icon, and this can be frustrating. Being the number one attraction at Wat Pho, the vihara is usually crowded. However, this tends to draw you closer to the statue's exquisite detail. The statue does not represent Buddha sleeping—as many assume—but his moment of enlightenment, when he entered nirvana. His joyous passing is represented by the reclining position and the languid, ecstatic smile on the finely modeled face of the statue.

Look closely at the soles of the feet. These are encrusted with mother-of-pearl inlays that—appropriately—describe the 108 *lakshanas,* or auspicious signs, that identify an enlightened one. ■

Wat Mahathat & Lak Muang

Wat Mahathat
- 66 C4
- Na Phra That Rd.
- Air-con bus: 8 or 12
- Chao Phraya River Express to Maharat Pier (Tha Maharat)

THE "TEMPLE OF THE GREAT RELIC" LIES MIDWAY BETWEEN the Grand Palace and the National Museum, but in architectural terms it's nothing special, having been rebuilt in the mid-19th century. Functionality takes the place of decoration, for this *wat* plays a central role in the study of *vipassana* (insight) meditation. it is also one of the most important centers of Buddhist teaching in the country, Mahachulalongkorn University.

The complex is also the seat of the Theravada sect of Buddhism—that is, the variation of Buddhism as practiced by most Thais. Introductory lectures in English and meditation retreats take place here each month.

Even if you are not interested in the practical skills of meditation, you should try to come here to stroll around the weekend market that is held on the grounds. Inevitably, the market specializes in Buddhist trappings such as medals, sacred images (often cast just across the river in Thon Buri), and monkish essentials—begging bowls, orange robes, and fans. This is also the place to seek out traditional herbal medicines.

LAK MUANG

Just opposite the Grand Palace is a moderately sized but very significant marble pavilion, housing a phallic-shaped icon that symbolizes the foundation stone of the city. All distances around the country are measured from this sacred monument.

The shrine is also the residence of the powerful landlord-spirits of Bangkok and, as many Thais believe the spirits possess the power to perform miracles, supplicants arrive daily to make offerings in support of wishes such as winning lottery numbers and the continued health of their children. It's intriguing to linger inside the pavilion to watch the pilgrims in action and to admire the performances of Thai classical dance sponsored by successful supplicants. The best times to see this are early morning and late afternoon, especially in the times immediately preceding events such as the lottery. ■

Buddhist amulets, images, and other religious items can be found for sale at Wat Mahathat's weekend market.

Mudras of the Buddha

The hand gestures (*mudras*) of the Buddha image complement the body position and give the faithful a pantheon of religious teachings in stone, not unlike the carved saints placed outside medieval Christian cathedrals.

Meditation mudra

The meditation mudra is a seated buddha with both hands folded in the lap, and the legs tightly crossed in the "lotus position." Several historical references can be made to this position, including the last period of meditation, and the moment of enlightenment as the Buddha sat under the

sacred *bodhi* tree. This serene position neatly summarizes the ecstatic goal of the ancient yoga, who withholds all spiritual disquiet in order to concentrate on the truth.

"Calling the Earth to witness" mudra

One of the most common positions depicts the Buddha with his right hand extended, the palm turned inward with the fingers extending down to touch the earth. The image is seated in a "half-lotus" position or, more rarely, in a "full lotus" with both feet elevated above the knees.

The four basic postures of Buddha icons are complemented by a number of hand gestures, which are essential to understanding the symbolism of Buddha iconography.

This mudra symbolizes the Buddha's victory over evil as personified by the demon Mara. According to legend, when the Buddha was on the verge of enlightenment, he was attacked by Mara, who demanded that he demonstrate his powers. The Buddha then touched the earth and summoned the earth goddess Torani, who wrung water from her hair and washed away the evil hordes.

"Turning the Wheel of the Law" mudra

A third seated position of the Buddha, in which both hands are raised to the chest, shows the position of the Buddha as he preached his first sermon in the deer park at Sarnath. The thumb and forefinger of the right hand are joined to form a circle, which represents the Buddhist "Wheel of the Law." This wheel symbolizes the setting in motion of Buddhist law, the endless cycle of birth and rebirth, and the principles of karma and nirvana.

"Triumph over evil" mudra

This mudra, generally depicted in a standing image, shows the Buddha with his right, left, or both hands held at shoulder level, palms turned outward, with the fingers stretched upward. According to legend, the Buddha was attacked by a mad elephant sent by his cousin

to trample him, but he raised his hand and stopped the beast in its tracks. The pose is also called Giving Protection, Dispelling Fear, or Granting Fearlessness.

"Dispensing favors" mudra

Symbolizing Buddha's vows of assistance and gifts of truth, this mudra is almost the same as the "triumph of evil" mudra—hands held out at shoulder level with palms turned outward—except the palm is exposed, open, and empty.

"Adoration" mudra

This mudra is performed by *bodhisattvas* (angels) giving homage to Buddha. The hand gesture is the same as the traditional Thai greeting, the *wai*—open hands pressed together at chest level.

"Calling for rain" mudra

This noncanonical mudra is sometimes encountered on Buddha images in Northern Thailand, especially Chiang Rai, Nan, and Phrae Provinces. The arms of a standing image fall downward at the sides of the body, with the palms facing the thighs. This posture and mudra signify the call for rain that will bring nourishment to rice fields. ■

Reclining Buddha icons—here at Ayutthaya—represent the Buddha at enlightenment.

National Museum

THE NATIONAL MUSEUM IS THE LARGEST AND MOST comprehensive museum in Thailand, and is an outstanding place to study its history, arts, and the religious symbolism of Buddhism. Visitors who intend to visit the ancient capitals of Ayutthaya and Sukhothai (see pp. 132–40 and 195–203) will find the museum an invaluable aid to their understanding of the country and its various schools of religious art. The complimentary guided tours in English, which start daily at 9:30 a.m., are highly recommended.

The museum is housed in several buildings around the central Wang Na Palace, including a beautiful 18th-century *wat* and three historic pavilions. Chronologically arranged displays range from the prehistory of the country to artistic movements of the Rattanakosin era.

After purchasing your ticket, your first stop should be the **Sivamokhapiman Hall** to the left, which functions as a quick introduction to Thai history, with dioramas and other displays on the various historical epochs from Sukhothai to the modern era. The prize exhibits are the famous Sukhothai inscription, or stele, of King Ramkamhaeng, which is the earliest known representation of the Thai script, and those describing the possible origins of the Thai people.

The **Gallery of Pre-Thai History** to the rear of the Sivamokhapiman Hall displays Paleolithic artifacts from Kanchanaburi (see pp.124–27), and the famous pottery and bronze creations discovered near the town of Ban Chiang (see pp. 182).

WAT BUDDHAISAWAN

Most important of the various examples of Thai architecture here is the centrally placed Wat Buddhaisawan, among the finest of the early monastic temples. The structure dates from 1787 and was built to contain a holy statue of the Buddha, the Phra Buddha Sing. The highlight is the spacious interior,

This Khmer-period lintel is part of the National Museum's expansive display of religious relics.

Red Pavilion

Sivamokhapiman Hall

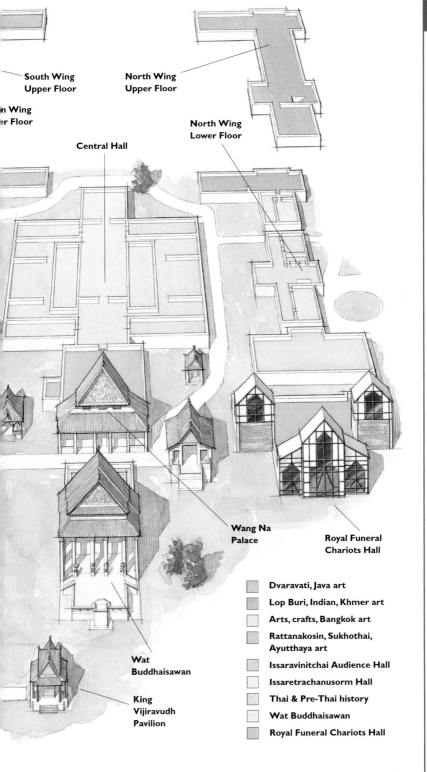

South Wing
Upper Floor

North Wing
Upper Floor

n Wing
er Floor

North Wing
Lower Floor

Central Hall

Wang Na
Palace

Royal Funeral
Chariots Hall

Wat
Buddhaisawan

King
Vijiravudh
Pavilion

Dvaravati, Java art

Lop Buri, Indian, Khmer art

Arts, crafts, Bangkok art

Rattanakosin, Sukhothai,
Ayutthaya art

Issaravinitchai Audience Hall

Issaretrachanusorm Hall

Thai & Pre-Thai history

Wat Buddhaisawan

Royal Funeral Chariots Hall

National Museum

66 C4

Na Phra That Rd., opposite the northern end of Sanam Luang Park

02-215-8173

Closed Mon.–Tues.

$

Air-con bus: 8 or 12

Chao Phraya River Express to Maharat Pier (Tha Maharat)

set with richly gleaming wooden floors and superb murals in warm, vivid colors, which give the room a wonderfully romantic atmosphere.

A return to the main museum route leads to the **Red Pavilion** (Taman Daeng). The former home of Rama I's sister, it is filled with the trappings of a royal residence of the late 18th and early 19th centuries.

CENTRAL HALL

Magnificent lacquered doors lead into the Wang Na Palace and the **Issaravinitchai Audience Hall,** once used by the surrogate monarch (the ruler's deputy). It now houses changing exhibits, such as recent archaeological discoveries. At the back of the hall is a small room filled with treasures discovered at Wat Ratchaburana in Ayutthaya (see p. 136).

The rear section has more than a dozen rooms filled with a variety of fine arts and more utilitarian creations. Most rooms have a core theme that helps reduce confusion as you explore the labyrinth.

The first of these is the **Phimuk Monthain Gallery,** filled with splendidly decorative litters used in funerals, and howdahs carried by royal elephants. The room to the left is filled with shadow puppets and other intriguing stage properties, such as *khon* masks worn by dignitaries of the court of Rama VI. .

The Central Hall also has rooms filled with European and Asian ceramics, glazed ware from Lop Buri, Sukhothai-period Sangkhalok stoneware and celadon, and brightly colored Rattanakosin-era porcelain called Benjarong. You will also find richly carved elephant tusks and models of white elephants, elephant battle armor covered with religious symbols, antique weaponry, more royal

regalia, carved teakwood, ancient inscribed stones, a collection of rare costumes and textiles from all regions of Southeast Asia, and Thai musical instruments, along with gamelans from Java and Bali.

SOUTH WING

After exploring the Central Hall, take a quick look at the first floor of the museum's South Wing. This particular section is dedicated to ancient artistic cultures of Thailand and its neighbors, including Cambodia and Java. The first room illustrates the importance of Indian culture on Thai art. Another concentrates on the role of various styles of Khmer art, from those known as Kompong Prae and Baphuon, to the pinnacle of Cambodian heritage, Bayon.

The second floor of the South Wing includes rooms filled with art of the Dvaravati period, and a small but worthwhile collection of images from central Java, including some exquisite examples of Hindu and Buddhist sculpture from Borobudur and Prambanan. A seventh-century stone Vishnu sculpture is a notable highlight.

NORTH WING

Artifacts from the later traditions of Sukhothai, Ayutthaya, and Bangkok are found in the North Wing, and are for many visitors the most impressive collections.

Among the highlights on the ground floor are printed and embroidered textiles from the Rattanakosin period; lacquerware, inlay-work, and ceramics; Bangkok-era statuary, with its elaborate headdresses and ethereal faces; and a room filled with Buddha statues from various epochs, of which the image carved in the Dvaravati style—seated in the "European" fashion with hands on knees—is

the most unusual. The numismatic gallery has displays of Thai coinage.

The upper floor of the North Wing contains the richest collection of Buddha images in the museum, ranging from the small but precise Lanna and Chiang Saen figures from Northern Thailand, to the grander creations of the Sukhothai Kingdom, regarded as the epitome of Thai art. Look for the magnificent bronze four-armed Vishnu and a statue of Harihara with eight arms arched in different *mudras*.

The final two rooms contain Buddha images from the Ayutthaya period, distinguished by their highly embellished headpieces and robes. Less interesting contemporary Buddhas complete the picture, and there are further examples of Rattanakosin craftwork.

Nearby are the **Funeral Chariots Hall,** full of magnificent chariots, and **Issaretrachanusorm Hall,** built for King Rama IV (*R.* 1851–1868), with his original European furniture in situ. ■

The sublime lines of a Buddha image dating from the Sukhothai period

Wat Saket

📍 66 D4

✉ Boriphat Rd.

💲 $

🚌 Air-con bus: 8, 11, or 12

Wat Saket &
the Golden Mount

AT THE NORTHERN END OF HISTORIC RATTANAKOSIN island is Wat Saket, undistinguished aside from its interesting carved windows. Nearby, the 260-foot (78 m) artificial hill known to Westerners as the Golden Mount, topped by a golden spire, is a clear landmark.

A monk climbs the 320 steps to the top of the Golden Mount, once the highest point in Bangkok.

The temple, like Wat Phra Kaeo and Wat Pho, was constructed by Rama I in the early 19th century and therefore ranks as among the oldest structures in the city. It was originally built outside the city walls to serve as a crematorium for commoners. Later, toward the end of the 19th century, it was used as a burial site for victims of a cholera epidemic. It follows a traditional style of architecture, with a principal sanctuary surrounded by a large and peaceful courtyard—a welcome escape from the city.

The interior of the temple is covered with fairly modern frescoes. They are well restored and reward close inspection. Look for the rows of angels on the upper levels, who are praying with their heads turned toward the altar.

Just outside the main cloister is another sanctuary, with a huge standing Buddha, which Rama I brought from the ruins of Sukhothai (see pp. 195–203). On the walls are paintings of Buddha's disciples. Behind the altar in the sanctuary, a seated Buddha image is surrounded by bronze statues of his disciples.

On the western side of the *wat*, the 320 steps leading to the summit of the Golden Mount—the highest point in Bangkok up until the 1960s—wind past gravestones, myriad Buddhist monuments, small mountains erected to recall the Khmer/Buddhist co-opted Hindu heaven of Mount Meru, and clutches of monks who often engage in conversation with visitors to improve their English. This artificial hill was created from mud, brick, and teak logs after a *chedi* being built on the orders of Rama III collapsed because the soft soil beneath it gave way. Rama IV subsequently built another small, unimpressive, chedi on the crest of the hill. The second chedi was expanded to house an Indian Buddha relic that was presented to Rama V by the British government in 1897. Each November, a festival held at Wat Saket features a candlelit parade up the steps to the summit of the Golden Mount.

It is worth the long climb to the top for the sweeping views over Bangkok—if, that is, the usual blanket of smog permits. ∎

Wat Suthat & the Giant Swing

Wat Suthat
- 66 C3, 66 D4
- Bamrung Muang Rd., just SW of Wat Rachanat
- Air-con bus: 8 or 12

THE LARGE *WIHAN* AND *BOT* OF WAT SUTHAT FORM one of the most impressive religious structures in Bangkok, a must-see after the splendor of the Grand Palace and Wat Phra Kaeo. The two buildings were started in 1807 by Rama I and gradually completed by his two successors.

Before entering the wihan, or main hall, spend a few minutes exploring the temple grounds, which hold a museum of stone carvings, bronze animals, and Buddha images. Highlights include Chinese statues of American sailors and Chinese warlords, 28 hexagonal Chinese pagodas, and four magnificent bronze horses.

The wihan is the biggest in Bangkok, and whatever it may lack in terms of gaudy glitter is more than compensated for in its refined style and good taste. The structure stands on a pair of rising platforms and is entered through tall teak-wood doors, carved in five exquisite layers to recall the mythological forest of Himavada. Rama II made one of these himself in an act of piety—it is on show in the National Museum (see pp. 80–83). The lavish interior radiates authority with marble pillars, high ceiling, and

frescoes. The 26-foot (8 m) bronze Buddha is a 14th-century master-piece from Sukhothai.

The bot, built about 1839, is famous for its murals. Painted with pre-Western treatments of perspective, panels between the windows relate tales about the early lives of the Buddha. Frescoes on the shutters depict the heavenly city of Indra, while those on the front wall concern the Buddha's temptation by Mara (see p. 79).

Priests would often ride the Giant Swing as part of a Hindu ceremony (shown above in an archive picture), but this dangerous practice was stopped in 1935.

GIANT SWING

Near the main entrance to Wat Suthat are two towering, red pillars. Dating from 1784, they were once capped with a crossbar from which hung a long swing. This was all part of a highly dangerous Hindu cere-mony involving monks and bags of gold coins. ∎

Spirit houses

M any Thai buildings have spirit houses—a home for spirits, or *phra phum*, to keep them from entering and causing trouble for the inhabitants. The spirit houses—ornate, dollhouse-size temples mounted on a pedestal in front of the main building—offer the spirits inviting daily gifts of food, flowers, and incense. Figurines inside symbolize the property's guardian spirits. ∎

More places to visit in Rattanakosin

LOHA PRASART

Loha Prasart is an unusual religious structure that resembles a large wedding cake, complete with candle spires. The pinkish monument, modeled on ancient temples in Sri Lanka and India, has a thousand rooms and was designed to serve as the home of Buddha and his disciples; this is the only surviving example of its type in the world. Although the exterior gate is generally locked, a resident monk will usually open it for you. Just behind Wat Rachanat.

🗺 66 D4 ✉ Mahachai Rd. 🚌 Air-con bus: 11 or 39

WAT RACHABOPHIT

Another unusual temple on Rattanakosin island is Wat Rachabophit, which has several buildings of interest, including a small chapel decorated in Italian Gothic style. Look for the particularly fine mother-of-pearl inlays in the doors and windows. In the royal cemetery next door, the tombs resemble miniature Asian temples or tiny European cathedrals. Best of all, you will probably be the only visitor there, and the attendant monks are usually pleased to show people around the temple grounds.

🗺 66 C3 ✉ Atsadang Rd. 🚌 Air-con bus: 3 or 12

WAT RACHANAT

Wat Rachanat, three blocks northeast of the Giant Swing (see p. 85), dates from 1846. It has some outstanding frescoes in the main sanctuary, and a *wihan* of an unusual design (thought to be modeled on Burmese structures), with Buddhas mounted on an elevated altar. Its amulet market rivals that at Wat Mahathat (see p. 77).

🗺 66 D4 ✉ Mahachai Rd. 🚌 Air-con bus: 11 or 39

WAT RACHAPRADIT

This peaceful minor temple is within easy walking distance of the Grand Palace and not far from Wat Suthat. Wat Rachapradit dates from the mid-19th century and was erected by King Mongkut to complement a pair of temples in Ayutthaya. It incorporates a variety of architectural styles, from older Thai traditions to Western motifs. The most interesting part is the interior murals, which depict lively scenes of mid-19th-century Bangkok, including the Giant Swing ceremony (see p. 85). A *prang* in the courtyard has an impressive carved image of the four-faced Brahma.

🗺 66 C3 ✉ Rachini Rd. 🚌 Air-con bus: 3 or 12 ■

British bobbies are part of the unusual collection of statues at Wat Rachabophit.

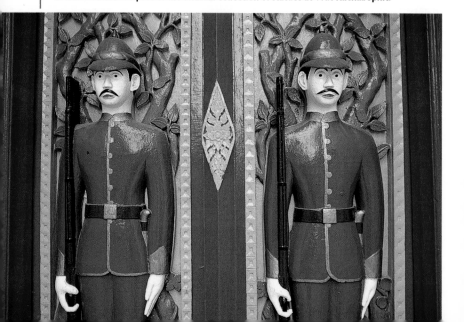

Arrive at Chinatown's Pak Khlong market before sunrise to catch it at its bustling best.

Chinatown

Chinatown is a district south of the Grand Palace, bounded on one side by the Chao Phraya, and by Charoen Krung Road on the other. It is rarely walked by foreign visitors, though it is one of the most exciting ethnic enclaves in Bangkok. Hidden behind the main streets, which now carry the dull look of modernization, are gaudily decorated temples filled with Taoist monks, creaky old pharmacies offering traditional Chinese medicines, gold shops piled high with chains and necklaces, and narrow alleys packed with all forms of street markets and peddlers of bric-à-brac.

Chinatown is also one of the oldest districts of the city, dating back to the late 18th century. When they were cleared from the land on which Rama I intended to build his Grand Palace and Wat Phra Kaeo, the Chinese merchants moved their shops southward. The first businesses were established along narrow Sampeng Lane, which doubled as a commercial zone during the day and an opium district at night. Most of the illicit operations have closed down, though sufficient sights and smells remain to make this one of the most exotic corners of the city.

Chinatown, however, is not a neighborhood for the faint-hearted or anyone who dislikes seething, frenetic, jam-packed quarters, where the scattered attractions and kaleidoscopic chaos make for a difficult

walking tour. Probably the most convenient introduction and starting point is Ratachawong Pier (Tha Ratchawong), from where you can walk up Ratachawong Road past several banks to the following attractions. You can turn right to walk down romantic Sampeng Lane, visit the famous Golden Buddha at Wat Traimit, and return up the more commercialized Charoen Krung Road. Be prepared to make lots of trips up the side lanes to visit temples and other historic structures, and remember, it's the small details of Chinatown that make it just about the most interesting section of Bangkok—far more intriguing and culturally rewarding than the shopping centers and modern highrises that now characterize so much of this rapidly changing city. ■

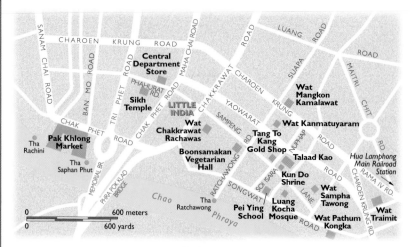

Chinatown highlights

Chinatown

 66 D3

Air-con bus: 1 or 7

Opposite: Bangkok's ethnic Chinese patronize well-stocked herbal medicine shops.

Boonsamakan Vegetarian Hall (*Krai Soi*) is a small and very peaceful, old, yellow temple containing magnificent examples of Chinese woodcarving. The carvings are seen in the entrance porch and around the altars inside, and depict dragons and other mythological Chinese creatures. There are also miniature reproductions of traditional opera scenes and tilework gaily painted to portray Chinese legends. Octagonal doors on each side of the main altars lead into auxiliary chambers, including crypts and private rooms of worship.

The temple comes to active life once a year in the fall, during the Vegetarian Festival, to honor the nine chief deities. Traveling opera troupes perform at this time on the stage opposite the main entrance.

Sampeng Lane, also known as Soi Sampeng or Soi Wainit 1, runs parallel with the river. Built in the 1870s, it was the first street in Chinatown. It offers an authentic experience to all the senses and some unusual shops. It is far too narrow for regular traffic but perfect for pedestrians—who must make their way through the piles of merchandise that spill out from the intriguing old shop-fronts, dodging the porters who madly haul their heavy loads. Fabric markets and clothing merchants predominate, and at the western end of the lane is the fabulous Pahurat Cloth Market, full of exotic silks and batiks.

Tang To Kang Gold Shop, a teetering but impressive seven-story structure designed by a Dutchman, was the original gold exchange for the neighborhood.

The **Kun Do Shrine** on Soi Isara Nuphap features a large grinning gilded horse head that is said to bring luck to those who bring him offerings of vegetables.

Talaad Kao, or Old Market, (*Soi 16*) is best visited in the early morning, when Chinese merchants and housewives come to trade all manner of produce, poultry, and fresh seafood. Come here before 10 a.m. to catch the best action of the day. Lanternmaking, an old tradition that has now largely disappeared from Thailand, survives in the small alley off Soi Isara Nuphap.

Large, busy streets through Chinatown belie its maze of narrow, intriguing alleyways jam-packed with colorful temples, gold shops, traditional pharmacies, and open-air markets.

Pei Ying School, located just off Sampeng Lane, is a large building of European design, housing a junior school founded by Chinese immigrants in 1916 to foster their language and customs. Chinatown also has a small Indian community, and Muslims gather on Friday afternoons at **Luang Kocha Mosque,** two blocks south of Pei Ying School, to perform their weekly absolutions. Ancient Islamic tombstones in the graveyard behind the mosque are worth seeing.

Wat Sampha Tawong, also known as Wat Koh, features an impressive, modern multistoried *bot*. Farther south, **Wat Pathum Kongka** straddles Songwat Road and dates from the Ayutthaya period, almost a hundred years before the founding of Bangkok.

Most visitors make the requisite stop to see the famous **Golden Buddha** inside **Wat Traimit** (*Tri Mit Rd.*), at the southern end of Chinatown and just across a canal from Hua Lamphong train station. The complex has the air of a rather seedy tourist trap, and the image itself, despite its claim to the

biggest golden Buddha in the world, is undistinguished. Dating from the 13th century, it stands 13 feet (4 m) high, weighs an estimated 5.5 tons, and is believed to be made of solid gold. According to legend, the Buddha had long been hidden under a disguising layer of stucco, until it was accidentally dropped from a crane in 1955, and a metallic core was revealed.

After paying your respects to the Golden Buddha, walk north up busy Charoen Krung Road, passing elaborately decorated gold stores and traditional Chinese wedding boutiques to **Soi Isara Nuphap** (*Soi 16 Market*), which is like a mini Sampeng Lane, with its crazy bazaar atmosphere. Food is the main item sold here—everything from fresh raw ingredients to ready prepared Chinese snacks.

The Chinese highly venerate the impressive **Wat Mangkon Kamalawat,** or "dragon flower temple" (*Soi 21, off Charoen Krung Rd.*). The central complex is filled with a fascinating collection of religious icons, from a fat Buddha to Taoist Star deities. ∎

Bangkok's Indian community worships in the Hindu temples of Little India.

More places to visit in Chinatown

HUA LAMPHONG STATION

The city's major train station, built by Dutch architects shortly before World War I, is Bangkok's most impressive art deco building. It features huge vaulted ceilings, massive skylights, and wide entrances that give a feeling of airiness. The inexpensive bars and restaurants on the mezzanine floor have the best view.
🅰 67 E3 & map p. 88 ✉ Rama Rd. IV 🚍 Air-con bus: 1, 7, or 29

LITTLE INDIA

Most Indians in Thailand have integrated into local society, and purely Hindu neighborhoods are now quite rare, with the exception of this small district between Chakkrawat and Chak Phet Roads, and pockets of Hindu culture near Silom and Charoen Krung Roads. On **Chak Phet Road,** which runs from the Central Department Store down to the river, shops sell traditional wedding gear for Hindu ceremonies as well as elaborate Thai dance costumes. The white **Sikh temple** stands seven stories high. Dozens of inexpensive food stalls and cafés line both sides of Chak Phet.
🅰 Map p. 88 ✉ Between Chakkrawat and Chak Phet Rds. 🚍 Air-con bus: 1 or 7

PAK KHLONG MARKET

The city's largest wholesale fruit and vegetable emporium overflows with basketloads of exotic produce. Come early in the morning to see it at its best. Visitors love the displays of flowers.
🅰 66 C3 & map p. 88 ✉ Chak Phet Rd. near Memorial Bridge 🚍 Air-con bus: 3 or 9 🚤 Tha Rachini

WAT CHAKKRAWAT RACHAWAS

Chinese funerals are held every day, it seems, at Wat Chakkrawat Rachawas. The most notable feature of the *wat* is its crocodile pond, just off the main courtyard.
🅰 Map p. 88 ✉ Chakkrawat Rd. 🚍 Air-con bus: 1 or 7

WAT KANMATUYARAM

This interesting little temple in a side street opposite the Cathay department store dates from 1864 and is chiefly visited for its striking Sri Lankan-style *chedi.* The temple has some of Thailand's most important murals, untouched since first painted. To see them, ask a monk to unlock the door to the interior.
🅰 Map p. 88 ✉ Mangkorn Rd. 🚍 Air-con bus: 1 or 7 ■

Colonial-style architecture, including the East Asiatic Company building, lines the Chao Phraya

Eastern Bangkok

Beyond Chinatown, Bangkok continues eastward on its mad sprawl. Office towers, hotels, and condominiums rise from a seemingly endless urban landscape. Traffic clogs the roads with more intensity than elsewhere, and masses of people crowd the potholed sidewalks, dodging motorcycles and muscling past myriad food vendors.

Beyond all this, there are numerous—albeit dispersed—attractions. The modern, air-conditioned Skytrain whisks you close to many. The line begins at the Chao Phraya river at the end of Sathorn Road near the gracious old *farang* quarter (see pp. 98–99). It heads east along the financial and entertainment district on **Silom Road,** home to world-famous **Patpong** and its side streets of go-go bars, massage parlors, restaurants, and night market. It then crosses Rama IV Road, past the exclusive **Royal Bangkok Sports Club** and the popular Erawan Shrine (see p. 96) to the major shopping district at Siam Square (see p. 93).

At Siam station you can change lines for a trip above the arterial Sukhumvit Road. The Sukhumvit area, especially side streets Soi 4 to Soi 40, palpitates wildly with bars, restaurants, and discos. The **Nana Entertainment Plaza** is at Soi 4. Here you'll experience a rowdy, in-your-face confrontation with

Bangkok's notorious sex industry—a raunchier scene than Patpong. Across Sukhumvit Road, in a number of lanes off Soi 3, the city's small Arab community gathers to smoke from hookahs and drink coffee at some excellent Middle Eastern restaurants. Farther down Sukhumvit, notably on Sois 13, 23, 24, and 33, are numerous restaurants—some converted from traditional Thai houses—offering excellent Thai and other cuisines.

Take the Skytrain from Siam station in the opposite direction to Morchit, at the end of the line. Here is the sprawling **Chatuchat** weekend market, an absolute must for shoppers, which sells, among other things, antiques, aquarium fish, fighting roosters, arts and crafts, clothing, paintings, kitchenware, and novelties. To get a perspective, pick up a map at the market's tourist center. Crowds can be intolerable on Sunday afternoons—it's best to arrive on Saturdays, mid-morning. ■

Siam Society & shopping centers

ESTABLISHED IN 1904, THE SIAM SOCIETY IS THAILAND'S premier cultural organization. It publishes books and the scholarly *Journal of the Siam Society*, and works to preserve all facets of traditional Thai culture. For those seeking a serious study into the history and culture of Thailand, a visit to its headquarters can be rewarding.

An excellent research library and archive is maintained on two floors at the society's headquarters in the Chalerm Phrakiat Building. Anything you need to find out about Thailand will be housed here. There is also an art galley and lecture and performance hall in the building, with lectures given by both Thai and Western scholars. Perhaps best of all are the regular excursions offered by the society to places of historical and cultural importance, including temples and archaeological sites, and to festivals around Thailand. Guided tours head deep into detail and incisiveness, and visitors can join in.

On the grounds of the society's headquarters is 175-year-old **Kamthieng House.** This traditional Thai wooden stilt house was dismantled in Chiang Mai, in Northern Thailand, by the Siam Society in the 1960s, moved to Bangkok, and reassembled here. It houses an ethnological museum that provides a fascinating record of rural life in Northern Thailand, with exhibits that include woodcarvings and an assortment of northern hill-tribe costumes.

SHOPPING AROUND RAMA I ROAD

Some of the best areas for shopping can be found around the junction of Praya Thai and Rama I Roads. **Siam Square,** in an area of upscale hotels, is the oldest shopping complex in Bangkok. It is a colorfully crowded mix of bargain-priced clothing and designer labels, movie theaters and bookstores, as well as a plethora of restaurants—many of which specialize in a Chinese favorite, shark's-fin soup.

Across the road is the smaller and more upscale **Siam Center.** Locals flock to the Mahbonkrong, or MBK *(just south of Siam Square on Praya Thai Rd.)*, for its maze of outlets and bargains. The enormous **World Trade Center** *(corner of Rama I and Ratchadamri Rds.)* provides much more of the same in a floor-after-floor shopping odyssey. ∎

Kamthieng House (Siam Society)
- 🅰 67 H3
- ✉ 131 Soi Asoke
- ☎ 02-258-3491
- 🕐 Closed Sun.–Mon.
- 🚌 Air-con bus: 1, 8, 11, or 13

Siam Center, Siam Square, World Trade Center
- 🅰 67 F3
- ✉ Rama 1 Rd.
- 🚌 Air-con bus: 1, 8, 11, or 13

A spirit house stands outside the Zen department store, one of a cluster of large retail outlets in Siam Square.

Jim Thompson's House

🅰 67 E3

✉ Soi Kasem San 2,
Rama I Rd.

☎ 02-612-3742 or
02-612-3743

💲 $

🚌 Air-con bus: I or 8

Jim Thompson's House

THIS IS THE MODEST BUT ATTRACTIVE FORMER HOME OF Jim Thompson (1906–1967), an American architect and military officer who settled in Bangkok at the end of World War II. Credited with reviving the fortunes of the ailing silk industry across Thailand (see pp. 178–79), Thompson disappeared in 1967 while hiking in the Cameron Highlands in Malaysia; no trace of his body was ever found, despite a massive search.

The home of Jim Thompson, the man who revived Thailand's silk industry after World War II, is now a museum.

Khlong Saen Saeb, with a simple entrance courtyard and finely crafted gardens. The wooden houses were dismantled and brought here from the countryside, and all have been carefully preserved to retain their traditional charm, complete with the high and slightly curved roofs and polished teakwood floors that are typical of Central Thailand. The overall effect is of an intimate and stylishly decorated residence.

In his quest for authenticity, Thompson adhered to particular customs of the early Thai builders, such as the elevation of the houses a full story above the ground—a practical precaution to avoid flooding during the rainy season. Thompson also had roof tiles specially made in Ayutthaya, employing a design that was common centuries ago but is rarely seen today. The exterior walls of the house were painted in a red preservative paint once commonly used on old buildings.

Thompson also insisted that the proper traditional religious procedures be followed during the construction process. Even the date of dedication was chosen by local astrologers as one that was auspicious. Within a few years of its occupation in the spring of 1959, the house and its fine art collection had become such a point of interest in Bangkok that Thompson opened his residence to the public, donating proceeds to local charities. ■

Thompson was an avid collector of Southeast Asian art and antiques, and his interconnecting maze of seven old teak houses is now a private museum full of assorted antiques, pottery, and other valuable curiosities. Highlights include the sixth-century headless Buddha that stands in the garden, Thompson's collection of Ming dynasty blue and white porcelain, and early 19th-century paintings of tales from the *Jataka*.

The house stands on the banks of an attractive, if noisy, canal,

Suan Pakkad Palace

DON'T BE PUT OFF BY THE LITERAL TRANSLATION OF THIS palace's name—*suan pakkad* means "cabbage patch"—for this collection of five traditional pavilions set in richly landscaped gardens forms one of the finest examples of traditional domestic architecture in Bangkok. The principal house was originally the residence of a wealthy northern family. Prince Chumbhot, a notable art collector, dismantled it and had it moved south from Chiang Mai.

Suan Pakkad Palace
- 🗺 67 F4
- ✉ 352 Sri Ayutthaya Rd.
- ☎ 02-245-4913
- 🕐 Closed Sun.
- 💲 $
- 🚌 Air-con bus: 4

The most striking building on the grounds is the 450-year-old **Lacquer Pavilion,** which was rescued from Ayutthaya (see pp. 132–40). It was originally the library of a temple located between Ayutthaya and Bang Pa-in.

The glossy black and gold structure is a unique example of Siamese decorative art, the only example of its kind to survive the ravages of time and warfare. Today it is admired not only for its fine proportions, but also for its remarkable lacquerwork murals, ornamented with intricate designs in gold. These panels, conceived and executed with great decorative ingenuity, show thousands of minutely observed people in stylized surroundings.

The formal gardens around the Lacquer Pavilion provide a most welcome relief from the heat and pollution of Bangkok.

The other pavilions—at one time serving variously as a bedroom, reception area, chapel, and dining room—hold a wide assortment of Thai artifacts, of which the highlights are Bronze Age pottery uncovered at Ban Chiang (see p. 182), Khmer sculpture, the Sangkhalok ceramics, and multicolored Benjarong ceramics. Other artifacts include musical instruments, finely crafted reproductions of royal state barges, and antique drums that date back to the Dong Son era of ancient Vietnam. The pavilions also house antique Thai

furniture, bronze and stone statues (of which those from the Dvaravati and Khmer periods are considered particularly fine), Chinese and Thai porcelain, swords that once belonged to Siamese warriors, and delicately crafted fans used by priests in Buddhist rites.

The prince's family lived here for several decades, and after his death the whole site was converted into a public museum. Most of the collection is displayed in an informal style that reflects the personal tastes of the former owners. ∎

Beautiful lacquerware adorns the walls of Suan Pakkad Palace's unique Lacquer Pavilion.

Erawan Shrine

THIS SMALL BUT HIGHLY REGARDED SHRINE, ON ONE OF the busiest intersections in the city and just outside the Erawan Grand Hyatt hotel, is an extraordinary spot dedicated to the mysterious and all-pervasive forces of animist spirits and Hindu deities.

People flock to the Erawan Shrine to make offerings and wishes for good fortune.

The shrine was erected in the 1950s to honor the Hindu god Brahma and to halt the string of disasters that had occurred during the construction of the original hotel at this site—such as the sinking of a ship carrying marble for the lobby and the deaths of several construction workers. Along with spiraling costs, these disasters threatened to stop completion of the hotel, and

Hindu Brahman priests were summoned to lift the curse. The shrine was built on their advice and the hotel's troubles came to an end.

Today, the shrine is a madcap scene of religious frenzy. Groups of devotees arrive with gifts of smoking incense and bunches of flowers. Little carved wooden effigies of elephants are left for Erawan, the highly venerated three-headed elephant god who carried Brahma. Pilgrims ask for blessings or give thanks for good fortune. Traditional dancers stand by—those whose prayers have been answered may pay for them to perform.

Photographers are welcome at this attraction, and the gaily costumed dancers will be some of the best you may see during your travels in Thailand. ■

Buddha amulets

Thais believe Buddha amulets worn around the neck can protect them from evil spirits (*phi*, pronounced PEE), misfortune, and danger. The small icons can cost hundreds of dollars depending on their perceived power, which is attained by being blessed by a monk or by being issued by a powerful organization such as the army or police. Taxi drivers wear them to protect against accidents; thieves don them to ward off arrest; soldiers clench them between their teeth before entering battle. The amulet trade is big business: At all markets, stalls trade in the symbols. ■

Lumphini Park

LUMPHINI PARK, ONCE LITTLE MORE THAN RICE FIELDS ON the edge of town, covers 140 acres (56 ha) of some of the best real estate in Bangkok. While the city has sprawled around it, Lumphini has survived as the city's most popular park, an easy escape from the incessant crowds, noise, and pollution of Bangkok's streets.

The park, bounded by Rama IV Road to the south, Sarasin Road to the north, Withayu Road to the east, and Ratchadamri Road to the west, was earmarked as the site of the First Siamese Trade Exhibition and was presented to the people in 1925 by Rama VI. In gratitude, city fathers put a statue of Rama VI at the main entrance, on the corner of Rama IV and Ratchadamri Roads.

Lumphini Park is named after the Buddha's birthplace in southern Nepal, reputedly an enchanting garden. While not particularly enchanting, areas of Lumphini are certainly tranquil. The central feature is a large artificial lake; you can hire boats for a row or a paddle. Generous, well-kept lawns, lush wooded areas, and walking trails surround the lake.

If you arrive before 7 a.m., you'll find Chinese practicing t'ai chi, joggers getting their exercise around a 2-mile (3 km) circuit, and vendors setting up stalls to sell snake blood and bile, a morning health tonic favored by ethnic Chinese Thais. Muscular young men lift weights in the exercise area, while others play soccer. A splash of color is added during the kite-flying season, February to April, when people head here to fly their kites. You can buy inexpensive kites from vendors and join in. The park has an open-air café and picnic tables.

An intriguing structure is a Chinese pagoda-style clock tower. Chinese philanthropic organizations were responsible for its construction—and for many other buildings in public venues. ∎

Lumphini Park

🏛 67 F2

✉ Main entrance at corner of Rama IV Rd. & Ratchadamri Rd.

🚌 Air-con bus: 4, 5, or 7
Skytrain: Silom

A walk around the old *farang* quarter

A fairly short but interesting walking tour can be made along the Chao Phraya river, around the attractive old commercial and diplomatic enclave that once comprised the original *farang* (foreigner) community within the city of Bangkok.

Start at the world-famous **Oriental Hotel** ❶, where you can spend some time exploring the palm-filled **Authors' Lounge** (early 20th-century luminaries such as Joseph Conrad, Noël Coward, and Graham Greene stayed here), or enjoy breakfast on the veranda overlooking the Chao Phraya. Just where Oriental Avenue terminates at the river, a Dutch flag flies over the whitewashed former headquarters of the **East Asiatic Company** ❷, built in 1901. Founded by

Dutch investors in 1897, this mercantile company was one of the first to set up permanent offices in the city.

Pass through the arch of the East Asiatic Company building and walk parallel to the river. Follow the alleyway around to the left to reach the pink and white confection of **Assumption Cathedral** ❸. There has been a Catholic cathedral on this site since the first Europeans settled around here in 1822, though the present structure dates from 1910. The brightly painted rococo interior has a marble altar imported from France—visitors are welcome.

Turn left on Oriental Lane, and bear left onto Oriental Avenue, then immediately right, to pass the Oriental Hotel on your left. Tucked on the next corner, just beyond the hotel, is the lovely old **French Embassy** ❹, built in the mid-19th century and the second oldest embassy in Bangkok. With its spacious rooms, shuttered windows, and upper verandas overlooking a well-tended garden, this building evokes an older, more elegant age.

Turn left down Soi 36 toward the river, then take a right to pass before the finely

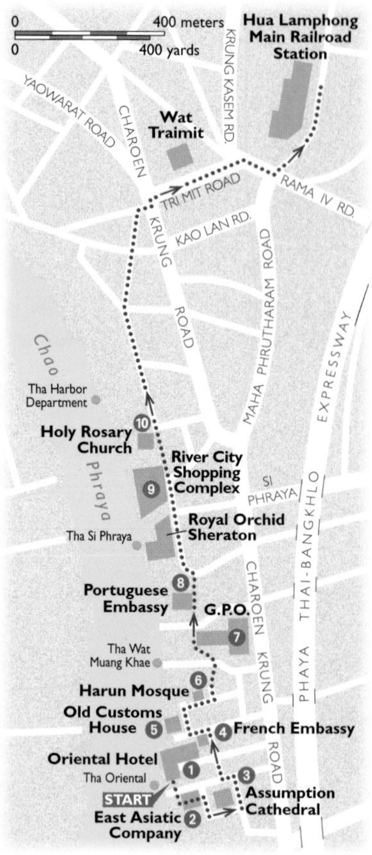

Map showing walking route with the following labels:

0 — 400 meters
0 — 400 yards

Hua Lamphong Main Railroad Station

YAOWARAT ROAD
CHAROEN KRUNG
KRUNG KASEM RD.
Wat Traimit
TRI MIT ROAD
RAMA IV RD.
KAO LAN RD.
MAHA PHRUTHARAM ROAD
EXPRESSWAY
Chao Phraya
Tha Harbor Department
Holy Rosary Church ❿
River City Shopping Complex ❾
SI PHRAYA
Royal Orchid Sheraton
Tha Si Phraya
CHAROEN KRUNG
THAI-BANGKHLO
PHAYA THAI-BANGKHLO
Portuguese Embassy ❽
G.P.O. ❼
Tha Wat Muang Khae
Harun Mosque ❻
Old Customs House ❺
Oriental Hotel ❶
Tha Oriental
START
East Asiatic ❷ Company
French Embassy ❹
Assumption ❸ Cathedral

▲ See area map p. 66 D2–E3
▶ Oriental Hotel
↔ 1 mile (1.5 km)
⏱ 1½ hours
▶ River City Shopping Complex

NOT TO BE MISSED

- Authors' Lounge, Oriental Hotel
- Assumption Cathedral
- French Embassy
- Old Customs House
- Harun Mosque
- Antiques at River City Shopping Complex

The venerable Oriental is consistently ranked among the world's best hotels.

proportioned **Old Customs House ⑤**. Built in the 1880s, this was Bangkok's primary customs house, until more modern port facilities were developed downriver at Khlong Toey. Today the building is used by the Bangkok Fire Brigade, which docks several fireboats along the waterfront.

Beyond the Customs House, turn right, away from the river, and weave through the narrow alleys to reach the little **Harun Mosque ⑥**. Bangkok's small community of Muslims gather here on Fridays to worship. Small paths lead on, away from the river, toward the **General Post Office ⑦**, through a neighborhood where many Indians and Pakistanis live. Small cafés provide fine opportunities for a stop on your walking tour.

You might want to make a quick visit to the G.P.O. to wander around its cavernous interior and perhaps purchase some Thai commemorative stamps, or check your mail at Poste Restante.

A few steps up from the G.P.O. is the **Portuguese Embassy ⑧**, which dates from 1820 and is the oldest foreign embassy in Bangkok. The Portuguese were the first Europeans to open trade relations with Siam in the 16th century, from their base in the Malaysian city of Melaka, and the first to be granted land for a trading post and then a consulate in Bangkok, during the reign of Rama II. You can peer over the embassy walls to see portions of the original construction.

One block beyond the G.P.O., narrow alleys wind back to the river and the **Royal Orchid Sheraton** hotel, and then continue to the nearby air-conditioned **River City Shopping Complex ⑨**. River City is Bangkok's premier outlet for Southeast Asian antiques, best picked up at the monthly auctions (check details in the *Bangkok Post*). Art exhibitions are held on the ground floor.

River City makes for a convenient finish to your walking tour, though a handful of other sights are within a few blocks up the river. The **Holy Rosary Church ⑩** stands on the site of a church built in 1787 by Portuguese Catholics, who had fled the destruction of Thon Buri by the Burmese. Known locally as Wat Calavar, this small but elegant Gothic-style church features some fine stained glasswork.

From here, you could also continue along the riverside for the short distance (½ mile/ 0.8 km) to **Wat Traimit,** the temple of the Golden Buddha (see p. 90), and then to the restored **Hua Lamphong** train station (see p. 91) and Chinatown (see pp. 87–90). ■

More places to visit in Eastern Bangkok

MAHA UMA DEVI TEMPLE

This small and extremely colorful Hindu temple lies right in the middle of the tourist district, on Silom Road. The temple was constructed by Tamil immigrants from India in the 1860s and features a brightly ornamented and colorful *gopuram* tower, covered with a twisting mass of bulging Hindu gods and goddesses and capped with a golden dome. The temple is usually bustling with life—an oil-lamp ritual is held daily at noon; and on Fridays at 11:30 a.m., vegetarian food is blessed and handed out to the faithful in a ceremony called *prasada*.

🔼 67 E1 ✉ Silom Rd. at Pan Pan Rd.
🚍 Air-con bus: 2, 4, or 5

MONK'S BOWL VILLAGE (BAN BAT)

Rama I established three villages in Bangkok to provide housing for the craftworkers who made bowls for the local community of monks. Only a single village remains, Ban Bat, near Wat Saket and the Golden Mount. A handful of remaining craftsmen continue to

Snakes at the Queen Saowapha Snake Farm are used for research as well as shows.

fashion bowls of polished silver, each traditionally and laboriously made from eight separate pieces of metal. These can be seen in use by local monks making their morning rounds to collect alms of rice and other food. The monks' bowls are also sold at Wat Suthat.

🔼 66 D3 ✉ Soi Ban Bat, near Bamrung Muang Rd. 🕐 Bowl production most days until around 6 p.m. 🚍 Air-con bus: 8, 11, or 12

QUEEN SAOWAPHA SNAKE FARM

One block from Lumphini Park is the former Pasteur Institute, Thailand's leading facility for the development of vaccines against diseases such as cholera, smallpox, typhoid, and rabies. More interesting for visitors, it is also a center for education about the local poisonous snakes, and anti-snakebite serum is made here.

Over 1,000 snakes are kept here by the Thai Red Cross for both research and educational uses. Snake demonstrations for the public are held twice a day (once a day on weekends). After watching a 20-minute slideshow giving the center's background, visitors are led into a circular demonstration room. Handlers bring out a variety of snakes, including the mesmerizing Siamese king cobra, and "milk" them spectacularly, waving them within inches of the audience. The snakes' fangs seep poisonous venom harmlessly into prepared glass jars, providing some highly unusual shots for photographers. Over a dozen other species of indigenous venomous and nonpoisonous snakes are displayed in the adjacent vivarium.

🔼 67 F2 ✉ Rama IV Rd. ☎ 252-0161 💲 $
🚍 Air-con bus: 4, 5, or 7

ROYAL THAI AIR FORCE MUSEUM

Strictly for fans of military aircraft, this collection includes rare examples of a Japanese Tachikawa trainer, a Spitfire, and several Breguets. There are the only two such collections in Thailand—the other is the Warbirds Museum at Chiang Mai International Airport (see p. 221).

🔼 67 G6 ✉ Don Muang Airport, Wing 6
🕐 Closed weekends 🚍 Airport Bus: A1, A2, or A3 ∎

Dusit

In the northern part of Bangkok, this fascinating neighborhood, also known as the New Royal City, is home to many of the important government offices and royal residences that were moved here at the beginning of the 20th century, away from the more crowded area around the Grand Palace (see pp. 72–74). The broad, tree-lined avenues and spacious mansions and public buildings give this leafy section of Bangkok a curiously European flavor.

Dusit is one of the few districts of Bangkok to show any signs of urban planning, and open green areas situated between the government buildings provide a calm dignity that has been lost from the rest of the capital. Public offices, universities and private schools, royal palaces, and public parks dominate the area. Although land speculation, and the construction of modern houses and high-rise offices, has inevitably changed the character to a certain degree, Dusit is one of the few places where you can get a glimpse of the garden aspects of the city, which made it so remarkable to the early travelers.

The most popular visitor attractions are Chitralada Palace (where King Bhumibol Adulyadej lives today), the beautiful wooden Vimanmek Palace, the outstanding Marble Temple (Wat Benchamabophit), the National Assembly (Parliament) building, and Dusit Zoo. These are all found close together, making Dusit surprisingly convenient to explore. The parks, with their lakes and shady trees, provide welcome relief from the heat.

Most visitors arrive via Ratchadamnoen Nok Road, which leads past the headquarters of the Tourism Authority of Thailand (T.A.T.), then the Ratchadamnoen Boxing Stadium, and finally the Khlong Phadung Krung Kasem canal, before reaching the old National Assembly building. Just before this, look for an impressive equestrian statue of King Chulalongkorn, the man responsible for the planning and construction of Dusit. Amporn Park is just opposite the statue, while Vimanmek Palace and Dusit Zoo flank the National Assembly. Chitralada Palace is a few blocks east, on the far side of the zoo. ■

This 105-foot-high (32 m) Buddha statue at Wat Indrawihan offers great views of Dusit.

Dusit Park

ON THE GROUNDS OF DUSIT PARK ARE A CLOCK MUSEUM, a display of King Bhumibol's photographs (he is a keen photographer, and many pictures of his family are included), and the Royal Carriage Museum, which houses an eccentric and entertaining array of ceremonial vehicles. However, the highlights are the zoo and the lovely Vimanmek Palace.

DUSIT ZOO

With its modest but growing collection of animals from across Southeast Asia, Thailand's largest zoo provides a welcome change if you are satiated with a steady diet of historical buildings. It has large mammals such as rhinos, monkeys, elephants, tigers, and bears, as well as deer and other indigenous species, including gaur (a species of ox) and serow (antelope), housed in a reasonably sensitive environment. Visitors can also enjoy the hundreds of birds and the extensive reptile collection.

The zoo has a children's playground, several small cafés, and an artificial lake with recreation facilities. It is a shady place bisected by several decorative waterways, which provide the setting for a competition of floats for the Loy Kratong festival in the fall.

As with so much else in Dusit Park, the zoo was created by King Chulalongkorn, who was inspired after a series of visits to the zoological gardens of Europe to start his own, believing in their power to educate. The king traveled to Indonesia in 1909, where he purchased a handful of star deer; they were returned to Bangkok and allowed to roam around the private royal botanical gardens. After the coup of 1932, the new government petitioned the king to transfer the gardens and park to the municipality of Bangkok for the use of the people, rather than remain a private reserve for the royal family.

The zoo was duly opened to the public in 1938 but was still limited to the star deer and a few other animals that had been allowed to wander around the royal grounds. The Bangkok authorities quickly added representative species of Thailand, and within a few years the zoo also had white monkeys, bears, and a crocodile pond. The zoo was greatly expanded after the creation of the Zoological Organization of Thailand in 1954. This organization went on to open another zoo in Chiang Mai (see p. 222) and an "open zoo" in Khao Khieo, Chonburi Province.

VIMANMEK PALACE

If there is a house filled with memories in Bangkok, the beautiful and serene L-shaped Vimanmek (it means "castle in the clouds") must be the one. Once the royal residence of one of Thailand's most beloved and progressive monarchs, King Chulalongkorn, this gracious old building of precious golden teak seems haunted by the memories, and the exquisite refinements, of its courtly inhabitants.

It also survives as a delicate architectural balance between the last sector of the 19th century and the modernization of the early 20th century. The original structure was built on the resort island of Ko Sichang, started in 1893 on orders of Chulalongkorn, who named the teak pavilion Mundhat Ratanaroj. It was designed by a German architect and built without a single nail.

Dusit Zoo
- 🏛 67 E5 & map p. 105
- ✉ Ratchawithi Rd.
- 💲 $
- 🚌 Air-con bus: 10

Vimanmek Palace
- 🏛 67 D5 & map p. 105
- ✉ Ratchawithi Rd.
- 💲 $
- 🚌 Air-con bus: 10

Construction unexpectedly came to a halt the following year, after a diplomatic crisis brought French warships sailing into the Gulf of Siam, rendering further royal visits to Ko Sichang impossible.

The unfinished structure lay abandoned until 1901, when the king ordered that the golden teak be dismantled, hauled to Bangkok, and refashioned into the present structure, which was renamed Vimanmek. Incredibly, it took only seven months to rebuild and complete the world's largest golden teak building, which, with its open galleries, gingerbread-house fretwork, charming porticoes, grand stairways, and delightfully spiraled staircases, clearly shows a European and Victorian architectural influence. Daily tours include fewer than half

the 80 rooms but give a good flavor of this extraordinary home.

The king and his family (and concubines) lived here until they could move into the nearby Chitralada Palace. Closed up and neglected, Vimanmek was on the point of final collapse when Queen Sirikit came to its rescue in 1982; it was beautifully restored to its former glory as part of Bangkok's bicentennial celebrations. Today it is a museum filled with a rich collection of royal artifacts and personal items belonging to Chulalongkorn, from antique photographs of the last elephant hunt to Thailand's first shower.

You can arrange for an English-language tour of Vimanmek Palace at the entrance gate. It costs a little over $1. ■

With its 80 rooms, Vimanmek Palace is believed to be the largest golden teak building in the world.

Many consider Wat Benchamabophit the most impressive example of modern Thai architecture.

A walking tour of Dusit Park

Dusit Park and its environs provide a number of worthwhile sights compacted within a small area. The sights are varied: a glorious temple, seats of government, royal palaces, both outlandish and exquisite architecture, a zoo, and cool parks and gardens.

Start your walk at **Wat Benchamabophit** ❶ *(corner of Rama V Rd. and Sri Ayutthaya Rd.),* one of the most elegant and refined pieces of modern religious architecture in Thailand. It was commissioned by King Chulalongkorn in 1899, to the designs of his half-brother, Prince Naris, and Italian architect Hercules Manfredi. The facing of Italian white Carrara marble gave the temple its nickname—the Marble Temple.

Proceed down the side road that runs parallel to Rama V Road for 5 minutes and turn right onto Thanon Luk Luang. The tree-lined boulevard has a parallel road separated by the wide Khlong Phadung Krung Kasem (laughing children may well be seen thrashing around in the canal). Both roads run past the sprawling complex at **Government House** ❷, dominated by the Gothic Thai Koo Fah Building. With an exterior of extravagantly ornate arches, domes, pillars, and eaves, this extraordinary building looks more like a

European palace than the office of Thailand's prime minister. The surrounding area is often filled with resilient protestors: a mixture of farmers from the impoverished Northeast, trade unionists, and activists who spend months at a time in makeshift shelters.

At the corner of Thanon Luk Luang and Ratchadamnoen Nok Road, a small, elegant bridge curves over the canal. Green wrought-iron barriers on each side of the bridge run to small, thick columns veneered in marble. Streetlights, wrapped in more intricately worked wrought iron, sit atop patterned steel and concrete poles. Turn right, down elegant, abundantly tree-lined Ratchadamnoen Nok Road for about 5 minutes to Dusit Park (take care crossing busy Sri Ayutthaya Road).

Dominating the **Royal Plaza** ❸ at the entrance to Dusit Park is an equestrian statue of King Chulalongkorn. Every December 5, the plaza trumpets pomp and ceremony with the Trooping of the Colors, when the Royal

Guard Regiment affirms its oath of loyalty to the king and queen, who attend the event.

Behind the plaza is the amazing **Ananta Samakorn Throne Hall ④**. Overdone in Italianate architecture, it almost appears as a parody. A huge green dome supported by a ring of Roman columns crowns the building. Set on expansive, manicured lawns, it is ridiculously ornate and wonderfully outrageous—but rarely open to the public. Its former stables, reached by taking a path to the left off Uthong Nai Road, now house the **Royal Elephant National Museum.** Exhibits include the gigantic tusks of the elephants of Ramas III, IV, and V.

Farther down the path, over a tiny bridge, is the **Abhisek Dusit Throne Hall ⑤**, whose imposing facade features a veranda carved in exquisite timber latticework. The building now houses the **SUPPORT Museum,** which displays traditional crafts such as nielloware, woodcarving, and textiles.

Beyond the museum is the extraordinary **Vimanmek Palace ⑥,** a marvel of

traditional architecture and the world's largest teak building (see pp. 102–103). A little farther up Uthong Nai Road is the **National Assembly,** built in 1970s concrete bunker-style—worth a cursory glance. Cross on to Uthong Nai Road and backtrack to the **Dusit Zoo ⑦** (see p. 102), pay your $1.20 entrance fee, and hire a small foot-paddle boat for a cool trip around the zoo's delightful lake.

Adjacent to Dusit Zoo, across busy Rama V Road, is **Chitralada Palace ⑧,** the king's official residence *(closed to the public).* ∎

> ⚠ See area map pp. 66–67 D5
> ▶ Dusit Park
> ↔ 1.6 miles (2.6 km)
> ⏱ 2 hours
> ▶ Dusit Park
>
> **NOT TO BE MISSED**
> • Wat Benchamabophit
> • Abhisek Dusit Throne Hall
> • Vimanmek Palace

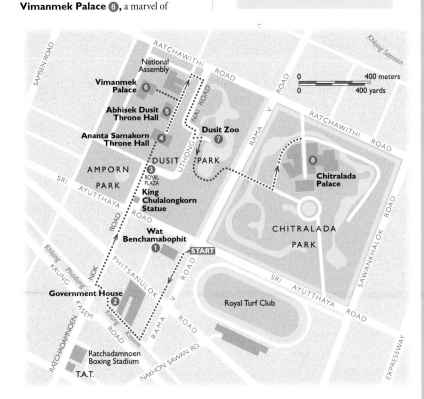

The royal family

King Bhumibol Adulyadej (Rama IX) was born on December 5, 1927, in Cambridge, Massachusetts, where his father was studying medicine at Harvard University. At the time, succession seemed unlikely. Bhumibol stood in the royal line behind his uncle, the reigning King Prajadhipok; his father, Prince Mahidol; and elder brother, Prince Ananda. Fate intervened when Mahidol died unexpectedly in 1929, and Prajadhipok abdicated without a direct heir in 1935. Ananda succeeded to the throne, reigning until his mysterious death in 1946, when the crown was passed to Bhumibol, who at the time was a student at Lausanne University in Switzerland.

Bhumibol, the longest reigning king in Thai history, has his own privy council made up of 14 appointees who advise and assist with the king's royal duties. The king and his wife, Queen Sirikit, have four children: Princess Ubol Ratana (born 1951), Crown Prince Maha Vajiralongkorn (born 1952), Princess Mahachakri Sirindhorn (born 1955), and Princess Chulabhorn (born 1957).

The son, Prince Maha Vajiralongkorn, is heir to the throne. If he declines ascendancy or is unable to take the crown owing to illness or death, the king's eldest daughter, Ubol Ratana, would be next in line. (Ubol Ratana fell out of royal favor in 1972 when she married American Peter Jensen against palace wishes, but her royal rank was later reinstated.)

Although negative comments about the monarchy are punishable by law, Thais feel no inhibitions about gossiping about members of the royal family in private. Many want to see Princess Mahachakri Sirindhorn as the next monarch (though traditional rulings make this unlikely). The princess—who has never married—is the most admired of the king's children because of regular visits to the countryside and her down-to-earth nature.

King Bhumibol and other members of the present royal family have done more than any other Thai royal family to give the institution a human face. Although deference to the monarchy has a lot to do with traditional reverence and esteem, their genuine concern for ordinary and less wealthy Thais has enhanced the institution's status. During his reign, the king—more often than not accompanied by his much-loved wife—has visited most places in Thailand, listening to the concerns of local officials and farmers. His travels have inspired the construction of hundreds of small-scale public works programs around the country under his patronage.

The extensive grounds of Chiltralada Palace, the royal family's home, have been turned into an agricultural research center, where scientists work on projects to improve Thailand's primary industries. Queen Sirikit works to promote the country's unique arts and crafts industry. Also on the palace grounds, there are workshops where craftsmen are passing on their skills to selected rural students in education schemes set up with royal patronage.

As a constitutional monarch, Bhumibol's status is ceremonial, but he can wield great influence in political life. Two attempted coups d'etat in the 1980s were thought to have failed because they could not garner the king's implicit approval. The coup of 1991, which overthrew a woefully corrupt (even by Thai standards) government, is believed to have had palace approval.

The most visual demonstration of the king's political influence was in May 1992, at the height of the bloody pro-democracy demonstrations in Bangkok (see p. 47). Bhumibol summoned the then (unelected) prime minister, Suchinda Kraprayoon, and Bangkok's governor and protest leader, Chamlong Srimuang, to his residence at Chiltralada Palace. Recorded on video footage that was seen around the world, the two men—looking more like contrite schoolboys than men of power—lay prostrate before a stern-looking Bhumibol. The madness on the streets outside the palace subsequently ceased. Suchinda resigned in disgrace and, within a few months, Thais went to the polls to elect a new, democratic government. ∎

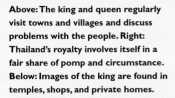

Above: The king and queen regularly visit towns and villages and discuss problems with the people. Right: Thailand's royalty involves itself in a fair share of pomp and circumstance. Below: Images of the king are found in temples, shops, and private homes.

More places to visit in Dusit

DEMOCRACY MONUMENT

The rallying point of Thailand's democracy movements over the past 30 years, the Democracy Monument was built in 1939 to commemorate the overthrow of absolute monarchy in 1932. The imposing 78-foot (24 m) monument, a city landmark, rises out of the center of a frantic traffic circle. Its sharp lines, reliefs of diligent, muscular, citizens carrying out their duties with pride, and a display of military hardware point more to overblown examples of fascist and communist architecture than any notions of democracy. Still, the monument remains a potent symbol. Gracious Ratchadamnoen Road, between the monument and Sanam Luang (Royal Field), has been the scene of many public protests over the years, including the Black May pro-democracy demonstrations in 1992 (see p. 47), when at least 50 protesters were killed by the military.

🗺 66 D4 ✉ Pracha Thipatai and Ratchadamnoen Klang Rds. 🚌 Air-con bus: 11, 12, or 44

KHAO SAN ROAD

The market along this crowded little street is legendary to budget travelers and backpackers—not only can you buy anything from Thai handicrafts to airplane tickets at bargain prices, but you can also sell your old designer blue jeans, Walkmans, and so on. Its lively action and busy trade can be enhanced only by the popularity of the ultimate backpacker movie, *The Beach* (2000).

🗺 66 C4 🚌 Air-con bus: 3, 9, or 11

WAT BOWONNIWET

Wat Bowonniwet is situated on the northern edge of Rattanakosin, not far from the Democracy Monument and a worthwhile stop en route between Rattanakosin and Dusit. The temple holds an important place in the hearts of Thai people, for this is where many royal princes studied and served their monkhood, including the current king, Bhumibol.

Bowonniwet dates from the mid-19th century and is architecturally unremarkable. It might have remained in obscurity, but the popularity and status of future king Mongkut, who chose to serve part of his monkhood here, changed all that. Mongkut became the chief abbot, a tenure that put a seal on the significance of the monastery.

Today, the temple is the residence of Thailand's Supreme Patriarch, the recognized leader of Buddhism in the country. It is also the headquarters of the Thammayut sect of Buddhism, a small but strict order that inspires great respect, as it is widely considered to be purer and more spiritually unpolluted than the majority, Theravada, branch.

The great golden *chedi* at the temple's heart enshrines sacred relics and ashes of Thai royalty. The two *wihans* are generally closed to the public. The unusual T-shaped *bot* holds a magnificent Sukhothai-period Buddha, cast in 1257 to celebrate freedom from the Khmers.

The most impressive features of Bowonniwet for the visitor, however, are the dark and imaginative three-dimensional murals on the interior walls of the bot, which break all of the previous rules used by painters in the country. Murals up to this point had traditionally been light and cheery, strictly limited both in their subject matter and perspective style. Monk-artist Khrua In Khong, court painter to King Mongkut, introduced Western perspective values, bringing a sense of realism to traditional Buddhist topics, and preferred mysterious, moody shading over the more commonly seen bright hues.

🗺 66 C4 ✉ Phra Sumen Rd. 🚌 Air-con bus: 11

WAT INDRAWIHAN

This minor temple, a 15–20-minute walk north of Wat Bowonniwet, is in a lovely, peaceful residential area, offering an escape from the more commercialized zones of the city. Take a walk through the smaller alleys here for an insight into the lifestyle of the average Thai. The wat itself is dominated by an ungainly, standing Buddha statue created in 1830, which can be entered and then climbed (for a small donation). The lack of artistic merit in the plastered statue is compensated for to some degree by the sweeping views from the top of the 105-foot (32 m) image.

🗺 66 D5 ✉ Wisut Kasat Rd. 🚌 Air-con bus: 3, 6, or 9 ∎

Longtail boats can be chartered for trips along the Chao Phraya river and the nearby canals.

Thon Buri

The former capital of Thailand spreads down the western shore of the Chao Phraya, linked to the newer city by bridges and ferry boats. Thon Buri was the original Bang Kok ("riverside village of the wild olive"), and lent this name to its newer neighbor. Much of the old capital retains its traditional charms and is built on a network of rivers and canals called *khlongs*, all in a state of bustling activity.

Thon Buri was founded in 1767 and served as the capital of Siam for 15 years after the fall of Ayutthaya. Then Rama I moved his court across the river for safety. Over the ensuing two centuries, while Bangkok received commercial input, Thon Buri was allowed to sleep on almost completely untouched by the forces of modernization. The first bridge between the two was not built until 1932. Other bridges followed, as did the construction of roads and shophouses. Later, in the 1980s and 1990s, came condominiums. But development in this surprisingly peaceful and rarely visited part of Bangkok has not greatly affected its ancient canal network, and much of it still remains intact.

Highlights of Thon Buri include the world-famous Wat Arun and the Royal Barges Museum, as well as the *wats* of Suwannaram, Kalayanimit, and Dusitaram.

Exploring Thon Buri can be tricky, as the smaller roads that lead to the most interesting temples are often little more than patchy lanes without formal demarcation. However, wandering around the alleys and planked walkways can be an excellent experience, as the people are friendly and invariably hospitable to the visitors who find themselves off the beaten track. In fact, getting lost is almost a blessing, as locals are more than happy to point out the correct direction to the temple of your choice.

The best way to explore Thon Buri is via a combination of water transportation, such as a motor-powered "longtail" water-taxi, and on foot through the maze of alleys. Longtail boats can be hired at most of the piers on the Bangkok side of river, but be aware that few boatmen speak enough English to serve as an adequate guide. ■

Royal Barges Museum

THIS REMARKABLE COLLECTION OF MORE THAN 50 elaborately decorated longboats is displayed in a vast, covered dry dock near Khlong Bangkok Noi. Painted, carved, and gilded, the boats were modeled after various mythological creatures from the Thai epic, the *Ramakien,* and come out only on the grandest of ceremonial occasions—for example, a procession on the Chao Phraya in December 1999 to celebrate King Bhumibol's 72nd birthday, the start of his 6th 12-year cycle of life, an auspicious age in Buddhism.

The tradition of royal barge processions dates back to the heyday of the Ayutthaya Kingdom, when King Narai the Great led a flotilla of 147 boats along the Chao Phraya, to accompany a diplomatic delegation sent to Siam by the great French king Louis XIV (R.1643–1715). At this time the royal barges served a dual purpose, both as decorative and ceremonial means of transportation and as the naval fleet. The barges were also used in boat races for entertainment and in religious rites such as the annual festival of Tod Kathin.

During the war of 1767 with the Burmese, which destroyed

Ayutthaya, the royal barges were wrecked along with other treasures. Fortunately, when Rama I ascended the throne in 1782, he regarded the renewal of national arts and crafts as a priority, and initiated the construction of new barges. By the mid-19th century, the royal barge procession had expanded to 269 boats, which required more than 10,000 oarsmen. The barges sustained severe damage during the bombing of Bangkok in World War II but were reconstructed and restored by King Bhumibol.

The most significant barge, known as **Supphanahongsa,** is 165 feet (50 m) long and weighs over 15 tons. The vessel is carved from a single piece of teak, with the exception of the gilded figurehead, which depicts the mythical golden swan Hamsa, after which the craft is named. This enormous boat requires the services of 54 oarsmen to pull it through the water, along with two helmsmen, two officers, one flagman, and a rhythm keeper who taps the butt of his silver spear on the deck in time with the chanting of ancient songs.

One of the best times to see the boats in action is during the royal Kathin ceremony at the end of Phansaa—the Buddhist rains retreat—during the October or November new moon. The festival features the magnificent **Anantanagaraj,** a 145-foot-long (44 m) barge with a multi-headed *naga* serpent on its prow, which is used to carry new robes that are offered to monks. ■

Above: Ornate barges are used in royal ceremonies. Below: The tradition of royal barges dates back to the Ayutthaya era. Opposite: Intricately carved figureheads have always featured on the barges.

Wat Arun

🏛 66 C3

✉ Arun Amarin Rd.

💲 $

⛴ Ferry from Tha Tien to Wat Arun Pier

Wat Arun

WAT ARUN, ALSO KNOWN AS THE TEMPLE OF THE DAWN, looms 286 feet (86 m) above the west bank of the Chao Phraya in an unmistakable silhouette that has become a striking symbol of Bangkok itself. It is even found on the 10-baht coin. The towering *prang*, built in the rather solid Khmer style, dates from the reign of Rama I and represents Mount Meru, mythological home of the Hindu gods. It was constructed on the grounds of an Ayutthaya temple, Wat Makok, which was at one time the home of the Emerald Buddha. When Taksin and his army reached the monastery following the destruction of Ayutthaya, the king renamed it Wat Jang (*jang* means "dawn") after the moment of his arrival—exactly at dawn.

Wat Arun's soaring prang is made of a brick core covered with plaster and embedded with broken bits of Chinese porcelain.

Rama II was responsible for initiating the building of the tall central spire, but he did not live to see it completed. This was done by Rama III in 1842, and King Mongkut, who finished off the structure by covering it with thousands of donated fragments of Chinese porcelain. He also renamed the shrine, calling it Wat Arun Rajavararam. Arun is more precise than jang, and it also reflects the Hindu god of the dawn, Aruna.

The huge central prang, surmounted by a Hindu *vagra* (thunderbolt), rests on three levels of terraces, surrounded by four smaller corner prangs, interspersed with four *mondops*. The combination of central prang, trident, and four lesser prangs represents the Buddhist universe and the four great seas of the physical world. Eight sets of stone steps, guarded by fierce Chinese figures, lead up to the first terrace, with the minor prangs at each corner. Giants and monkeys of traditional Thai design encircle the lower sections of the first terrace, along with images of other gods and Siamese mythological creatures.

The second terrace has a lovely pavilion, with four statues that illustrate important events in the life of the Buddha—his birth, enlightenment, first sermon, and moment of entering nirvana at his death. Visitors are limited in their climb to the third terrace, from where there are great views back over the river to the Oriental hotel. Above, the symbolic layers continue, with the Traiphum representing existence across the three worlds of the Buddhist universe; the Travatisma Heaven, guarded at all four corners by further vagras; and the Devaphum right at the top, symbolizing the peak of the seven realms of happiness. ■

Stilt houses edge still waters in Thon Buri—a world away from the Bangkok's loud streets.

A boat trip along the Chao Phraya

A ride on the commuter ferry service, the Chao Phraya River Express, is an inexpensive and easy way to explore the river and nearby sites that could otherwise be missed. Stay on the boat as far as Nonthaburi, a pleasant town on the city's northern outskirts or, to see a gentler side of Bangkok, take a water taxi to explore Thon Buri's maze of canals.

The white and red Express boats run every 20 minutes, 6 a.m. to 6 p.m. Start at **Tha (pier) Sathon,** where Sathon Road meets the Chao Phraya at Taksin Bridge, and head upriver. You pay the fare once aboard. The Express soon makes its first stop, at Tha Oriental, named after the venerable hotel (see p. 98). The nearby Old Customs House, the East Asiatic Company building, and, a little farther north near Tha Mueng Khae, the General Post Office are fine examples of colonial architecture. Also from Bangkok's colonial era is **Holy Rosary Church** ❶, just beyond the riverside Royal Orchid Sheraton hotel. Portuguese Catholics, who moved over from Thon Buri to the new capital of Bangkok, built the church in 1787.

On the river's Thon Buri banks you can see two rarely visited Ayutthaya-style temples. **Wat Thammachat** features impressive murals depicting scenes dating from the reigns of Rama III and Rama IV. **Wat Thong Noppakhun** is notable for its bronze panels detailing the Buddha's life. The Express glides under **Memorial Bridge** to Tha

Saphan Phut. Opened in 1932 by King Rama VII (Prajadhipok), to commemorate the 150th anniversary of the Chakri dynasty, the bridge was the first to span the river. At Tha Saphan Phut you can jump ship and visit the colorful **Pak Khlong Market** ❷, immediately behind the pier, and the nearby **Little India** neighborhood. You can also hop onto longtail taxi boats for inexpensive journeys across the Chao Phraya to the maze of *khlongs,* or canals, in Thon Buri (see p. 114).

At Tha Rachini shuttle boats carry passengers to Thon Buri and three notable sites. **Wat Prayun** ❸, built in the early 19th century under Rama III, is memorable for its central hillock planted with small *chedis* and frangipani trees. Around the hill is a pond full of turtles that are regularly fed by worshipers to gain merit. The temple's two *vihans* have doors inlaid with mother-of-pearl and extensively ornate gables (see also p. 116). Just north of Wat Prayun is **Santa Cruz Church** ❹, another place of worship constructed by Portuguese Catholics fleeing the Burmese

The sun sets behind Wat Arun.

Canals *(khlongs)* of Thon Buri

Leading off the western banks of the Chao Phraya river and into Thon Buri is a fascinating network of canals where you see stilted wooden houses and ancient temples set among rice fields, vegetable gardens, and orchards.

Three primary canals lead west from the Chao Phraya and arch around Thon Buri: Khlong Bangkok Noi, Khlong Bangkok Mon, and Khlong Bangkok Yai. These are bisected by numerous smaller arteries that reach otherwise hidden communities. **Khlong Bangkok Noi** river taxis leave from Tha Maharat, cross the river passing the Royal Barge Museum, and into the khlong—the farther you go, the more rustic the scene.

From Tha Tien, river taxis go up **Khlong Bangkok Mon** for similar sights. Most head up Khlong Bangkok Mon and then turn off into smaller canals before terminating. Stay aboard to return to Tha Tien. Water taxis to **Khlong Bangkok Yai** leave Tha Tien or Tha Rachini, and pass Wat Intharam, unusual for its *bot's* gold and black lacquerwork doors and a *chedi* housing the ashes of assassinated King Taksin.

River taxis ply these routes every 30 minutes 6 a.m. to 6:30 p.m. (less than 50 cents) or long-tails can be hired from river piers (a one-hour excursion should, depending on bargaining skills and number of passengers, cost around $10). ■

invaders of Ayutthaya. **Wat Kalayanimit 5**, next to Santa Cruz Church, houses an immense Buddha image and more murals from the time of Rama III (see p. 116). Just before Tha Tien, near Wat Pho and the Grand Palace and hidden in thick foliage, is **Chakrabongse House.**

Built in 1909 by Rama V, it is one of the last royal residences on the Chao Praya. From Tha Tien you can explore **Wat Pho, Wat Phra Kaeo,** and the **Grand Palace 6** (see pp. 69–74 and 75–76), take a shuttle boat to **Wat Arun 7** (see p. 112), or a longtail water taxi for a trip to the khlongs (see p. 114).

On the Thon Buri side, the Express stops at Tha Rakhang, near **Wat Rakhang Kositharam 8.** This little-visited temple is noted for its superb library consisting of three late 18th-century timber buildings, the residence of Rama I before he became king. The library also features intricate murals dating to 1788 and depicting scenes of the *Ramakien* and Buddhist cosmology. From the temple grounds you get a fine view of the Grand Palace, Wat Phra Kaeo, and Wat Pho.

Exit at Tha Maharat for **Wat Mahathat 9** (see p. 77), the **National Museum** (see pp. 80–83), and **Thammasat University.** Thammasat is the most prestigious university in Thailand after Chulalongkorn. It has witnessed its share of unrest and bloodshed: In 1973 students led protests that overthrew the military government, and in 1976 it was the awful scene of right-wing revenge, when more than 200 students were murdered by vigilantes and paramilitaries. ∎

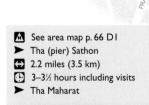

- See area map p. 66 D1
- Tha (pier) Sathon
- 2.2 miles (3.5 km)
- 3–3½ hours including visits
- Tha Maharat

NOT TO BE MISSED
- Pak Khlong Market
- Canals (khlongs) of Thon Buri
- Wat Prayun
- Wat Rakhang Kositharam

More places to visit in Thon Buri

FLOATING MARKET

For generations, the people of lower central Thailand conducted much of their commerce on the network of canals that crisscrossed their land. It is only in the past few decades that roads have replaced the functionality of the canals.

Bangkok had an active floating market once, but this largely disappeared in the 1960s as roads were constructed and vendors moved into modern shopping centers. The demise of the traditional floating market within the city limits inspired tour operators to create an artificial market, hiring local women to paddle around each morning and pretend to bargain for their produce. Although this attraction has more in common with the theme park than authentic experience, visitors with limited time might consider a half-day tour of this market, which also includes opportunities for shopping in the attached souvenir stalls. For an authentic floating market, head south to the town of Damnoen Saduak (see p. 123). ✉ Khlong Bangkok Yai ⏱ Closes at noon 💲 $ 🚌 Organized tours only

WAT KALAYANIMIT & WAT PRAYUN

Two interesting temples are situated near the banks of the Chao Phraya and can be easily toured in a morning with a rented longtail boat. The Chinese-influenced Wat Kalayanimit is located near the opening of Khlong Bangkok Yai and is therefore easily accessible by public or private boat. This vast *wihan* houses a huge sitting Buddha, but the temple is best known for the giant bronze bell, the biggest in Thailand, which hangs in its white tower. Both the wihan and the *bot* have reasonably well-preserved frescoes dating from the mid-19th century. Nearby Wat Prayun is much more modest but features some intriguing exterior details, such a hill reputedly modeled on melted wax from Rama III's candle and covered in miniature temples, and a pool filled with carp and turtles. The turtles are bought and released here as a way of gaining merit for a future life. 🗺 66 C3, 66 C2 ✉ Soi Wat Kanlaya 🚢 Ferry from Rachini pier

WAT SUWANNARAM & WAT DUSITARAM

Wat Suwannaram, near the Thon Buri train station, is architecturally significant as it represents an evolution from the forms favored at Ayutthaya to the more extravagant styles of contemporary Bangkok. The temple was finished in 1832 and is chiefly noted for its superb interior murals, some of the most original and refined in the city. The work of Luang Vichit Chetsada and Krua Khonpae, they are full of lively detail, depicting *Jataka* tales as well as the Buddhist cosmology and the defeat of Mara. Frescoes of great sensitivity, telling the traditional tales from the life of the Buddha, can also be seen inside Wat Dusitaram, near the Royal Barges Museum. 🗺 66 B4, 66 C4 ✉ Soi Suwannaram 🚢 Ferry to Rot Fai Pier ■

The murals of Wat Suwannaram are noted for such lively detail as this prancing horse.

Within a few hours of Bangkok is an array of top attractions that exemplify the natural beauty, culture, and history of Thailand.

Around Bangkok

Dome, Phra Pathom Chedi

Fertile plains near Bangkok bless the area with abundant vegetable crops.

Around Bangkok

THE AREAS TO THE WEST AND NORTH OF BANGKOK OFFER PLENTY OF cultural, historic, and natural sites to keep visitors occupied. Indeed, places such as the magnificent old Thai capital of Ayutthaya, the immense Phra Pathom Chedi at Nakhon Pathom, and the beautiful and evocative Kanchanaburi Province are regulation stops on a trip to Thailand.

All the sites described in this chapter are within easy reach of Bangkok. Visits to all of them can be arranged as part of organized excursions booked through the tour desk at your hotel.

A good way to get to Ayutthaya—the great cultural center and capital of Thailand from 1350 to 1767—is to take a leisurely cruise up the Chao Phraya river from Bangkok by luxury boat. At Ayutthaya switch to a longtail boat for a trip along the waterways that surround the old city. Then move ashore to take in the city's magnificent buildings.

North of Ayutthaya is the historically important center of Lop Buri, one of Thailand's oldest cities, which has been continuously occupied since the sixth century.

Just 30 miles (50 km) west of Bangkok is Nakhon Pathom, famed for its *chedi*: the tallest Buddhist monument in the world and one of the most revered in Thailand. The chedi is the centerpiece of some other wonderful Thai monuments, including a number of impressive Buddha statues.

West of the capital, Kanchanaburi is a place with a surfeit of natural attractions, making it a popular weekend getaway for Bangkok residents. Among visitors the area is famous for its River Kwae bridge and the Thailand–Burma Railway, otherwise known as the Death Railway, built for the Japanese during World War II by Allied and Asian prisoners of wars at a terrible cost of human life. ■

Bangkok

Area of
map detail

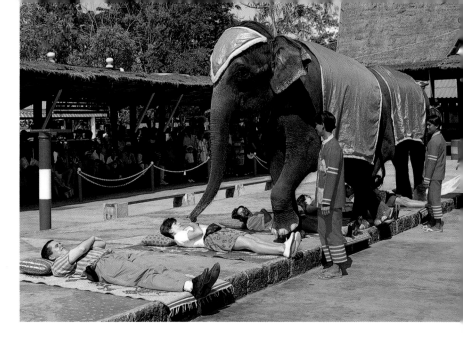

Tourists take part in an elephant show at Samut Prakan Crocodile Farm.

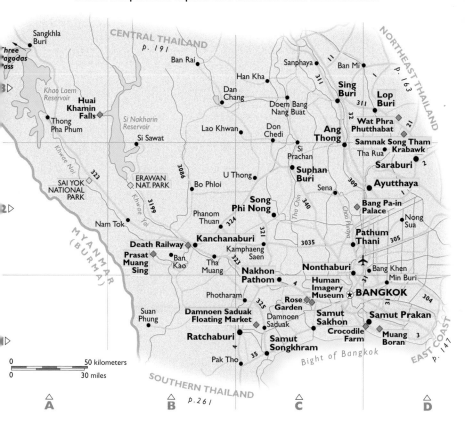

CENTRAL THAILAND
p. 191

NORTHEAST THAILAND
p. 163

Sangkhla
Buri

Three
Pagodas
Pass

Ban Rai

Han Kha

Sanphaya

Ban Mi

Sing
Buri

Lop
Buri

311

11

Khao Laem
Reservoir

**Huai
Khamin
Falls**

Dan
Chang

Doem Bang
Nang Buat

Wat Phra
Phutthabat

311

32

Thong
Pha Phum

Si Nakharin
Reservoir

Lao Khwan

Don
Chedi

**Ang
Thong**

Samnak Song Tham
Krabawk

Si Sawat

Si
Prachan

Tha Rua

Saraburi

2

3086

U Thong

**Suphan
Buri**

Sena

Ayutthaya

309

**SAI YOK
NATIONAL
PARK**

Khwae Noi

323

**ERAWAN
NAT. PARK**

Bo Phloi

**Song
Phi Nong**

Tha Chin

340

**Bang Pa-in
Palace**

Nong
Sua

Nam Tok

3199

Khwae Yai

Phanom
Thuan

324

321

**Pathum
Thani**

305

Chao Phraya

Kanchanaburi

Kamphaeng
Saen

3035

Nonthaburi

Bang Khen

Min Buri

**Prasat
Muang
Sing**

Ban
Kao

Tha
Muang

323

**Nakhon
Pathom**

**Human
Imagery
Museum**

BANGKOK

304

31

4

Photharam

325

**Rose
Garden**

**Samut
Sakhon**

Samut Prakan

Suan
Phung

**Damnoen Saduak
Floating Market**

Damnoen
Saduak

**Crocodile
Farm**

**Muang
Boran**

3

Ratchaburi

4

**Samut
Songkhram**

35

Bight of Bangkok

EAST COAST
p. 147

Pak Tho

MYANMAR
(BURMA)

0   50 kilometers

0   30 miles

SOUTHERN THAILAND
p. 261

A   B   C   D

Nakhon Pathom

Nakhon Pathom
 119 C1
Frequent buses from Southern Bus Terminal, Bangkok. Train from Hua Lamphong Station, Bangkok

Visitor information
Tourism Authority of Thailand, 4 Ratchadamnoen Nok Ave., Bangkok
02-2829774, 02-282 9775, or 02-282 9776

Phra Pathom Chedi
Ratchadamnoen Rd.

ONE HOUR WEST OF BANGKOK, THIS LARGELY UNDISTIN-guished provincial city is visited almost exclusively for its towering Phra Pathom Chedi, the tallest Buddhist structure in the world and one of the most revered monuments in the country. Nakhon Pathom is believed to be one of the oldest settled sites in Thailand for, according to tradition, the city was founded several centuries before the Christian era as a seaport for the mythical kingdom of Suwannaphum.

Nakhon Pathom is important to the people of Thailand as the birthplace of Buddhism in the country. It is believed that during the reign of King Asoka the Great (R.272–32 B.C.), two senior monks were sent from India to introduce Theravada Buddhism to the residents of the lower Chao Phraya plains. They probably traveled through the Three Pagodas Pass on the border of Myanmar (Burma) and Thailand, and made their first converts in the villages around Nakhon Pathom. A stupa was built around this time.

In the sixth century, the site flourished as a capital of the mysterious Mon people (whose Dvaravati Empire dominated Central Thailand in the 6th–13th centuries). Several stone inscriptions survive, along with small stupas and a coin inscribed with the words *Lord of Dvaravati.*

Nakhon Pathom was conquered by Khmer King Suryavarman (R.1011–50) in the early 11th century and became part of the Khmer Empire. The city fell again in 1078, to Burmese invaders, who abandoned it soon after. Its potential as a defensive outpost against Burma was recognized, and the town was reestablished in the 17th century by the Siamese. It was King Mongkut, however, who realized the importance of the stupa built by the converts to Buddhism. He ordered the stupa's preservation

and restoration in 1860, encasing it in the bulbous Phra Pathom Chedi, which dominates the town today.

PHRA PATHOM CHEDI

The magnificent *chedi* of Nakhon Pathom, rising almost 395 feet (120 m) into the skies, is covered with golden-orange tiles. It is sometimes compared to the Shwedagon in Yangon, Myanmar, but it is taller and is surrounded by an intriguing complex of auxiliary *bots*, Buddha images, and other curious substructures. The tower is topped by a gold trident, symbol of the Hindu god Siva, with a superimposed Royal Crown of Thailand highlighting its national status and importance.

The monument is best approached from the north side, which faces the train station, across a long field flanked by minor religious sites and usually thronged with pilgrims. Left of the main entrance are amulet salesmen, toothy old palmists who can divine the future for both Thais and Western tourists, and stalls serving refreshing glasses of iced coffee.

Past the two ceremonial halls, and up the Grand Staircase into the **north wihan,** is the revered **Phra Ruang Rochanarit,** or standing Buddha. Its modern bronze body was especially made to match the much older stone hands, feet, and head. In the nearby temple offices a mural

Opposite: The golden Phra Pathom Chedi is considered the most sacred Buddhist site in Thailand.

Elegant Buddhas adorn Phra Pathom Chedi.

points to the principal features of Phra Pathom Chedi. A display in a public hall presents the history of the chedi's restoration.

The circular **cloister** that separates the chedi from the walkway houses a series of impressive bronze Buddha statues, in various positions, set into its walls. At the **east wihan,** an enlightened Buddha is placed at an altar, while being shaded by a mural of a spreading *bodhi* tree. Beyond the wihan, the east terrace contains the amazing **Dvaravati seated Buddha,** powerful and skillfully carved in white quartzite, and positioned in the "European" seated fashion—a particular, closed-kneed posture believed to have been developed from Greco-Roman statues. A European influence is discernible in robe contours and facial expressions. Nearby are a museum with Dvaravati-period relics of some interest, a *sala*, and a Chinese temple.

Standing in the courtyard at the southern entrance is a model of the original stupa—which has been surmounted by a Khmer-style

prang. Next to the prang is another large Dvaravati seated Buddha.

The wihan at the southern entrance to the chedi has a Buddha image in an earth-touching pose, surrounded by disciples. In an inner chamber a Khmer-style Buddha receives shelter under a hooded *naga.* At the **west wihan** is a highly venerated 29-foot-long (9 m) reclining Buddha. An interior chamber is generally crowded with pilgrims paying homage to a smaller Buddha. In the courtyard are monks' quarters built in timber.

Surrounding the huge chedi are 24 bells, often rung by pilgrims.

About 1 mile (1.6 km) west of Phra Pathom Chedi is **Sanam Chan Palace,** built by Rama VI at the end of the 19th century (entry is not permitted into the palace buildings). The palace is a collection of generously proportioned buildings in Thai and European design, surrounded by neat gardens. One curious aspect is a statue of the reputedly feisty Vajay, Rama IV's beloved pet dog, who was poisoned by palace staff because of his fierce nature. ∎

Around Nakhon Pathom

A NUMBER OF ATTRACTIONS CAN BE FOUND WEST OF Bangkok en route to Nakhon Pathom. They are best explored as part of tour packages—easily arranged at your hotel—from the capital. These provide an excellent reason to escape Bangkok for the day.

DAMNOEN SADUAK FLOATING MARKET

The image of a traditional Thai floating market is a powerful one for visitors. While those in Bangkok have been re-created to serve the tourist trade, the Damnoen Saduak market remains the real thing.

The town lies between Nakhon Pathom and Samut Songkhram, some 68 miles (109 km) southwest of Bangkok, and in fact has several floating markets in different neighborhoods. Most visitors head directly to the biggest, at Ton Kem.

The best way to experience the floating market is to stay overnight in a hotel in nearby Damnoen Saduak, but you could rise early and hire a taxi from Bangkok. The market is at its busiest and best in the early morning—before the tour groups arrive. The "stalls" are the traders' open sampan boats, which bustle up and down the narrow canals selling a range of deliciously fresh produce, mainly fruit and vegetables. The boats are paddled mostly by women, who wear lamp-shade hats and the familiar blue shirts of the farming community.

Visitors can watch the parade of sampans, piled high with produce and flowers, either from the bridge that crosses over the canal or from the produce shed on the right.

ROSE GARDEN

The Rose Garden is in a lovely setting on the banks of the Nakorn Chaisri river. This well-designed resort complex has landscaped gardens set around a large lake, an aviary with over 300 species of exotic birds, orchid and rose nurseries, a championship 18-hole golf course, and a model village where craftsworkers demonstrate weaving, carving, and basketry.

The highlight is the twice daily cultural show (11 a.m., 2:45 p.m.), when a hundred performers delight the crowd with their displays of traditional dance, music, and martial arts. This is one of the best such

shows in Thailand, squeezing a wedding, the ordination of a Buddhist monk, sword-fighting, and boxing into the space of one nonstop hour. Close by are the **Human Imagery Museum** and **Samphran Elephant Ground & Zoo** (see p. 146).

PHRA PHUTTA MONTHON

Also southeast of Nakhon Pathom, on the Bangkok road, this Buddhist "theme park" has re-creations of Buddha's journey from birth, enlightenment, and first sermon to nirvana. A 133-foot (41 m) walking Buddha dominates the park. ■

Damnoen Saduak Floating Market
- 119 C1
- Sukhaphiban 1 Rd., Damnoen Saduak
- Market active daily sunrise–noon
- Bus: 78 from Southern Bus Terminal in Bangkok

Rose Garden
- 119 C1
- 20 miles (32 km) W of Bangkok, off Hwy. 4
- 02-295-3261
- $; extra for show
- Bus: 83 & 997

Dancers at the Rose Garden carry *krathongs*, which are floated on waterways during the Loy Krathong festival in November.

Phra Phutta Monthon
- 119 C1
- Hwy. 3310, between Hwys. 4 and 338
- Bus from Southern Bus Terminal, Bangkok

Kanchanaburi & around

THIS RELAXED TOWN TO THE WEST OF BANGKOK SITS IN A beautiful setting of forests and picturesque hills. It is best known for its connections with the notorious Thailand–Burma Railway—the Death Railway—built during World War II with forced Allied labor. Kanchanaburi is the site of a bridge over the River Khwae (Kwai), made famous by David Lean's Oscar-winning film of 1957. More recently it became the focus of world attention when proposals for a massive dam threatened to destroy significant areas of wildlife habitat. After an environmental outcry, the project was scrapped.

The first inhabitants of this area were neolithic tribespeople, and fragments of their lives—pottery and simple tools—are displayed at the **Ban Kao Museum,** 22 miles (35 km) west of Kanchanaburi (see p. 130).

The main historic trade route to India, via the Three Pagodas Pass, lies along the Khwae Yai Valley. During the 13th century the area fell under the control of the Khmer Empire, and a magnificent fort was erected at Muang Sing. Khmer rulers were replaced by Ayutthayans, who constructed a military citadel to the west of Kanchanaburi (both sites have been restored and can be visited). In 1548 the Burmese invasion army marched into Siam through here. It was Rama I who set up a military

camp at Kanchanaburi, however, and the town grew up as a major defensive center.

The main focus of a visit to Kanchanaburi is likely to be the notorious bridge, 2 miles (3 km) north of the town center. For a fuller understanding of the story behind its construction, the men who worked on it, and the bridge's part in the wider history of the Death Railway (see pp. 128–29), it is well worth visiting some of the associated sites first.

JEATH WAR MUSEUM

An excellent place to start is the JEATH War Museum, in Kanchanaburi. The title is an acronym formed from the names of some of the nations involved in the building of the railway: Japan,

Kanchanaburi

⬛ 119 B2

Visitor information

✉ Tourism Authority of Thailand, Saeng Chuto Rd., Kanchanaburi 71000

☎ 034-511200

🚌 Bus from Southern Bus Terminal in Thon Buri. Train from Bangkok Noi station (also Thon Buri); frequent service on weekends (reserve seats); limited service during the week

England, Australia/America, Thailand, and Holland.

The museum is informal, with three bamboo huts revealing something of the feel of the original prison camps. Memorabilia displayed inside the huts includes paintings and drawings by the prisoners that graphically depict the horrors of camp life, and letters written by the P.O.W.s, telling of sacrifice and deprivation on the railroad and grisly tortures inflicted by the Japanese.

JEATH War Museum may be modest in scale, but it is a moving and unforgettable memorial to the 12,000 Allied prisoners of war and 100,000 Asian laborers who died here under such appalling conditions in the construction of the Thailand–Burma Railway.

KANCHANABURI WAR CEMETERY

This vast graveyard, midway between downtown Kanchanaburi and the famous bridge, is the final resting place for nearly 7,000 Allied P.O.W.s (mainly British and Australian) who died building the railroad. The graves are immaculately maintained by a dedicated team of gardeners under the auspices of the Commonwealth War Graves Commission in London. Simply reading the inscriptions on the tombstones brings a lump to the throat. At Chung Kai there is a smaller cemetery. (See also Konyu Cemetery, Hellfire Pass, p. 130.)

KHWAE YAI RIVER BRIDGE

The present bridge and railroad are largely modern constructions that

Above left: Monument to the notorious Death Railway. Above: Waterfalls enhance the natural beauty of the countryside around Kanchanaburi.

JEATH War Museum
✉ Pak Phreak Rd., Kanchanaburi
💲 $

Kanchanaburi War Cemetery
✉ Soang Chuto Rd., Kanchanaburi

**Khwae Yai River
Bridge**

✉ Saeng Chuto Rd.,
Kanchanaburi.

🚉 See Kanchanaburi,
p. 124

**The bridge on
the Khwae Yai
river has been
immortalized in
books and film.**

replaced the original work of the
Japanese. The Thai government
eventually took over responsibility
for it all after the end of the war,
tearing down some of the bridge
and the railroad as far as
Nam Tok for the scrap iron. The
government later requested help
from the Japanese in the form
of war reparations, and these
included the replacement of the
central girders with the present flat,
boxy structures.

Although the story of the
construction and destruction of the
bridge is charged with emotion (see
pp. 128–29), the modern-day crossing can be a disappointment—just
a seemingly run-down wood and
iron bridge mounted on ungainly

concrete pillars. It comes to life
when the twice-daily train departs
Kanchanaburi and slowly makes it
way across the rickety structure, on
its way north to the terminus at
Nam Tok. You can walk onto the
wooden planks of the bridge, but
it's also used by local motorcyclists,
so be careful.

AROUND THE BRIDGE
Several minor but worthwhile
sights are located near the famous
bridge. These include an old steam
engine, which dates from the 1940s,
and a curious Japanese supply
truck that could run on both road
and rails. Just south of the bridge,
cafés overlook the river, and
there are souvenir shops. An art

gallery nearby is notable for its contemporary murals.

A Japanese memorial in the area, raised in 1944, is euphemistically dedicated to those who "died through illness during the course of the construction."

BUDDHIST TEMPLES

Several Buddhist temples situated to the south of Kanchanaburi are worth a brief visit, if only to experience their sense of kitsch and unbridled commercialism (which seems to characterize an increasing number of temples in the country). **Wat Tham Monkam Thong** (meaning "cave temple of the golden dragon") features a Buddhist nun and her disciples,

who float in water while meditating and whistling—the steady stream of pilgrims consider this a neat trick. Behind the temple complex, steps lead to an series of limestone cliffs filled with the exquisite Buddha images and providing fine views over the river.

Near the town of Tha Muang, a pair of very striking temples perch on the edge of the valley on a limestone outcrop. The temple on the left, **Wat Tham Sua,** is chiefly noted for its Chinese pagoda and spacious courtyard, which is dominated by a rotund Buddha. **Wat Tham Kao Noi** has been constructed in classic Thai style, with a massive *wihan* holding an immense Buddha image. ■

Wat Tham Monkam Thong
✉ Chukkadon Rd., Kanchanaburi
🚐 Mini-truck from Kanchanaburi

Wat Tham Monkam Thong employs such gimmicks as this floating, meditating nun to attract pilgrims.

Death Railway

Kanchanaburi's chief attraction, and one of the most famous World War II memorials in Southeast Asia, is the simple girdered bridge at the north end of town. The original wooden bridge was part of a much more ambitious project, which gained notoriety at the center of one of the most terrible and tragic stories of the war.

The Japanese conceived a plan in fall 1942 to build a 255-mile (414 km) railroad across Thailand to Thanbyuzayat in Burma (now Myanmar). Allied operations around Singapore and in the Straits of Malacca had effectively blocked sea routes used by the Japanese between mainland Southeast Asia and points west, such as Burma and—the final goal—India. The Japanese had quickly conquered Burma at the beginning of the

conflict and badly needed to provide supplies to their bases and troops.

The construction time of the serpentine rail line, through jungle and over mountain passes, was initially estimated at five years, but this was overruled by the Japanese High Command, who ordered that the link be completed in just 12 months (in fact, it took 16 months). Allied prisoners were brought in from Singapore, Hong Kong, and other British territories, while Asians were shipped in from all corners of the region under Japanese control. The forced labor was essential to the success of the scheme, and men were treated as expendable—the appalling treatment, working and living conditions, malnutrition, and tropical diseases such as malaria, cholera, and dysentery killed thousands of laborers. The cost in human lives

About 7,000 allied soldiers who died during the construction of the Death Railway are buried in Kanchanaburi.

A train still runs along the remains of the Thailand–Burma railway.

across the most difficult sections was later dubbed "a life for every sleeper"—a dead man for every railroad tie.

The first bridge built by P.O.W.s over the River Khwae (Kwai) was a rickety affair of wood, replaced in 1943 by a stronger iron structure imported from Java, which remains today. The bridge was the regular target of United States B-24 bombers, which knocked out the central span in 1945. It was rebuilt after the war with Japanese cooperation as reparation. The railroad itself operated for just two years—today only the 47-mile (77 km) stretch between Kanchanaburi and Nam Tok remains in regular use.

Most visitors' views are colored by the famous Academy Award-winning movie (it won six awards) *The Bridge on the River Kwai* (1957), by English director David Lean

(1908–1981). The epic film is based on a novel by French author Pierre Boulle (1912–1994) called *Le Pont de la rivière Kwai* (*The Bridge on the River Kwai*) and takes a number of liberties in its retelling of history.

The central character of the movie— Colonel Nicholson, played so movingly by Alec Guinness (1914–2000)—never existed and was invented for the purposes of the story. The film also suggests that the Allied prisoners were responsible for the engineering of the bridge, but in fact it was highly trained Japanese engineers who designed the project.

The film hinges on Nicholson's obsession with constructing a perfect bridge that will be a tribute to its builders, but in reality the prisoners sabotaged and delayed the project at every possible turn.

The film also weaves an imaginative story about an American maverick, played by William Holden (1918–1981), escaping from the P.O.W. camp and then making his way to Ceylon (Sri Lanka), before returning to Kanchanaburi to blow up the bridge. The true story is that no one escaped the Japanese internment camp at Kanchanaburi and lived to talk about it. Perhaps the most tragic aspect of the book and the film was not the liberal retelling of the saga, but the fact that neither medium made much mention of the tremendous loss of Asian lives during the construction of the railroad bridge. ■

On the road to the Myanmar border

HIGHWAY 323, RUNNING 150 MILES (250 KM) NORTHWEST from Kanchanaburi to the Myanmar (Burma) border at Three Pagodas Pass, takes you through some stunning scenery. Lush mountain outlooks prevail along the route, which cuts through the river valley of the River Khwae Noi and follows the trail of the "Death Railway" (see pp. 128–29) line to Myanmar, passing the enormous man-made Khao Laem Reservoir.

About 22 miles (35 km) on Highway 323 from Kanchanaburi, take Highway 3229 and then 3455 to the small **Ban Kao Museum,** which houses a fascinating collection of neolithic tools and utensils collected from nearby digs and dating back 3,000 to 4,000 years. Four miles (7 km) farther west along Highway 3455 are the expansive remains of the 13th-century Khmer temple at **Prasat Muang Sing.** The site, attractively set on the banks of the Khwae Noi river, was at the western extremities of the Khmer Empire and was most likely set up as a trading outpost. It sprawls over 170 acres (70 ha), with the remains of ramparts still guarding the complex. Four entrances *(gopura)* lead to the main shrine in the center.

Back on Highway 323, about 50 miles (80 km) from Kanchanaburi, is **Hellfire Pass,** so named by the Allied and Asian prisoners of war building the Death Railway because of the light thrown onto the bare rock face by the flames of the torches used by the workers at night. At Konyu Cutting, prisoners of war carved the way through solid rock. At the pass is a memorial to the hundreds of Australian and British soldiers who died constructing this section of the railroad and who are buried at the nearby **Konyu Cemetery.**

A trail follows the remains of the track through the pass, then carries on up to a hill for an overhead view. A quaint train still runs along a section of the railroad from Kanchanaburi through attractive scenery to the town of **Nam Tok** near the pass. From Pak Sang pier at Nam Tok, longtail boats can be hired for a journey upriver to the popular **Sai Yok National Park,** about 24 miles (38 km) from Nam Tok. At the park you will find peaceful stands of forest on the banks of the broad Khwae Noi river. Follow the signs from the information center to the nearby suspension bridge for admirable views of Sai Yok Noi waterfall tumbling down a limestone cliff into the river.

Highway 323 continues northeast along the contours of the vast Khao Laem Reservoir (Krung Kravia Lake), dammed to power a huge hydroelectric turbine, to **Sangkhla Buri,** 137 miles (220 km) from Kanchanaburi, at the northern end of the lake. The small town, mainly populated by Mon, Karen, and Burmese, holds its charm in its isolation and position on Khao Laem Reservoir. Its major attraction is a colorful morning market, dealing mainly in contraband, and a Mon village on the banks of the reservoir (from the center of town, head east over

Ban Kao Museum
- 119 B2
- Hwy. 3455
- Closed Mon.–Tues.
- $

Prasat Muang Sing
- 119 B2
- Hwy. 3455
- $
- Bus from Kanchanaburi

Sai Yok National Park
- 119 A2
- Off Hwy. 323
- Bus, train from Kanchanaburi
- Boat from Pak Sang pier, Nam Tok

an impressive wooden bridge). You can arrange boat tours of the reservoir at guesthouses in the town.

Three *chedis* mark the Thai/Myanmar (Burma) border at the appropriately named **Three Pagodas Pass,** the historical transit point of invading Burmese armies into Thailand. These days the pass is a major point for cross-border smuggling, and rebel activities sometimes result in temporary closure of the border crossing.

ERAWAN NATIONAL PARK

The superb waterfalls at this national park—about 50 miles (80 km) north of Kanchanaburi, on Highway 3199, parallel to Highway 323—are the most popular in Thailand. A rock formation at the top of one cascading waterfall recalls the shape of the sacred elephant Erawan and gives the park its name. The superior, higher falls are almost deserted, while those at the bottom are usually busier; swimming is possible in the lowest pools. As with all waterfalls in Thailand, Erawan is best visited during the rainy months, from July to November, when water is at its most plentiful.

Stretching north of these spectacular falls is the vast reservoir **Si Nakharin,** formed from the creation of a dam. The lake is popular with Bangkok residents, who arrive on weekends in great numbers to fish, hike, enjoy boat tours, or relax in the raft hotels—some of which are luxurious—on the shoreline. ∎

The road from Kanchanaburi to the border with Myanmar (Burma) travels through striking scenery.

Erawan National Park
- 119 B2
- ✉ On Hwy. 3199, 40 miles (65 km) from Kanchanaburi.
- $ $
- Bus from Kanchanaburi

Ayutthaya

Ayutthaya

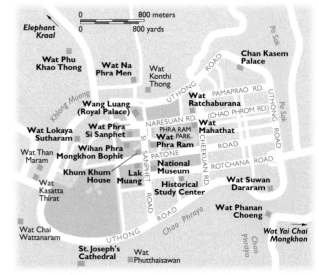 119 D2

Visitor information

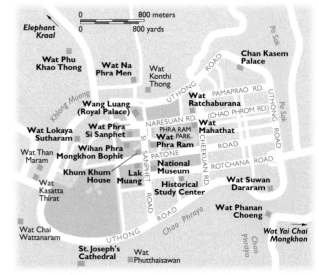 Tourism Authority of
Thailand, 108/22 Mu
4, Pratu Chai,
Ayutthaya 13000

☎ 035-246076

🚌 Bus from Northern
Bus Terminal,
Bangkok.
Train from Hua
Lamphong Station,
Bangkok

🚤 River boat from
Bangkok

THIS ROMANTIC RUINED CITY, SURROUNDED BY A MODERN town, is one of Thailand's national treasures. It attests to the power and splendor of an empire that dominated Southeast Asia for almost 400 years. In the bloody aftermath of a Burmese onslaught, most of the city was destroyed by fire, its people killed or taken to Burma as slaves. It was a catastrophic loss on a scale now hard to imagine.

The city began as a Khmer military and trading outpost. Ramathibodi I made it his capital about 1350. Ayutthaya was ideally located within the protective surroundings of several rivers, which were diverted and channeled into smaller canals, to create a waterbound and almost impregnable fortress.

Ramathibodi named it after a mythical kingdom portrayed in the *Ramakien* and soon began the building of royal palaces and temples. To honor his belief in Theravada Buddhism, he invited monks from Sri Lanka to direct most religious activities in his royal city.

During its four centuries of existence, Ayutthaya was ruled by a succession of 33 kings, who in their turn erected new, and embellished existing, temples and palaces, while maintaining large armies to increase the national borderlands. Ayutthayan kings conducted almost continual warfare against Burma, as well as fighting with the Laotian, Cambodian, and Muslim empires to the south. By the end of the 15th century Ayutthaya controlled most of Southeast Asia.

Ayutthaya developed as an important commercial center for mainland Southeast Asia and was visited by international trading groups from all over Europe. Dazzled emissaries of French king Louis XIV reported that the city was comparable to European capitals.

Finally, after four centuries of power and glory, Ayutthaya slipped into decline. For two years it withstood a Burmese siege but fell at last in 1767. ■

Opposite:
Ayutthaya reigned as the Thai capital from circa 1350 to 1767.

Architecture & sculpture of Ayutthaya

The four centuries of the Ayutthayan period were an important era for art and architecture, encouraged and patronized by wealthy temple-building kings who saw themselves as the cultural inheritors of previous Southeast Asian empires. The result was an architectural gold mine, plus a high level of achievement in sculpture, painting, and other fine arts.

Central to the Hindu belief in many separate, parallel universes is the image of the magical Mount Meru, mythical home of the gods—the Mount Olympus for Asian religions. Ayutthaya was therefore constructed as a giant mandala, surrounded by ramparts and moats to symbolize great seas, with the royal palace as the heavenly center and lesser buildings and even cities spread around in cosmological order.

Priceless artifacts were discovered beneath the prang of Wat Ratchaburana in 1957.

such as homes and businesses were made of wood. This is the chief reason why only religious structures have survived the ravages of time.

Ayutthayan architects borrowed forms from the Khmers (such as the cob-shaped *prang*) and from Sri Lanka (notably the bell-shaped *chedi*). These foreign designs were modified and refined into unique expressions of Siamese style. Thus squat Khmer prangs and heavy unadorned Ceylonese chedis with an elongated elegance combined to form a new definition of Asian religious architecture.

Architecture

If sculpture was the high point of the Sukhothai Empire, then Ayutthaya's crowning glory was its architecture. European visitors reported that the city had over 600 major monuments and temples of extraordinary design. Most of the monuments were initiated during the founding reign of King Ramathibodi (R.1350–69) and completed during the next 150 years.

When looking at these remarkable structures, it helps to understand that, throughout Southeast Asia, it had long been the fashion to construct temples in stone, while royal palaces and utilitarian structures

Sculpture

Ayutthayan sculpture is not in the same league as that of Sukhothai but is still important. Early artists continued the traditions of the Uthong school of art, which owed its inspiration to the Mon and Khmers. Later sculpture was influenced by the Sukhothai style, and some of the most successful work dates from this time.

As the artistic influence of Sukhothai waned, late Ayutthayan images became over-ornamented, lacking the sensitivity of earlier styles. Yet Ayutthayan sculptors also introduced remarkable innovations—such as the depiction of the Buddha in a wider variety of poses—and proved themselves masters in casting bronze images on a large scale. ∎

**Above right: Clothing a Buddha image at Wat Phra Si Sanphet brings merit.
Right: Royalty used Wat Phra Si Sanphet as a private place of worship and for ceremonies.**

Highlights of Ayutthaya

Chan Kasem Palace

- 🅰 Map p. 132
- ✉ Uthong Rd.
- 🕐 Closed Mon.—Tues.
- 💲 $
- 🚖 Tuk tuk from Ayutthaya city center

Ayutthaya National Museum

- 🅰 Map p. 132
- ✉ Rotchana Rd.
- 🕐 Closed Mon.—Tues.
- 💲 $
- 🚖 Tuk tuk from Ayuttthaya city center

Ayutthaya Historical Study Center

- 🅰 Map p. 132
- ✉ Rotchana Rd.
- ☎ 035-245124
- 🕐 Closed Mon.
- 💲 $
- 🚖 Tuk tuk from Ayutthaya city center

A TRAVELER FROM EUROPE AT THE END OF THE 17TH century estimated Ayutthaya's population at over a million, with some 1,700 temples, some 30,000 priests, and more than 4,000 Buddha images, all of them cast in gold or covered with golden gilt. Tragically, most of the temples and icons were destroyed by the Burmese, but around 50 temples remain in various states of repair and restoration, along with miscellaneous monuments such as giant reclining Buddhas. Three excellent museums are filled with smaller Buddha images and other important archaeological discoveries.

CHAN KASEM PALACE

Ayutthaya's oldest museum is inside a palace originally built as the future home of King Naresuan (R.1590–1605), one of the most powerful of all Ayutthayan kings. Like so much of the city, it was destroyed in 1765 but was reconstructed in the 19th century.

The displays are somewhat modest, though the complex of buildings has architectural interest. To the left of the main entrance, the **Chantura Mukh Pavilion** houses an impressive standing Buddha. Behind this, the **Piman Rajaja Pavilion** is filled with rare Thai shadow puppets and smaller Buddha images. The nearby **Pisai Sayalak Tower** was an astronomical observatory.

WAT RATCHABURANA

One of Thailand's great archaeological discoveries took place in this unremarkable temple, constructed in 1424 by King Borommaracha II (R.1424–1448) to honor his brothers, who had killed each other in a fight for the throne. The central *prang* was built shortly after the king had conquered and looted the great Khmer capital, Angkor Thom.

Borommaracha apparently hauled his plunder back to Ayutthaya and stored it inside a secret crypt below the prang. In 1957, a fabulous treasure trove of priceless gold objects, bronzes, Buddhas, and other items, both from Angkor Thom and created by the craftsmen of Ayutthaya, was discovered by accident when thieves broke in. Much of the surviving treasure is now displayed in the Ayutthaya National Museum (see p. 137). Steps still lead down into the crypt where the artifacts lay hidden for so many centuries.

WAT MAHATHAT

King Borommaracha I (R.1370–1388) constructed this Khmer-influenced "Temple of the Great Relic" in 1374. The temple was leveled by the Burmese and today largely lies in ruin. However, the scale of the floor plan suggests the impressive size and relative importance of this central temple complex. Look for the broken Buddha head in the southeast corner, which appears to be growing out of a tree trunk. *(Naresuan/Cheekuan Rds.)*

WAT PHRA RAM

This modest temple dates from 1369 and was built on the funeral site of Ayutthaya's King Ramathibodi (R.1350–1369), by his son, Ramasuen (R.1369–1395). The extraordinary corn-cob prang, adorned with mythical figures and Buddhas, was added around 100 years later. Wat Phra Ram is less

impressive than some of the larger temples at Ayutthaya, but it is in a stunning location—on a grassy peninsula that extends into a pond covered in giant water lilies. (*Si Sanphet Rd.*)

AYUTTHAYA NATIONAL MUSEUM

The funds for this major museum, formally known as the Chao Sam Phraya, were raised from the sale of less important artifacts discovered in the haul at Wat Ratchaburana (see p. 136). The collection, spread over the two floors of the main building, is representative of all the major movements in Thai art. Highlights to look out for include golden treasure from the Wat Ratchaburana hoard and a massive bronze Buddha head. As with many Thai museums, the displays are arranged in chronological order.

AYUTTHAYA HISTORICAL STUDY CENTER

This academic center, opened in 1990, promotes research into the history of Ayutthaya. Its principal building serves as a museum, open to the public, while other buildings to the rear are reserved for students, researchers, and academics. Exhibitions range from the history of ancient Ayutthaya to the role of the Ayutthaya Empire in international relations. Miniatures of seafaring vessels include a Chinese merchantship, and scale models of various structures depict old Ayutthaya, including a reconstruction of Wat Phra Si Sanphet (see p. 138) and a typical Thai village.

A tree encases the head of a Buddha at dilapidated Wat Mahathat.

LAK MUANG & KHUM KHUM HOUSE

Ayutthaya's city pillar, Lak Muang, stands by the National Museum and is believed to be the home of ancient spirits that live in the ground under the modern city. This means it is an animist or Hindu shrine, rather than a religious structure dedicated to the Buddha.

Nearby Khum Khum House was built in 1894 as the city jail, and it remains an outstanding example of traditional domestic architecture. It is now home to the Fine Arts Department, and visitors are welcome to explore the grounds.

WIHAN PHRA MONGKHON BOPHIT

One of Thailand's largest and most highly revered Buddhas is located inside this unimaginative building *(Si Sanphet Rd.)*, immediately south of the far more elegant Wat Phra Si Sanphet. The original building on this site was erected during the Ayutthaya period but collapsed in 1767. It was reconstructed in 1951. Head inside to enjoy the power of the immense image, covered with a thick black coating and gilded with gleaming mother-of-pearl eyes.

WAT PHRA SI SANPHET

Similar in purpose to Wat Phra Kaeo in Bangkok (see pp. 69–72), this famous trio of 15th-century *chedis* once formed the core of the most important temple complex in Ayutthaya. The *wat* was both the private chapel and ceremonial courtyard for royalty, who would

arrive on gilded palanquins from the nearby Royal Palace. The finely proportioned, symmetrically domed chedis stand on a long central platform, separated by square *mondops*, and are an image used widely on film—from Thai television commercials to American movies. The chedis were built to enshrine the ashes of important kings. The ruins are overgrown but one of the great sights of Ayutthaya.

ROYAL PALACE

At no other place in Ayutthaya is the destruction of the city more evident than on the grounds of the old Royal Palace, where nothing remains but some scattered foundations connected by a series of small paths. It was built in the mid-15th century by King Borommatrailokanat (*R.*1448–88) and expanded over the following centuries. Today, there is little that hints at its former opulence.

WAT NA PHRA MEN

One of the few great monuments to escape the destruction of 1767 is this soaring monastery on Khlong Sabua, opposite the Royal Palace. Believed to date from the late 15th century, it has been restored several times. Rarely visited by tourists, Wat Na Phra Men features a large *bot* beside a small but significant *wihan*. The larger building boasts magnificent Ayutthayan architectural details in its gateways, elaborate porticoes, and refined pediments. The interior, with its gilded supports, gleaming floors, and roofs carved with lotus buds, is just as remarkable. A gilded, Ayutthaya-style Buddha sits at the center.

The smaller wihan is noted for its extraordinarily rare Dvaravati Buddha, which is seated, with spread feet and hands curiously placed on the knees—a powerful image that richly deserves its reputation as a masterpiece of Mon art (*north part of town off Uthong Rd.*).

WAT LOKAYA SUTHARAM

The site of this wat, to the west of Auytthaya's main attractions, is marked by the 67-foot (20 m) figure of a reclining Buddha. The somewhat ungainly image was once protected by a wooden wihan, of which only the octagonal pillars survive—now a coat of whitewash is all that keeps him from the elements. Reclining Buddhas are usually associated with the Buddha's entry into nirvana, but this one relates to a particular story about the Buddha's growing huge in order to defeat an enemy.

ST. JOSEPH'S CATHEDRAL

During Ayutthaya's heyday, Western merchants and emissaries lived outside the city walls, and could only enter with official permission. As a result, various European communities grew up beyond the river boundary, and the 17th-century Catholic cathedral belongs to this time. Rebuilt in the 19th century, it continues to operate as a church (*Bung Phra Ram Rd., across the river, south side of city*).

WAT PHANAN CHOENG

One of the oldest and largest temples in Ayutthaya, Wat Phanan Choeng was constructed in 1324 specifically to house a massive seated Buddha, the gift of a Chinese emperor. The powerful and inspiring image has been restored many times, and a steady stream of Thai and Chinese pilgrims arrive daily to make offerings. An adjoining wihan to the left of the main temple has several rare and valuable Sukhothai statues (*south of town at ferry crossing*).

Little remains of the Royal Palace's original grandeur.

Royal Palace

- Map p. 132
- Si Sanphet Rd.
- $
- Tuk tuk from city center

Lak Muang & Khum Khum House

- Map p. 132
- Si Sanphet Rd.
- Tuk tuk from city center

Elephant Kraal

Map p. 132

Old Lop Buri River Rd., in Ban Phaniat

$

Tuk tuk from city center

WAT YAI CHAI MONGKHON

Southeast of town, towards the train station, is a monastery established in 1360 for local monks who, in the spirit of the new Buddhism, wished to emphasize meditation rather than the study of the Buddhist canon. Today it is home to a large community of Buddhist nuns *(mae chi),* who maintain the lawns and buildings. The wat's main feature is a huge reclining Buddha, exposed to the skies.

WAT SUWAN DARARAM

This small temple in the southeast quarter of the old city is worth seeking out for its magnificent interior murals, which date from the reign of Rama II. They depict events from the *Vessantara* and *Suvanasama Jatakas.* More modern murals commissioned by Rama VII show scenes from the life of King Naresuan. *(Uthong Rd.)*

WAT PHU KHAO THONG

Situated in rolling countryside some 3 miles (5 km) west of town is the gigantic chedi of Phu Khao Thong, the "golden mountain." The soaring 266-foot (80 m) structure was erected by the Burmese but later modified into a Thai style. Renovation projects over the centuries have not been kind to the chedi, but visitors who make the tiring hike to the summit will be rewarded with outstanding views over the plains.

ELEPHANT KRAAL

Ayutthaya's elephant enclosure—one of the last surviving teak stockades—was built to hold and train wild elephants for military use and was not abandoned until the mid-19th century. The stockade has been restored but is unexciting without its chief inhabitants. The shrine at the center is dedicated to the elephant guardian Ganesha. ∎

Cosmic symbolism in Thai architecture

Thai architecture may at first appear to be confusing and haphazard to the visitor, but in fact nearly every religious structure has been carefully designed to follow traditional elements that symbolize Theravada Buddhism and the underlying belief in Hindu cosmology. Almost everything about ancient and modern Thai architecture can be traced back to Hindu architectural concepts, which borrowed from the Khmers and were adapted by Thai builders.

Thai temples are filled with numerous Buddha images, which follow Hindu symbolism and concepts of cosmology. This may seem a strange combination, but animism underpins Buddhism in Thailand. Thus, while Thai kings honored Buddhism in their spiritual beliefs, they followed the animist traditions of Hinduism in their building designs.

Hindu cosmology dictates the architectural structure of all Thai temples. A massive tower that represents Mount Meru must always be the centerpiece, with 33 tiers that symbolize the 33 levels of heaven. *Prangs* were surmounted by a thunderbolt trident, the heavenly symbol of Indra, while *chedis* were capped with a circular orb to represent the core of nirvana. Moats symbolized ancient oceans separating the human race from the home of gods. Interpreted with the Thai love of curvature and extravagance, the results are an outstanding architectural triumph. ∎

Bang Pa-in Palace

MONARCHS WORLDWIDE HAVE SOUGHT A RETREAT FROM the confines of their royal capitals since time immemorial. So Philip II of Spain (R.1556–1598) built his Escorial palace, and Louis XIV of France his Versailles. For centuries, Siamese kings chose to escape the worst of the hot season in the riverine town of Bang Pa-in.

The habit of maintaining retreats and summer palaces started in the 17th century with King Narai (R.1656–1688), who received French envoys not only in his royal palace in Ayutthaya, but also at his great upriver retreat at Lop Buri (see p. 144). Narai also maintained a summer palace downriver at Bang Pa-in, a site established by his father, King Prasat Thong (R.1629–1656) in honor of Narai's birth. Narai's summer palace served the royal family until the fall of Ayutthaya in 1767, and the site lay neglected until its revival by King Mongkut in the mid-19th century.

Mongkut and his successor, King Chulalongkorn, enjoyed the advantages of the site and its easy access from Bangkok, revitalizing the area with new construction that can be seen today. Bang Pa-in could be reached by boat up the Chao Phraya or, later, via the railroad that ran from Bangkok to Chiang Mai.

Royalty retreated from the duties of Bangkok at Bang Pa-in Palace.

Bang Pa-in Palace

- ⓜ 119 C2
- ✉ Hwy. 32
- 💲 $
- 🚌 Bus from Northern Bus Terminal in Bangkok

Bang Pa-in is of secular rather than religious importance. The small collection of royal buildings that make up the palace are an easy stopover between Bangkok and Ayutthaya, and most reflect Chulalongkorn's fascination with European architecture. The overall impression is a mixture of French neoclassic, Victorian Gothic, imperial Chinese, and traditional Thai styles. The lovely grassy parklands are, in turn, formal French, rustic English, and classic Chinese.

Most of the buildings at Bang Pa-in date from 1872 to 1899—the swansong of European monarchy, but for Siam an era that embraced both traditional culture and the innovations of the West. The architectural range from château to summerhouse, pagoda to lighthouse, and Chinese mansion to Thai *sala* may sound like a 19th-century Disneyland, but the reality is a place of charm and dignity.

PHRA THINANG AISAWAN THIPPA-AT

The highlight of Bang Pa-in Palace is this little pavilion, which appears to float in the shimmering pool that surrounds the complex. Translated as "the divine seat of personal freedom" and designed in classic Rattanakosin style, the delicate pavilion is an icon of Thai architecture—and a great place for photos. The building is, in fact, a copy of a pavilion in Bangkok's Grand Palace (see pp. 72–74) and houses a statue of King Chulalongkorn in the uniform of a field marshal.

PHRA THINANG WEHAT CHAMRUN

Nicknamed the Peking Palace, this mansion is a copy of a monument in the Beijing Imperial Court, presented to King Chulalongkorn in 1889 by Chinese merchants and imported lock, stock, and barrel

from China. It is one of the few buildings open to the public, with interesting displays of lacquer tables, Chulalongkorn's fantastically carved bed, Ming porcelain, and a superb collection of jade.

PHRA THINANG WAROPHAT PHIMAN

The "excellent and shining abode" is a European-style palace set between the lake and the river, erected by King Chulalongkorn to replace King Mongkut's two-story royal residence. A grand porticoed structure, it was Chulalongkorn's official residence and throne hall. Memorials honor important events in national history.

HO WITHUN THASANA

This curious Royal Observatory tower is where the keen astronomer King Mongkut spent his evenings observing the stars. The tower is what remains of a wooden palace destroyed by fire in 1938.

QUEEN'S MONUMENT

Chulalongkorn's first queen is honored with a white marble memorial across a small bridge, inscribed with Thai and English eulogies composed by the king. Queen Sunandakumariratha drowned in a tragic swimming accident in 1880, within the reach of would be rescuers who were absolutely forbidden to touch the royal personage.

WAT NIVET THAMAPRAWAT

A small cable car takes you over the river from the main group of buildings to this unusual neo-Gothic-style temple that looks more like a Christian church than a Buddhist temple. Note the stained-glass window featuring King Chulalongkorn (the builder). The *wat* is unique in that it is the only one in Thailand buit in a European style. ∎

Wat Phra Phutthabat

Wat Phra Phutthabat

🅰 119 D3
✉ Saraburi
☎ 036-268915 or 036-268916
🚌 Bus from Northern Bus Terminal in Bangkok

LOCATED BETWEEN THE UNINSPIRING TOWN OF SARABURI and Lop Buri (see p. 144), north of Bangkok, this *wat* is one of the country's most revered. The temple was constructed by King Song Tham about 1620–28, to honor a wandering hunter's miraculous discovery of a footprint left by the Buddha during his time on Earth. According to the legend, the hunter reported that scars and wounds across his face and body vanished immediately after he bathed in the waters held within the immense footprint.

The miraculous powers assigned to the footprint over the centuries have turned it into a sort of Lourdes of Thailand, attracting a steady stream of pilgrims. Today the wat is one of the holiest shrines in the country (along with the temples at Chiang Mai, Nakhon Phanom, and Nakhon Si Thammarat).

An elaborate *mondop* shelters the 5-foot-long (1.5 m) gilded footprint, which is reached via a walkway guarded by mythological snakes. The hall is impressive inside—it was restored in the 18th century. Pilgrims throw coins into the footprint to improve their karma and toss in special sticks to divine their fortune. Electronic fortune-telling machines have also been installed in the mondop and other buildings within the temple complex.

Wihan Luang, within the same complex, is a museum of assorted religious relics. Smaller *chedis* and *bots* are dedicated to the Buddha and the Hindu god Kala.

Phra Phutthabat is the focus of two festive pilgrimages each year, in February and late March. Held for more than 400 years, the festivals draw up to 800,000 people. ∎

A *naga*-lined staircase leads to a mondop where a Buddha footprint, believed to have miraculous healing powers, is housed.

Lop Buri

Lop Buri

 119 D3

Visitor information

✉ Tourism Authority of Thailand, Narai Maharat Rd.

☎ 036-422768

🚌 Bus from Northern Bus Terminal in Bangkok

SOME 102 MILES (164 KM) NORTH OF BANGKOK, THIS IS THE site of one of Thailand's most ancient cities, continuously occupied since the sixth century. Lop Buri, originally known as Lavo, is thought to have been the capital of the Dvaravati Empire. The Khmers took over the town in the 11th century but permitted it to continue the cultural and religious traditions of the Dvaravati Empire. It was during this period that most of the major monuments were built.

After the fall of the Khmer Empire, the city lay abandoned until its revitalization in the 17th century by Ayutthaya's King Narai. He transformed the ancient city into an alternative capital, where he invited Europeans to visit and help create his summer "Versailles of Siam." French architects assisted in the building of his new residence, and exquisite gifts were exchanged with Louis XIV of France. This golden era ended with Narai's death in 1688, and Lop Buri slipped into the backwaters of history. Today, a lively modern town has grown up to the east of the ancient city.

Phra Narai Ratchaniwet (Royal Palace)

✉ Sorasak Rd.

🕐 National Museum closed Mon.–Tues. (palace open daily)

💲 $

PHRA NARAI RATCHANIWET

Narai's enormous **royal palace** complex displays a strong blend of traditional Khmer and European architecture.

To the right of the main entrance is the Chanthara Phisan Pavilion, built in 1665 and now the **Lop Buri National Museum,** with an interesting collection of Buddhas, and displays of Uthong, Khmer, and Ayutthayan art. The **Audience Hall** to the left of the museum was a reception hall. Now little more than teetering stone walls, it was once lined with grand mirrors in imitation of Versailles.

Opposite: Resident monkeys are the guests of honor for a feast at Wat San Phra Khan.

WAT PHRA SI RATTANA MAHATHAT

This 12th-century Khmer temple is Lop Buri's most significant piece of architecture. The towering central *prang*, decorated with elaborate stuccowork, survived clumsy renovations during the Ayutthaya and Sukhothai periods, and is an outstanding sight. A brick *wihan* was built for King Narai, and its unusual pointed window arch clearly shows European and Persian influence *(Naprakan Rd.)*.

WAT SAN PHRA KAN

Also known as the Kala Temple, the site includes the remains of a 10th-century Khmer prang, a smaller temple with a particularly ornate doorway, and a modern temple built in 1953, with a gilded statue of the four-armed Hindu god Kala. Most visitors come here to see the unruly and sometimes aggressive army of monkeys that has been allowed to take over virtually every nook and cranny of the temple *(Wichayen Rd.)*.

CHAO PHRAYA WICHAYEN

This European-style palace was built by King Narai for a French ambassador of Louis XIV but gained fame later as the residence of a Greek, Constantine Phaulkon (died 1688). Phaulkon exerted considerable influence over the king and hoped to convert him to Christianity. The king's death sealed his own fate, however—his rivals promptly had him executed. The palace was demolished at the same time *(Wichayen Rd.)*. ■

More places to visit around Bangkok

CROCODILE FARM

A few miles from Muang Boran is the world's largest reptile farm, established in 1950 to preserve endangered crocodiles, and now so successful it runs a side business manufacturing crocodile-skin wallets, briefcases, shoes, and handbags, which are sold on the site. The 30,000 crocodiles, which lie around in murky pools waiting for feeding time (4:30–5:30 p.m.), include species from all around the world. The crocodile-wrestling show is popular; the trained chimps and elephants are less appealing to the modern visitor. Try crocodile meat in the restaurants on the site.

⚠ 119 D1 ✉ Old Sukhumvit Hwy., Samut Prakan ☎ 02-703-5144 or 02-703-5145 $ $$ 🚌 Bus: 7, 8, or 11 to Samut Prakan

HUMAN IMAGERY MUSEUM

This is like a waxworks, but the figures from Thai and Asian history—including Chakri kings and famous monks—are made of fiberglass. It is 19 miles (31 km) west of Bangkok, near Samphran Elephant Ground & Zoo (see right) and the Rose Garden (see p. 123).

⚠ 119 C1 ✉ Km. 31, Hwy. 4 ☎ 034-332607 $ $ 🚌 Bus: 83 or 997 from Southern Bus Terminal in Bangkok

MIN BURI

Two great escapes from the concrete jungle of Bangkok are **Safari World** and **Siam Park,** both in the suburb of Min Buri, 6 miles (10 km) northeast of the capital. Safari World is a drive-through wildlife park, offering glimpses of tigers, elephants, and zebras in different habitat settings. Siam Park is a waterpark with water slides, a small zoo, and botanical gardens—a great place to cool down.

⚠ 119 D1 ✉ Min Buri ☎ 02-518-1000 $ $$$$$ 🚌 Bus: 26 or 27 from Victory Monument, Bangkok

MUANG BORAN

Also called Ancient City, this exclusive outdoor historical and architectural theme park features 65 faithful reproductions of significant buildings from around the country. Most are reduced in scale by about two thirds. Some depict buildings that no longer exist,

such as the Grand Palace of Ayutthaya. This is a great place to get a quick overview of the important architectural sights in the country. It is 20 miles (33 km) southeast of Bangkok.

⚠ 119 D1 ✉ Sukhumvit Rd., Bangpu Samut Prakan ☎ 02-226-1936 $ $ 🚌 Bus: 7, 8, or 11 to Samut Prakan

NONTHABURI

About 6 miles (10 km) north of Bangkok, this small town retains some of the charm of old Siam, with its riverside market, stylish old buildings, royal boathouse, and—on the opposite shore—picturesque temple ruins amid orchards of breadfruit trees.

The town is also the home of Thailand's favorite beer, made at the Singha Brewery. A small but intriguing museum in the prison shows methods of torture and execution from the Ayutthaya period to more modern times. The town is best reached by river (see p. 113).

⚠ 119 C2 ✉ Hwy. 305 🚌 Bus: 5 or 6 🚤 Chao Phraya River Express from Bangkok

SAMPHRAN ELEPHANT GROUND & ZOO

Crocodile wrestling and animal-themed magic shows are part of the attraction of this small farm. But it is the elephant games that are the most unusual, with a tug of war, a mock-round-up, and the re-creation of a historical battle fought on elephant-back. The park is close to the Human Imagery Museum (see left) and the Rose Garden (see p. 123). Shows at 1:45 p.m. and 3:30 p.m.

✉ Km. 31, Hwy. 4 ☎ 02-284-1873 $ $ 🚌 Bus: 83 or 997 from Southern Bus Terminal in Bangkok

SAMNAK SONG THAM KRABAWK

About 15 miles (25 km) north of Saraburi toward Lop Buri, this is Thailand's most famous drug rehabilitation center, claiming a 70–80 percent success rate for opium and heroin abusers. It uses a radical combination of herbal ingestion, counseling, and spiritualism. When they leave, patients vow to stay drug free lest they incur the wrath of the spirit world. Visitors are welcome.

⚠ 119 D3 ☎ 036-267198 ■

A rambunctious and famous international resort, beach towns where locals spend their weekends away from Bangkok, and peaceful, idyllic islands await visitors to Thailand's east coast.

East Coast

Fishing boat in Rayong harbor

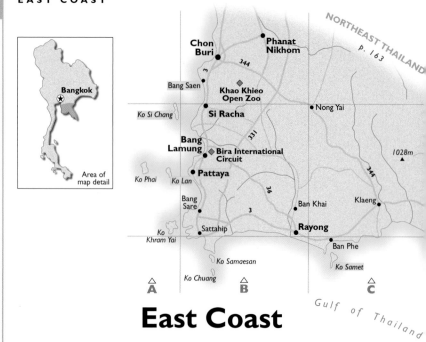

Bangkok

Area of map detail

Chon Buri

Phanat Nikhom

NORTHEAST THAILAND P. 163

Bang Saen

Khao Khieo Open Zoo

344

Nong Yai

Ko Si Chang

Si Racha

331

Bang Lamung

Bira International Circuit

1028m

Ko Phai   Ko Lan   Pattaya

344

Bang Sare

36

Ban Khai   Klaeng

Ko Khram Yai   Sattahip

3

Rayong

Ko Samaesan

Ban Phe

Ko Samet

Ko Chuang

A   B   C

Gulf of Thailand

East Coast

THAILAND'S EASTERN COASTLINE STRINGS TOGETHER AN ALMOST unbroken stretch of sand that runs from southeast of Bangkok to Hak Lek, a village that sits on the Cambodian border in Trat Province. The coast closer to Bangkok is the industrial heartland of Thailand, where huge manufacturing, power, and oil refinery plants predominate. Where the factories end, the famous resort city of Pattaya begins. Beyond Pattaya lies a crop of uncluttered islands that attract visitors—Thai and foreign— who are looking for quieter locations.

All towns along the east coast lie on or near Sukhumvit Highway (Highway 3), which stretches 399 miles (638 km) from the heart of Bangkok as far as the Cambodian border. After cutting through the urban southeast of Bangkok, Sukhumvit Highway emerges into traces of countryside before it reaches the coastline, a narrow strip of land wedged between the Gulf of Thailand and the Dongrek Mountains, which rise abruptly just a few miles inland. Here government planners have set in motion a package of schemes that will transform this section of the eastern seaboard from a collection of fishing villages to Thailand's major industrial zone.

While deepwater ports, natural gas and oil refineries, and industrial estates may have little appeal for the visitor, the resort city of Pattaya certainly does. The honeypot

of the east coast, Pattaya provides an enormous range of activities for visitors, from superb golf courses and excellent scuba diving to theme parks for the kids. Reasonable diversions can be made from Pattaya to the modest beach at Bang Saen and to the island of Ko Si Chang, just a short boat ride from Si Racha.

The coast beyond Pattaya unveils a couple of island gems—Ko Samet and Ko Chang—and a number of towns with varying degrees of appeal.

Rayong is an unremarkable town, though it provides the gateway to the nearby island of Ko Samet. This is a favorite stop for Thai students, who bring their guitars with them and stay in the moderately priced bungalows that flank the island.

Farther east again is the large town of Chanthaburi, located in an area famed

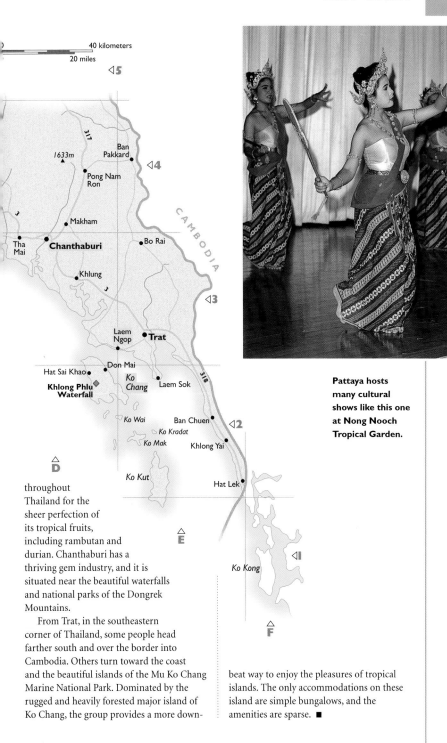

40 kilometers

20 miles

◁5

317

Ban
Pakkard

1633m ▲

◁4

Pong Nam
Ron

Makham

Bo Rai

Tha
Mai

Chanthaburi

CAMBODIA

Khlung

◁3

Laem
Ngop   •**Trat**

Don Mai

Hat Sai Khao•

*Ko
Chang*   Laem Sok

**Khlong Phlu
Waterfall**

318

◁ Ko Wai   Ban Chuen

◁2

○ Ko Kradat

Ko Mak   Khlong Yai

△
D

Ko Kut   Hat Lek

△
E

◁1

Ko Kong

△
F

Pattaya hosts
many cultural
shows like this one
at Nong Nooch
Tropical Garden.

throughout
Thailand for the
sheer perfection of
its tropical fruits,
including rambutan and
durian. Chanthaburi has a
thriving gem industry, and it is
situated near the beautiful waterfalls
and national parks of the Dongrek
Mountains.

From Trat, in the southeastern
corner of Thailand, some people head
farther south and over the border into
Cambodia. Others turn toward the coast
and the beautiful islands of the Mu Ko Chang
Marine National Park. Dominated by the
rugged and heavily forested major island of
Ko Chang, the group provides a more down-
beat way to enjoy the pleasures of tropical
islands. The only accommodations on these
island are simple bungalows, and the
amenities are sparse. ■

Stonemasons are in high demand for creating sculptures for theme parks and other tourist attractions.

Bang Saen

SUKHUMVIT HIGHWAY CUTS ACROSS WHAT LITTLE remains of the rice fields that once characterized the area southeast of Bangkok, until it reaches the large industrial city of Chon Buri, known on the tourist circuit only for its annual water-buffalo races. A few miles beyond is one of the oldest beach resorts in Thailand, the modest stretch of sand and casuarina trees at Bang Saen.

Bang Saen

🗺 148 B5

Visitor information

✉ Tourism Authority of Thailand, 609 Mu 10 Phra Tham Nak Rd., Tambon Nongpue, Amphoe Bang-Lamung, Chon Buri

☎ 038-427667 or 038-428750

🚌 Bus from Ekamai (Eastern) Bus Terminal, Bangkok

Before the completion of the road to Pattaya in 1969, Bang Saen was the most popular weekend beach escape in the kingdom. Even today it attracts big crowds of Thais, who appreciate its proximity to Bangkok and its almost total lack of tourists.

The beach here is clean, but the waters on any particular day can vary from clear to murky. Vendors are always on hand to rent umbrellas and bamboo furniture to go along with the mats on which families spread out picnics. Visitors are a rarity, so you can expect to be invited to join a group of Thais who will probably be cracking open mussels and consuming prodigious quantities of Mekong whiskey.

Khao Khieo Open Zoo (*Rte. 3144, tel 038-338390*), 12 miles (18 km) inland from Bang Saen, opened in 1973 to provide overflow facilities for the cramped Dusit Zoo in Bangkok (see p. 102). ∎

The *wai*

The graceful wai—hands placed together in a prayer-like posture, accompanied by the bowing of the head—is the traditional greeting in Thailand and is still widely used. It appears to be simple, but the wai is tied up in a complicated set of social rules involving age, community status, wealth, and power. Who wais first, whether a wai is returned, how high the hands are held, and how long they remain in that position, as well as the length and depth of the bow, depend on your status and that of the person you are greeting. ∎

Si Racha & Ko Si Chang

THE SMALL BUT ACTIVE FISHING VILLAGE OF SI RACHA IS famous as the production center of a pungent fish concoction called *nam phrik si racha*—the most popular sweet and spicy sauce in Thailand. The town itself has little of great interest, but it is the launching point for boats across to the historic island of Ko Si Chang.

While waiting for the boat for Ko Si Chang, spend an hour wandering around Si Racha, visiting a few temples and exploring the colorful waterfront (look for the unique motorcycle trishaws).

The only real attraction of note is the famous offshore island of **Ko Loi,** linked to the mainland by a 1-mile (1.5 km) bridge. The island has a temple—Wat Ko Loi—which is popular with Thai tourists, who flock here to honor the memory of a deceased monk. According to local folklore, the monk possessed miraculous healing powers. You can see his wax statue at the temple.

KO SI CHANG
This island, which lies 8 miles (13 km) offshore from Si Racha, became popular with wealthy Thais and royalty in the mid-19th century—so popular that King Chulalongkorn built a **summer palace** here in 1892 (royalty previously stayed on steamships offshore). The end result—you can see it to the right as you arrive on the island from Si Racha—was impressive: the two-story Wattana Palace, the eight-sided Phongsri on a nearby hill, and the Aphirom with dual porches were part of a compound that included 14 royal domiciles and four throne halls built in teak, plus a hillside *chedi.* Wells were dug, a lighthouse was constructed to aid passing ships, and roads were built to connect the residences.

But it all fell into disrepair after it was abandoned when the French occupied the island from 1893 to 1904. One of the four throne halls was dismantled and moved to Bangkok in 1910, where it now serves as Vimanmek Palace (see pp. 102-103). Its foundations and stairway remain at Ko Si Chang. Other surviving palace buildings, or what's left of them, are partly overgrown, but they still form an appealing site.

Another site worth searching out is a Chinese temple called **San Chao Por Khao Yai.** This is a gathering point for thousands of Chinese Thais who come every year during Chinese New Year. The temple, at the top of steep climb, has a number of shrine caves. The views over the island are spectacular.

The most popular beach is **Hat Tha Wang** at the western end of the island, 1.25 miles (2 km) from the main pier, near the palace. ∎

Si Racha

⚑ 148 B4, 148 A4

Visitor information

✉ 609 Mu 10 Phra Tham Nak Rd., Tambon Nongpue, Amphoe Bang-Lamung, Chon Buri

☎ 038-427667 or 038-428750

🚌 Regular buses from Ekamai (Eastern) Bus Terminal, Bangkok

Shrimp farms

Shrimp farms proliferate in the coastal areas of Thailand and are considered a major cause of environmental destruction. Mangrove forests are cut down and wetlands dredged to make way for the farms, leading to the destruction of these important habitats and exposing the coastline to erosion. Local species are affected and migratory birds—which once came in their thousands—no longer return. The farms are often in "protected" parks, where unscrupulous businessmen pay off politicians to allow their construction. ∎

Pattaya

FIFTY YEARS AGO, PATTAYA WAS A SOMNOLENT FISHING village reachable only by boat from Bangkok or other towns near the estuary of the Chao Phraya. The town's chief claim to fame was that it served as a resting place for King Narai during his military campaign to oust Burmese forces from his country.

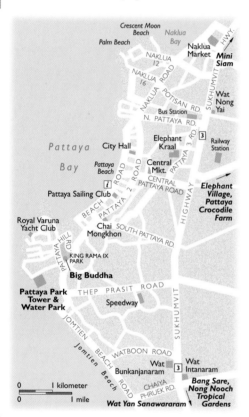

as a rest and recreation spot during the Vietnam War. By the 1970s locals and tourists were starting to discover its charms. Hotels were built along the shoreline, together with restaurants, nightclubs, and bars. By the 1980s Pattaya had become one of Thailand's most popular tourist resorts.

Today, three million visitors flood this rambunctious resort every year to enjoy its highrise hotels, simple guesthouses, roaring discos, fine restaurants, souvenir shops, and countless nightclubs, which complement several world-class golf courses and every imaginable activity connected with the ocean. Those who seek perfect quiet on a lonely tropical island should skip Pattaya and head down to Ko Chang (see pp. 160–61). But visitors who desire comforts and pleasures, along with nonstop entertainment, will love Pattaya, one of Southeast Asia's great party towns.

The most accessible beach resort near Bangkok, Pattaya is in the process of changing itself from a rather seedy destination for single men into a highly varied retreat favored by couples and families. But no one can hide the problems that Pattaya faces. Because of reckless development over the years, its main beach became so polluted that people were warned not to swim there. For a long while, the city was probably the only beach resort in the world where the beach was out of bounds. Pattaya also suffers from its image as a sex

Pattaya

148 B4

Visitor information

✉ Tourism Authority of Thailand, 382/1 Mu 10 Chaihat Rd., Pattaya City

☎ 038-427667 or 038-428750

🚌 Bus from Ekamai (Eastern) Bus Terminal, Bangkok

In 1959 a group of American GIs from a U.S. military base in Nakhon Ratchasima (Khorat) arrived in Pattaya, renting houses in the southern part of town. On their return to Khorat, they spread the word about the white sands and clear waters of Pattaya beach. The visit kickstarted Pattaya's tourism drive. More U.S. servicemen from military bases scattered throughout Northeast Thailand used the town

center and is a favorite haunt for men from abroad looking for sex.

City fathers face a constant battle with the resort's image, launching campaign after campaign to try to convince people that it has cleaned up its act. And to some extent it has. You can now swim at Pattaya Beach. The city has become one of Asia's premier golf centers, with a dozen quality courses attracting people from all over the region. There is a myriad of water sports, and on nearby offshore islands, sparkling beaches and gardens of coral are great for diving

Water scooters—one of numerous modes of water fun available in Pattaya—line Jomtien Beach.

and snorkeling. There are amusement parks and plenty of other tourist sites in and around the town. And—if you keep an open mind—you will encounter a lively and enjoyable nightlife.

Pattaya Beach is narrow and less impressive than beaches in Southern Thailand. However, a few hours relaxing under an umbrella, munching on Thai snacks, makes for a pleasant diversion.

For excellent views over Pattaya, head up Pattaya Hill Road, at the southern end of town, to Wat Pra Yai, with its **Big Buddha** statue.

Off Pattaya Hill Road, not far from Wat Pra Yai, at the northern Jomtien beachfront on Thapphraya Road, **Pattaya Water Park** (*Jomtien Beach, tel 038-251201*), with its water slides and whirlpools, is something the entire family will enjoy. Next door is **Pattaya Park Tower** (*Jomtien Beach, tel 038-251201*), which features a revolving restaurant on the 53rd floor. After a buffet lunch, you can ride the elevator down to the ground or jump out of the window and descend to earth on the seemingly perilous "sky shuttle."

AROUND PATTAYA

Pattaya Crocodile Farm (*Siam Country Club Rd., tel 038-249347*) has rare animals, as well as crocodiles, and a botanical garden. In Pattaya, turn off Sukhumvit Road at the Kilometer 140 signpost to Chaiyaphonwithi Road (Highway 3024) for 3 miles (5 km).

Mini Siam (*Sukhumvit Hwy., tel 038-726202*), on the left of Sukhumvit Road traveling south, at the Kilometer 143 signpost, features almost 100 miniature models of famous Siamese temples and other historical structures, including Wat Phra Kaeo (see pp. 69–72), the bridge over the River Kwai (Khwae; see pp. 125–26), and the Khmer

temple at Phimai (see pp. 170–71). The park also has models of worldwide icons such as the Eiffel Tower and the Statue of Liberty.

From Mini Siam, head south on Sukhumvit Road, past North Pattaya Road; then turn left on Pornprapanimitr Road toward the Siam Country Club to the popular **Pattaya Elephant Village** (*Siam Country Club Rd., tel 038-428645*). See demonstrations of the unique skills of the Thai elephant, and take a two-hour ride through the adjacent jungle. An elephant ride, jungle trek, and river-rafting package is also available.

Bira International Circuit (*Hwy. 36, mobile tel 01-587-7448*) is on Highway 36—the main Pattaya–Ranong road—about 9 miles (14 km) north of town. It sponsors international motor-racing events and is home to a popular race school. Rental choices range from go-carts to Formula 3 models.

About 10 miles (16 km) south of Pattaya off Sukhumvit Road, **Wat Yan Sangwararam** features seven unique structures in various Asian and Western styles, and a magnificent museum filled with Chinese paintings, scrolls, bronzeware, carved wall reliefs, and a small-scale model of the excavated tomb in Xian, China.

A few miles south, still on Sukhumvit Road, turn left at the Kilometer 163 signpost to **Nong Nooch Tropical Gardens** (*Rte. 3, tel 038-709358*), another well-managed tourist resort, with gardens, a small zoo, an orchid house and aviary, several restaurants, and a daily cultural show that ranks among the better of its kind.

Bang Sare, a small fishing village 3 miles (5 km) south of Nong Nooch Tropical Gardens, is the departure point for many fishing trips sponsored by a local game fishing association.

KO LAN

After visiting some of the more commercialized attractions of Pattaya, many visitors choose to spend a day out on one of the nearby islands, where the sand is much cleaner and inviting than at the municipal beach. Of the half-dozen islands offshore, the most popular is **Ko Lan** ("coral island"), which has several beautiful beaches, clear water, and an abundance of coral. You can view the coral from a glass-bottom boat, snorkel, or organize a trip at one of the dozen scuba-dive centers in Pattaya.

Tour boats from Pattaya head to **Ta Waen Beach** on the northeast coast of Ko Lan, the island's best and most popular beach (avoid weekends, when it gets packed). Restaurants and outlets offering watersports line most of the beach. Besides glass-bottom boat tours of the nearby coral crops, you can hire snorkeling gear, try parasailing, go water skiing, or hire a water scooter. At the southwestern end of the island is the clean and tranquil (on weekdays) **Laemtien Beach.** South again are the smaller, more secluded Samae and Nual beaches.

GOLF COURSES

The most highly regarded are **Siam Golf and Country Club** (*Siam Country Club Rd., tel 038-249381*), **Bang Phra International Golf Club** (*45 Mu 6, Tambon Bang Phra, tel 038-341149*), and **Great Lake Golf & Country Club** (*77 Mu 5, Mabyangpon, Amphur Pluek Daeng, Rayong, tel 038-662630*). ∎

Young Thais congregate in one of Pattaya's many beer bars.

Ko Samet

KO SAMET IS A SMALL, WEDGE-SHAPED ISLAND JUST OFF-shore from Ban Phe. Graced with superb sandy beaches and crystal-clear aquamarine waters, it sits below rocky headlands that are typical of the arid interior. Samet's appeal also lies in its relatively close proximity to Bangkok and in its simple, rustic lifestyle, which is a marked contrast to the livelier atmosphere of Pattaya.

Foreign visitors know Ko Samet for its unpretentious charms, but Thais associate the island with their greatest poet, Sunthorn Phu (1786–1855), who based his earliest and most famous epic poem, *Phra Aphaimani*, on his experiences while living on the island. Sunthorn wrote this in the mid-19th century, at a time when Samet functioned as the last customhouse for junks and other ships sailing between China and Siam. The island and its adjoining straits were also the haunt of brigands who raided the cargo-laden vessels. Captured pirates were executed near the customhouse on the north side of Samet.

Ko Samet lay largely off the tourist trail until the early 1970s, when young Thais seeking quiet and solitude traveled down from Bangkok to live in simple shacks on the deserted beaches. An attempt was made to develop the island with resorts, but the outcry from local environmental groups forced the National Parks Division of the Forestry Department to declare the entire island a national park in October 1981, effectively halting large-scale development. Despite these legal measures, developers continued to encroach on the island without permits, and local authorities did little to stop the building of bungalows and resorts, watersports facilities, and even a few small nightclubs.

The confrontation between private resort developers and government officials peaked in May 1990, when a special police task force raided the island and closed dozens of bungalows as illegally constructed facilities. Although the blitzkrieg was short-lived and ultimately doomed to failure, it helped raise a national consciousness about the preservation of the environment and the threatened overdevelopment of a once-unspoiled paradise.

Ko Samet today remains in a quandary about its future: Whether large-scale development will over-run the island or controlled simplicity will remain the common theme are questions that remain unanswered, as they do on many other small islands. The completion of a large freshwater reservoir in 2000 has given credence to the claims of local resort owners that their historic rights must supersede those of the Forestry Department. Today, the island receives almost 30,000 visitors per month and has some 50 illegal resorts of more than 1,500 rooms.

Despite the fact that political controversies continue to swirl, the island remains an essentially quiet and easygoing destination, without the high-tech thrills of other commercially developed islands in the kingdom.

Visitors arrive on converted fishing trawlers, which leave hourly from the creaky pier at Ban Phe. Most of the boats are chartered by the more upscale resorts and pro-ceed directly to their destinations.

Ko Samet
🗺 148 C3
Visitor information
✉ Tourism Authority of Thailand, Ban Gon Ao, Tambon Pae, Rayong
☎ 038-653034
🚌 Buses to Rayong from Ekamai (Eastern) Bus Terminal, Bangkok

The **Na Dan ferry landing** on the north shore of Ko Samet is the most professionally developed enclave on the island, with hotels and resorts in all price ranges, and watersports that cover the whole spectrum, from windsurfing and boat excursions to snorkeling and scuba diving.

Ko Samet's finest beaches and cleanest waters are found along the east coast, starting with **Hat Sai Kaeo** ("diamond sand beach") at the northeastern tip of the island and just a 10-minute walk from the Na Dan ferry landing. Hat Sai Kaeo has the longest and most impressive beach, and has become the favorite stop for many of the families with children and moderately affluent travelers who come down from Pattaya for a day visit.

South of Hat Sai Kaeo are a number of smaller beaches and coves packed with everything from primitive wooden huts to deluxe resorts with swimming pools and air-conditioned restaurants. **Phai Beach,** also known as Paradise Beach, is a typical small cove with a handful of small bungalows to rent, and basic services including a travel office and a post office with poste restante facilities. **Tub Tim** and **Pudsa Beaches,** farther south, offer a quieter atmosphere plus relatively easy walking access to the near deserted beaches of the west coast—the perfect place for dramatic sunsets. **Wong Deuan, Candlelight, Wai,** and **Kui Beaches** round out the possibilities on the lower stretches of the east coast. ∎

Formerly called **Ko Kaew Phitsadau** ("vast jewel isle"), a reference to the island's glorious white sand, Ko Samet takes its present name from the abundant *samet,* or cajeput, trees.

Chanthaburi

CHANTHABURI ("CITY OF THE MOON"), A BUSY commercial enclave on the highway to Cambodia, makes an interesting stop on the long drive to Ko Chang (see pp. 160–61). It has a thriving gem industry, durian plantations (the smelly fruit so loved by many Thais), and a significant population of Vietnamese Christians who fled Vietnam in the late 19th century.

Fruit and vegetable vendors in Chanthaburi vie for customers with more modern retail outlets.

Chanthaburi

🅰 149 D3

Visitor information

✉ Tourism Authority of Thailand, 153/4 Sukhumvit Rd., Amphoe Muang, Rayong

☎ 038-655420 or 038-655421

🚌 Bus from Ekamai (Eastern) Terminal, Bangkok

With its utilitarian architecture and modern conveniences, the town appears unremarkable on the surface. In fact, Chanthaburi figured prominently in battles with the French, who occupied this section of Thailand between 1893 and 1904.

Chanthaburi's riverside district and lush parks are relaxing places to while away a few hours, watching the local people and visiting the limited range of attractions that reflect the region's history. Top draw for most visitors is the historic Catholic **Church of the Immaculate Conception,** constructed in French style between 1906 and 1909 by Vietnamese immigrants who had flocked here to escape the religious persecution of Emperor Gia Long. The

delightfully cheerful color scheme on the exterior seems very French, an impression born out by details of the interior, from the stained-glass windows (imported from Europe) to the shellwork chandeliers and 26 Moorish-style arches. And it's refreshingly cool inside this Gothic-style monument.

Gems and precious jewelry have long been associated with Thailand, which remains an important source for both the gems themselves and for gem processing. While precious stones are now rarely found in large quantities within Thailand, rubies, emeralds, and sapphires continue to pour into the country from Myanmar (Burma) and Cambodia. The gems are mined just across from Chanthaburi in the lower Cambodian hills and brought to the city for cutting and then merchandising by the jewelry dealers, who arrive daily in steady numbers. Chinese gem dealers can still be observed at work in their sidewalk stalls and inside modern stores just off Sukaphiban Road, near the bridge.

Visitors with extra time may want to explore the old-style houses—notable for their intricate woodcarvings and elaborate wooden altars—which are situated along Sukaphiban Road, just behind the Kasem Sarn I hotel. Several of these atmospheric old homes still have colonial shutters and filigree plasterwork, reflecting the French and Vietnamese origins of the town. ■

Trat & Laem Ngop

TRAVELERS HEADING DOWN TO BEAUTIFUL KO CHANG (see pp. 160–61) must pass through Trat, a small but thriving commercial enclave, and the sleepy port village of Laem Ngop, the launching point for ferries across to the island. Neither place offers much charm, though the intricacies of transportation in this part of Thailand may necessitate an overnight stop in one or the other.

Trat has played a surprisingly important role in Thai history, most notably after 1767, when it was the launching point for a counterattack against the Burmese conquerors of Ayutthaya.

The city also figured in the French colonial conquest of Indochina, when it was ceded to France in 1894 in exchange for Chanthaburi. It returned to Thai control in the early days of the 20th century, when it was exchanged with the French for Cambodia. A treaty signed that year by King Chulalongkorn ceded the Cambodian provinces of Battambang, Sisophon, and Siem Reap in exchange for Trat, Ko Chang, and Ko Kong. France later attempted to take back Ko Chang, sparking a sea battle off the southern coast of the island in 1941. Thailand lost three warships in the confrontation but retained sovereignty over Ko Chang.

Trat today is the only town in Thailand that celebrates an independence day. This commemorates the day in March 1906 when the town and province were "liberated" from their French colonial overlords.

Attractions are in short supply, but the stranded visitor may enjoy a visit to the bustling and reasonably clean market, with its inexpensive foodstalls. There is an impressive fish market in the rear. The town also has a pair of night markets that provide a degree of interesting diversion.

Wat Bupharam, also known as Wat Pai Klong, is the only historical building of note, having been constructed in 1652, during the reign of King Thong of Ayutthaya. This temple is 2 miles (3 km) west of town, on the road just opposite the Trat hotel.

LAEM NGOP

Laem Ngop, 11.5 miles (18 km) south of Trat, chiefly functions as the departure point for ferries and fishing boats to Ko Chang and other smaller islands toward the Cambodian border. Most visitors arrive at the pier and hang around the small cafés, waiting for the next departure to Ko Chang. The 1941 battle between the Thai and the French navies mentioned above is noted by a sign in the parking lot. ■

The coconut industry thrives on East Coast islands. Here, coconuts are unloaded at Laem Ngop's port.

Trat

🅰 149 E3

Visitor information

✉ TAT, 100 Mu 1, Trat-Laem Ngop Rd., Tambon Laem Ngop, Amphoe Laem Ngop, Trat

☎ 039-597255 or 039-597259 or 039-597260

🚌 Bus from Ekamai (Eastern) Bus Terminal, Bangkok

Ko Chang

Ko Chang

🅰 149 E2

Visitor information

✉ Tourism Authority of Thailand, 100 Mu 1, Trat-Laem Ngop Rd., Tambon Laem Ngop, Amphoe Laem Ngop, Trat

☎ 039-597255 or 039-597259 or 039-597260

✉ Laem Ngop tourism office: Ban Hin Ta Boy, Laem Ngop, Trat

☎ 039-538100

⛴ Ferries from Laem Ngop (see p. 159)

KO CHANG ("ELEPHANT ISLAND") HAS MANAGED TO maintain much of its wilderness feel despite the development of tourism over the last decade. The island—at 197 square miles (492 sq km) the second largest in Thailand after Phuket—is carpeted in thick rain forest that climbs a steep wall of hills laced with waterfalls. The hills run though the center of the island, splitting it in two. Closer to the waterline, mangroves and beach forests proliferate, and crystalline water laps up on lovely white-sand beaches.

Ko Chang and the numerous small islands nearby, which together make up **Ko Chang Marine National Park,** can thank their environmental survival to relative isolation and the protection afforded by park status (about 85 percent of the main island is national park land, but borders are often blurred when it comes to development). Whether this protection can be maintained as Ko Chang grows in popularity remains to be seen. A paved road virtually rings the island now, and the main island's beaches (most have bungalow accommodations) are easily accessible by motorcycle, taxi, hired motorbikes, and *songthaew* buses. Ferries regularly leave the pier at Laem Ngop (see p. 159), on the mainland, and stop at a number of beaches around the island. Most people dock at Ao Sapporot—the most convenient destination, at about 45 minutes from Laem Ngop—at the northern tip of the island and fan out to beaches from there. Despite development, Ko Chang remains one of the most beautiful islands in Thailand and is well worth the effort of a long overland journey from Bangkok.

The longest and most popular beach on the island is **Hat Sai Khao,** or White Sand Beach, which extends from the northwestern tip of Ko Chang down the upper one-third of the island. Hat Sai Khao has the largest choice of accommodations and the best restaurants. **Hat Khlong Phrao,** just to the south over a hillock, is a beach with a greater degree of peace and solitude. South of Hat Phrao, smaller, but by no means less appealing stretches of sand, can be found at **Hat Bae** and **Hat Kruat.**

Most visitors are content to relax on the sands, but there are several natural attractions that make interesting diversions. You can hike from Khlong Phrao Beach into the rain forest to **Khlong Phlu Waterfall;** longer treks over the mountainous spine of the island require guides, who can be arranged through bungalow owners. Attractions on the east coast include an almost deserted visitor center with a 3D model of the island, the six-level **Tham Mayom Waterfall** with a small swimming pool at its base, and modest **Don Keo Waterfall** in the northeast corner of the island, past the main town of Don Mai.

ISLANDS NEAR KO CHANG

Over a dozen largely deserted or sparsely developed islands lie in the warm waters of the Gulf of Thailand, between Ko Chang and Cambodia. Ferries to most of these can be taken from Laem Ngop and are frequent from December to April, the tourist high season. Ferries also island-hop at this time. During

the wet season (May to November) some resorts close down and transportation is difficult.

Ko Kut, the second largest island in the archipelago, is not under the supervision of the National Parks Division and is therefore the most developed in the region. Fortunately, the island's large size and inaccessibility have preserved the environment and left most of the beaches, coves, and lagoons in almost perfect condition. Beaches with bungalows or superior resorts are mostly located on the north and northwest coasts.

Several rivers with waterfalls snake down from the central mountain ridge and plunge into the sea along the west coast. Other waterfalls, such as **Khlong Chao** and **Khlong Anamkok,** can be

reached by taking a boat to Khlong Chao and then a short hike through the jungle. The island also has some striking coral beds.

Ko Mak is smaller and flatter than Ko Kut, but is still the third largest island, and one of the most developed, with some upscale resorts. It is blessed with fine beaches, coconut groves, and colorful coral reefs off its northern tip.

The other, smaller islands in the Ko Chang archipelago are within the marine national park. **Ko Kradat** ("paper island") has a 4-mile (6.5 km) beach, with decent diving among the coral. This island, along with the smaller islands south of Ko Chang, is often visited on day trips. Other islands with overnight facilities are **Ko Phrao, Ko Ngam, Ko Laoya,** and **Ko Wai.** ■

Listing coconut palms and gleaming white sand grace Ko Chang's beaches.

Road to Cambodia
149 E2, 149 E3
Visitor information
✉ 100 Mu 1, Trat-
Laem Ngop Rd.,
Tambon Laem Ngop,
Amphoe Laem Ngop,
Trat
☎ 039-597255 or
039-597259 or
039-597260

**Ko Kong
International
Casino**
 149 F1
✉ Ko Kong Island
🚌 Bus to Hat Lek
from Trat, then
speedboat or ferry
from Hat Lek

The road to Cambodia

EAST, AND THEN SOUTH, OF TRAT, SUKHUMVIT HIGHWAY—
under the guise of Highway 318—runs down a sliver of land hemmed
between attractive beaches along the Gulf of Thailand and the
Cambodian border. The area, once restricted because of Khmer
Rouge activity, is now open for travel. Thais flock to a casino on the
Cambodian side of the border.

Several small towns are located
along the 60-mile (100 km) road
that runs south from Trat to Hat
Lek, a village at the southeastern-
most tip of Trat province.

At **Hat Ban Chuen,** about
40 miles (60 km) south of Trat, is
an inviting, long stretch of sand.
Other beaches, including the
appealing sounding Hat Sai Si
Ngoen (Silver Sand Beach), Hat Sai
Kaew (Crystal Beach), and Hat

Thaptim (Sapphire Beach) are
spread along the coast before Ban
Chuen. These beaches, backed with
casuarina (sea pine) and eucalyptus
trees, are fine in their own right
but do not match the quality of
Ban Chuen.

At the Kilometer 70 signpost,
just off the highway, a road climbs
to **Jut Chom Wiw,** a lookout
that offers panoramic views of the

coast and Cambodia. A little
farther south is **Khlong Yai,** the
last sizable town in the area; it is
notable for its smuggling activities
and its big border market. The
beaches here are not as attractive
as those farther north. At Khlong
Yai you can catch boats to Ko
Kut and other islands of the Ko
Chang Marine National Park (see
pp. 160–61).

Like Khlong Yai, **Hat Lek**
enjoys the benefits of a thriving
smuggling industry and a busy
border market. But the village is
also notable for a steady influx of
Thais who are more intent on
gambling than sightseeing. The
village sometimes resembles a
more than a parking lot as both
private vehicles and tour buses
unload tourists for trips to nearby
Ko Kong, across the border in
Cambodia and, in particular, to the
**Ko Kong International
Casino and Resort.**

The casino—one of a number
strung along the Thai border with
both Cambodia and Myanmar to
circumvent Thailand's ban on casi-
nos and encourage the Thais' love
of gambling—attracts over 1,000
visitors a day. They board boats at
Hat Lek for the short trip to the
island of Ko Kong. Foreign visitors
can visit the casino without acquir-
ing a Cambodian visa.

From Ko Kong, speedboats
are available to Sihanoukville in
Cambodia. From here, there are
bus services to Phnom Penh, the
country's capital. ■

**Rubber being
tapped at one of
the numerous
plantations
near Trat**

The Northeast remains a mystery to most visitors to Thailand. Untangle that mystery and you will find a place full of rural charm, crisp forested mountains, ancient temples, and one of the world's great rivers.

Northeast Thailand

Traditional dress made from Northeastern silk

Northeast Thailand

THE NORTHEAST OF THAILAND—KNOWN AS ISSAN TO THAIS—HAS NEVER been a big-ticket number on the international visitor's agenda. Of the nearly ten million tourists who pour into the country each year, fewer than 4 percent venture into the region. The reasons point more to the bounty of attractions all over Thailand, rather than the lack of any in Issan. On a visit to this vast and unpretentious region you will find a polite, independent people clinging to the traditional ways of Thailand with a tenacity not seen in other parts of the country.

Issan is the largest, most populated, and poorest region of Thailand, and its rural inhabitants forge a hard-earned living growing rice, tapioca, and cotton. Mulberry trees bear leaves to feed worms that spin silk, which is then woven into cloth of the highest quality. The region sprawls across 66,000 square miles (171,000 sq km) on the high sandstone Khorat plateau, which reaches north to the Mekong River and south to the Dongrek Mountains, on the Cambodian border. It can be a harsh place. Droughts are as frequent as flooding, and hardships and deprivation have forced many to quit the land and move to the cities in search of work.

Yet this vast region holds many pockets of great beauty, especially on the heights of its mountainous national parks. Peaceful monastic retreats hide among the forests;

fascinating remnants of past civilizations dot the area; and there are plenty of lively, bustling cities. Issan's detachment from tourism is more of a bonus than a hindrance, sharpening its frontier feel.

In the late 1950s, with help from the United States, the Friendship Highway was built from Bangkok to Nong Khai, on the banks of the Mekong River and bordering Laos, opening up the region. During the ensuing war with Vietnam, untold amounts of money were pumped into the region as the U.S. military set up bases. Towns like Nakhon Ratchasima and Udon Thani boomed overnight. The Friendship Highway is the arterial route into the region, and along its veins you find the riches of Issan.

Principal among these are the extraordinary monuments of the Khmers. Ruled by a

Children celebrate the festival of Phi Tha Khon in Loei.

0 | 100 kilometers
0 | 75 miles

succession of god-kings, the Khmer Empire (802–1431) at one stage stretched from Angkor in Cambodia, west across Thailand to Myanmar (Burma), south to the Malay Peninsula, and north to the Laotian capital of Vientiane. Over 300 sites have been located in Thailand's northeast. Some have been painstakingly restored, to reveal a culture of remarkable cosmological architecture, presented in a symmetry of structures that are festooned inside and out with wildly imaginative and intricate sculptures and stone carvings. Either of the two best examples, Prasat Hin Phimai or Prasat Phanom Rung, alone is worth a visit to Issan.

The Mekong River, which runs along much of Issan's border with Laos, is another draw.

The opening up to tourism of neighboring Laos in recent years now allows travelers to cross the Mekong at several points, notably the Friendship Bridge near Nong Khai. At the end of the rainy season in October, communities celebrate their affinity with the river in colorful and hotly contested boat races, during a series of raucous festivals. ■

Khao Yai National Park

KHAO YAI IS THAILAND'S OLDEST NATIONAL PARK, founded in 1961; it is also one of the country's most ecologically diverse and wildlife-abundant areas. The park's 840 square miles (2,176 sq km) straddle four provinces along the eastern Dongrek Mountains, at the southwestern edge of the vast Khorat plateau, the dominant geological feature of Issan.

Khao Yai National Park

🅰 165 A1

Visitor information

✉ National Park Division of the Royal Forestry Department, Paholyothin Rd., Bangkhen, Bangkok

☎ 02-579-5734 or 02-579-7223

The park is a convenient wilderness, only 125 miles (200 km) northeast of Bangkok, just off the Friendship Highway (Highway 2); turn off 3 miles (5 km) before the town of Pak Chong. Consequently it gets about 1.5 million visitors a year. On weekends and holidays, people escape the gasping capital and besiege the park, so it is best avoided at these times.

The crowds have placed great strains on the park's resources over the years. Between 1992 and 1993 overnight stays were stopped for 12 months because rangers could not cope with the numbers. Khao Yai's outstanding natural beauty is also forced to withstand the problems of land encroachment, illegal logging, poaching, under-staffing and corrupt officials that exist within many of the country's national parks.

As you would expect from a place called Khao Yai ("big mountain"), the park is generally mountainous, rising from near sea level at its southeast perimeter to 4,432 feet (1,351 m) at the summit of **Khao Laem.** While mountains in the north slope gently to its northern boundary, those in the south and west form a steep escarpment that drops to agricultural plains outside the park. The long wall-like mountain, Khao Kamphaeng, bounds the northeast.

Many of the park's 13 hiking trails, from 1 mile to 6 miles (1.5 km to 9.5 km) long and originally tramped by elephants, take you through lush tangles of monsoon forest, along numerous streams to tumbling waterfalls, past caves, and up to evergreen rain forests and spectacular viewpoints on the hillsides. High up on the ridge tops, cooler temperatures encourage stands of pine woodlands. Hikes take from about 90 minutes to 7 hours, depending on the trail. Many of the numbered trails, with routes set by colored markers, radiate from the park headquarters and visitor center, or the nearby Kong Kaeo Waterfall.

Some routes (numbers 6, 7, 8, and 9) loop back to, or near, the visitor center. On others, be prepared to backtrack or organize transportation to return to the start point. Some trails are poorly marked or confusing, so a guide is needed. The visitor center can advise on this; it also has trail maps.

The 3.5-mile (6 km) Trail 6, from the visitor center to Nong Phak Chi wildlife observation tower, is relatively easy and one of the most popular, taking about 3 to 4 hours. Easy to follow, Trail 8 is about 1 mile (1.5 km) long, takes 90 minutes, and returns you to park headquarters. Trail 9 (1.5 miles/ 2 km and 60 minutes) is similar. Trail 11, from the old restaurant up to Tat Ta Phu Waterfall, is more testing. This 5-mile (8 km) trek will take all day and follows a stream to the falls, then backtracks (a guide is required).

Much of Khao Yai's wildlife congregates near the park headquarters. Elephants—their numbers estimated at 250–300—are not difficult to spot, nor are the mouse deer and barking deer that congregate in the evening at Nong Phak Chi observation tower. The park's 50 or so tigers are rarely, if ever, sighted. You are also unlikely to see the leopards, leopard cats, marbled cats, and shy Asiatic black bears.

Khao Yai has tens of thousands of white-handed and pileated gibbons, however. The latter, which generally live in insular family groups, often gather in a unique 6-mile-wide (9.5 km) contact zone around Lam Ta Klong stream. Other primates include the pig-tailed macaque, a sociable, highly intelligent monkey known for its great variety of calls and numerous facial expressions; and the arboreal, nocturnal slow loris, with its slow-motion movements, brown fur, and large round eyes. There are also Asiatic wild dogs and giant flying squirrels. One of the park's most amazing sights is the dusk eruption of myriad wrinkle-lipped bats, which fly out from a large cave at Khao Luk Chang.

Guided excursions are the best option, especially if you want to reach deeper into Khao Yai to view wildlife from observation towers in the evening or to climb higher into the mountains. There are tour companies and accommodations at Pak Chong. Wildlife Safari is recommended *(39 Pak Chong Rd., tel 044-312922).* ∎

Wild boars are a familiar sight in the national park.

Nakhon
Ratchasima
(Khorat)
 165 B2
Visitor information
✉ Tourism Authority
of Thailand,
2102–2104
Mittaphap Rd.,
Nakhon Ratchasima
☎ 044-213666 or
044-213030

Nakhon Ratchasima (Khorat)

NAKHON RATCHASIMA—OFTEN ABBREVIATED TO KHORAT by losing the first syllable of the first word and the last three of the second—is the thriving gateway to Issan. The province is scattered with ancient Khmer monuments, including Thailand's most famous at Phimai, and is renowned for its silk industry. Khorat is the largest province in Thailand, and its burgeoning capital, the first major stop on the arterial northeast route, the Friendship Highway (Highway 2), is the commercial heart of the region.

The capital (also called Nakhom Ratchasima—in Thailand provincial capitals carry the same name as the province) concerns itself with progress, but interesting remnants of its past remain. Presiding over a square in the city's center, at the 10th-century Chumphom gate and reconstructed town wall, there is a statue of Khunying Mo, known as **Thao Suranari** ("Brave Lady"). In 1826, Prince Anuwong of Vientiane captured Khorat and threatened to enslave its residents. The feisty Khunying, wife of the deputy governor, persuaded the young women of the city to seduce the invaders and involve them in drunken revelry. That done, the women killed the soldiers while they slept. The springtime Thao Suranari Festival, Khorat's most popular, celebrates this triumph with musicians, dancers, parades, fireworks, and a beauty contest.

A curious vestige of Khorat's more recent history is found behind the doors at the **VFW Café** (167 Poklang Rd., tel 044-256522). The city's airfield was one of seven in Northeast Thailand used by U.S. troops to launch raids on Laos and Vietnam during the 1960s and 1970s. A legacy of those turbulent times—along with the ample collection of huge neon-pulsing massage parlors—the VFW (Veterans of Foreign Wars) Café is a U.S. roadhouse-style restaurant

locked in the 1960s. It's also the base for a close-knit band of Vietnam veterans who retired there after the Vietnam War.

South of the Thao Suranari monument on Ratchadamnoen Road, a small but edifying collection of artifacts and archaeological discoveries from surrounding Khmer ruins are housed in the **Maha Weerawong National Museum** (closed Mon.–Tues.). The museum is on the grounds of Wat Suthachinda, just south of the intersection with Mahad Thai Road. Its more memorable displays include a statue of the female Hindu deity Uma, Siva's consort, and Mahayana Buddhist images from Prasat Hin Phanom Wan.

More Khmer icons are found at Khorat's oldest monastery, **Wat Phra Narai Maharat,** west of the Thao Suranari statue on Prachak Road. Here is a collection of sandstone images taken from other nearby Khmer ruins.

The central sanctuary at **Wat Sala Loi,** built in 1973, deviates imaginatively from the typical temple style. Perhaps because of its location by the Lamtakhong River, 440 yards (402 m) past the northeastern end of the city's moat, it is shaped like a Chinese junk.

While overshadowed by the bigger and more celebrated Khmer monument of Prasat Hin Phimai (see pp. 170–71), **Phanom Wan,**

Khorat's heroine Thao Suranari led a revolt against occupying Laotian forces in 1826. Here her statue is decked with offerings.

set in a peaceful rural area off High-way 2, about 12 miles (19.5 km) northeast of the city, is still impressive. Venerated Buddha images in saffron-colored wraps, food offerings, and glowing incense sticks remind visitors that Phanom Wan, unlike most Khmer temples, has been in use for worship since the ninth century. The best time to visit this peaceful temple is when soft morning or late-afternoon light brings out the colors and textures of the sandstone and laterite.

Twenty miles (32 km) south of Khorat, along Highway 304, **Pak Thong Chai** is a thriving center of the silk-weaving industry, with more than 70 silk factories spread around the district. A variety of silks, including the beautiful hand-dyed *mutmee*, are woven here. The Silk Weavers Association has a museum and cultural center where weavers demonstrate their skills. Local retailers are not necessarily less expensive than those in Khorat or Bangkok. ■

A giant Buddha statue overlooks the entrance to Wat Teppitak Punnaram in neighboring Saraburi Province.

Prasat Hin Phimai

THE RESTORED KHMER SANDSTONE SANCTUARY AND temple of Prasat Hin Phimai is a spectacular revelation into the grandeur of one of Asia's great civilizations. The town itself sits at the Thai end of the fabled Royal Road, the major route of the Khmer Kingdom that led 140 miles (224 km) from its capital at Angkor in Cambodia.

On the banks of the Mun River, some 37.5 miles (60 km) north of Khorat, Prasat Phimai is probably the most significant of all Khmer buildings. It was once a vice-regal center for an empire that dominated this part of Southeast Asia for over 600 years, until its final defeat in 1431. Buildings at Phimai date from the late 11th and the 12th centuries—the height of the empire. The last great Khmer king, Jayavarman VII *(R.1181–1220)*, was a fervent Buddhist, and he built on the largest scale ever known in the empire, remodeling temples honoring Hindu gods to serve the Tantric gods of Mahayana Buddhism—a style widely seen in Phimai.

Phimai was built in the 12th century as the temple of the city of Vimayapura; its outer enclosure is in fact the old city wall. Phimai is still surrounded by a community, and its layout is believed to be based on the old city plan.

The temple complex consists of two rectangular walled enclosures, with the inner enclosure housing the dominant, cone-shaped *prang*, the central structure of all Khmer temples. The main entrance into the temple is a *naga* (serpent) bridge, a cross-shaped terrace with rearing naga heads symbolizing the transition from the temporal world into the domicile of the gods. The bridge leads to the heavily embellished southern *gopura* (entrance pavilion), the main entrance to the outer enclosure.

This outer enclosure spreads over 10 acres (4 ha) and contains four large ponds. At the southern corner, a pond once lined with stone blocks gives a clear view to the inner enclosure, with the magnificent prang reflected in its waters. A causeway dividing the ponds leads to the inner southern gopura, its entrance dominated by a lintel with a central design of a giant holding a pair of elephants aloft, and standing over the head of the demon guardian Kala. In the central courtyard, the elaborately carved white sandstone prang lies directly ahead, flanked by two minor towers.

In and around the buildings of the inner enclosure, Khmer mythology unfolds in a treasury of exquisitely carved lintels and pediments. On one lintel, for example, troops build a bridge across the sea to the mythical Lanka, in a tale from the *Ramakien*. Monkey warriors carry boulders to throw into the sea, symbolized by fish and dragons. A pediment above depicts a battle scene from the same epic. Another shows the hero Rama parading home, victorious from his battles with the Lankans, and being blessed by a gathering of the gods Siva, Brahma, Indra, and Vishnu.

Kings asserted their royal authority by building the grandest of structures, and Khmer mythology does not only lie in these superb carved details, but in the entire layout of the temple

Prasat Hin Phimai
🅜 165 B2
✉ 35 miles (60 km) NE of Khorat
Visitor information
✉ Tourism Authority of Thailand, 2102–2104 Mittraphap Rd., Nakhon Ratchasima
☎ 044-213666 or 044-213030

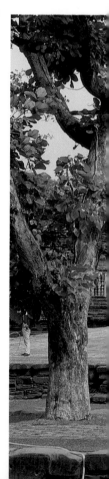

compound (see p. 52–53). The meticulous construction of the temples reflects the Khmer belief in cosmology. Phimai stands as the Khmer Hindu/Buddhist model of the universe: Concentric mountains and seas surround a single continent, from which rises the central Mount Meru (represented by the prang), the five-peaked home of the gods. Moats, ponds, and enclosing walls all play a part in this microcosmic universe.

The **museum** (*closed Mon.–Tues.*) at the northern end of town is an essential part of a visit to Phimai. It houses more beautifully carved lintels from the monument and relics from other temples in the Northeast. ■

Rocket festivals

Rocket festivals (*bun bang fai*) are held throughout the Northeast—usually in the second week of May—to celebrate the end of the dry season and appease the rain god Phaya Than. Rockets are traditionally fashioned from bamboo filled with saltpeter and charcoal. Huge timber launching pads are erected, and missiles are launched to the delight of spectators. Similar events were held during the reigns of Khmer kings. The festival is most fervently celebrated in Yasothon, a province neighboring Ubon Ratchathani (see p. 177). ■

Extensively reconstructed, this once great Khmer shrine conveys a sense of its original scale and majesty.

Surin & around

165 C2

Surin & around

Visitor information

Tourism Authority
of Thailand,
2102–2104
Mittraphap Rd.,
Nakhon Ratchasima

044-213666 or
044-213030

THOUSANDS FLOCK TO SURIN ON THE THIRD WEEKEND OF November to witness Thailand's internationally famous Elephant Roundup, when hundreds of elephants lumber into town for a festival of fun and games. While it is this festival that has put the town of Surin on the map, evocative Khmer monuments and thriving basketry and silk industries in the province—on the frontier with Cambodia—make it well worth a visit.

The Elephant Roundup celebrates the ethnic Suay people's affinity with the beasts. The Suay, who came mainly from neighboring Cambodia, have been hunting and training elephants since the Ayutthaya era. The festival is unabridged fun. Elephants are paraded through town with their handlers (mahouts), then herded into Surin's Sports Park. Here they entertain with soccer games, dancing, races, an elephant-versus-people tug of war, and colorful processions. The carnival attracts up to 40,000 visitors, and hotels are booked months ahead. After the show, tourists take elephant rides around town. Besides the enjoyment of it all, the roundup provides a rare opportunity to see a large number of elephants in one place.

Surin's Elephant Roundup offers a rare opportunity to see large groups of pachyderms.

Some of the elephants that take part in the roundup are trained at **Ta Klang Elephant Village,** 36 miles (58 km) northeast of Surin town *(tel. 01-999-1910).* A museum and elephant educational center go some way to explain the importance of the great beasts in Thai culture and their sad plight, which has threatened their existence in modern Thailand (see box below).

Centers of Surin's silk and basket-weaving industries are within easy reach of the capital. **Khawao Sinarin,** east of the town off Highway 226, and **Ban Chanron,** southeast on Highway 2071, both produce quality silks using traditional hand-weaving techniques. You can watch the silk being made at factories and buy the finished product. Just off Highway 226, 8 miles (12 km) east of Surin, villagers at **Butom Basket Village** make tightly woven and intricately designed baskets, and sell them to visitors at bargain prices.

Remnants of the Khmer Empire stud Surin Province. Three such sites are on the Cambodian border, about 56 miles (90 km) south of the town along Highway 214. These are intensely atmospheric and evocative places, set in thick, rapacious jungle. Passing an armed military checkpoint on the approach road, and posted warnings not to stray into the jungle because of land mines, add a certain edge to the experience. Khmer Rouge rebels occupied the area in the 1980s and pillaged many of the monuments' carvings.

Ta Muan Thom, right on the Cambodian border, is the largest and earliest of the three temples, constructed during the reign of Udayadityavarman II *(R.1050–1066).* The most impressive view is from the bottom of its steep, wide staircase, framed by solid laterite ramparts, which leads to the main entrance pavilion.

Ta Muan Toch, a hospital temple *(arogayasala),* and **Ta Muan,** an overnight rest house *(dharmasala),* were built a century later by Jayavarman VII, whose Buddhist beliefs necessitated a building spree of public works throughout the empire. Arrange tours to all three sites at Pirom's House guesthouse *(272 Krung Sri Rd., Surin, tel 045-515140).*

These two smaller monuments near Ta Muan Thom confirm this area was part of the famed Royal Road from Angkor. ∎

Threatened elephants

At the beginning of the 20th century, Thailand had 100,000 elephants. Today, there are fewer than 5,000. Half of those are domesticated, while the rest find protection inside national parks. The elephant's decline is due to the loss of its natural environment, to hunting, and to poaching. In 1989 Thailand banned logging, and the elephants—which had been used to shift logs in the forests for centuries—were no longer needed for work.

Many owners have turned to tourism for income through popular trekking camps and shows, while others lead their beasts along the choking highways into the heart of Bangkok to beg. Tourism is a way to maintain elephant numbers until the authorities quit their lip service and make real attempts at preservation. Most operators treat their elephants well, and demands for the beasts in the industry affords them protection—something they have lacked in the past. ∎

Prasat Phanom Rung

🅰 165 B1
Visitor information
✉ Tourism Authority
of Thailand,
2102–2104
Mittraphap Rd.,
Nakhon Ratchasima
☎ 044-213666 or
044-213030

Prasat Phanom Rung

SIXTEEN YEARS OF RESTORATION BETWEEN 1972 AND 1988 transformed Prasat Phanom Rung into the most spectacular Khmer site in Thailand. Its towering *prang* rises from the crest of an extinct volcano, 1,250 feet (381 m) above sea level, with views over flat farmlands to the Dongrek Mountains and the Cambodian border in the south. Its elevated position realizes Hindu cosmology, symbolizing Siva's home on Mount Meru.

Phanom Rung—30 miles (48 km) south of Bur Iram, off Highway 218—was constructed between the early 10th and the late 12th centuries. Various inscriptions at the monument offer sketchy accounts of its history. A battle scene carved on one of the upper pediments above the southern entry of the central prang indicates an alliance of powerful local ruler Narendraditya with the fiercely combatant Khmer King Suryavarman II (*R*.1113–50), builder of Angkor Wat. The scene depicts war elephants, one of which is crushing an enemy soldier with its trunk.

Narendraditya's allegiances allowed him to maintain suzerainty over Phanom Rung for some time after Suryavarman claimed the throne at Angkor, a situation confirmed by more iconography devoted to the exploits of Narendraditya and his family. These carvings suggest that he gave up his warring ways after the birth of his son, Hiranya, and became a yogi and guru.

Phanom Rung is strung out along an east–west axis in an amazing 550-yard (500 m) journey from a laterite terrace along a system of causeways and promenades, steps and terraces to the eastern *gopura*, and into the central prang. The complex has an imposing, almost intimidating, grandeur. Its dramatic stairway entrance, ornate carving, and spiritually inspired design reflect the power and arrogance

needed to expand and control an empire for five centuries.

The first significant point is the **White Elephant Hall,** down the slope from the visitor center in the direction of the first cross-shaped terrace. This large rectangular building of laterite and sandstone, with its porches, galleries, and walls, derives its name from the royal predilection for keeping rare and sacred white elephants. Just south of the hall, at the cross-shaped terrace, a 175-yard-long (160 m) laterite-paved causeway, lined with 67 lotus bud-tipped boundary stones, draws you toward a large raised stone terrace and bridge. Intricately carved five-headed *nagas* form the bridge's balustrade, symbolically transporting the visitor from the temporal world into the divine.

From the bridge, the stairs begin their spectacular rise to the enclosure, a climb interrupted by five leveled sections. The wide, grass-covered terrace at the top holds four ponds, arranged symmetrically and probably used in some sort of ritual. A second bridge here has three more naga balustrades facing north, east, and south. Like the first bridge, the nagas are exquisitely carved from stone, although with subtle differences in design. The bridge takes the visitor up to the eastern entrance pavilion, which broadens, joins, and then wraps around the entire main temple ground.

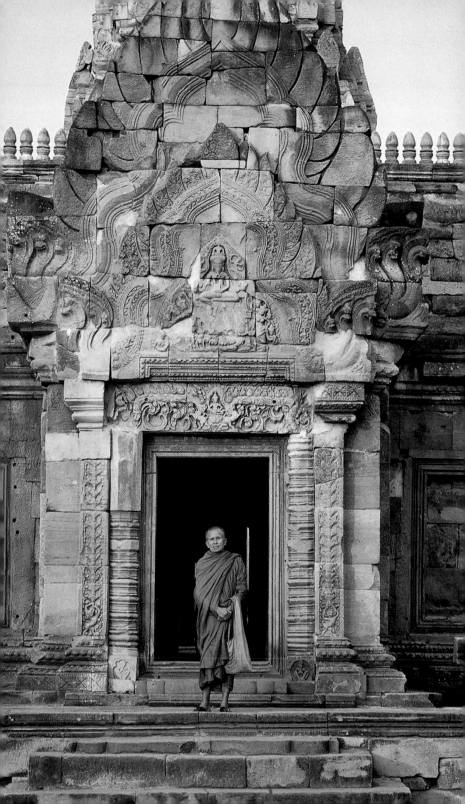

The eastern gopura is the most important of four that cut through the middle of each side of the rectangular wall protecting the enclosure. Significantly, it faces the sunrise and is aligned with the succession of doorways that run the length of the temple's axis through to the exit at the western gopura.

The main pediment of the eastern gateway is of a Hindu yogi, surrounded by female attendants and celestial dancers representing Siva. More iconography can be seen on the other gopuras and around the galleries that surround the complex. The lintel below the pediment shows a divinity seated over demon guardian Kala, gripping the hind legs of a pair of disconcerted lions.

Passing through the door of the gopura and crossing a third naga bridge, you come almost immediately to the antechamber to the main prang (*mandapa*), which has an extraordinary pediment and lintel, sublime examples of Khmer craftmanship. The pediment depicts the ten-armed Siva-Nantaraja enthralled in a cosmic dance. At Siva's feet are Ganesh, the divinity's elephant-headed son, and two female disciples. Below the pediment is the famous Nara lintel (see box) depicting Vishnu reclining on a naga. Brahma rises from the reclining Vishnu on a lotus flower, while Lakshmi, Vishnu's wife, cradles his legs. The two motifs on either side of Vishnu show Kala issuing garlands, and two elegantly carved parrots. Nagas, winged garudas, elephants, and monkeys crowd the lintel with amazing precision.

From here you move toward the main prang. On each of its four sides are gallery entrances (each gallery is a smaller version of the main prang), which, in turn, have entrances into the prang. The galleries, along with the towering prang, represent the five peaks of Mount Meru, the center of the Khmer universe and home to the Hindu gods.

The gallery entrances are set with intriguing carvings, a number of which highlight the anguishes and triumphs of Rama, the earthly incarnation of Vishnu and hero of the romantic *Ramakien*. One scene depicts monkey warriors triumphantly swooping down on the enemy. The interior of the prang has a number of Khmer statues and an altar on which priests poured holy waters and laid offerings of garlands and fruit.

Outside, a wild conglomerate of sculptured Sivas, dancers, charging elephants, *rishis* (Hindu sages, usually hermits), and other Khmer icons climb up the sandstone walls of the prang. ∎

Nara lintel

The Nara lintel disappeared from Phanom Rung sometime between 1961 and 1965, ending up in the Art Institute of Chicago. Investigations showed U.S. art benefactor James Alsdorf had donated it. It was not until December 1988, six months after the completion of Phanom Rung's restoration—and after strong protests from the Thai government and others—that the Alsdorf Institute decided to return the lintel, at a cost of $250,000 (donated by U.S. interests). Around that time, a Thai rock group, Caraboa, had a hit with a protest song that included the line: "Take back your Michael Jackson, and give us back our Phra Narai." Rumor has it that six of the seven Thais involved in the original theft have met "unnatural" deaths. ∎

Ubon Ratchathani

Ubon Ratchathani

🗺 165 D2

Visitor information

✉ Tourism Authority of Thailand, 264/1 Kuang Thani Rd., Ubon Ratchathani

☎ 045-243770

UBON RATCHATHANI IS ONE OF A NUMBER OF NORTHEAST cities where growth was spurred by the presence of the U.S. armed forces during the Vietnam War. It sits at the eastern corner of Issan, near where two major rivers, the Chi and Mun, converge before flowing about 30 miles (48 km) east to the Mekong, at the border with Laos. Ubon has been tagged the gateway to the "Emerald Triangle," a tourist-luring invention to describe the province's abundance of forests and its borders with both Laos and Cambodia.

Established by the Khmers, Ubon came under Ayutthayan control in the 15th century. The **Ubon National Museum** *(Kheuan Thani Rd., tel 045-255071, closed Mon.–Tues.)* gives insight into these developments. The museum, housed in a former summer palace of Rama VI, was opened in 1989, the first provincial museum in the Northeast. Rooms are devoted to regional geography, geology, prehistory, and local handicrafts, with a handsome collection of art from the 6th to the 17th centuries. A highlight is the huge fourth-century ceremonial bronze drum.

The most impressive of Ubon's temple compounds is **Wat Supattanaram Worawihan,** on the banks of the Mun River. Built in 1853 by Vietnamese craftsmen, it has an appealing confusion of Thai, Western, and Khmer architectural styles.

Beyond the Upparat Road bridge and about 9.5 miles (15 km) southwest on Highway 2193, **Wat Pa Nanachat Beung Rai** ("temple of the international forest") is one of the more curious forested wats hidden among the thick woodlands of Ubon Province. The North American, European, and Japanese monks here follow the strict tenets laid down by Ajaan Man (1870–1949), a monk who has inspired over 40 forested wats in Issan, with simple teaching methods that opened the Buddhist faith to many Westerners. Lay people are welcome to stay, but it's best to contact the abbot beforehand in writing *(Wat Pa Nanachat, Ban Bung Wai, Amphur Warin, Ubon Ratchathani 34310).*

At the start of the Buddhist lent, in July, temples construct floats holding huge candles and wax carvings, and parade through town in a two-day Candle Festival. ∎

A group of stilt shelters on the Nam River makes a picturesque spot for relaxing.

Silk

Silk weaving is a Thai tradition dating back centuries. It has thrived since the days of the Khmer Empire (802–1431) and wove its way into the conventions of subsequent Sukhothai, Ayutthaya, and Chakri dynasties. In many villages in Thailand's Northeast, silk production has changed little. Silk worms still feed on the leaves of hardy mulberry trees which thrive in the area's harsh conditions. Villagers still pluck the worms' cocoons from the tree, and spin them into smooth, glossy, and flexible threads. And ancient looms still clack with the sound of yarns, cleaned and dyed, being woven into fabulous silk fabrics.

Spools of silk. American Jim Thompson revived the country's silk industry.

Today silk remains a valuable trading commodity, and the silk of the Northeast is famous worldwide for it beauty, artistry, patterns, and colors.

But the industry's survival has been by the narrowest of margins. A wave of cheaper factory-produced fabrics from China and Japan flooded the markets toward the end of the 19th century, and despite attempts by King Chulalongkorn to keep the craft alive, the silk industry fell into serious decline, and almost extinction. Silk production, an intricate, time-consuming process, simply could not compete with the price and availability of mass-produced fabrics.

The revival and subsequent international acclaim for Thai silk is attributed to the most unlikely of characters: an American ex-serviceman and member of the Office Strategic Services—O.S.S., the precursor to the C.I.A.—named Jim Thompson (1906–1967).

After serving with the U.S. military in Europe during World War II, Thompson, an architect and native of Delaware, arrived in Asia as part of a force formed to liberate Thailand from potential Japanese occupation. He then joined the O.S.S. and was stationed in Bangkok for a short time before moving to New York. But he was soon back in Thailand, where his entrepreneurial spirit and eye for the exquisite beauty of the local silk would lead to the industry's resurgence in Thailand and introduction to the rest of the world.

Thompson devoted the next 30 years of his life to promoting Thai silk. He sent samples to London, Milan, New York, and Paris, gradually building up a worldwide clientele. A gifted designer and innovator, he introduced colorfast dyes that preserved the distinctive luminosity and brilliant jewel colors. He also introduced new colors and weaves for the Western market, and created a new market for heavy silks to be used for upholstery.

Thompson recognized silk weaving as an art form, a cottage industry, and part of a traditional way of life. At Pak Chong, in Nakhon Ratchasima Province, his company, Jim Thompson Thai Silk Co., built the largest hand-weaving facilities in the world. More than 70 factories are now spread around the district, making it the major silk-producing area in Thailand.

On March 27, 1967, Jim Thompson disappeared without trace while hiking alone in Malaysia. Thailand's current queen, Sirikit, a tireless promoter of traditional Thai art and handicrafts, took up the baton in the 1970s, pushing Thompson's work into a new dimension. Her public appearances in updated designs of traditional Thai silk styles prompted a new popularity among fashion-conscious Thai women, ensuring the survival of this very special fabric. ■

Above: Silk worms are fed the leaves of mulberry trees, which thrive in the Northeast. Right: Yellow silkworm cocoons soak in water. Individual strands are then gathered into raw silk thread. Below: Thailand's world-famous silk comes in a rainbow of shimmering colors and designs.

That Phanom's lively riverside market features bamboo products.

That Phanom

IN 1975 THE GRAND *CHEDI* AT WAT PHRA THAT PHANOM collapsed after four wild days of torrential rain. Local authorities soon gathered into action: This talismanic symbol, one of the most revered in Issan, was too important to leave a crumbled waste. With the help of Thailand's Fine Arts Department, the chedi's reconstruction was completed in 1979. Pilgrims once more flocked to the small Mekong River town of That Phanom.

That Phanom
🗺 165 D3
Visitor information
✉ Tourism Authority of Thailand, 184/1 Sunthon Wichit Rd., Nakhon Phanom
☎ 042-513490

Thousands of people come from all over the Northeast and across the Mekong River from Laos every full moon of the third lunar month (February or March), crowding into the town for its annual fair, to pay homage at the rebuilt chedi.

Legend places the construction of Wat Phra That Phanom back 2,500 years ago, when a wandering monk, Maha Kasapa, arrived in the area with the Buddha's breastbone. The bone was subsequently placed inside the gold-tipped spire of the chedi. Archaeologists, however, date the construction of the wat back only about 1,500 years.

Whatever the date, the chedi is still an imposing and beautiful structure. It reaches 185 feet (57 m), dominating the town. Its sharpened tip—decorated with

240 pounds (109 kg) of gold—plays late-afternoon glinting games with the scorching sun. With the Mekong River a few hundred yards away and the clay-red harshness of the Issan terrain all around, this Lao-style chedi takes on a wondrous aspect.

That Phanom earns its stripes as a border town on Mondays and Thursdays, when hundreds of Laotians cross the Mekong and set up a lively market near the pier. Opposite the market is a collection of French-Lao buildings.

Nearby, a scaled-down version of Wat Phra That Phanom is found at the cotton- and silk-weaving village of **Renu Phanom,** some 10 miles (16 km) away. At a weekly market, weavers gather here to sell their wares. ■

Nakhon Phanom

THE MEKONG RIVER REACHES ITS PANORAMIC BEST along the landscaped promenade of its banks at Nakhon Phanom. Views here look across the busy river traffic to smoke-blue craggy mountains rising behind the small town of Tha Khaek in Laos. The U.S. armed forces launched rescue and reconnaissance missions from Nakhon Phanom's air base during the Vietnam War, but the town has long since retreated into its more familiar relaxed character.

On the full moon of the 11th lunar month (usually late October), at the end of the rainy season and Buddhist retreat, Nakhon Phanom gets a wake-up call and takes to the river. The Nakhon Phanom Festival features the evening launch of thousands of *reua fai,* or fire boats. The tiny boats, crafted from banana logs or bamboo and carrying offerings of rice, cakes, and flowers, glide silently down the Mekong, illuminating and crowding the river with thousands of glorious dots of light.

Nakhon Phanom's restaurants and cafés, fronting the river along **Sunthon Wichit Road,** near the clock tower and main passenger pier, are a good place to try the river's prize catch, the giant Mekong catfish, or *pla buk* (great and powerful fish). The fish is the largest of its type in the world, growing up to 10 feet (3 m) in length and weighing 660 pounds (300 kg). It once thrived all along the Mekong, but numbers have now diminished. The New Suan Mai *(271 Sunthon Wichit Rd., tel 042-511202)* is one of the best places to taste this local specialty.

It is possible to visit the Laotian town of **Tha Khaek,** which lies directly across the river and is interesting for its French-style architecture. Travel agents in Nakhon Phanom will organize visas, which takes from a few hours to a day. Count on paying $50 plus, but the ferry costs less than a dollar. Before the Communists came to power in 1975, the casino at Tha Khaek prospered with the gambled cash of Thai visitors. ■

Tobacco—one of numerous crops grown in the Mekong River area—dries in the sun.

Nakhon Phanom

▲ 165 D3

Visitor information

✉ Tourism Authority of Thailand, 184/1 Sunthon Wichit Rd., Nakhon Phanom

☎ 042-513490

Udon Thani

Udon Thani

🗺 165 B3

Visitor information

✉ Tourism Authority of
Thailand, 16/5
Mukmontri Rd.,
Udon Thani

☎ 042-325406

THE ESTABLISHMENT HERE OF A HUGE U.S. AIR BASE during in the 1960s and 1970s was the springboard for Udon Thani's development. The base, on the outskirts of the city, was passed over to the Thai authorities in 1976 and now serves as an important civilian airport and Royal Thai Air Force facility for this bustling regional center.

Pottery unearthed at the village of Ban Chiang, which archaeologists believe thrived 3,500 years ago

The American influence lingers, albeit on a much smaller scale. A number of U.S. citizens, mainly ex-military and diplomatic personnel, have chosen Udon Thani as a place to retire. There is a U.S. consulate *(35/6 Suphakit Janya Rd., tel 042-244270)*, a Veterans of Foreign Wars association, and a huge Voice of America radio transmitter that dispatches news, views, and music throughout Asia. The city offers the usual urban indulgences of cinemas, restaurants, and malls.

About 30 miles (50 km) east of Udon Thani is the archaeological site of **Ban Chiang.** This tiny hamlet was propelled into the world's spotlight in the 1970s with the discovery of bronze relics purportedly dating back to

3600 B.C. The startling find predated the earliest recognized Bronze Age civilizations in the Middle East and China, and threw accepted historical notions into controversy. But many dispute the findings, suggesting between 2500 B.C. and 2000 B.C. to be a more accurate date. The **Ban Chiang Historical Museum** *(closed Mon.–Tues.),* near the excavations, displays an extensive collection of local relics including bronze tools, human skeletons, and unique swirling red-on-buff painted pottery.

About 40 miles (64 km) northwest of Udon Thani, elaborate Buddhist shrines mingle in and around delightfully weird rock formations that jut from the sandstone foothills at **Phu Phrabat Historical Park. ∎**

PHU PHRABAT WALKING TRAIL

Phu Phrabat has a two-hour walking trail to lead you around the park. Caves in the rocks there have prehistoric paintings.

Nong Khai

Nong Khai
165 B4
Visitor information
Tourism Authority of
Thailand, 16/5
Mukmontri Rd., Udon
Thani
042-325406

LEAFY NONG KHAI LOUNGES ALONG THE BANKS OF THE Mekong River. Its proximity to the Laotian capital of Vientiane has blessed it with French-Laotian architecture and a distinctly French culinary fraternity with its ex-colonial neighbor. A few of the town's bakeries turn out baguettes, croissants, and other pastries, and restaurants serve thick, strong Lao-style coffees.

A pleasant place to take in the colorful action on the river is at the timber-decked restaurants that jut over the water on **Rimkhong Road.** The street is home to the old immigration and customs building, and a pier where small rickety boats, flying Thai and Lao national flags, ferry locals and Lao people back and forth—foreigners need to cross at the nearby Friendship Bridge (see pp. 186–87). The building still serves as a departure point to Tha Deua in Laos, but business is slower since the opening of the Friendship Bridge in 1994. Also worthwhile is the sunset river cruise (Mekong sunsets amaze with stunning deep red and yellow hues) on board the floating restaurant, which departs at 5 p.m. daily from behind Wat Hai.

The floating restaurant churns past **Phra That Nong Khai,** a *chedi* that slid into the river over a span of 150 years. For those who want to explore the Mekong further, information desks at guesthouses along Rimkhong Road will arrange trips.

Just east of the immigration and customs building at the end of Rimkhong Road is a long and narrow daily **market** brimming with Laotian and Issan handicrafts, along with the usual souvenirs, inexpensive clothes, cheap electrical appliances, and kitchen utensils. The market eventually opens up to an unexpected brick-paved, unshaded river promenade.

In the late 16th century a revered Buddha image was being transported across from Laos when

A gate, sculpted as an open mouth, is one of the bizarre offerings at Hindu-Buddhist Wat Khaek.

A worshiper makes merit by lighting candles at a Nong Khai temple.

the boat sank in a storm. According to local legend, the image miraculously resurfaced some years later and was eventually placed in **Wat Pho Chai,** just past the bus terminal, off Prajak Road in the eastern part of town. Murals in the *wat* recount the tale of the icon's travels from the interior of Laos to its current resting place on an altar bedecked with elaborate carvings and mosaics.

Nong Khai's star attraction is the bizarre **Wat Khaek,** also called Sala Kaew Ku, about 3 miles (5 km) southeast along Highway 212. It is the masterpiece of Vietnamese monk Luang Pu Bunleua Surirat (died 1997). The wat, begun in 1978, is a thematic merger of Hinduism and Buddhism, splashed with unfettered imagination and humor, and with a bewildering mix of Buddhist and Hindu statues. The core theme is the life of the Buddha before he left India on his travels through Asia, over 2,500 years ago.

Where else would you see Buddha, surrounded by his disciples—scantily clad women—

being tempted by their gifts? The "Enlightened One" can also be found sitting on top of a peacock. One statue has Hindu god Vishnu atop a parrot. The most imposing statue, 82 feet (25 m) high, is of the Buddha perched on a coiled, seven-headed serpent. The *naga* is protecting Buddha against rain and wind for seven days and seven nights as he meditates. There are hundreds of other fantastic offerings at Wat Khaek, and it's easy to spend a few hours wandering its pathways, captivated by the inventiveness and skill of Luang Pu and his followers.

A good time to visit Nong Khai is during its hectic annual boat races, which are held toward the end of October to celebrate the end of both the Buddhist lent and the rainy season. Scores of sleek naga-headed boats are frantically powered along the river, with as many as 40 oarsmen in each. People come from all over the province to enjoy the spectacle. (Many other towns along the Mekong also celebrate the end of the Buddhist lent in this fashion.) ■

Mekong River Valley

THAILAND'S CONTACT WITH THE MEKONG MAY BE confined to its fringes, but it is still a rewarding flirt with the world's 12th longest river. The Northeast remains the most convenient place to view the Mekong along part of its 2,600-mile (4,200 km) journey, which begins in Tibet and ends with a multiveined exit into the South China Sea at the southern tip of Vietnam.

After briefly skirting the far north of Thailand, the Mekong River turns east into Laos, before switching south to rejoin the country near the provincial city of Loei. From here, its middle reaches flow along the Thai–Laotian border, then it abruptly moves back into Laos at its confluence with the Mun River, near Udon Ratchathani.

Thailand has had a volatile relationship with Laos over the years, but these days the two are cozy neighbors, and the river thrives. People crisscross the waterway almost at will, and international tourism, especially since Laos opened up a number of outposts along its borders, is on the rise.

The river joins the Thai border at tranquil **Chiang Khan,** about 30 miles (48 km) north of Loei. Timber homes and shops nestle comfortably here in an attractive forest and river setting. The town is known for its delicious bananas, a fact celebrated every fall with its Miss Banana Beauty Contest.

About 3 miles (5 km) downriver are the **Kaeng Kut Khu** rapids, where you can sit on raised decks above the river. **Pak Chom,** farther downstream, is a village that encapsulates much of the rural charm of Issan's river communities. During the dry season, locals pan for gold on Don Chom Island, at the mouth of a confluence of the Mekong and Chom Rivers. Stark evidence of the once volatile relations between the Mekong neighbors is found at the now-closed **Ban Winai Refugee Camp.** The camp once held 30,000 Hmong tribespeople, displaced from Laos after the Communist Pathet Lao took power in 1975.

Highway 2186 continues along the banks of the Mekong to **Si Chiangmai,** where a large Laotian and Vietnamese immigrant population has turned the town into one of the world's leading manufacturing and export centers for springroll wrappers. The wrappers, hung over bamboo racks to dry, can be seen all over town. A little farther downstream, the important market town of **Tha Bo** shows what the richly fertile Mekong flood plains can conjure. Here banana and vegetable plantations and tobacco fields flourish.

Continuing downstream from Nong Khai (see p. 183), the Mekong widens in places to nearly half a mile (1 km), its placid flow occasionally interrupted by minor rapids. Many small towns dotting the river route take on the prefix of *Nong* or *Beung,* terms referring to freshwater ponds fed by streams running in from the Mekong. Vietnamese and Thais, wearing conical straw hats, tend rice fields and vegetable plots on the riverbanks.

Beyond Nakhon Phanom (see p. 181) and the revered *chedi* of That Phanom (see p. 180), more beautiful riverside scenery reveals itself at **Mukdahan,** the last sizable Thai town on the Mekong. Opposite the Laotion city of Savannaket,

Mekong River Valley

🅜 165 A4, B4, C4, & D4

Visitor information

✉ Tourism Authority of Thailand, 16/5 Mukmontri Rd., Udon Thani

☎ 042-325406

✉ Tourism Authority of Thailand, 184/1 Sunthon Wichit Rd., Nakhon Phanom

☎ 042-513490

Preparing springroll wrappers in Si Chiangmai. The town is one of the world's largest producers of the product.

Mukdahan bustles as a major trade link between the two countries. A second bridge over the Mekong is planned for the town, which would open an avenue along Route 9 in Laos, stretching to the Vietnamese port of Danang.

At Mukdahan, Highway 2034 continues beside the river. About 10 miles (16 km) on, near the village of Ban Na Kam Noi, is **Mukdahan National Park,** a 20-square-mile (52 sq km) area strewn with bizarre rock formations and with prehistoric paintings on its cave walls.

At the village of **Khong Chiam,** a site called Mae Nam Song Si ("two-color river") is where the relatively clear waters of the Mun clash with the Mekong's muddy flow. You can rent boats for short river excursions. Nearby is **Pha Taem,** a sheer cliff with paintings of uncertain origins depicting fish, elephants, and buffalo; it dates back 2,000–3,000 years.

FRIENDSHIP BRIDGE

The Thai–Lao Friendship Bridge extends over the lower reaches of the Mekong River at Nong Khai and is spanned with good intentions. When it was completed in the mid-1990s, its was effectively and symbolically to link two countries that, despite sharing strong cultural ties, had been at each other's throats for much of the previous 30 years. Its opening was a defining moment in reconciliation and was viewed as a facilitator for a new and prosperous era of trade and commerce.

Construction began in 1991, three years after Thailand and Laos ended hostilities that had flared sporadically since the end of the Vietnam War in 1976. The two had been ideological enemies since then. Thailand was a robust capitalist economy, striding—and often stumbling—along the path to modern democracy. Laos had bolted its doors to the West and embraced socialism. By the late 1980s, relations improved after then Thai Prime Minister Chatichai Choonhavan (1922–1988) announced his "turn battle-fields into marketplaces" policy. And Laos cautiously opened up to foreign investment in an attempt to kick start its moribund economy.

At the opening in April 1994, Buddhist monks performed *rote nam,* a water-blessing ceremony ensuring *mong-kon* (an auspicious future) in front of Thailand's revered monarch King Bhumibol, Prime Minister Chuan Leekpai, and the then Australian Prime Minister, Paul Keating (Australia provided the 30 million dollars for the bridge's construction).

The Friendship Bridge, at the Bangkok–Nong Khai railhead, was to signal a new era for Issan, which would now flourish as the gateway to tourism and trade in Indochina. A railway would be built through Laos to Vietnam, connecting Singapore to China. Foreign investors would be enticed to land-locked Laos with the promise of easier access to port facilities in the Gulf of Thailand, and trade would flow both ways over the bridge.

Today, few of the lofty ambitions of the 3,851-foot (1,174 m) bridge have been realized. The decimating 1997–99 Asian economic crisis stalled the dream, but perhaps more pivotal is the cautious stance taken by the Lao authorities. Laos has a population of just 4.5 million, governed by a mix of half-hearted market economics and debilitating bureaucracy. Fear of outside influences importing divergent views and exploiting natural resources is holding up traffic on the Friendship Bridge.

Tourists can cross into Laos by paying either $30 or $50

(depending entirely on bureaucratic whims) for a 14-day visa at the Laos immigration point. You'll need to fill out visa application forms and produce two passport photos. Minibuses carry passengers over the bridge for about 20 cents, but private or rental cars are restricted from crossing. Just off the Laotian end of the bridge, the road performs a neat trick at a traffic circle, and vehicles suddenly find themselves on the right-hand side of the road (in Thailand vehicles travel on the left side, in Laos on the right). At the end of the bridge, fixed-fare taxis leave for the capital, **Vientiane,** about 20 miles (32 km) east.

Outside of Hanoi, in Vietnam, Vientiane maintains some of Southeast Asia's best examples of French colonial architecture. A plethora of Buddhist temples testifies to the Communist government's failure to purge the state of religion after it took power in 1975. Not that it tried very hard—Laotians are devout, and any wholehearted attempts to destroy Buddhism would have alienated a significant portion of the population. The country's sustained fling with the Soviet Union presents itself in drab, worn-out Stalinist architecture. Sidewalk cafés sell amphetamine-strength Laotian coffee and croissants, and mountains of freshly baked baguettes are sold at the city's morning market. Add all this to a Mekong frontage and a rambunctious city center, and Vientiane makes a funky diversion. ■

The Mekong River skirts Thailand on its route between Tibet and Vietnam.

National parks of Loei

▲ 165 B3, 165 A3, 165 A4

Visitor information

✉ Tourism Authority of Thailand, 16/5 Mukmontri Rd., Udon Thani

☎ 042-325406

✉ National Park Division of the Royal Forestry Department, Paholyothin Rd., Bangkhen, Bangkok

☎ 02-579-5734 or 02-579-7223

National parks of Loei

IN THE PAST, BEING SENT TO LOEI, IN THE FAR NORTHEAST near the Laotian border, was the connotative equivalent of being trucked off to Siberia. For government workers posted there it meant isolation, inhospitable terrain, searing summers and frigid winters, few creature comforts, troublesome Communist insurgents, and the not-so-subtle hint that their careers were on the rocks. Now the province, with its rugged mountains and fertile valleys along the western edge of the Khorat Plateau, is recognized for the beauty of its mountainous national parks.

PHU KRADUNG NATIONAL PARK

The prize among these parks is the 138-square-mile (359 sq km) Phu Kradung National Park, established

A reveler in a spirit mask at Loei's Phi Tha Khon festival, which celebrates the Buddha's association with spirits, or *phi*.

in 1962 to protect its unusual and diminishing temperate fauna. The park—peaking at 4,462 feet (1,360 meters)—embraces a gently hilly sandstone plateau atop a steep-sided mountain, and the surrounding fertile lowlands. On the plateau, as you wander past azaleas and rhododendrons and through carpets of wildflowers, it is hard to remember or imagine being in tropical Thailand.

Phu Kradung is ably set up for hiking, with 30 miles (48 km) of well-marked trails. The visitor center at Si Than, 50 miles (80 km) south of Loei, has maps and blankets, stores baggage, and arranges porters and guides. The park gets busy on weekends and holidays, so try to visit on weekdays.

The 4.5-mile (7 km), steep climb to Phu Kradung begins at the visitor center and takes about three hours (ladders and stairs ease the chore at more difficult points). You pass communities of mixed deciduous, hill evergreen and cloud forests, and tracts of bamboo, before pulling over the top of the plateau's ridge. It's another 2 miles (3 km) to the park headquarters. Here you buy provisions and rent bungalows. Trails snake out onto the plateau through meadows, stands of pine, patches of evergreen forest, oak and birch, and ground flora of violets, orchids, and daisies, to some breathtaking mountain and valley views at the summit. Bring warm clothes, food, a flashlight, candles, and insect repellent. The park closes from June to September, when rains make the trails slippery and dangerous.

PHU LUANG NATIONAL PARK

About 12.5 miles (20 km) north of Phu Kradung, near the village of

Wang Saphung, Highway 2250 turns southwest for about 16 miles (25.5 km) before heading into Phu Luang National Park. The park shares many of the features of Phu Kradung but is less visited. It comprises a steep-sided sandstone plateau rising to 3,600 feet (1,100 m)—and upwards to its 5,154-foot (1571 m) summit—scattered with numerous rocky outcrops and boulders. Mini-trucks from Loei rumble about halfway up the mountain, from where you climb a tough trail for three to four hours before reaching park headquarters. On the plateau, park rangers have blazed trails through swaths of shrubland interspersed with deciduous pine and occasional stands of bamboo. The trails lead to waterfalls, freshwater springs, and spectacular cliff edges with expansive mountain and valley views.

Humid conditions promote a jungle growth packed with ferns, mosses, and the park's most treasured natural attribute—over 1,500 species of wild orchid. Phu Luang is also credited with an abundance of wildlife, including large, long-tailed deer called sambars, elephants, tigers, leopards, Asiatic black bears, and about 140 species of migratory and resident birds.

Phu Luang is not as popular as Phu Kradung, simply because access is more difficult. Tours arranged by park rangers *(tel 042-841141 or 042-879032)* are recommended. The three-day, two-night tours cost about $20 per person and include transportation from Loei town, food, guides, and accommodations in park bungalows.

PHU RUA NATIONAL PARK
This largely mountainous park is about 30 miles (48 km) west of Loei. From park headquarters, a three-hour climb passes through tropical, evergreen, and pine forests to the 4,511-foot (1,375 m) summit, where a jutting slab of cliff hangs out over fine mountain vistas. Although the 75-square-mile (121 sq km) Phu Rua is isolated from the much larger Phu Luang National Park, fauna is similar and includes tigers, Asiatic black bears, and sambars. ■

Over 1,500 species of wild orchid grow in the mountains of Phu Luang National Park.

Khon Kaen

Khon Kaen

⚠ 165 B3

Visitor information

✉ Tourism Authority of Thailand, 15/5 Prachasamoson Rd., Khon Kaen

☎ 043-244498

THE FOURTH LARGEST CITY IN THAILAND, KHON KAEN IS the gateway to Issan for travelers moving across the country from Northern Thailand. Speared by both the Friendship Highway (Highway 2) and the other major Issan route, Highway 12, it could also claim to be at its crossroads. Add a modern airport and an important rail stop on the far-reaching Bangkok–Nong Khai line, and you have a city that binds into a convenient base from which to explore the Northeast.

Khon Kaen's unbridled growth over the past decade has pushed it to the regional fore in transportation, communications, finance, and education. The sprawling 2,000-acre (810 ha) Khon Kaen University is Issan's largest. Khon Kaen is not an unpleasant place, but besides the customary urban diversions of a modern Thai city, and boat rides and picnicking at the expansive **Khaen Nakhon Lake** on the city's outskirts, it has little to offer in the way of attractions.

An exception is the well-managed **Khon Kaen National Museum** (*Lungsun Rachakhan Rd., tel 043-236741, closed Mon.–Tues.*). Artifacts include superbly complex lintels from the Ku Suan Taeng temple in Buriram Province, built by the Khmer King Jayavarman VII. Jayavarman, a devout Buddhist, initiated a network of public works, including 102 hospitals. A stone stele at the museum identifies one such structure. A 12th-century conch shell laden with Mahayana Buddhist motifs and small votive deities is among the museum's more exquisitely quirky relics. There is also a collection of artifacts excavated from Ban Chiang (see p. 182).

Away from the capital, provincial Khon Kaen quickly slips into Issan's calming rural heartland. **Chonnabot** (*35 miles/57km SW of Khon Kaen on Hwy. 229*) is known throughout Thailand for its tie-dye *mutmee* cotton and silk. The process involves dyeing individual threads of silk before weaving. Examples are displayed at Chonnabot's handicraft center on Pho Sii Sa-aat Road, opposite Wat Pho Sii Sa-aat. In the nearby streets a number of weaving houses sell similar products at better prices. ■

An Issaner blows on traditional Kaen pipes.

Central Thailand is home to the magnificent old capital of Sukhothai and the golden age of Thai civilization. This is where the Thai nation was born.

Central Thailand

Elephant statue, Wat Chang Lom, Si Satchanalai

Central Thailand

CENTRAL THAILAND IS WHERE THE ANCIENT KINGDOMS OF SIAM AROSE. IT IS considered the essential source of the country's culture, pride, and religious traditions, and of traditional Thai values, including the generosity and humanity that permeates life today. The landscape is unremarkable, but rich soil and plentiful rainfall make it the breadbasket of the country, and its rice and corn crops are a vital source of national income.

The area has a complicated system of rivers and canals that have long helped the people to support themselves in the agricultural sector. Although the area is fairly prosperous and modernized, most residents still make their homes in rural villages, where life centers on family, farming, and the Buddhist faith.

Central Thailand's greatest attraction is the ancient city of Sukhothai, the original capital of the first true Thai nation in a period recognized as the golden era of Thai history. The splendid and remarkable ruins give an insight into the magnificence of Sukhothai culture of the 13th and 14th centuries. Sukhothai Historical Park is a collection of the finest and most intriguing ruins in the land.

Nearby Phitsanulok is a bustling commercial center that briefly enjoyed status as the capital of the country after the fall of Sukhothai and before the rise of Ayutthaya. It is best known today as the home of one of the most famous Buddha images in the world.

Within striking distance of Sukhothai are two more destinations of great architectural

Young monks take a break at Sukhothai Historical Park.

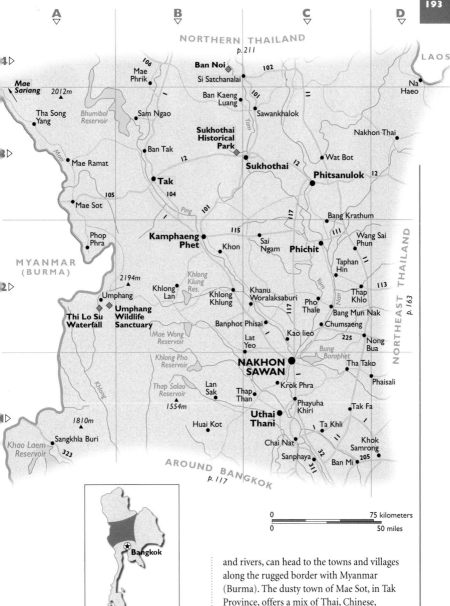

LAOS

A B C D

Mae Sariang 2012m

106 Mae Phrik

Ban Noi

Si Satchanalai 102

Na Haeo

Tha Song Yang

Bhumibol Reservoir

Sam Ngao

Ban Kaeng Luang

101

Sawankhalok

Moei

Mae Ramat

Ban Tak

12

Sukhothai Historical Park

Yom

Nakhon Thai

Wat Bot

Sukhothai

12

Phitsanulok 12

Tak

105 104

Mae Sot

Ping 101

Bang Krathum

MYANMAR (BURMA)

Phop Phra

Kamphaeng Phet

115

Khon

Sai Ngam

Phichit

117

Wang Sai Phun

Taphan Hin

NORTHEAST THAILAND   p. 163

2194m

Khlong Klung Res.

Umphang

Khlong Lan

Khlong Khlung

Khanu Woralaksaburi

Nan

Thap Khlo

113

Thi Lo Su Waterfall

Umphang Wildlife Sanctuary

Moe Wong Reservoir

Banphot Phisai

Pho Thale

Bang Mun Nak

Khlong Pho Reservoir

Lat Yeo

Kao lieo

117

Chumsaeng

225

Nong Bua

Khlong

NAKHON SAWAN

Bung Boraphet

Tha Tako

Thap Salao Reservoir

1554m

Lan Sak

Thap Than

Krok Phra

Phaisali

1810m

Huai Kot

Uthai Thani

Phayuha Khiri

Ta Khli

Tak Fa

Sangkhla Buri

Khao Laem Reservoir

323

Chai Nat

Sanphaya

32

311

Ban Mi

Khok Samrong

205

| 0 | | 75 kilometers |
| 0 | | 50 miles |

Bangkok

Area of map detail

interest: Si Satchanalai, a vice-regal seat in the Sukhothai period, and Kamphaeng Phet, the final part of the Sukhothai Kingdom.

Visitors wanting to explore some of Thailand's remoter areas, including jungles and rivers, can head to the towns and villages along the rugged border with Myanmar (Burma). The dusty town of Mae Sot, in Tak Province, offers a mix of Thai, Chinese, Indian, and Burmese, plus Karen and other hill-tribe ethnic groups. It is the center of the gem and jade trade along the border and has a tinge of appealing frontierism. Just outside the town, right on the border, you'll find one of the most colorful markets in Thailand. To the south, isolated Umphang, well off the conventional tourist track, is a good place to organize trekking and river-rafting trips. ■

Traditional houses fringe the Nam River in Phitsanulok, one of Thailand's oldest towns.

Phitsanulok

CENTRAL THAILAND'S LEADING BUSINESS CENTER AND regional transportation hub, this sprawling, friendly city sits on the banks of the Nan River, 235 miles (376 km) north of Bangkok. Phitsanulok today appears to be a modern enclave with all the conveniences of home, yet the city is among the oldest and most historic towns in Thailand. It was an early Khmer military outpost and, during the Sukhothai era, was a military garrison for the first Siamese kingdom. King Naresuan the Great was born here.

Phitsanulok

▲ 193 C3

Visitor information

✉ Tourism Authority of Thailand, Surasi Trade Center, 209/7–8 Borommatrailokanat Rd., Amphoe Muang, Phitsanulok

☎ 055-252743

Phitsanulok's major attraction is the exquisite and highly revered image of the **Phra Phuttha Chinarat,** housed inside the equally impressive **Wat Phra Si Rattana Mahathat** (or Wat Yai) (*Phutthabucha Rd.*), one of the few Ayutthaya-period structures to survive a catastrophic fire that took place in 1955.

Entry is via a pair of elaborately carved doors into a stunning interior, resplendent with decorated black and gold columns, a richly colored red roof, delightful murals of courtesans and hunters, and a dramatic architectural scheme that points toward the central image.

Phra Phuttha Chinarat is one of the finest examples of Sukhothai art, with its extraordinary casting and mesmerizing beauty, and should not be missed.

An amazing collection of rural artifacts is displayed in **Sergeant Major Thawee's Folk Museum** (*Wisuth Kasat Rd., closed Mon.*) in the southeast section of town. Objects range from fish traps and musical instruments to sculpted coconut grinders and clunky elephant bells.

Opposite the folk museum, the Buddha **foundry** (*Wisuth Kasat Rd., closed Mon.*) still makes bronze Buddha images. ■

Sukhothai Historical Park

SUKHOTHAI IS TO THAILAND WHAT ANGKOR IS TO Cambodia, Tikal to Mexico, and Giza to Egypt. Lying 281 miles (450 km) north of Bangkok, Sukhothai ("dawn of happiness") was the center of Thailand's first independent kingdom and birthplace of the Thai nation, and is probably the most impressive and popular archaeological site in the country. In this vast national park, you will find superb examples of artistic and architectural achievements of a kingdom that spread far west to Vientiane in Laos, east to Pegu in Myanmar, and south to Nakhon Si Thammarat.

Sukhothai Historical Park
▲ 193 B3
⑤ $, or $$$ for admission pass to all sites

Visitor information
✉ Tourism Authority of Thailand, 209/7–8 Surasi Trade Center, Borommatrailokanat Rd., Amphoe Muang, Phitsanulok
☎ 055-252743

Formerly a strategically well-placed Khmer military outpost, the city was established in 1238 by two Thai princes who sought independence from Khmer rule. The city would flourish until it was swamped by the rise of Ayutthaya in 1378.

Over a relatively short period, Sukhothai successfully conquered many small principalities in the region to create the most powerful nation in Southeast Asia at that time. Early kings preached a philosophy of political power share rather than military might and the importance of respecting the wishes of the people—in direct contrast to the ruthless oligarchy practiced by both the Khmers and the Burmese.

The golden age of Sukhothai—a time of remarkable political, cultural, and religious freedoms—came under the leadership of King Ramkamhaeng (R.1278–1318), famous throughout Thai history for his enlightened rule and wide-ranging accomplishments. Not only did Ramkamhaeng make his mark as a successful warrior, but he also was an economic revolutionary who introduced a free-trade economy and is credited with inventing the modern Thai alphabet. A great religious leader, too, he actively promoted the

pure sect of Theravada Buddhism, the national religion of today. Unlike his predecessors and

contemporaries across Southeast Asia, who reigned from a position of godlike terror, Ramkamhaeng ruled with a surprising degree of humanity. It is said that he ruled from his throne, and citizens could seek his judgment by ringing a bell just outside the palace.

Subsequent Sukhothai kings had less impact overall than Ramkamhaeng, but some left their mark in other fashions. It was

A colossal Buddha dominates Wat Mahathat, Sukhothai's spiritual center.

during the reign of King Mahalithai in the mid-14th century that the art and architecture of Sukhothai reached its dizzying heights, and the city developed its role as the largest center of Buddhism in the world. The kingdom continued to thrive until 1378, when it started to be subsumed by the emerging power base of Ayutthaya. A handful of minor kings ruled the slowly declining empire until 1438, when the final king abdicated in favor of an Ayutthayan prince, and Sukhothai's fate as little more than a subservient outpost to the rising Ayutthayan Empire was sealed.

Sukhothai faded into history and was largely forgotten by the Siamese people until 1782, when the Chakri dynasty became established in Bangkok. To legitimize his power through royal and religious kinship, Rama I (R. 1782–1809) collected hundreds of Sukhothai images to grace his newly constructed temples and monasteries. Several of his building projects were designed to reflect Sukhothai prototypes, and the mythology of the earlier kingdom was actively promoted to inspire and unite the people.

King Mongkut promoted the memory and reverence of Sukhothai after he visited the abandoned site in 1833, returning with stone tablets that confirmed the brilliance of the ancient empire.

In 1977 work began to restore the historical site, and 16 years later the Sukhothai National Historical Park, covering some 28 square miles (70 sq km), opened to the

Two large standing Buddhas flank the principal *chedi.*

Remains of a large, square-based, stepped *chedi*

The different hand gestures, or *mudras,* **of Buddha images carry different meanings.**

public. Today the splendidly restored buildings of this UNESCO World Heritage site—top of most visitors' must-see list—give a revealing insight into Sukhothai's golden past.

Sukhothai-style Buddha images are considered the most sublime.

Classic Sukhothai lotus-bud finial

Principal chedi ringed by eight smaller chedis

Ruins of the main _wihan_

Plan of Sukhothai Historical Park. The shaded area near the center represents Wat Mahathat.

RAMKAMHAENG NATIONAL MUSEUM

An excellent introduction to the history, arts, and crafts of Sukhothai, Si Satchanalai, and Kamphaeng Phet is given in this modern and spacious building at the entrance to the central zone of the Sukhothai Historical Park. The well-planned museum features graceful Sukhothai Buddhas, treasured Sawankalok ceramics from Si Satchanalai, ancient Khmer statues, and other archaeological artifacts from Central Thailand.

A highlight is the magnificent bronze walking Buddha that faces the front entrance. Noteworthy exhibits on the main floor include models of the old city and a reproduction of the four-sided pillar that claims fame as the first example of written Thai script. Household utilities and farming implements show the degree of sophistication of the common people in early Sukhothai. The second floor is largely devoted to Buddha images in the slender-waisted Sukhothai style, which emphasized simplicity and grace.

Sculpture around the grounds of the museum ranges from a rare Khmer phallic shrine to a collection of stucco temple elephants gathered from local shrines. A statue of King Ramkamhaeng, seated on a replica of the Manangasila throne, is located west of museum. The historic throne, imbued with magical properties, was discovered in 1833 by King Mongkut, and the highly revered original is now in the National Museum in Bangkok (see pp. 80–83).

WAT MAHATHAT

The spiritual center of old Sukhothai was the huge complex of Wat Mahathat, which was both the royal temple and the most important Buddhist monastery in

Southeast Asia. Though largely in ruins as a result of the ravages of war and the effects of the elements, Wat Mahathat remains important as the religious focus of the most brilliant of all Thai kingdoms. The temple monastery was constructed by Sukhothai's first king, Si Intharathit (R.circa 1240–1270), and was expanded and remodeled by subsequent rulers, including Ramkamhaeng and King Lo Thai (R.1298–1346).

To appreciate its former splendor, imagine the *wat* in its prime, when it boasted almost 200 *chedis* erected to protect royal remains, around a dozen *wihans* for public worship and an impressive central *bot*, surrounded by moats. Today, large Buddhas sit serene amid the crumbling masonry. The highlight is the soaring central chedi, erected by Lo Thai to house two sacred Buddha relics donated by a Sri Lankan monk. The monument has been modeled in the Sinhalese style, with a bulbous, lotus bud-shaped outline that is now considered the classic architectural motif of Sukhothai.

MORE LOCAL SIGHTS

Just west of Wat Mahathat are the rough foundations of **Ramkamhaeng's Royal Palace.** Constructed almost entirely of wood, it has not survived. Only religious structures were built of stone, and so almost all historic royal and domestic architecture has disappeared. King Mongkut discovered the famous Manangasila throne here in 1833.

One of the most interesting and evocative structures on the site is **Wat Si Sawai,** a striking Khmer-style sanctuary of three closely set, corncob *prangs* erected by King Jayavarman VII of Angkor, and completed in the 14th century. Enclosed within a deep moat, this intriguing shrine first honored Hindu Brahmanic deities favored by the Khmers but was adapted in the 15th century to suit Buddhist sensibilities. The central nave and trio of complementary brick prangs follow the classic motif found in many Khmer temples in Thailand.

Perhaps the most beautifully situated temple at Sukhothai is **Wat Traphang Ngoen** ("silver lake monastery"), which rises gracefully on a small island in the center of an artificial lake, and today is the focus for the November festival of Loy Krathong. The monastery features an elegant lotus-bud chedi, modeled after that crowning Wat Mahathat.

Another temple in a superb watery setting is nearby **Wat Sa Si,** which overlooks a lake. The temple features a well-restored, large Buddha image, and on the temple grounds is a small black Buddha image in the famous Sukhothai walking style.

The Khmers also left behind another laterite temple of the Hindu type, **San Tapa Daeng,** with its four porticoes and Angkor Wat-style statuary that dates the monument to the early 12th century. The Angkor deities have been removed and are now displayed in the Ramkamhaeng National Museum.

Wat Sorasak, constructed in 1412, is known for its base—which is made up of reconstructed elephant buttresses—and its classic Sri Lankan-style chedi. ∎

The festival of Loy Krathong originated in Sukhothai. On a full-moon night in November, tiny banana-leaf boats, shaped like lotuses and containing flowers, incense, lighted candles, and a coin, are floated on Thailand's rivers for good luck.

Arts of Sukhothai

Beginning in the late 13th century Sukhothai developed into a major center of artistic creativity. Drawn out of a need to assert its cultural identity over the once dominant Khmer, Sukhothai eschewed the Khmer's Mahayana Buddhism and embraced Theravada Buddhism from Sri Lanka. It fused artistic influences from other Asian cultures, principally from the Indian subcontinent and, ironically, the Khmers, to create Thailand's first indigenous art.

Despite the short duration of the Sukhothai Kingdom, it was prolific and varied in its artistic endeavors. Through its architecture, sculpture, ceramics, and paintings—although few signs of the latter have survived—it produced a remarkable sense of beauty and grace that has proved to be both profound and enduring.

Artists of the Sukhothai period created elegant walking Buddha images.

SCULPTURE

Perhaps the best example of this—indeed, some suggest it is the most notable of all Sukhothai artistic expressions—is the design of Buddha icons. Influenced by Sri Lankan style, Sukhothai Buddha sculptures were marked by a fluid, almost ethereal design; their lithe curves and cylindrical forms produced a weightless elegance. Other distinguishing characteristics were wide shoulders tapering to narrow waists, a head crowned with flame ornamentation, and the flap of the robe draped over the left shoulder and ending in a wavy pattern at the waist. Also notable were the facial expressions—elongated heads with strongly defined noses, eyes, and mouths. These expressions captured, more than any other style of Buddha iconography before and, arguably, since, an amazing degree of serenity and spirituality.

Sukhothai Buddhas typically come in four postures: seated in the half-lotus posture with right hand performing the earth-touching gesture; standing; reclining; and walking—the posture recognized as the greatest design achievement by Sukhothai artists. Although this image had existed before, it was almost always carved in relief and was not used as a canonical type. Sukhothai artists created a sublime image frozen in a moment of movement. With one heel raised and one foot planted on the ground, Buddha appears to move forward in a supple, but essential surge. Most of the walking Buddhas from Sukhothai temples have been moved to museums in Sukhothai and Bangkok, but a few are still seen on their original monuments.

CERAMICS & OTHER CRAFTS

Similar craftsmanship are found in rare woodcarvings on doors and ceilings, and in slate engravings. Finely crafted, if faded, stucco reliefs can still be seen in some of Sukhothai's temples: the best examples are at Wat Traphang Tong Lang (see p. 202)—the southern panel shows the Buddha's descent to Earth, surrounded by angels and bodhisattvas.

The works of the kingdom's ceramicists are also notable. Craftsmen, who learned the trade from the Chinese, used Sukthothai's and Si Satchanalai's expansive kilns to make exquisite ceramics in brown, white, and celadon, or with a painted design known as Sangkhalok. These ceramics and other forms of decorative pottery, sometimes molded into animal and human shapes, were exported to Malaysia, the Philippines, Indonesia, and Japan. Artifacts recovered from shipwrecks in the Gulf of Thailand and off the coast of Indonesia and the Philippines attest to this trade.

Sukhothai architects refined architectural styles developed by earlier kingdoms.

ARCHITECTURE

Sukhothai architects seemed intent on developing fresh and more delicate styles, improving on the heavy stupas from Sri Lanka and the Khmer *prangs*.

The most distinguishable forms of Sukhothai architecture can be found in the lotus-bud motifs crowning *chedis*, a style that evolved from Khmer and Burmese Bagan influences. Khmer prangs were modified and enhanced to form bell-shaped chedis. Their square bases were adorned and buttressed with elephant stucco carvings. Taking the cue from the Lanna period, stupas were designed with square redented bases. The main body of the stupa was indented with alcoves in which Buddha statues were housed. The bell-shaped stupas were crowned with ornamental rings.

The crafting of Buddha footprints in stone and bronze was popular during the reign of Li Thai (*R*.1347–1368). The footprints were richly symbolic, identifying the presence of Lord Buddha. Temples where the footprints are placed became highly revered. ∎

Around Sukhothai

Around Sukhothai

193 C3

Visitor information

✉ Tourism Authority of Thailand, 209/7–8 Surasi Trade Center, Borommatrailokanat Rd., Amphoe Muang, Phitsanulok

☎ 055-252743

SOME OF SUKHOTHAI'S FINEST MONUMENTS LIE outside the old city walls, north of town. Several more noteworthy temples are situated to the west, south, and east of the central zone, although few compare to those previously mentioned and the distances deter some visitors. One way to get around is to hire a bicycle near the east gate—you can then escape the beaten track to experience a simpler, less commercialized version of the old city.

Wat Phra Phai Luang ("temple of the great wind"), almost a mile (1.6 km) north of Wat Mahathat, was once a Buddhist monastery second only to Wat Mahathat in importance. Built in the 12th century by the Khmers as a Hindu religious shrine, it was converted into a Buddhist monastery after the fall of the Khmer Empire. Only one of the three laterite *prangs* remains. Sadly, looters stole many valuable Hindu and Buddhist images in the 1950s.

A number of huge **pottery kilns** make a welcome change from temple touring. Believed to predate Sukhothai, they were used to produce an outstanding range of ceramics, from glazed tiles to Sangkhalok bottles.

Among the most impressive Buddhist monuments in Sukhothai is the gigantic Buddha image inside the square *mondop* of **Wat Sri Chum.** The image, dating from the late 14th century, is seated in the attitude of subduing the evil goddess Mara and is still an active religious icon for Thai pilgrims.

To the west of the old city are several brick temples that show signs of vandalism by robbers and an ancient reservoir, which has been renovated and now serves as the main source of fresh water for modern Sukhothai.

The trek up a very steep hill to **Wat Saphan Hin** ("temple of the stone causeway mountain") is a tiring one, on a confusing landslide

of stone steps, but those who reach the top are satisfied with a giant Buddha image and superb views over the entire valley. The Buddha, with its raised hand in the aspect of ensuring peace, seems to be blessing the valley, the city, and even the odd Western visitor who makes the tough climb up the dusty hill.

Monuments to the south are also rather modest, chiefly renowned for their traces of rare and fine stuccoes. The remoteness of the area means that it has suffered from pillagers, who have stripped most of the ancient monuments of their priceless stucco works, including divinity figures, standing elephants, and superb *garudas.* Most impressive of the remaining structures is **Wat Chetuphon,** which has two tall, upright stucco Buddas; the walking image is particularly fine.

Although the distances to the eastern sector are great, and the landscape rugged and dry, most of the temples here remain blessedly free of restoration and display more of their original character than monuments found elsewhere in the old city. Highlights are the *chedi* of **Wat Chang Lom,** with its sculpted elephants; the beautifully proportioned chedi of **Wat Chedi Sung; Wat Traphang Tong,** with its highly revered footprint of the Buddha; and **Wat Traphang Tong Lang,** known for the superb stucco decorations on the walls of the mondop. ■

Opposite: Mudras, or Buddha image hand gestures, help instruct devotees.

Si Satchanalai

Si Satchanalai

THIS MEMORABLE AND RARELY VISITED SET OF ANCIENT ruins provides a complementary overview of early Siamese architecture and makes for an excellent day excursion from Sukhothai, which lies some 35 miles (56 km) to the south. Si Satchanalai has fewer ruins than Sukhothai, and the site is smaller, too—about 3 square miles (7 sq km). However, the setting on the west bank of the Yom River and the sheer isolation of the old city make for a very evocative tour.

Si Satchanalai

⚠ 193 C4

✉ On Hwy. 101, 35 miles (56 km) north of Sukhothai

💲 $

Visitor information

✉ Tourism Authority of Thailand, 209/7–8 Surasi Trade Center, Borommatrailokanat Rd., Amphoe Muang, Phitsanulok

☎ 055-252743

Si Satchanalai's history is inextricably linked with that of Sukhothai. Both towns were founded by the Khmers for use as military and administrative centers. A rebel force was raised by two Siamese princes in 1238, to drive the Khmers finally

Sangkhalok ceramics were produced at kilns in Si Satchanalai.

from the area, and their first target for release was Si Satchanalai, which would serve as a springboard for the successful attack on Sukhothai.

The princes divided their army into two contingents, one of which battled the Khmers at the midway point between the two cities, while the other marched into an unoccupied Sukhothai. This clever strategy worked as planned, and Sukhothai was transformed in a short time to become the first Siamese kingdom. One of the

leaders renamed himself King Sri Indraditya and began to build both Sukhothai and Si Satchanalai.

Si Satchanalai enjoyed a steady building boom over the ensuing century, and the sheer number of temples and the grand proportions of the royal monastery demonstrate that the city enjoyed great political and religious significance. Si Satchanalai fell from favor after the rise of Ayutthaya and, after repeated attacks from Burmese forces, was almost completely forgotten by the 18th century. After centuries of disuse, most of the ruins were carefully renovated in the mid-1980s by the Fine Arts Department.

Si Satchanalai today has three areas of historical and architectural interest, with the vast majority of the ancient ruins found inside the central laterite walls that mark the first outlines of the township.

The cozy **museum** near the entrance has a scale model of the old city and is a useful place to get your bearings before exploring.

At the center of Si Satchanalai is the Sri Lankan-style *chedi* of **Wat Chang Lom** ("temple surrounded by elephants"), constructed in 1285 by King Ramkamhaeng while his eldest son ruled over the city. The handsome bell-shaped structure rises above a tier of stucco elephants, after which the structure was named. Situated on the upper terraces are what remains of almost a dozen stucco Buddhas.

Monks wander among the ruins of Wat Chang Lom, built in 1285.

Paths and grassy lawns lead to all the following attractions. Start at **Wat Khao Phnom Phloeng** ("temple of the mountain of fire"), in the northern quadrant. Climb the 114 steps to the summit for splendid views over the scattered ruins of the ancient city. To the west is a smaller hill, topped by the ruins of **Wat Suwan Khiri.** A Sinhalese-inspired chedi known as the Temple of the Golden Mountain dominates the site. Here, too, there are excellent views. You can then walk back to Wat Chang Lom and continue south to **Wat Chedi Chet Thaeo,** with its numerous chedis (the temple name means "seven rows of chedis") and the impressive lotus-bud crown on the main chedi—a distinctive Sukhothai style. The smaller chedi behind the main

chedi houses faded murals depicting the lives of Buddha and dignitaries of the Sukhothai period. Reproductions can be found in the National Museum at Sukhothai (see p. 198). Wat Suan Kao Utayan Yai dates from the mid-15th century, its crumbling chedi done in Sri Lankan style. The large Wat Nang Phaya, also dating from the 15th century, contains an elegant bell-shaped chedi, and a south wall has some fragments of stuccowork.

South of the central ruins is the old Khmer military outpost at **Chaliang,** while to the north are impressive pottery kiln sites, **Ban Noi** and **Ban Pa Yuang,** where Sangkhalok ceramics were produced. (You need a rental bicycle or private transportation to reach the kiln sites and Chaliang.) ■

Kamphaeng Phet

LYING 53 MILES (85 KM) SOUTHWEST OF SUKHOTHAI, Kamphaeng Phet, along with Si Satchanalai (see pp. 204–205), once served as a satellite city of Sukhothai. Li Thai, the fourth king of the Sukhothai dynasty, founded it in 1347. Essentially he raised the status of the existing town by installing relics of the Buddha in the *chedi* at Wat Phra Boromathat. Kamphaeng Phet saw intense construction work for several decades, until it was abandoned to the dominating forces of Ayutthaya. It continued to serve as a regional capital.

The old city of Kamphaeng Phet is a short distance north of the uninspiring commercial district of the modern town. The site of this **historical park** comprises several notable structures inside the original walls, along with more unusual temples to the north of the walls, just off the highway to Sukhothai. Kamphaeng Phet is too distant from Sukhothai for a day trip, and most visitors prefer to stay overnight in the modern town on the banks of the Ping River.

The ideal first stop of any tour is the finely stocked **Kamphaeng Phet National Museum** (*Ratchadamnoen Rd., closed Mon.–Tues.*), located inside the old walled city. Among highlights on the ground floor are a highly regarded bronze statue of Siva, cast in 1510, and a superb Buddha in the U-Thong style, at the far end of the hall. There are exhibits of prehistoric terra-cotta, iron, and stone artifacts, and tools 2,000 to 4,000 years old. Dvaravati-period (eighth–ninth centuries) coins have faces stamped in images of the moon, *naga* heads, and flowing water. The second floor has 16th-century bronze statues of Hindu deities Vishnu and Lakshmi from excavations in the area. More recent terra-cotta (14th–18th centuries) and ceramics of the same period are on display, including 15th-century Sangkhalok jars (see box).

Near the National Museum and often called the Golden Teakwood Museum for the abundant use of teak throughout both exterior and interior is the **Kamphaeng Phet City National Museum** (*Ratchadamnoen Rd, closed Mon.–Tues.*). Opened in 1997, it focuses on the history, ethnology, and handicrafts of the province.

Two Buddhist temples situated within the old crenellated city walls are worth inspection. **Wat Phra Kaeo,** the royal chapel, has largely crumbled away, but the wonderfully eroded Buddhas elevated on brick pedestals are both elegant and evocative. **Wat Phra Thak,** opposite the National Museum, has

Sangkhalok ware

S ukhothai potters learned their skills from Chinese craftsmen brought to Thailand by King Ramkamhaeng. Under the guidance of the Chinese, potters began modeling glazed ceramic wares, of which Sangkhalok was the most famous. Sangkhalok pale blue or off-white porcelain features floral, foliage, and fish designs. Kilns in Si Satchanalai and, later, Kamphaeng Phet also produced pieces for architectural decoration, as well as "Sangkhalok dolls." Sangkhalok ware was exported all over the region. ■

Kamphaeng Phet
▲ 193 B2
Visitor information
✉ Tourism Authority of Thailand, 193 Taksin Rd., Tambon Nong Luang, Amphoe Muang, Tak
☎ 055-514341 or 055-514342 or 055-514343

Ruins at Wat Phra Boromathat. Kamphaeng Phet thrived for only a few decades before it succumbed to the forces of Ayutthaya.

a splendid chedi with an octagonal base, surrounded by pillars.

The remaining religious structures are north of town and require local transportation. **Wat Phra Non** once featured a large reclining Buddha, but it has largely eroded away. However, its well-preserved chedi, behind the reclining Buddha's *vihara*, with lotus-leaf tiers and bell-shaped crown, is a fine example of Sukhothai craftsmanship. Also impressive are the huge laterite columns, among the largest ever found in Thailand. **Wat Phra Si Iriyabot** ("temple of the four postures") is notable for its fragmented statue of a walking Buddha in Sukhothai style and a particularly fine standing Buddha statue in fairly good condition.

Wat Sing, close by, has a trio of badly weathered standing Buddhas.

A good hike northwest of **Wat Sing** is **Wat Chang Rop** ("temple surrounded by elephants"), set on a hilltop with superb views over Kamphaeng Phet. The reward for a tough climb is an huge ruined chedi supported by 68 crumbling elephants of brick and stucco. Taken together, they are the most impressive monument in Kamphaeng Phet. Superbly crafted stucco images of demons, divinities, and other heavenly beings make this a must-see attraction.

Wat Nak Chet Sin, Wat Awat Yai, and **Wat Tuk Praman,** near the northern entrance to the park, are under reconstruction and will be worth a visit when work is completed. ∎

Tak & Mae Sot

Tak & Mae Sot

⚐ 193 B3, 193 A3

Visitor information

✉ Tourism Authority of Thailand, 193 Taksin Rd., Tambon Nong Luang, Amphoe Muang, Tak

☎ 055-514341 or 055-514342 or 055-514343

THESE TWO TOWNS, IN THE WESTERN BORDERLANDS OF Central Thailand, are rarely visited. An increasing number of young backpackers, however, are being drawn to this remote corner by the sense of adventure and a desire to enjoy the nearby national parks.

Tak was an outpost of the Sukhothai Kingdom, and, after its decline, it came under the influence of the northern Lanna Kingdom. Today, it is a busy provincial capital with little to see, apart from a handful of splendid old teakwood houses. The town was the birthplace of the revered King Taksin, who defended Thailand against Burmese invaders. He is honored at **Phra Chao Taksin Maharat** (*on Phaholyothin Rd., between Taksin and Mahathai Bamrung Rds.*), where a venerated shrine houses a seated Taksin, with a sword lying in his lap.

Tak has long been a major teakwood distribution point, owing to its fortuitous location on the Ping River, which runs from the forests of Myanmar (Burma), via the Chao Phraya, all the way to the processing plants in Bangkok. This happy state of affairs has long allowed local citizens to construct their houses and businesses with this valuable and very beautiful wood; some of the best are along **Mahathai Bamrung** and **Taksin Roads,** and in the network of alleyways just south of the town park. Enjoy these remarkable structures while you can—collectors of historic houses regularly visit Tak to buy, dismantle, and then move them to the buyers' hometowns.

The lively border town of **Mae Sot** is much more charming and colorful than the modernized commercial enclave of Tak and lies just 3 miles (5 km) east of the Myanmar border, on the banks of the Moei River. It is inhabited by a fascinating mix of ethnic groups, from Thais and Burmese to Chinese merchants, and minority tribes such as the Karen and Hmong. The best introduction to this ethnic melding is the morning market, where traders offer food, Burmese handicrafts, and glittering gems, from sapphires to rubies, smuggled in from Myanmar.

Several Burmese-style temples are scattered around town, most notably **Wat Chumphon Khiri,** which gleams in its covering of golden tiles. **Wat Mae Sot Luang** has a reclining Buddha, covered in small brass tiles. **Wat Maune Pai Son** is covered in little *chedis*, reminiscent of Loha Prasart in Bangkok (see p. 86). ∎

Mae Sot's Wat Maune Pai Son is one of the town's many Burmese-style temples, reflecting the influence of neighboring Myanmar (Burma).

Umphang

THE MORE INTREPID TRAVELERS TO THIS REGION HEAD TO the area of jungles and rivers some 102 miles (164 km) south of Mae Sot, near a village called Umphang. For almost a decade, Umphang and its vicinity have been hosting increasing numbers of hardy visitors who prize the untouched corners of the kingdom. The winding and sometimes treacherous Highway 1090 from Mae Sot to Umphang—once known as the Death Highway because of guerrilla activity—takes in some magnificent mountain scenery.

Umphang

🗺 193 A2

Visitor information

✉ Tourism Authority of Thailand, 193 Taksin Rd., Tambon Nong Luang, Amphoe Muang, Tak

☎ 055-514341 or 055-514342 or 055-514343

Umphang is a very simple village, situated at the confluence of the Mae Khlong and Umphang Rivers, and surrounded by some of the most pristine countryside in all of Thailand. Some people come here just to pass the time relaxing on the riverbanks, while the more active join group expeditions to raft down the raging waters or trek through ancient forests to visit some of the remote hill-tribe villages. The region also has magnificent roaring waterfalls—best seen during the rainy season—and isolated caves engulfed by thick jungle.

Umphang is a base camp for ecotourism explorations around the region, which mostly head south of town into protected reserves such as **Umphang Wildlife Sanctuary** and a nearby park that combines two further wildlife sanctuaries— **Thungyai Naresuan** and **Huai Kha Khaeng.** The vast, largely untouched regions make up one of the largest protected forests left in Southeast Asia.

Rough roads suitable only for four-wheel-drive vehicles cross some of the region, and while elephant trekking is a popular activity, most visitors choose to explore the jungles and waterfalls on one of the daily river-rafting expeditions. These organized adventures typically start in Umphang and proceed down the Umphang River. Where this river intersects with the Mae Khlong, it picks up volume, continuing south through untamed tropical jungle to a series of outstanding natural wonders: waterfalls, hot springs, limestone cliffs, blood-red karsts, and secretive caves.

The highlight of a visit to Umphang is a sight of the lofty **Thi Lo Su Waterfall,** one of the best limestone waterfalls in Southeast Asia. The falls are so remote that they were discovered only in 1987 by a low-flying helicopter, but they can be reached in two days by raft and on foot. ∎

It takes a two-day journey on raft and by foot to reach the magnificent Thi Lo Su falls.

Road to Mae Sariang

🗺 193 A3

Visitor information

✉ Tourism Authority of Thailand, 193 Taksin Rd., Tambon Nong Luang, Amphoe Muang, Tak

☎ 055-514341 or 055-514342 or 055-514343

The road to Mae Sariang

ADVENTUROUS TRAVELERS CAN HEAD NORTH FROM MAE Sot, following the road that runs parallel with the Moei River to Mae Sariang. Highway 1085 offers a rare journey through one of the remotest districts in Thailand. Buses and trucks leave Mae Sot in the morning and wind their way along this backdoor entry to Northern Thailand, an unusual approach that avoids the tiresome return to Tak or Phitsanulok, and links up with connections to Mae Hong Son, Pai, and, finally, Chiang Mai.

Along this rough and untamed section of Thailand, Highway 1085 winds alongside the Moei River before climbing into verdant hills that are clothed in stands of teak forest and dotted with hill-tribe villages clinging to their traditional lifestyles. Eventually it arrives in Mae Sariang, 141 miles (226 km)

Terraced rice paddies are carved into the rugged terrain between Mai Sot and Mae Sariang.

north. The largest hill-tribe group is the Karen, who continue to challenge the Myanmar (Burmese) government for control of their homelands across the Moei River. The river itself is an oddity, as it flows north—rather than south, the typical direction—until it changes course in the Dawana Range, to flow south through the interior of eastern Myanmar.

You can arrange treks into the surrounding hills at villages along the way—including Mae Ramat, Mae Sarit, Tha Song Yang, and Ban Sop Ngao—but most travelers prefer to wait until arrival in Mae Sariang and seek out treks organized by local guesthouses.

MOEI RIVER MARKET

Before setting out on Highway 1085, it is worth making the effort to take a side trip by *samlor* or *songthaew* to colorful markets on the Myanmar border post, 4 miles (6 km) west of Mae Sot. Visitors will find a large variety of goods in this dusty outpost, including gems (including jade), an abundance of handicrafts, and foodstuffs. From the market you can walk along the Moei River and take in views of the Myanmar town of Myawaddy.

A concrete and steel bridge was completed here in 1999, much to the delight of traders in Mae Sot, who rely on business carried over these waters. Unfortunately, the sometimes shaky relations between Myanmar and Thailand often cause the closure of the bridge. The construction of the bridge was tagged as a major part of the ambitious Pan-Asian highway, known as Asia Route 1, which promises some day to link Singapore with Istanbul, providing all the countries along the way with a land crossing. ■

Northern Thailand is a delightful corner of the kingdom, with fantastic landscapes of mountains and valleys, distinctive art, and two capital cities of the ancient Lanna Kingdom.

Northern Thailand

Detail of a woodcarving, a Chiang Mai specialty.

Northern Thailand

NORTHERN THAILAND HAS ALWAYS BEEN A WORLD APART, PHYSICALLY AND emotionally separate from the rest of Thailand, with a sense of grace and style uniquely its own. Historically, the North managed to remain independent of Siamese control until the early part of the 20th century and instead was ruled by a distinguished kingdom known as Lanna.

The North has famously attractive landscapes of rolling hills, soaring mountains, crashing rivers, thick jungle, and other variations of a natural environment that are not found anywhere else in the country. Among the people of the region there is a wide variety of ethnic types, whose identity is preserved in the remote corners of this mountainous region. The tribes are associated with a wide range of handicrafts and other traditional forms of artistic expression. It used to be said that the people here considered themselves superior to the lowlanders of Bangkok and the central plains—and notably for the great beauty of their women—though this attitude is no longer commonplace.

The main city is the old Lanna capital of Chiang Mai, full of cultural interest as well as good shopping and traditional dining.

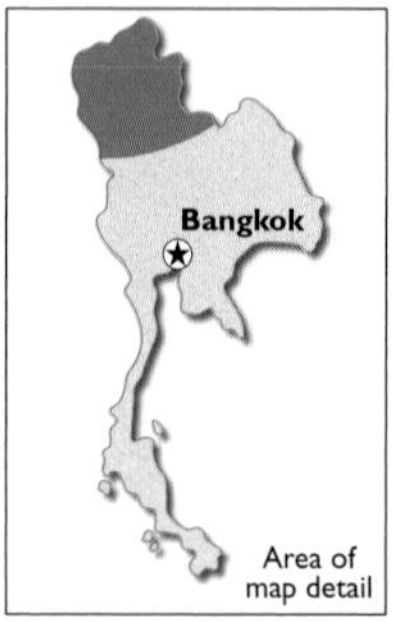

Bangkok

Area of map detail

MYANMAR (BURMA)

LAOS

Mae Sai
Doi Tung
Sop Ruak
Chiang Saen
Chiang Khong
Mekong
Mae Salong
Mae Chan
Tha Ton
2285m
Kok
Fang
109
Chiang Rai
3▷

Pha Sua Waterfalls
Mae Aw
THAM LOT NAT. PARK
Soppong
107
Doi Chiang Dao
Chiang Dao
Mae Suai
Phan
Thoeng
Ing
Tham Pla
Pai
Pa
Chiang Dao Elephant Training Center
Phrao
118
Wat Si Komkan
Chun
Pong
Tha Wang Pha
1980m
Chiang Klang
Na Soi
Mae Hong Son
Mae Taeng
2030m
Phayao
Nam
Nong Bua
Pha Pang Hot Springs
Mae Sa Valley
CHIANG MAI
Ngao
Yom
Nan
Mae Charim
2▷
108
DOI SUTHEP-DOI PUI NATIONAL PARK
Khun Yuam
Hang Dong
2565m
San Kamphaeng
DOI INTHANON NATIONAL PARK
San Pa Tong
Lamphun
Song
Sa
101
Na Noi
Mae La Noi
Chom Thong
108
Pa Sang
Young Elephant Training Center
Rong Kwang
Wat Phra That Lampang Luang
Lampang
Phrae Muang Phi
Na Mun
Salween
108
Wang Lung
Ko Kha
11
Long
Phrae
Ban Khok
Mae Sariang
106
Mae Tub Reservoir
Li
Wong
Wang Chin
Den Chai
Siri Kit Reservoir
1▷
Moei
Sop Moei
Ping
101
Nam Pat
Om Koi
Bhumibol Reservoir
Thoen
Uttaradit
102
Tron
2012m▲

△
A
△
B
CENTRAL THAILAND
p. 191
△
C
△
D

0   100 kilometers

0   50 miles

Northern farmers winnow rice. Thailand is the world's largest rice exporter.

Chiang Mai has grown tremendously in recent years but remains the heart and soul of the North, and is the key destination for most visitors.

Just south and southeast of Chaing Mai are the historic towns of Lamphun and Lampang, where some of the most elegant examples of Mon and Burmese architecture are seen—and, as a bonus, there is the elephant training ground en route to Lampang.

West of Chiang Mai are the previously remote towns of Mae Hong Son and Pai, where trekking and river rafting remain the principal draws.

North of Chiang Mai are Chiang Rai and the notorious region known as the Golden Triangle, once home to the world's most powerful opium smugglers. Beyond these easily accessible destinations are the smaller towns that skirt the Mekong River, such as Chiang Saen and Chiang Khong, and interior towns rarely visited by foreigners, including Phayao, Phrae, and Nan.

The North awaits the adventurous. ■

Fine examples of domestic Thai architecture can still be found in the North.

Chiang Mai

FIRST STOP FOR MOST VISITORS TO NORTHERN THAILAND will be Chiang Mai, heart and soul of the ancient Lanna Kingdom, which flourished from 1250 to 1860. Along the banks of the Ping River and within the confines of the original city you will discover elegant religious structures, cultural emporiums for demonstrations of local dance and music, and very special forms of food and festivals.

Chiang Mai is tucked away in a lush valley surrounded by rivers and green hills. As it is set at a higher altitude than Bangkok and the cities of the south, it has a drier, cooler climate and brings welcome respite for visitors.

Yet it is the people of Chiang Mai that make this city—indeed, all of Northern Thailand—such a warm and wonderful destination. Their cultured dignity and intrinsically gentle nature is often attributed to the city's association with the independent kingdom of Lanna.

Chiang Mai was officially founded in 1292 by Mengrai, a Thai-Laotian prince from Chiang Rai who absorbed the early Haripunchai Empire to establish the Lanna Kingdom. In his five decades of rule, Mengrai constructed a royal city resplendent with

Chiang Mai

🗺 212 B2

Visitor information

✉ Chiang Mai National Tourist Office, 105/1 Chiang Mai—Lamphun Rd., Chiang Mai

☎ 053-248604 or 053-248605 (fax)

palaces and Buddhist temples, and left behind an empire that continued to rule most of Northern Thailand for the next two centuries.

The reign of King Tilok was the next highlight in Lanna's history, ushering in a golden age of arts, crafts, and Buddhism. Chiang Mai suffered through years of warfare with its neighbor Burma, which ruled the area from 1556 to 1774. Lanna was finally absorbed into the burgeoning empire of Bangkok. Subsequent kings of Thailand acknowledged the historic roots of the Lanna Kingdom by reviving the region's hereditary line of rulers, and most of Northern Thailand—including Chiang Mai—was allowed to remain a semi-autonomous state until 1939.

TEMPLES ON THA PHAE ROAD

Several small but significant temples are situated on this busy and very narrow commercial thoroughfare, which connects the Ping River with the Tha Phae Gate. It soon becomes clear that there are some distinct architectural treatments in the temples of Chiang Mai, such as the use of Burmese decoration and elegantly mounted roofs that swoop down much lower to the ground than their counterparts elsewhere. Other unique traits are the use of much more muted colors and flamboyant woodcarving, which is closer to Burmese than Thai styles.

Wat Saen Fang is typical, incorporating Burmese-style architecture in its *chedi* and monastery, along with more modern Thai styling in the brightly painted *wihan*, which is gilded with abstract *nagas*. Across the street stand the three wihans of **Wat Bupparam,** including a very modern and very garish structure

Bargaining—here at Chang Klang market in Chiang Mai—is the norm in Thai markets.

on the left that demonstrates every bad cliché of modern Thai architecture, and a far more refined, much older wooden wihan on the right. This 17th-century gem is worth a close look for its elegant proportions and the workmanship in its exterior stucco decorations.

Two other temples of note are farther west on Tha Phae Road, en route to the restored gateway. **Wat Mahawan** is a small complex that neatly combines Burmese influence in its gaily decorated wihan with later Lanna-Thai styling in its *bot* and monks' residences. Among the details are the monumental elephants encircling the chedi and wooden filigree on many exterior facades. Across the road is **Wat Chedowan,** noted for its trio of chedis donated by wealthy pilgrims and an elegant wihan that has outstanding woodcarvings on the gables and naga posts.

Tha Phae Road ends at a large town square, fronted by the recently restored **Tha Phae Gate,** which marks the formal entrance into the old city. Most of the original walls have collapsed over the centuries, but the rectangular network of protective moats has been excavated, and several of the ancient gateways rebuilt. This is an excellent place to take a break, at one of the several good cafés and restaurants found here.

TEMPLES IN THE WALLED CITY

The following temples are widely scattered within the walled city; it is necessary to hire a three-wheeled rickshaw *(samlor),* motorized three-wheeler *(tuk tuk),* or other form of private transportation to reach them all.

Wat Cha Si Phum *(Chaiyaphum Rd.)* is worth a quick look, for its buildings include a chedi graced with highly unusual

Romanesque columns. The temple complex of **Wat Pa Pao** *(Mani Noppharat Rd.)*, just outside the northeastern walls, is rarely visited and somewhat difficult to locate, with a richly decorated monastery and a romantic chedi set with gleaming blue tiles.

Wat Chiang Man *(Ratcha Phakhinai Rd.)*, within the city walls, was the original residence of King Mengrai. Most structures were rebuilt in the 18th and 19th centuries, but the older wihan with its elaborately carved wooden gable is worth close inspection—it depicts the elephant god Erawan. The modern wihan has a pair of highly venerated Buddha statues: a crystal Buddha endowed with miraculous rainmaking powers, and a bas-relief marble Buddha from the eighth century. On the grassy grounds are a 19th-century *bot* filled with valuable bronzes, an elevated wood and lacquer library, and a 15th-century chedi supported by life-size elephants.

Two smaller monuments worth a quick stop are **Wat Duang Di** *(Phra Pok Klao Rd.)*, for its baroque pediments, and the wihan at **Wat Pan Tao** *(Phra Pok Klao Rd.)*, for its masterly Lanna woodcarving.

Next to Wat Pan Tao is the vast ruined chedi of **Wat Chedi Luang** *(Phra Pok Klao Rd.)*, built in 1401 to a height of 299 feet (90 m) but reduced by half in an earthquake in 1545. Restoration work over the last few decades has reconstructed some of the structure and brought back the elephant buttresses and naga-lined staircase, but it looks like it will never be completed. Chiang Mai's **Lak Muang Shrine** is in the grounds of the temple, situated under the shade of an enormous gum tree.

Chiang Mai's most famous building is the temple complex of **Wat Phra Sing**, or "monastery of the lion lord" *(Singharat Rd.)*. According to tradition, the site was established in 1345 to house the ashes of King Kham Fu and to mark the religious center of the Lanna Kingdom. The modern wihan at the entrance has little architectural significance, but the library next door is among the finest in the country, both for its brilliant stucco *devas* (heavenly beings) and for the flowery scrollwork around the foundation. A Lanna-style bot constructed on an unusual perpendicular axis and a large whitewashed stupa are also on the grounds. Wihan Kham is a small chapel in the southwest corner. This striking building, which dates from 1811, is noted for its superb interior murals and its central Buddha statue, the powerful **Phra Buddha Sing.**

Two minor temples are worth a visit. **Wat Phapong** *(Singharat Rd.)*, beside Wat Phra Sing, has sensitively carved teakwood windows and doors, while the 17th-century Chinese-influenced **Wat Puak Hong** *(Samlan Rd.)* has traces of original stucco on its upper terraces. ◼

Betel nuts

Betel nuts come from the areca palm, widely grown in Southeast Asia. A small piece of the areca palm's fruit is wrapped in a leaf of the betel pepper, along with lime, to cause salivation and release stimulating alkaloids. Cardamom or turmeric may be added for flavor and stimulation. Chewing betel nut produces a slight narcotic effect. Users carry their betel chew in boxes made of worked silver or brass, sometimes highly decorated. Antique betel-nut boxes are much prized collector's items. ◼

A walk through the heart of Chiang Mai

This walk avoids heavy traffic areas while giving you a chance to experience the different aspects of inner Chiang Mai, from the peace of the Chiang Mai First Church to the contrasting bustle of Worowat Market; the frantic pace of Tapae Road to the aura and quietude of the many temples along the way.

Wat Phra Sing was built in the 14th century as the religious center of the Lanna Kingdom.

Beginning at the **Chiang Mai First Church** on the eastern bank of the river, cross over the Nawarat Bridge, keeping to the northern (right-hand) side. As you reach the city side, turn right and continue along the pleasant, though usually fairly untidy riverside path, passing in front of the police station and onto the pedestrian overbridge, 50 yards (150 m) upriver.

Cross over the bridge, descend to the left, and then turn right at the bottom of the steps into **Warowot Market ❶**. Following this path from the bridge will take you past fresh seafood stalls, then across Wichayanon Road and through into the next section of the market, where fruit sellers have set up among the clothes, toys, and other stalls in a cheerful muddle. Feel free to wander deeper into the market on your own; provided you keep your bearings, it is easy enough to find your way back onto the main path.

Leave the main market building by the exit onto Kuangmane Road, and turn left. You may notice a Chinese influence here, and as you walk down Kuangmane Road you will come to the **Kuan U Shrine ❷** on your right. This small Chinese temple is open at sunrise every day *(closes 5 p.m.)*, and it is worth a look to experience a change from the more traditional Thai temples. Continue along Kuangmane Road, and turn right at the three-way intersection to come out at Tha Phae Road.

Busy Tha Phae Road is at the heart of Chiang Mai's commercial district. Along the road on the right side you will come to **Wat Saen Fang ❸**; be careful as you cross over Chang Moi Road, as the traffic switches over to the right side—be sure to look left first before you cross. Stay on Tha Phae Road. Farther down from Wat Saen Fang you will soon reach **Wat Chedowan ❹**. Wat

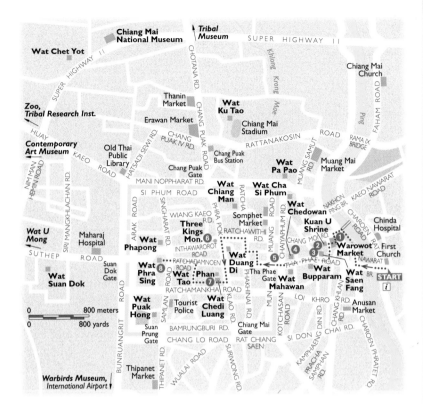

Mahawan, just across Tha Phae Road, is also worth seeing.

At the end of Tha Phae Road, you will find yourself in the more touristy Tha Phae Gate area. The walk continues through the rebuilt **Tha Phae Gate ⑤**—you may want to climb to the top of it for a look, before crossing over Mun Muang Road to continue up Ratchadamnoen Road, directly opposite. After passing the American University Alumni (A.U.A.) building and Chiangmai Fellowship Church, leave the main road and turn right into Rachadamnoen Soi 5. Turn left at the red cobbled path (Mun Muang Lane 5), then right at Ratcha Phakinai Road and left again at the traffic lights. Continue ahead until you arrive at the **Three Kings Monument ⑥**, a popular place of worship for the kings of the old Lanna Kingdom.

Continue southward along Phra Pok Klao Road to reach **Wat Chedi Luang ⑦** on the right, whose huge *chedi* is a long-term restoration project. Leave the temple by the

Also see area map p. 212 B2
► Chiang Mai First Church
2.5 miles (4 km)
1.5 hours
► Wat Pra Sing

NOT TO BE MISSED
- Warowot Market
- Wat Chedowan
- Tha Phae Gate
- Three Kings Monument
- Wat Chedi Luang
- Wat Phra Sing

back entrance so that you exit onto Jhaban Road. Walk just 30 yards (100 m) to your right, then turn left at the intersection, past the Chiang Mai Metropolitan Police Station and directly on to the last attraction of this walk, **Wat Phra Sing ⑧**, Chiang Mai's most famous temple complex. ∎

Chiang Mai museums

CHIANG MAI'S (AND THAILAND'S) HISTORY AND CULTURE are reflected in a number of museums scattered throughout the city. At these places you will encounter both modest and exuberant displays. Traditional national museums, displays of contemporary art, exhibitions of hill-tribe life, and presentations of the more offbeat can be found.

Chiang Mai National Museum

🅰 Map p. 219
✉ Hwy. 11
☎ 053-408568
🕐 Closed Mon.–Tues.
💲 $

This terra-cotta statue is part of the Chiang Mai National Museum's fine collection.

CHIANG MAI NATIONAL MUSEUM

This small but worthwhile museum on the outskirts of town, on the very busy "superhighway," is the main repository for the arts and crafts of Chiang Mai and Northern Thailand. The Lanna-style concrete building was opened in 1973 by the king and queen, and it was designed to be not only the guardian of regional arts but also an education center for both Thais and visitors.

The museum has been under reconstruction for several years, and the focus has been expanded to include displays on the natural and cultural history of the Lanna Kingdom, the trade and economy of recent centuries, and modern developments in banking, education, and public health. Among the more traditional themes, most of the classic Thai art movements are represented here, from early Mon sculpture to Bangkok-era styles, with an emphasis on local Lanna art.

As with most museums in Thailand, the Chiang Mai National Museum chiefly features bronzes, sculptures, and early pottery on the ground floor, and handicrafts and household goods on the upper floor. A pair of 15th-century pottery kilns has been installed on the grounds.

Displays on the ground floor include Sangkhalok ceramics, pottery shards discovered near Kanchanaburi (see p. 124) just after World War II, an impressive collection of Chiang Saen images, and terra-cotta figurines from the Haripunchai and Srivijayan Empires. Perhaps the most striking item is a massive Buddha head, uncovered at Wat Chedi Luang, in Chiang Mai, which—to judge from its impressive dimensions— must have been part of an enormous image.

Displays on the second floor are more utilitarian, but they do an excellent job of portraying the lifestyles of the ordinary Thai. Along with a small room devoted exclusively to Burmese-Shan arts, there are intriguing (if simple)

displays of betel-nut boxes, a richly carved ox cart, traditional coffin covers, a modest presentation on the hill tribes of Northern Thailand, and some examples of royal regalia, including giant Dongson drums and elaborately carved beds.

CHIANG MAI CONTEMPORARY ART MUSEUM

This historic city's most recent addition to its cultural scene is the concrete modern art museum on the grounds of Chiang Mai University. While the exterior belies the sensitivity of traditional Lanna architecture, the displays are quite impressive, as Chiang Mai is home to some of Thailand's most talented modern artists. Much of the artwork is generated by local students, with contributions from professional artists—both local and international.

The museum also sponsors art education workshops in both Thai and English.

WARBIRDS MUSEUM

Another recent addition to the local museums is the Warbirds— the collection of restored airplanes that occupies three hangers at Chiang Mai International Airport. The collection of primarily military aircraft is owned and operated by members of the Royal Thai Air Classics Association. Among the more interesting aircraft are a Douglas Dakota DC 3 and a Cessna Dragonfly A-37. Six Birddogs and T-28 Trojans make up the core of the collection.

The museum was the suggestion of Princess Chulabhorn's husband, who had admired an old Trojan, and had the derelict aircraft restored and reflown in 1991. In 1993, the association was registered as a foundation and

placed under the royal patronage of the king.

Visitors register at the front gate, where they must leave some form of identification, and then tour the classic aircraft with an escort. It is best to bring a Thai-speaker or guide with you, as the military guards here speak little, if any, English. The best time to visit is around 9 a.m. on Tuesday and Friday, when the maintenance team tests the engines of several of the old airplanes.

TRIBAL MUSEUM

In a beautiul location overlooking a lake, in the northern section of town, the small but fascinating Tribal Museum is a modern structure designed to resemble a Lanna-style *chedi*. It has displays about the major hill tribes of Northern Thailand (see pp. 234–35) and is an excellent place to visit for some research before participating in an organized trek.

The well-presented exhibits include a range of handicrafts, colorful costumes, textiles, musical instruments, and farming implements. English-language boards explain the histories and traditions of the major tribal groups of the area.

The museum also has exhibits on the contributions of the king and his family concerning the health and welfare of the hill tribes, and research projects sponsored by various government and non-governmental agencies.

Those with a particular interest in the hill tribes may also enjoy a visit to the **Tribal Research Institute** (*Chiang Mai University, tel 053-221933, closed weekends*). It has a modest display of hill-tribe culture, and a limited amount of research information is available in English. ∎

Chiang Mai Contemporary Art Museum
- 🅰 Map p. 219
- ✉ Nim Man Hemin Rd.
- ☎ 053-944833
- 🕐 Closed Mon.–Tues.

Warbirds Museum
- 🅰 Map p. 219
- ✉ Opposite entrance to Chiang Mai Inernational Airport
- ☎ 053-201538
- 🕐 Closed Sat.–Sun.

Tribal Museum
- 🅰 Map p. 219
- ✉ Chang Puak Rd., Ratchamangkala Park
- ☎ 053-221933
- 🕐 Closed Sun.
- 💲 $

Wat Ku Tao's chedi combines Burmese and Chinese architectural styles.

More places to visit in Chiang Mai

CHIANG MAI ZOO

Located on the western edge of town, at the base of the mountains, this is Thailand's second largest zoo. It has a reasonably good collection of local wildlife, including an abundance of monkeys and other creatures, such as crocodiles, miniature deer, and Asiatic elephants, always eager to pick up the occasional banana. The original ensemble of endangered animals was donated by a concerned Westerner, and the Thai government has made efforts to expand the zoo in recent years. Zoo conditions may still appear substandard to some visitors.
🅰 Map p. 219 ✉ Huay Kaeo Rd. ☎ 053-222479 💲 $

WAT CHET YOT

Among all the religious structures in Chiang Mai, perhaps the most significant in regional terms is this oddly constructed, seven-spired *chedi*. Wat Chet Yot dates from 1455 and, according to local tradition, was modeled after the famous Mahabodhi temple in India. Its religious importance derives from a convention held here by King Tilok in 1477, which commemorated the 2,000th year of the Buddhist era. All of the old gold ornamentation was stripped out during the following century by Burmese invaders, but Wat Chet Yot's 12 stucco figures of seated divinities—its main glory—have survived the ravages of time, making the *wat* an important stop for all visitors interested in the aristic heritage of the region.
🅰 Map p. 219 ✉ Superhighway ☎ 053-211464

WAT KU TAO

While this peculiar 17th-century structure may not be the most elegant in Chiang Mai, it certainly wins awards for its unique five-orbed chedi, which combines Burmese and Chinese architectural elements to enshrine the remains of a Burmese leader who once ruled the province. The five-melon monument is in an

Originally built in the 14th-century, Wat Suan Dok has been much restored and enlarged.

odd location, just north of the White Elephant Gate, up a poorly marked alley, and close to the Chiang Mai stadium.

Map p. 219   Chang Puak Rd.   053-211842

WAT SUAN DOK

Another significant site with ancient and modern relics is situated outside the old city walls, in the southwestern corner of Chiang Mai, along Suthep Road. Wat Suan Dok, the "monastery of the flowers," dates from 1383 and was constructed to honor a relic of Buddha—hair and a fragment of collarbone.

Today the largest building within the enclosure is a massive open-air *wihan* raised in 1932, housing a particularly fine collection of Buddhas, including the highly regarded 500-year-old **Phra Chao Kao Tue.** Dozens of gleaming white miniature chedis and cenotaphs adorn the neighboring garden— they entomb the remains of Chiang Mai nobles and important Buddhist leaders. Traditional Thai massage is provided by old women in the large wihan, which was erected

by the same Buddhist monk who inspired the construction of the hillside Wat Doi Suthep (see p. 226).

Map p. 219   Suthep Rd.   053-278304

WAT U MONG

Thai monks have traditionally constructed their temples, monasteries, and religious retreats either in the city or out in the country to escape the distractions of urban life. One of Thailand's most famous forest monasteries is Wat U Mong, at the edge of Chiang Mai, and at the base of a magnificent mountain. Established about 1380, it is still an active retreat for Buddhist pilgrims.

This fascinating destination, rarely visited by foreigners, has a welcome hall with a map of the site and Buddhist literature. On the site are dozens of tiny wooden huts, inhabited by robed monks, and some much older caves carved into the mountainside, where the most ascetic of residents choose to make their homes. Meditation classes in English are given here by a team of Western monks.

Map p. 219   Suthep Rd.   053-277248 ∎

National parks of the North

Northern Thailand's national parks are sparkling, cool, mountainous retreats, a world away from the tropical heat at lower altitudes. The best are easily accessible from Chiang Mai and make agreeably peaceful getaways.

The most renowned is **Doi Inthanon,** some 36 miles (58 km) southwest of Chiang Mai, on the road to Mae Sariang. The park was created to protect four of the Mae Ping's main tributaries and Thailand's highest mountain, a granite massif named after Chiang Mai's last ruling prince, which soars skywards to 8,400 feet (2,565 m). With its rivers and mountains, Doi Inthanon offers vast ranges of evergreen montane forests, acres of wildflowers in the spring, several impressive waterfalls, great views from the summit, and a range of interesting wildlife.

As the highest mountain in Thailand, Doi Inthanon is the only place where notable montane forests thick with oaks, chestnuts, and magnolias grow—vegetation more usually associated with temperate climates. The range of flora is extended by varieties that thrive in the cool, damp climate on the fog-enshrouded mountain, such as epiphytes, lichens and mosses, and orchids.

This protected area is also rich in birdlife, including blue-winged minlas, green cochoas, red-headed trogons, and green-tailed sunbirds, which congregate at the summit in a sphagnum bog, the only one in Thailand. Naturalists and bird-lovers come in droves to watch the nearly 400 bird species that make their home here. The park is also home to the Assamese macaque, monkeys and gibbons, and endangered mammals such as the Asiatic black bear and the Szechuan burrowing shrew.

After passing through the entrance gate, near the base of the long, winding road to the summit, visitors first encounter **Mae Klang Falls,** and then the spectacular **Vachiratarn Waterfall** on the Mae Klang River. With a total drop of 164 feet (50 m), Vachiratarn is one of the park's most exciting sights, and an excellent place to observe birds that favor rocky, rushing streams.

The road continues up the mountain, following the course of the Mae Klang River as it winds its way through deciduous and evergreen forests, to reach **Sriphum Falls** at the midway point. From Sriphum, the road continues past several Karen and Hmong villages, where the inhabitants operate an experimental farm, until it reaches the summit. The views are spectacular.

About 3 miles (4 km) before the summit is Phra Mahathat Naphamethanidon, built to commemorate the king's 60th birthday. The two marble chedis feature terra-cotta reliefs. Mountain views are spectacular.

Doi Suthep-Doi Pui National Park, covering some 100 square miles (261 sq km), is the pride of Chiang Mai, as few modern cities in Southeast Asia can boast such a splendid backdrop. The park includes two high mountains—Doi Pui and Doi Suthep— which rise majestically from the floor of Chiang Mai valley to 5,527 feet and 5,497 feet (1,685 m and 1,676 m) respectively.

Easily accessible and only 10 miles (16 km) from the historic capital, Doi Pui is thickly covered with a forest that includes deciduous and evergreen trees, with some semi-evergreen cover in the gullies and waterways at lower elevations. The park supports a remarkable flora, with over 2,000 species of flowering plants, some of which are unique to the park. Among the fauna are small mammals, some of the largest moths in the world, and a profusion of exotic birds, including the audacious blue magpie, the changeable hawk eagle, and the red-faced liocichla.

The park is well organized—you can pick up a map at the park headquarters (where there are accommodations in dormitories or bungalows) and enjoy a variety of hikes, including a challenging trail that leads past remote Hmong villages to the summit of Doi Pui. A funicular railway leads to the *wat* that stands on top of Doi Suthet (see p. 226). ∎

Monks view Vachiratarn Waterfall, one of the most breathtaking sights in Doi Inthanon National Park.

Around Chiang Mai

AS YOU WOULD EXPECT OF ONE OF THAILAND'S MAJOR tourist destinations, the area surrounding Chiang Mai is crowded with attractions, all easy to visit thanks to the city's excellent tourism infrastructure. You can choose from scenic, sometimes spectacular, drives into cool mountain areas, dozens of magnificent temples, and seemingly limitless shopping opportunities.

DOI SUTHEP–DOI PUI NATIONAL PARK

Several day excursions are possible from Chiang Mai. The most popular leads 10 miles (16 km) northwest to a mountain named after a highly revered hermit, who once lived on the slopes and inspired the construction of the winding road up to the temple. Doi Suthep rises to a summit elevation of 5,497 feet (1,676 m), while the temple—the primary destination—clings to the mountainside at a more modest 3,454 feet (1,053 m). Clean air and spectacular panoramic views are the big draws for this excursion, as well as a visit to the golden temple of **Wat Doi Suthep.**

The temple is reached via a monumental 304-step staircase, flanked by fantastical undulating *nagas.* Alternatively, you can make the trip via a restored tramway. Although the temple is modest by Thai standards, the site is highly venerated as it contains a sacred Buddha relic. The central stupa is the most dazzling structure in Northern Thailand.

Many visitors simply make the climb up to the temple and then return to town, but Doi Suthep has several other interesting attractions, including the beautifully tended rose and orchid gardens on the grounds of the **Phuping Royal Palace,** 3 miles (5 km) beyond the temple *(Doi Suthep Rd.).*

Three miles (5 km) farther again is the turnoff down to the small and scruffy **Doi Pui** Hmong village. Although the village is highly commercialized and almost exclusively geared to tourists, lifestyles remain traditional, and some interesting attractions have been specially built, including a replica opium den and a small museum dedicated to the northern hill tribes (see pp. 234–35). The village may be worth a visit if you are not intending to make a hill-tribe trek and see the real thing.

En route to Wat Doi Suthep is another modest attraction, **Monthathon Falls,** 8 miles (13 km) from Chiang Mai and reached by a winding, unsealed road that leads to the foot of the falls.

HANDICRAFT VILLAGES

Chiang Mai is well known as the handicrafts center of Southeast Asia, rivaled only by the Indonesian island of Bali. It's a wonderful place to shop for a mind-boggling array of items, including fabulous woodcarvings, fine filigree and silverwork, glazed ceramics, top-quality Thai silks, and other examples of crafts that have made this region so famous.

The best place to learn about these crafts—and empty your wallet—is along Highway 1006, between Chiang Mai and the silk-weaving village of **San Kamphaeng,** a 12-mile (18 km) stretch of road with over 50 major shops and factories. Here you can watch the craftsperson at work, and then, with some sharp bargaining

Doi Suthep–Doi Pui National Park
🗺 212 B2
Visitor information
✉ Tourism Authority of Thailand, 105/1 Chiang Mai-Lamphun Rd., Chiang Mai
☎ 053-248604 or 053-248607

skills, purchase his or her products at excellent prices (or at least less than you would pay in Bangkok). Although this district is highly commercialized and almost entirely dedicated to tourists, it is unquestionably the best place to watch the creation of silk, learn about the skills required for pounding out silver bowls, witness ceramics creation, and watch young women paint splashy flowers on bamboo umbrellas.

San Kamphaeng marks the end of the "handicraft highway" and makes for an excellent place to lunch and observe the local silk-weaving industry—and perhaps visit one of the large silk factories. A few miles before San Kamphaeng is the umbrella village of **Bo Sang,** so called because of its numerous

umbrella manufacturers. As well as thousands of painted umbrellas, the town's shops sell fans, straw handicrafts, silverware, bamboo and teak products, celadon, and lacquerware. Standards vary from tacky to excellent.

Several other villages near Chiang Mai produce handicrafts, including **Muang Kung,** 6 miles (10 km) south of Chiang Mai. The small village—just off Highway 108—has a reputation for the quality of its pottery, especially the giant water jugs (nam ton). Take a walk around, and you will notice potters shaping clay with wheels under their stilted homes. At **Hang Dong,** 8 miles (13 km) down Highway 108 from Chiang Mai, wickerware and, to a lesser degree, woodcarvings are for sale in

Gilded Wat Doi Suthep sits atop Doi Suthep mountain, promising fine aerial views of Chiang Mai on clear days.

its many stores and stalls. **Ban Tawai** and a clutch of nearby villages are famed for their woodcarvings, which are exported worldwide. Here, hundreds of houses and shops carve, chip, and sand wood into an incredible range of products—everything from delicate spoons to near life-size elephants. Ban Tawai also has several large factories that churn out impressive imitation antiques, which have fooled many a shopper.

Mae Sa Valley

🅰 212 B2

Visitor information

✉ Tourism Authority of Thailand, 105/1 Chiang Mai–Lamphun Rd., Chiang Mai

☎ 053-248604 or 053-248607

Queen Sirikit Botanical Gardens

✉ Old Sameong Rd., Mae Sa Valley

☎ 053-298179 or 053-298171

💲 $

Mae Sa Elephant Camp

✉ Mae Sa Valley

☎ 053-97060

💲 $$

MAE SA VALLEY

A wonderful day excursion, easily arranged at your hotel desk, can be made to the beautiful Mae Sa Valley, 17 miles (27 km) north of Chiang Mai, which features a number of attractions. A short way into the valley, several orchid farms and nurseries offer the chance to learn about the art of orchid cultivation. The biggest and most famous is the **Queen Sirikit Botanical Gardens,** which display a wide variety of orchids and other flora common to Northern Thailand. Several orchid farms have creatively expanded their offerings by adding small butterfly enclosures, thereby attracting both the fauna and the flora crowds.

Mae Sa Valley also has a small snake farm, with several shows scheduled daily. But the most popular stop is the **Mae Sa Elephant Camp,** situated in the middle of the valley, by a river and under the cool shade of a towering forest. Twice-daily shows take the elephants gently through their paces, with a display of training and bathing games in the river. The shows are followed by optional rides for the tourists. Elephants once hauled teak in Thailand, but now that logging has been sharply curtailed, tourism is the only form of employment left to them.

Shortly before the elephant camp, **Mae Sa Waterfall** is worth a stop. It tumbles down through the trees in eight steps, past a visitor center. The road continues through the valley in a counterclockwise direction to reconnect with Chiang Mai. This makes a full day of driving, through some very remote countryside. There are more orchid gardens to see, a waterfall, a Meo tribal village, another village with café and gasoline station, and a half-dozen mid-range resorts chiefly geared to local travelers. Eventually, the road comes out at the back of **Doi Suthep** (see p. 226), joining Highway 108 near Hang Dong.

ALONG THE CHIANG MAI–LAMPHUN ROAD

Several worthwhile attractions lie southeast of Chiang Mai along the road to the ancient Haripunchai capital of Lamphun. The old Chiang Mai–Lamphun Road is far more attractive than the newer trunk line, which provides faster access but misses most of the sights.

History enthusiasts may enjoy a visit to the diggings at **Wiang Kum Kam,** an ancient village 6 miles (10 km) out of Chiang Mai. Founded by King Mengrai and long forgotten after centuries of neglect, the lost town has been excavated and partly restored, to reveal extensive building foundations and significant religious structures, including early stupas and elegant Lanna-style *chedis.*

Just past the remains of the village is the **McKean Leper Institute,** established in 1908 by Presbyterian missionaries to treat what was then a fairly common disease. The grounds are spacious and splendidly set with magnificent trees, which soar over the small cottages where the patients live. Visitors are welcome

The many organized tours out of Chiang Mai include river rafting.

to tour the patient facilities, the medical clinics, and the historic church on a small island in the middle of the Ping River.

TO THE SOUTHWEST

Travelers heading southwest from Chiang Mai to Doi Inthanon National Park or onward to Mae Sariang or Mae Hong Son can also make some interesting stops. Just past the town of **San Pa Tong,** 15 miles (24 km) south of Chiang Mai, is a large collection of wooden pens where Northern Thailand's largest cattle market is held every Saturday morning. This traditional event has expanded in recent years into a gigantic flea market, selling Japanese electronic goods and the latest CD-Roms from Hollywood alongside the livestock.

The turnoff to Doi Inthanon National Park is marked by the small town of **Chom Thong**— 36 miles (58 km) south of Chiang Mai—and its magnificent and well-maintained Wat Phra That Si Chom Tong. The gilded Burmese chedi was built in 1451 and its bot about 55 years later. Also done in Burmese style, the bot is one of the most beautiful in Northern Thailand, highlighted with masterfully crafted woodcarvings along the eaves and inside the ceiling, which is supported by massive painted teak columns. The Lanna-style altar resembles a miniature *prasat*. In front of the altar are finely carved statues of Buddha. More Buddha images and antique Thai weaponry can be found in display cases in the room behind the altar. ∎

Mae Sariang

Mae Sariang

🗺 212 A1

Visitor information

✉ Tourist Police Office,
Singhanat Bamrung
Rd., Mae Hong Son

☎ 053-611952

ONE OF THE MOST POPULAR DRIVING ROUTES FROM Chiang Mai heads southwest, past the turnoff for Doi Inthanon National Park, to the sleepy little town of Mae Sariang. It then turns north up to popular Mae Hong Son, before completing the loop by returning to Chiang Mai via the lovely and rarely visited town of Pai. Most of this excursion passes through Mae Hong Son Province, one of the most mountainous regions in the country. This is also one of the most ethnically diverse districts in Thailand, with some dozen major hill tribes scattered among the hills and mountains, notably the Karen, Hmong, Lisu, and Lahu.

Elephants were once widely used to shift logged timber. Since logging was banned in 1989, the beasts are now more widely seen demonstrating these skills in elephant shows.

Mae Sariang, 117 miles (188 km) southwest of Chiang Mai, is a typical one-horse town with a handful of guesthouses and small cafés, many of which face the scenic Yuam River. There is not a lot to see, but it is a pleasant enough base from which to explore the area.

A quick stroll around town reveals several noteworthy temples, mostly constructed in Burmese-Shan style. Among them, both **Wat Sri Bunruang** (*Mae Sariang Rd.*) and the adjacent **Wat Chong Sung** (*Mae Sariang Rd.*) are the work of Burmese laborers, who composed the majority population here before the influx of Thais arrived in the early 20th century.

Mae Sariang's best example of Burmese monastic architecture is down by the bridge, at the sprawling **Wat Chong Kham** (*Wai Wueksa Rd.*). The original wooden roof was replaced with tin several decades ago.

Mae Sariang is a departure point for hikes to the hill-tribe villages (see pp. 234–35). Treks are organized by guesthouses in town and chiefly head north to visit the villages around **Mae La Noi** and **Khun Yuam,** roughly midway to Mae Hong Son. This district also has several large waterfalls and is famed for its profusion of yellow sunflowers in the spring.

The town is also a base for river-rafting journeys down the nearby **Salween, Thanlwin,** and **Yuam Rivers.** Most excursions start with a dusty truck ride down to a nearby waterway, from where rafts and noisy longtail boats head up and down the rivers, passing simple Myanmar (Burmese) villages, re-mote waterfalls, and logging camps with working elephants (despite the ban on logging imposed in 1989). ∎

Mae Hong Son

Mae Hong Son

212 A2

Visitor information

Tourist Police Office, Singhanat Bamrung Rd., Mae Hong Son

053-611952

A THRIVING COMMERCIAL ENCLAVE TUCKED AWAY IN THE mountains near the Myanmar (Burma) border, Mae Hong Son has recently developed into a major tourist destination, largely in response to a government-sponsored campaign to portray the town and region as Thailand's mystical and hidden Shangri-La. While the hype doesn't quite match the reality, Mae Hong Son, 230 miles (369 km) south of Chiang Mai, is an ideal center from which to explore the mountains and rivers, to enjoy trekking to hill-tribe villages, and to visit nearby caves and waterfalls. The city is well supplied with guesthouses and hotels, cafés and restaurants, and souvenir shops.

Mae Hong Son started as an elephant herding camp in 1831, and it wasn't until the completion of the tortuous road south from Chiang Mai in 1965 that either Thai or Western tourists made the long journey to this extremely isolated spot. In fact, the village had long been a place of exile for disgraced government officials, who dubbed it the "Siberia of Thailand." Today, the place is jammed with backpackers, vacationers, travel agencies, and local entrepreneurs offering trekking and anything else they can dream up to part visitors from their cash.

Most of the attractions can easily be seen in a full day of walking, starting with the striking **Chong Kham Lake,** just two blocks off the main road. This placid lake was originally the elephants' bathing pool, but today is mostly the focus of a local fitness park, and a number of budget guesthouses now surround it.

On the far side of Chong Kham Lake stands a pair of extremely striking temples constructed in classic Burmese style, with multi-tiered roofs, elaborate filigree woodwork on the facades and lintels, and gilded images of Burmese spirit gods. The 19th-century **Wat Chong Klang** is notable for its array of 35 *Jataka-*

inspired wooden figures, which were carved in Burma and brought to Mae Hong Son in 1857. The images range from Buddhas to galloping horses. The temple just to the east is **Wat Chong Kham,** built by the Shan people about 200 years ago. This large monastery features a huge, 16-foot-high (5 m) seated Buddha, a tiered roof, and flamboyant woodwork.

Dramatic views over the valley can be enjoyed from the hilltop of

A Hmong woman sells her wares at Mae Hong Son, now one of the North's most popular tourist locations.

Temperate fruits such as tomatoes can be grown in the North's cooler climes. Here, a family of Karen sell their crop.

Doi Kong Mu, at the western end of town, where two *chedis* were constructed in the mid-19th century to mark the admission of the town into the Thai Kingdom. **Wat Doi Kong Mu** reveals its Burmese origins in its exterior construction and immaculately carved, white alabaster Buddha, which is placed on a gilded palanquin. The hike up the steps of the hill is exhausting, but the views over the misty valley in the morning are unforgettable.

It's well worth visiting the two temples at the base of Doi Kong Mu for their unusual construction and their highly venerated Buddhas. **Wat Moytu** is well known for its magnificent bronze Buddha and four highly stylized chedis that are covered from top to bottom with small chambers. These would once have held Buddhist amulets. Just a few steps down the road is **Wat Phra Nan,** a 19th-century Burmese-style temple complex constructed by a Shan ruler to house a massive reclining Buddha. The statue is quite different from its Thai counterparts, with its realistic, heavily painted face. The temple also has a small museum, and a pair of fierce Burmese stone lions stand at the base of an old footpath leading up the mountain.

Across the road from Wat Phra Nan is **Wat Kham Khor,** another delightful treasure trove of Burmese religious architecture and curiosities. Usually missed by visitors, this fascinating and strange place has countless Shan-style Buddhas, old paintings badly in need of restoration, black and white photographs that date from the early days of Mae Hong Son, and a carved peacock throne that is thought to be over a hundred years old.

The collapsing, multiroofed wooden temple of **Wat Hua Wiang,** in the middle of Mai Hong Son, is important for its highly venerated brass Buddha, which was made in Burma and hauled here across the mountains in the 19th century. The nearby market is a good place to buy local produce, including the cigars known as cheroots. ∎

Around Mae Hong Son

TREKKING TO THE REMOTE HILL-TRIBE VILLAGES IS particularly popular around Mae Hong Son. The local population is made up mainly of Shans, with other minority tribes including Karen, Lawa, Lahu, Lisu, and Meo. Most guesthouses, hotels, and tour agencies can arrange treks to these villages, which are far less commercialized than those near Chiang Mai and Chiang Rai.

Forested hills, rivers, and hill-tribe villagers make Mae Hong Son a popular trekking destination.

There are some commercialized attractions south of Mae Hong Son, including the **Pha Pang Hot Springs,** where visitors can bathe in the naturally hot water and lunch at one of the small cafés in the park. Several river-rafting companies operate from the resorts along the banks of the lazy **Pai River.** Two-hour trips are the standard, but longer odysseys are sometimes offered all the way to the Myanmar (Burma) border and beyond.

Most of the following destinations are off the main Mae Hong Son–Pai road and are best reached on an escorted tour or with private transportation such as a rented motorcycle or chartered mini-truck. The Shan village of **Na Soi** has been converted into a questionable tourist stop for the exploitation of Paduang women, whose necks are elongated by brass rings and who cheerfully pose for photographs after you've paid an admission fee to the village. This barbaric practice had died out, but has now been revived for the tourist market (see pp. 340–41).

Pha Sua Waterfalls provide a fine escape on a hot day but are at their best in the rainy season. Beyond the falls is the busy Hmong-Chinese village of **Mae Aw,** where opium production and trafficking were once the primary occupations. Caution should be exercised in this notoriously unstable region, which is just opposite the former army camp of opium king Khun Sa. ■

THAM PLA
Fed a steady diet of papaya by eager visitors, enormous carp swim in placid pools at Tham Pla "fish cave," 10 miles (16 km) north of Mae Hong Son on Highway 108. Just across the road is a vast limestone cave that can be explored with the aid of local guides.

Northern hill tribes

For many visitors, the highlight of a tour of Northern Thailand is to trek and spend time with the semi-nomadic hill tribes, the ethnic groups that inhabit the remote mountains. Hill-tribe trekking is well established in centers such as Chiang Mai.

Called *chao khao,* or mountain people by the lowland Thais, the tribes are not a homogenous group, but a series of separate cultural entities with distinct languages, religious beliefs, forms of dress, historical traditions, and even styles of architecture. Estimates of their total population vary—figures range from 500,000 to 800,000. The Thai government recognizes six major groups (Akha, Hmong, Karen, Lahu, Lisu, and Mien), while the Tribal Research Institute in Chiang Mai goes with ten, plus ten smaller subtribes.

Whatever term is attached to these people—hill tribes, mountain people, ethnic minorities—all are believed to have migrated south from Tibet, Myanmar (Burma), and China since the late 19th century, to escape famine, warfare, and the discrimination that has plagued these various groups since time immemorial. Despised by the lowland Thais, these displaced groups moved into the mountains of the North, living a nomadic existence of slash-and-burn farming and often supporting themselves through the cultivation of opium, a practice that has largely been eliminated since the early 1980s. Most are now agriculturists and settled in remote villages, still with remarkably little communication with the outside world.

Akha (Ekaw)

The Akha are distinguished by the dazzling costumes still worn by the women. Dark, long-sleeved jacket, skirt, and leggings are adorned with brilliant stitching and beadwork, with a sash of silver coins and a headdress of silver baubles and colored ribbon. Like most hill tribes, the Akha are animists who believe in the power of ghosts, nature, and departed ancestors, and so perform rituals, including the sacrifice of animals. Their relatively low level of education and refusal to integrate into Thai society have made them the poorest tribe, most discriminated against by the others.

Hmong (Meo)

The second largest group is the Hmong, who live largely around Chiang Mai and Tak Provinces and are often seen in the local night

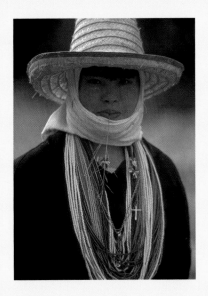

Thailand's hill-tribe people number between 500,000 and 800,000 and include the Akha (far left), the Lahu (left), the Karen (Pwo, above left), and the Palung (above right).

markets, selling their handicrafts, exquisite needlework, and tribal clothing. The women are notable for their bulky hairstyles, enhanced by hairpieces. Hmong, often seen on treks, divide themselves into the White and Blue subdivisions, based on the favored colors of their traditional costumes.

Karen (Yang or Kariang)

The largest hill tribe is the Karen, who are subdivided into smaller groups, including the Sgaw near Mae Hong Son, the Pwo south of Mae Sariang, and the Kayahs in Myanmar. Trekkers will probably notice the more obvious divisions based on the color of their clothing—White Karen, Black Karen, and Red Karen. The women are noted for their skillfully woven garments, the men for their tattoos. The Karen are a sophisticated group, which generally lives in the lowlands and practices crop rotation.

Lahu (Musser)

The Lahu are among the most assimilated of northern hill tribes, allowing them to move into the Thai mainstream and gain a degree of economic independence. A majority of these either animist or Christian peoples belong to the Black Lahu or Red Lahu linguistic groups, with a minority speaking variations on the Yellow Lahu dialect. Traditional costumes are black, with brilliant embroidery.

Lisu (Lisa)

The hill tribe with the greatest prosperity, as reflected by the conditions of their villages, is the Lisu, who are recognized for their business acumen and enterprising spirit. Their wealth is also evident in their beautiful and stylish clothing—blue skirts, red blouses, and extravagant turbans decorated with long strands of beads and multicolored yarn. All this is complemented by profuse silver decorations that cover almost the entire neck and chest of Lisu women.

Mien (Yao)

The Mien closely follow their origins in their use of Chinese script, obedience to the Taoist religion, and creation of Chinese-inspired scrolls that function as portable icons (similar to Tibetan *tankas*). Mien women are very stylish dressers in their bulbous black turbans, distinctive red boas, and richly embroidered baggy pants. ■

Tham Lot National Park

You need to take a boat ride to reach higher ground in the cavernous Tham Lot.

THE STUPENDOUS CAVES OF THAM LOT NATIONAL PARK attract an increasing number of visitors on the journey between Mae Hong Son and Pai. Most come to explore the park's most famous cave, Tham Lot, a breathtaking cavern wonderland of stalactites and stalagmites, originally cut by the Nam Lang River.

Tham Lot National Park

🅰 212 A3

Visitor information

✉ Tourism Authority of Thailand, 105/1 Chiang Mai–Lamphun Rd., Chiang Mai

☎ 053-248604 or 053-24860 (fax)

💲 $$

A labyrinth of auxiliary river canyons snakes off in all directions from the main chamber of Tham Lot, increasing the fascination of exploration. The intriguing journey through this cave is negotiated by boat—boatmen wait inside the cave—but with some wading involved. Guides are necessary for tours of Tham Lot and the dozen or so other caves in the park. You will find guides at the entrance to the park, or they can be hired at nearby guesthouses or in the town of Soppong, 5 miles (8 km) from the park. Soppong is also where you arrange transportation to the caves.

The caves are also famous for the teakwood coffins discovered here, believed to have been carved thousands of years ago by Lawa tribespeople, who inhabited the region long before the arrival of the Thais. For many years, locals believed that the mysterious coffins

Spirit Cave so important is the antiquity of the plant and seed remains, which were almost certainly cultivated. If Gorman's theories are correct, what is now Northern Thailand may well have been home to the earliest agriculturalists in Asia, more than 10,000 years ago.

It is very exciting to be at Tham Lot at dusk, when hundreds of thousands of Himalayan swiftlets swirl into the exit chamber of the river cave to roost, while thousands of bats fly out for their night's hunting—an impressive changing of the guard. All the while, large bat-eating hawks soar in the air above, hoping for a kill, while the sounds of the jungle mix with the incessant squeaks of the birds.

Its relatively easy access and calm waters make exploration of Tham Lot a breeze, but serious spelunkers can also explore many other caves in this remote corner. With the services of a professional guide, you can delve into the wonders of **Tham Nam Lang,** a 12-mile-long (19 km) cave that is one of the longest in Southeast Asia. Some years ago, a group of four Australian spelunkers climbed down into the cave, which runs almost half a mile (1 km) below the surface, walking through the darkness of the subterranean world and exploring vast chambers larger than football fields. They were lost for several days but fortunately managed to retrace their steps and emerge to safety. Their experience should serve as a warning to all.

Another challenging cave is the **Spirit Well,** named after its shape and intimidating dimensions. At almost 300 feet (91 m) across and more than 600 feet (182 m) deep, it is the largest known natural hole in Thailand. ■

Magnificent stalagmites and stalactites fill parts of Tham Lot.

had been carved by spirits who left behind these ungainly monuments, which seem to resemble rough dugout canoes. However, the spirit theory was thrown out after the archaeological work of American historian and archaeologist Chester Gorman, who excavated a small coffin cave near the Myanmar (Burma) border in the 1960s and found evidence of ancient human habitation.

Digging through layers of earth to the bedrock floor of the cave, Gorman discovered carbonized plant and animal remains, pottery shards, and stone tools. These were carbon-dated to show the slow evolution from basic hunting and gathering to the beginnings of agriculture, ceramics, and advanced stone production. What makes this

Pai & around

THIS SUPERFICIALLY UNEXCITING LITTLE TOWN IS SET IN A stunning location in a broad valley flanked by green mountains—a genuine beauty spot. This is one of the best places in the country to escape the tourist crowds and simply enjoy the wonders of nature, relaxing with almost nothing to do—probably the three sweetest words to any traveler who has spent too much time rushing from temple to temple, trying to absorb all the culture and sights. The Thais themselves are firm believers in the merits of *sanuk* (fun) and *mai pen rai* (never mind), and you'd be hard pressed to find a town that better exemplifies these traits than Pai, so take advantage of it and unwind in a setting of extraordinary natural beauty.

Some treks include rafting trips down the Pai River.

Pai
◭ 212 A2
Visitor information
✉ Tourism Authority of Thailand, 105/1 Chiang Mai–Lamphun Rd., Chiang Mai
☎ 053-248604 or 053-248605 (fax)

Most visitors to this small town, almost midway between Mae Hong Son and Chiang Mai, spend their days sitting on the porch of their guesthouse contemplating nature or thinking over where they might try a bowl of spicy chicken soup that evening (fast food has no place here!). Those with more motivation might wander over to the local market and inspect the chickens, or head down to the river and see if the fish are jumping. Pai is that kind of town.

Pai has just three streets and a few alleys to connect them. There's a bridge over the slow-flowing Pai River, as well as the necessary facilities such as a bus stop and post office, plus a handful of small travel agencies that can arrange local treks to hill-tribe villages and afternoon elephant rides. A few places near town might be worth a quick visit, but don't concern yourself if you feel inspired instead to spend your day lounging around your guesthouse.

A half-hour stroll west of town *(take Rajadamrung Rd. over the Pai River and continue along the adjoining road)* is the modern **Wat Phra That Mae Yen**, situated on top of a hill, with fine views over the Pai Valley on a clear and crisp morning. Late sleepers may

consider waiting until dusk to climb the 350-step staircase to enjoy a spectacular sunset over the distant mountains.

A welcome soak can be enjoyed in the evening at the **Tha Pai Hot Springs,** in a pleasant park along the same road as Wat Phra That Mae Yen, and about 5 miles (8 km) southeast of Pai.

AROUND PAI

After a few days of relaxation, some visitors elect to explore the surrounding countryside. Trekking and river rafting are the most popular activities, and all the necessary arrangements can be made locally.

Hiking around Pai is delightful as the region is less "trekked out" than Chiang Mai and Chiang Rai. Without an airport to shuttle in legions of visitors, the area remains a quieter trekking destination than even Mae Hong Son (see pp. 231–32).

Treks typically leave in the early morning and head northward, with overnight stops in Shan, Black Lahu, and Lisu villages. Some of the treks include either a short rafting trip down the **Pai River** or two hours' ride on the back of an elephant. However, if such gaudy tourism does not appeal, it is easy

enough to avoid any trek that includes these activities. Serious hiking enthusiasts can join a seven-day trek from Pai all the way down to Mae Hong Son, cutting through an interior district rarely seen by foreign visitors.

Rafting down the Pai River is perhaps the most popular diversion here, especially during the rainy months from July to December, when the river picks up some speed and produces some fairly exciting rapids. The rafting companies that operate from Pai are still in their early stages and generally use primitive bamboo contraptions rather than rubber boats. Unfortun-ately the bamboo sometimes disintegrates in the rapids, leaving passengers floating down the river. Fortunately, a few companies are starting to use rubber rafts as it is becoming more difficult and expensive to find bamboo in the jungles of Northern Thailand.

One of the best rafting adventures is a three-day excursion on rubber boats from Pai to Mae Hong Son, including stops at several waterfalls, caves, and a hot springs near the central camp, which is managed by the rafting company Thai Adventure Rafting *(tel 053-277178)*. The trip also passes through remote canyons and races at times down rapids that are graded at Class 3.

There are several elephant camps located around the town, offering rides through the local jungle. The most popular operation is to the southeast of Pai, near the hot springs. ■

A ride from one of Pai's elephant camps provides an excellent opportunity to appreciate the area's spectacular landscape.

North of Chiang Mai

MANY VISITORS HEADING NORTH FROM CHIANG MAI take a bus or private taxi directly to Chiang Rai. The adventurous traveler, however, may favor the more exotic route to Tha Ton, followed by a riverboat trip down to Chiang Rai, or even a motorcycle journey through the heart of the Golden Triangle (see p. 244) to Chiang Rai via Mae Salong.

CHIANG DAO ELEPHANT TRAINING CENTER

The excellent elephant camp on the Ping River, just south of Chiang Dao and 45 miles (72 km) north of Chiang Mai, is one of several places of interest on the road from Chiang Mai to Tha Ton. Thailand now has many elephant camps where you can watch the elephants display log-rolling and other talents once used in the harvesting of teak. But few are blessed with such a lovely forest environment as Chiang Dao. After the amusing and fascinating elephant demonstration, you can take a short elephant ride or sign up for the bamboo-raft excursions down the adjacent Ping River.

THAM CHIANG DAO

Chiang Dao is a small but active trading town, with the standard collection of shops and services. A narrow road leads west toward an immense limestone mountain called **Doi Chiang Dao,** at 7,500 feet (2,285 m) the third largest peak in the country. Tucked away at the base of this mountain is Tham Chiang Dao, several caves that—while they may not compare with those at Tham Lod National Park (see pp. 236–37)—are worth a quick inspection if you have private transportation.

Entrance to the caves is made from the lower parking lot, which is itself of some interest for its massive tamarind tree, old Burmese-style *chedi,* and small pool filled with giant carp. A covered stairway leads from the parking lot up to a series of caves filled with dozens of sacred Buddha statues, including several donated by Shan pilgrims who migrated over the years from their home in Myanmar (Burma) to new residences in Northern Thailand.

Tham Chiang Dao has two major caverns and several smaller openings, best explored with the guides—and their lanterns—who wait near the entrance. **Tham Num** features several impressive Buddhas illuminated by floodlights and some natural sunlight, while **Tham Ma** is a completely darkened cave set with stalactites and stalagmites, imaginatively named after their odd shapes.

THA TON

The road north from Chiang Mai reaches Tha Ton at a bend in the **Kok River,** a medium-sized body of slow-moving water that demarcates the southern boundary of the infamous Golden Triangle (see p. 244). Most travelers leave Chiang Mai in the morning, visit some of the natural attractions along the route, and overnight in Tha Ton, then depart the next morning for the river journey down the Kok to Chiang Rai.

Tha Ton is a very small, sleepy village set in a marvelous riverbank location, with soaring mountains to the north and west. Guesthouses and cafés are located on the road that faces the river, while more luxurious appointments are across

Chiang Dao Elephant Training Center
- 212 B2
- Hwy. 107 between Mae Taeng and Chiang Dao
- 053-862037
- $$

the bridge on the northern bank of the river. Looming over the town from a northern hillside are an immense white Buddha on the grounds of **Wat Tha Ton** and another gigantic golden Buddha farther up the hill. It's a long and tiring hike to reach them, though you will be rewarded with wonderful views over Tha Ton, the river, and the Golden Triangle.

It is possible to trek from here, without the need for a guide, to plenty of the lower elevation hilltribe villages, though walkers should exercise some caution as this region remains popular with opium smugglers. Few travelers are bothered by the local entrepreneurs, but avoid asking too many questions or photographing heavily laden mini-trucks.

KOK RIVER JOURNEY

For 30 years, travelers have stopped off at Tha Ton to join tours on the large bamboo rafts that make their way north to Chiang Rai on the Kok River, past small settlements in a region once strongly associated with the Golden Triangle.

Commercialization has perhaps reduced the romance factor on this river experience—and noisy longtails have largely replaced the old bamboo rafts—but this still remains one of the best little river trips in Thailand and certainly beats the mundane bus ride. One passenger boat leaves Tha Ton daily, but you can also charter boats for a reasonable price. Such boats give you more deck space and some flexibility when stopping at villages along the way. ■

The Kok River winds past Wat Tha Ton. Climb the hill to a gilded Buddha for the best views.

Chiang Rai & around

THIS IS ONE OF THE OLDEST CITIES IN THAILAND, established in 1262 by King Mengrai as the centerpiece of the first independent kingdom in the country, and heart of the Lanna Kingdom. Yet, after just 34 years of glory, Mengrai moved his capital south to Lamphun and then finally to Chiang Mai. Chiang Rai largely fell into disuse and was fought over by Siamese and Burmese until 1786, when it was finally incorporated into the Siamese Kingdom.

Lying 112 miles (180 km) northeast of Chiang Mai, Chiang Rai is a medium-size city with plentiful guesthouses, hotels, and cafés, nondescript urban architecture, and a handful of more interesting sights in the historic quarter on the banks of the Kok River. The town is reasonably compact and can be toured in a single day, perhaps before heading off for a trekking adventure (see below).

Most visitors start with a look at **Wat Phra Kaeo** *(Trirat Rd.)*, a locally venerated temple as it was once home to the Emerald Buddha, now housed in the identically named temple in Bangkok (see pp. 69–72). A model of the sacred image formerly displayed here has been moved to its own **Ha Phra Kaeo** (Jewel Buddha Hall), but the distinguished old wooden *bot* is worth a close inspection. The structure dates from 1890 and displays a large early Lanna-style Buddha statue.

Several other minor temples are worth a look, including **Wat Phra Sing** *(Singhakhrai Rd.)*, with its reproduction of the Phra Sing Buddha image from Chiang Mai; the seven-spired *chedi* at **Wat Chet Yot** *(Chet Yot Rd.)*, and a modern hilltop temple called **Wat Doi Chom Thong** *(Winitchaikul Rd.)*, which has particularly good views over the Kok River.

Probably more intriguing than these modest temples is the

Population and Community Development Association (P.C.D.A.) **Hill-tribe Education Center** *(620 Thanalai Rd., tel 053-719167)*, where volunteers from a non-governmental organization can help with questions about political and economic conditions of the hill tribes. The center has a small handicraft showroom and bookstore, and a very informative museum. Tribal craftwork can be bought here.

TREKKING AROUND CHIANG RAI

Most travelers use Chiang Rai as a base for visiting the hill-tribe villages in the vicinity (see pp.234–35). Over 20 agencies and guesthouses provide escorted trekking, which takes place chiefly in the rolling hills around **Doi Tung, Mae Salong,** and **Chiang Khong,** near the Mekong River.

You can undertake your own self-guided treks to hill-tribe villages with minimal planning, as the hills around Chiang Rai have been walked for years, and everyone in the area is familiar with independent trekkers. Route options include a river journey up the **Kok**—trekkers can strike out without a guide and follow well-marked paths from villages such as **Ban Ruammit.** Another option is to start from any of the popular hillside guesthouses west of **Mae Chan** or in Mae Salong.

Chiang Rai
🗺 212 C3
Visitor information
✉ Tourism Authority of Thailand, 448/16 Singhaklai Rd., Amphoe Muang, Chiang Rai
☎ 053-717433

MAE SALONG

This remote village, about two hours northwest of Chiang Rai, has an intriguing history. After their defeat in China by Mao Tse-tung's (1893–1976) Communists in 1949, members of the Chinese Nationalist Army—also called the Kuomintang (K.M.T.)—isolated in Yunnan Province, headed across the border to Myanmar (Burma) and Thailand, many settling in Mae Salong. In the early 1950s the K.M.T. received financial support and military equipment from the C.I.A. to stem the Communist threat. The group began taking over the Golden Triangle opium trade and by 1967 controlled 90 percent of the market in Thailand. A number of battles between rival groups loosened the K.M.T.'s control.

When opium warlord Khun Sa was driven into exile across the border into Myanmar in the 1980s, the town took on a new name, Santikhiree ("hill of peace") and a fresh identity.

So nowadays Mae Salong is no longer the lawless, opium-smuggling capital of Thailand that it once was. But it still looks like a pretty bamboo village somewhere in China's Yunnan, and there is a Chinese feel to the place rather than anything remotely Thai.

Signs of Chinese influence include the continued use of the Mandarin language by many residents and architectural features such as Chinese talismans and ying-yang mirrors. Tea, cabbages, and herbal medicines have replaced the opium crops. ∎

A modern temple high up in Mae Salong provides spectacular views of forested mountains.

Golden Triangle & Sop Ruak

🄰 212 C3

Visitor information

✉ Tourism Authority of Thailand, 448/16 Singhaklai Rd., Chiang Rai

☎ 053-717433

Golden Triangle & Sop Ruak

DESCRIBING THE EXPANSE OF HILLS AND MOUNTAINS OF North Thailand where it borders on Laos and Myanmar, the name Golden Triangle conjures an air of mystery and excitement, serving for many years as the hot buzzword for spy novels, drug movies, and lurid magazine articles about opium warlords and renegade armies.

The Golden Triangle, once famous as an opium-growing area, is now a major tourist destination.

The Golden Triangle's traditional apex is a small village called Sop Ruak, but the actual area spreads over hundreds of miles, covering a vast region that for years was the world's center of the opium and heroin trade. Most of the opium cultivation has moved across the border into Myanmar (Burma) and Laos, where small-scale farmers continue to produce much of the world's illegal opiates, which are then smuggled down to Chiang Mai and Bangkok, and from there on to the West.

Unfortunately, a recent growth of mass tourism has largely destroyed whatever aesthetic or romantic appeal Sop Ruak once possessed. Those lonely nights in some simple wooden hut, gazing out over the Triangle under a full moon, are but a distant memory. Luxury hotels are now the norm, and most visitors to Sop Ruak are brought here on tour buses, with just enough time to take a few photos and purchase a few trinkets from the local vendors. Fake hill-tribe children in snappy new costumes pose for the tourists, while the owners of the luxury accommodations desperately put out signs advertising huge discounts on their largely empty white-elephant hotels.

A stake was driven through the heart of the town a few years ago when, just over the border in Myanmar, on the spit of land that marks the exact tip of the Golden Triangle, Thai investors opened a massive hotel and casino complex geared to wealthy Thai and Chinese gamblers.

After decades of romance and intrigue, the reputation of the Golden Triangle should be laid to rest. ∎

Mae Sai

THE GOLDEN TRIANGLE AS TYPIFIED BY SOP RUAK MAY rank low in the authenticity stakes, but several other places nearby are worth exploration, including Mae Sai, the northernmost town in Thailand. Mae Sai is a large commercial enclave set with concrete hotels and modern shopping complexes, and yet it has far more mystery and romance than Sop Ruak, thanks to its location at the bridge crossing to Myanmar (Burma).

Mae Sai
✉ 212 C3
Visitor information
✉ Tourism Authority of Thailand, 448/16 Singhaklai Rd., Chiang Rai
☎ 053-717433

Mae Sai's focal point is the **bridge,** which crosses the Sai River to the Burmese town of **Tachilek.** The bridge buzzes constantly with traffic and traders who bring with them the exotic products of Myanmar, such as marionettes and antiques, fake jade Buddhas and mouse-ear mushrooms, sweet orange wine and peacock tails, stuffed armadillos and Mandalay cheroots. Some want to tell your fortune, others to provide healing reflexology treatment on your feet. Beggars plead for baht. Great masses of Burmese move across into Thailand, while Thais and foreign visitors can cross with little difficulty into Myanmar. Foreigners, after leaving their passports at Burmese immigration, receive permits and can pass into Tachilek. This is a great place to spend some time, even if you're not intending to make the crossing.

DOI TUNG

Visitors with private transportation may enjoy a scenic drive along the winding road that leads from Mae Sai up into the mountains to the west. About midway between Mai Sai and Mae Chan, a road heads west to Doi Tung, passing several Shan, Akha, and Lahu villages before reaching the tenth-century monastery of **Wat Phra That Doi Tung,** restored in the early 20th century. The shrine, with its fat Chinese Buddha statue, is not overly impressive, but the 11-mile

(18 km) drive from the main highway is an amazing journey, with wonderful views when visibility is good.

A short distance away from the monastery is **Doi Tung Royal Villa,** a summer palace constructed in 1988 for the king's mother. Up to

her death in 1995, she was very active in reforestation projects and in encouraging local hill-tribe farmers to raise alternative crops to opium. It was hoped that the presence of the royal family would move the opium fields back into Myanmar, away from the public eye. Although drug trafficking has been substantially reduced, visitors are advised to keep to main roads and trek only with a local guide. ■

The Mekong River and its rich bounty separate Mae Sai, in Thailand, from Myanmar (Burma). Visitors can cross the river for a short visit to Tachilek.

Orchids

Thailand is a land of sensual beauty, personified by its most famous flower, the orchid. Thailand's orchid industry is dominated today by a handful of large corporations near Bangkok, such as the Bangkok Flower Center, and by the many smaller operations in the Mae Rim Valley, just north of Chiang Mai. These smaller farms are excellent places to see the cultivation process and pick up some sprays to take back home.

Orchid refers to any member of the family Orchidaceae from the order Orchidales, a range of flowering plants that includes up to 800 genera of orchids and at least 35,000 documented species. Along with the obviously erotic shapes of the flower, the word orchid also has a male sexual connotation, for it is derived from the Greek word *orchis,* for "testicle," after the shape of the root tubers of some species. Orchids in Thailand are incredibly resilient and can be found from sea level up to 3,300 feet (1,000 m). Some grow on the floors of rain forests hidden from the sun, while others thrive in the arid plateau of Northeastern Thailand. They sprout from the ground, attach to trees, or grow out of crevices in mountain rocks.

The export of refigerated orchids started in the 1950s and now brings in over $100 million annually, with the primary markets in Japan, Europe, and the United States. Despite the fact that orchids are strikingly abundant in tropical countries such as Thailand, the industry remained largely unexploited until the mid-1980s, when local horticulturists decided to challenge the dominance of Singapore in this field. They soon discovered that the drier climate of Thailand was superior for orchid cultivation, and orchid farms boomed.

The major genus of the orchid family is the *Epidendrum.* These are mainly wild orchids with over 1,000 species. The next largest genus is the *Dendrobrium,* which can found as far north as the Himalayas and as far south as Australia. This group contains 900 species. Most species in the strikingly colorful *Cattleya* genus are hybrids, ranging in hue from violet and yellow to cream colored. The species of the *Cymbidium* group—of which there are about 40—are prized for multiple blooms found on one stem and their longevity. The *Brassavola* genus flowers are generally white and fragrant, and feature heavily fringed lips on the edge of the blossom.

Cut at dawn, flowers like these (far left, purple orchid; above left, yellow slipper; above, *Dendrobium*) are on sale the next day in San Francisco, London, and Tokyo.

Thai orchid growers concentrated on the production of *Dendrobium,* one of the few genus of orchids that can produce flowers within a single year and up to 30 orchid sprays within that time. (Most orchids produce only three sprays per year, leading to lower production and higher costs.) Another great advantage to *Dendrobium* sprays is their ability to live without water for up to a month, and the fact that the plants continue to blossom year round. Within a decade, Thailand had become the largest exporter of tropical orchids in the world.

Orchids can last for several weeks with proper care and refrigeration, but the finest flowers are those cut in the early morning hours inside vast cultivation sheds, packed in cardboard boxes with moisturizing agents, and then trucked to the Bangkok International Airport at Don Muang for immediate export.

To remain successful in the face of fierce competition from Japan and other countries, Thai orchid growers must not only run their export operations with military precision, but also be prepared to change their planting, cultivation, and export styles according to international trends. Throughout the 1990s, many of the more common orchid types declined in price as worldwide markets were flooded with an oversupply of classic favorites, such as the purple "Madame Pompadour"

Dendrobium. Faced with falling prices, cultivators shifted to more exotic species to maintain profit margins, including the *Mokkara, Alanda, Vanda,* and *Cattleya* genera.

Always seeking to maintain and perhaps improve profit margins in the highly competitive orchid industry, orchid farmers have recently moved into the world of controversial technology—the cloning of orchids into perfectly identical plantlets. Less complicated and headline grabbing than cloning sheep or dinosaurs, orchid cloning was quickly recognized as superior to seed reproduction, as it halved the time needed for maturation and ensured perfect production of disease-resistant plants. Cloning also provides the mechanism to produce exact replicas of the most attractive—and hence most profitable—species of the plants.

Knowledge gained in orchid cloning has spilled over into other important areas of cultivation, notably growing and exporting asparagus, decorative ferns, and exotic fruits. An industry that started with the exotic orchid has now expanded to include almost every fruit and vegetable in the kingdom. ■

Chiang Saen

Chiang Saen

✉ 212 C3

Visitor information

✉ Tourism Authority of
   Thailand, 448/16
   Singhaklai Rd.,
   Chiang Rai

☎ 053-717433

✉ Chiang Saen local
   tourist office, Hwy.
   1016, Chiang Saen

CHIANG SAEN IS A QUIET, CHARMING LITTLE TOWN IN A
pastoral setting on the banks of the Mekong River. Its attractions
include some intriguing historic ruins. The town consists of a
handful of almost deserted streets, with a few shops for essentials and
some simple guesthouses that welcome a steady trickle of
backpackers. It is a lovely place, overflowing with shady trees, with a
relaxed atmosphere that is all too rare in this bustling part of the
world. Chiang Saen may lack major monuments, and the
accommodation scene is basic, but the peace and quiet make an ideal
escape for the unhurried traveler.

The town dates from the 10th
century, when local chieftains
constructed a palace and a few
temples. After a brief run, this
settlement disappeared, and Chiang
Saen lay abandoned until 1328,
when a grandson of King Mengrai,
named Saenphu, reestablished the
city as a military post.

Saenphu hoped to prove
himself a devout Buddhist by
constructing a large number of
temples, the remains of which bear
witness to the former glory of this

Villagers along the Mekong River construct rafts from bamboo.

isolated town. Chiang Saen was later absorbed into the Lanna Kingdom, subsequently invaded and conquered by the Burmese in 1558, and then finally restored to Siamese control in 1804.

The **Chiang Saen National Museum** (*Chiang Saen Rd., closed Sun.–Mon.*) together with the nearby tourist office are useful places to pick up maps and to get your bearings before you explore the ruins inside the confines of the ancient city walls.

Among the highlights of the museum are a small but excellent collection of elegant Lanna-period Buddhas and some demon heads and *garudas* discovered in the ruins of Wat Pa Sak (see below). The Lanna bronzes and a large stone Buddha head are also excellent examples of local craftsmanship. Utilitarian objects such as gongs and bronze kettledrums are displayed in the back rooms, while collections on the second floor concentrate on lacquerware, works of rattan, and Lanna-era swords.

One of Chiang Saen's most impressive monuments is the immense octagonal *chedi* behind the museum, **Wat Chedi Luang** (*Chiang Saen Rd.*), built in 1331 by Saenphu and reconstructed shortly before the Burmese conquest of the town. The 190-foot (58 m) structure has partially collapsed, as has the nearby *wihan*, which houses a highly revered Buddha image. Despite its dilapidated condition, and the weeds that are eating their way up the walls, this is a monument of great power and grace.

The importance held by Chiang Saen before the rise of Chiang Mai and the Lanna Kingdom is demonstrated at **Wat Pa Sak** (*Chiang Saen Rd.*), outside the old walls. This is the city's oldest surviving structure, with a construction date estimated at 1295. It was here that many of the Buddhas now displayed in the local museum and the National Museum in Bangkok (see pp. 80–83) were discovered, and the extremely rare stepped pyramidal design makes this monument particularly important in Thai history. All of the Buddhas that once occupied the wall niches have been removed or stolen, and some of the restoration work has been shoddy. Nevertheless, the remaining stucco-work on the upper levels remains remarkable in terms of its execution and sensitivity.

Two other monuments that predate the founding of Lanna-era Chiang Saen are located northwest of town, on a small hill overlooking the Mekong River. **Wat Phra That Cham Kitti** and the smaller **Wat Cham Chang** have lost most of their original statuary and stuccowork, but four remaining standing Buddhas are in excellent condition and make the trek a worthwhile experience.

Back in town, near the banks of the river, stands **Wat Phra Khao Pan,** its four restored Buddhas standing in hollowed niches on the upper levels of the temple.

Several other minor monuments are worth visiting on foot or with a rented bicycle.

Wat Phra Buat, the unusually shaped temple opposite Wat Chedi Luang, has a gateway with a splendid stucco Buddha torso. **Wat Mung Muang** dates from the reign of the second Lanna king of Chiang Saen. **Wat Prachao Lanthong,** the "temple of a million golden weights," is now little more than an immense brick base that once supported a gigantic chedi. **Wat Sao Kien** is a scattered ruin, but it has a solitary, seated, and completely headless Buddha. ■

Chiang Khong

Chiang Khong
✉ 212 C3
Visitor information
✉ Tourism Authority of
Thailand, 448/16
Singhaklai Rd.,
Chiang Rai
☎ 053-717433

CHIANG KHONG IS ANOTHER SLEEPY TOWN ON THE south bank of the Mekong River, chiefly used by travelers as an exit point to Laos across the river at Huay Sai. The town actually comprises three villages strung together, which have maintained their individual monasteries as their commercial districts blended together over the years.

Despite its remote location, Chiang Khong's economic base has expanded recently, owing to increased trade between the town and Huay Sai—chiefly agricultural goods and livestock imported from Laos, in exchange for consumer goods and luxury items from Thailand. Most trade is conducted in town on Soi 5 and at the larger pier of Tha Rua Bak, at the far north end of town.

For many years, Western visitors were confined to the Thai side of the border and could only gaze across the river into Laos, wondering about the landlocked country and the mysteries it might hold. This situation has changed, and now travelers with a visa for Laos are permitted to take a small ferry across to **Huay Sai** and continue on into the country. Visas should be obtained in advance from the Lao Embassy in Bangkok, though guesthouses in Chiang Khong can quickly obtain them for a premium service fee.

Chiang Khong lacks much in the way of historical buildings, despite a long and somewhat remarkable history. The city began as a minor fiefdom in the early days of the eighth century and later played a subservient role to stronger empires in Chiang Rai and Chiang Saen. After a period of decline, Chiang Khong joined the Lanna Kingdom and served as a major military stronghold, until it fell to Burmese forces three centuries later. Returned to Siamese control in 1880, it was then ceded to the French in 1893, as French colonial forces seized most of the left bank of the Mekong River in their creation of Indochina.

Chiang Khong is a town long on views but short on sights. Among the small number of

A hill-tribe villager carries produce to market.

minor attractions is **Wat Luang,** a classic Lanna-style temple complex in the center of town. Dating from the 13th century, the *wat* was reconstructed in 1881 after Chiang Khong returned to Thai control. Local folklore alleges that a stupa has existed on this site since the early eighth century and that the original *chedi* once contained two hairs of the Buddha. A few blocks north is **Wat Phra Kaeo,** with guardian lions at the entrance, *nagas* crawling up both sides of the *wihan*, and rickety wooden monks' quarters to the rear of the temple compound.

A far more interesting place to visit is the old **Kuomintang Cemetery,** where around 200 soldiers of Chiang Kai-shek's (1888–1975) Chinese Nationalist Army (K.M.T.) are laid to rest.

As K.M.T. forces lost their battle against the Communist uprising of Mao Tse-tung in the southern Chinese province of Yunnan, thousands of soldiers fled south, finding refuge in Thailand. Most of the soldiers and their

families elected to establish outposts in remote districts such as Mae Salong (see p. 243) in the hills west of Chiang Rai, and here in Chiang Khong, where they served as a cultural and military buffer zone to hostile forces to the north.

Following the Chinese custom, the grave mounds and tombstones are elevated on a hill to ensure good *feng shui* and to provide eternal views in the direction of their homeland.

Another peculiarity of Chiang Khong is the *pla buk* (great and powerful fish), a monstrous species of catfish, possibly the largest of its kind in the world and increasingly rare. At the south end of town, in the village of **Ban Hat Krai,** fishermen occasionally snag one of these "monsters of the Mekong," which is then sold to local cafés and served up as a highly prized delicacy—the flesh is white and tasty. The fish can grow to 8 feet and weigh 650 lbs (2.5m, 300 kg), but the record is held by a fisherman who pulled in a 6-foot, 480-pounder (1.8 m, 218 kg). ∎

Goods and people can now readily cross the Mekong River into Laos.

Phayao

✉ 212 C2

Visitor information

✉ Tourism Authority of
Thailand, 448/16
Singhaklai Rd.,
Chiang Rai

☎ 053-717433

Phayao

PHAYAO IS A QUIET, RARELY VISITED TOWN. SET IN A
wonderful location on the edge of an immense lake, it has a majestic
view to the mountains on the far shore. Most visitors whiz past the
town in a fast-moving bus, but Phayao is a pleasant place to pause,
and it features several impressive temples down at the lakeside.

Phayao gains great benefit from its
large freshwater **Lake Phayao,**
which covers almost 15 square
miles (39 sq km) and provides a
wide range of fishing, sporting, and
economic opportunities, including
numerous fish farms that can easily
be spotted from the municipal pier.
Behind the placid lake looms **Doi
Bussacarun,** a 6,088-foot-high

**The few visitors
who stop in
Phayao enjoy its
impressive lake
and mountain
scenery.**

(1,826 m) mountain that gives
Phayao the air of a Swiss mountain
village. Over the mountain range is
the **Wang River Valley,** which
continues south, down to the rivers
and valleys of Chiang Mai.

The lakeside has been well
developed, with a promenade,
several popular seafood restaurants,
a public park with fitness games,

and a boat launch that rents
paddleboats and larger craft for a
day of leisure. The few visitors who
ever stop in this town are likely to
be approached by groups of
friendly young Thai students,
anxious to practice their English
and show you around the modest
collection of temples in the center
of town.

Phayao's great religious
attraction is **Wat Si Komkan,**
about 2 miles (3 km) north of city
center on the banks of Lake Phayao.
This is one of the most important
religious sites in Northern
Thailand, as the central *wihan*
holds a highly revered, 400-year-old
Buddha image, called **Phra Chao
Ton Luang.** This vast 52-foot
(16 m) statue of brick and stucco
is one of the biggest icons in
Thailand and is worth the effort to
reach, despite a poor-quality
restoration job by local monks.

Striking a humorous note,
the temple grounds have been
converted into a bizarre
wonderland of kitschy statues that
are intended to provide life lessons
to pilgrims visiting the temple.
Among the wonderfully silly images
are those of dinosaurs and the
character from the movie *E.T.,*
along with evildoers being tortured
by devils to teach devotees that life
is transitory and the ways of the
flesh impermanent.

The modern wihan has
exquisite murals painted by one
of Thailand's most famous
contemporary artists, Angkarn
Kalyanaponsga. ∎

Nan

THIS IS AN EXQUISITELY REMOTE AND RARELY VISITED town and province near the border with Laos, with enough rustic charm and character to keep some travelers happy for weeks on end. Some say it resembles the Chiang Mai of several decades ago, while others simply describe it as a world apart and would rather see the region kept a secret from visitors. The prosperous little town is surrounded by misty mountains and lush valleys filled with rice fields.

Nan today is a fairly modernized town, with a great deal of history preserved in its temples and other remains. The town was established in 1368 as an independent northern kingdom with close ties to Sukhothai (see pp. 195–99). After the demise of Sukhothai, Nan aligned itself with the Lanna Kingdom at Chiang Mai, with periods of control by the Burmese. In 1788 it was absorbed by the Chakri dynasty in Bangkok. Nan was allowed to remain a semi-autonomous kingdom until 1931, when it was integrated into the modern Thai nation.

Much of Nan's long and rich history can be navigated inside the confines of the **Nan National Museum** *(Phakwang Rd., closed Mon.–Tues.)*, in the center of town. The building itself is a renovated former palace, dating from 1903, and final home to the last two princes of a semi-independent Nan regency. Unlike many other regional museums in Thailand, this one has well-arranged exhibits, with explanations provided in both Thai and English. It has an outstanding collection of Buddhas, local ceramics, explanatory dioramas about provincial history, displays of Northern Thai textiles (including contemporary examples from local hill tribes), and a highly revered black elephant tusk on the second

Nan
☎ 212 C2
Visitor information
🛈 Tourist Information Centre, District Offices, Suriyaphong Rd., Nan
☎ 054-751029 or 054-773047

floor. This magical talisman was brought to Nan some 300 years ago and was the prized possession of the Nan rulers until they surrendered their authority to Bangkok.

Several venerable temples in the downtown area, near the National Museum, provide a historical context for the town, showing the

Unknown artists painted Wat Phumin's absorbing murals in 1893.

wide variety of local architectural styles. **Wat Phra That Chang Kham** *(Phakwang Rd.)*, across from the museum, dates from 1547 and is easily recognized by the stucco elephants supporting the primary *wihan*, in a manner similar to temples in Sukhothai, Si Satchanalai, and Kamphaeng Phet. The Buddha images are worth a look. They include a pure-gold statue 4.75 feet (145 cm) high, discovered by American archaeologist Alexander Griswold in 1955, when a plaster covering broke away to reveal the treasure hidden inside.

The highlight of Nan is the beautiful **Wat Phumin** *(Phakwang Rd.)*, a national treasure that dates from 1596, with extensive restorations in the 19th and 20th

centuries. The wihan is unusual, designed in a cruciform shape to accommodate the quartet of identical, gilded Sukhothai-style Buddhas, who sit back to back around a central column, facing the cardinal points. The interior is adorned with carved and painted pillars and coffered ceilings, but Wat Phumin's most famous attributes are its murals—not to be missed. Painted by unknown artists about 1893, the murals depict the *Jataka* tale of the Buddha's reincarnation as Khatta Kumara and scenes from life in Nan in the late 19th century. There are enchanting portraits of local people taking part in activities such as hunting, fishing, planting rice, playing musical instruments, and riding elephants. Just as fascinating are the depictions of the Buddhist hell, comical portraits of Western visitors and French diplomats, starving holy men, Catholic priests, and a famous scene of a young tattooed man courting an elegantly dressed woman.

Several other temples in Nan are worth a quick visit. **Wat Praya Phu** *(Suriyaphong Rd.)* has a pair of rare Sukhothai-style walking Buddhas dated 1426. **Wat Suan Tan** *(Mahayat Rd.)* has a soaring Khmer-style *prang* (unusual in this region) and a 15th-century wihan.

Just outside town, the 1862 Thai-Lue **Wat Nong Bua** is known for its murals, believed to be by the same artists who worked at Wat Phumin. The Thai Lue are an ethnic group famed for their distinctive woven textiles.

Visitors who feel ready for some exercise can climb the royal staircase, just southeast of town, to the top of Mount Phubhiang, to admire the 14th-century **Wat Phra That Chae Haeng.** Here, an elevated courtyard contains a vast golden *chedi* and multiroofed wihan. ■

Phrae

Phrae

✉ 212 C1

Visitor information

✉ Tourism Authority of
    Thailand, 448/16
    Singhaklai Rd.,
    Chiang Rai

☎ 053-717433

THE PROVINCIAL CAPITAL OF PHRAE IS A BUSY COMMERCIAL
town on the Yom River, long made prosperous from the exploitation
of its natural resources, notably coal and timber. Although the teak
has largely disappeared, Phrae thrives on its rattan industry, as well as
on the production of homespun blue farmers' shirts, worn all over
Thailand as a symbol of the rural roots of most citizens.

Like most towns in Central and
Northern Thailand, Phrae spent
time under Burmese control and
later welcomed large numbers of
Burmese immigrants. Their
influence is reflected in temples
such as the early 20th-century **Wat
Chom Sawan** (Ban Mai Rd.),
with its multitiered roofs and
ceilings gilded in Burmese designs.
Laotian influence is seen at the
18th-century *bot* at **Wat Phra
Bat** (Charoen Muang Rd.), where
the modern *wihan* contains the
most important Buddha image in
the province. Laotian design styles
are also obvious at **Wat Phra
Non** (Wichairacha Rd.), known for
its reclining Buddha image.

For a change of pace, visit the
**Ban Prathup Chai teakwood
house** just west of city center,
where a wealthy merchant created
one residence out of nine old
houses. It lacks unity, but you will
almost certainly never see so much
teakwood in one place again.

A real highlight of Phrae is **Wat
Phra That Chaw Hae** (Chaw
Hae Rd.), a hilltop temple complex
several miles east of town. You can
hike up the pathway past
undulating *nagas* to visit an
impressive *chedi* sheathed with
gilded copper plates and often
wrapped in heavy satin (chaw hae)
by pilgrims. A smaller shrine holds
the image of **Phra Chao Than
Chai,** believed to grant wishes.

Phrae Muang Phi, 12 miles
(18 km) from Phrae off a side road
on Highway 101, just before the
Kilometer 143 marker, is an eerie
wonderland of rock pinnacles. ■

**Nine teakwood
houses compose
Ban Prathup Chai.**

Lampang

AN EASY DAY EXCURSION CAN BE MADE FROM CHIANG MAI to the historic town of Lampang, distinctive for its Burmese-style temples, horse-drawn carriages, and nearby Wat Phra That Lampang Luang. Lampang has grown dramatically in recent years and is now the second largest city in Northern Thailand. It was originally founded in the seventh century, and traces of its long heritage can be seen in the inner core of the old city, near the banks of the Wang River.

The city owes its early prosperity to British merchants in the 19th century, who developed the district as the center of Thailand's teak industry. They employed thousands of Burmese workers, who left many of the temples and monasteries that still grace the old town.

Among the Burmese-style gems is **Wat Phra Kaeo Don Tao** (*Suchada Rd.*), in a residential neighborhood on the east bank of the Wang River. This is one of the finest examples of Burmese architecture in Thailand, as exemplified by its elaborately carved and ornamented *mondop* topped off by a nine-tier roof. In the same compound are several gilded *wihans*, a brightly painted Burmese-style reclining Buddha, and a surprisingly extensive museum filled with local artifacts.

A few blocks south, and also on the east bank of the Wang River, is **Ban Sao Nak** (*Phra Kaeo Rd., tel 054-227653*), a huge ancestral mansion of teak, known as the "many pillars house" for its supporting 116 square teak pillars. Furnished with Thai and Burmese antiques, it is now a museum.

Further significant temples constructed in the Burmese style include **Wat Pa Fang** (*Prabhat Rd.*), known for its alabaster Mandalay-style Buddhas, and **Wat Si Rong Muang** (*Takranoi Rd.*), a Burmese monastery with a dazzling multicolored exterior of carved wood, home to sacred images

presented by wealthy patrons. **Wat Chedi Sao** (*Khong Rd.*) is a simple temple in a peaceful location outside the city limits, with 20 whitewashed *chedis* crafted in a composite Burmese-Thai style.

WAT PHRA THAT LAMPANG LUANG

Lampang's greatest claim to fame is this 11th-century walled temple complex, 16 miles (25 km) south of town in a region of hot dry plains and scattered rice fields. Wat Phra That Lampang Luang is considered a masterpiece of Thai art for its wealth of decoration and purity of architectural style.

Originally part of an eighth-century fortressed city, the temple as seen today dates from the 15th–19th centuries. Entrance is via a staircase flanked by *naga* serpents, leading to a striking 15th-century monumental gateway lavishly decorated with stuccowork and gilded in brilliant hues of gold. The centerpiece of the courtyard is the huge open-sided wihan, its pillars lacquered and inlaid with gold, its main Buddha image enclosed in a Lao-style gilded *prang*.

A vast chedi looms behind it, and spread around the temple grounds are more structures of great artistic interest: the 16th-century **Wihan Nam Tam** is perhaps the oldest wooden building in Thailand, and the beautifully carved Lanna-style **Wihan Phra Phut** is a treasure house of

Lampang
🅰 212 B1
Visitor information
✉ Lampang Tourist Office, 2nd Floor, District Office Bldg., Rawp Riang Rd., Lampang
☎ 054-218823

A procession carries Buddha images through the streets of Lampang during its Luang Wiang Lakon festival in February.

priceless Lanna-era Buddhas. Several more chedis, bots, and wihans are set around the walled compound, along with a dusty old museum, and a huge *bodhi* tree.

YOUNG ELEPHANT TRAINING CENTER

One of the better elephant camps, the Young Elephant Training Center is just 23 miles (37 km) from Lampang on the Chiang Mai road.

Over the course of five years, elephants are trained to stack, carry, and pull logs, and will go on to have a working life of about 50 years. There are daily demonstrations between 10 a.m. and noon, except for the dry months from March to June. A small museum gives a useful background to the story of working elephants in Thailand. ■

Young Elephant Training Center

🅰 212 B1 & B2

✉ On Chiang Mai Rd., 23 miles (37 km) NW of Lampang

☎ 054-228034 or 054-228035

☎ $$

Siamese twins

The most famous Siamese twins, Chang and Eng, were born in 1811 on the outskirts of Bangkok. In 1829 an opportunist British trader, Robert Hunter, took them to the United States Having earned a fortune making public appearances, the twins became farmers in North Carolina, married sisters, and fathered numerous children. The pair had very different personalities and toward the end of their lives were fighting constantly. Chang, a heavy drinker, died from a cerebral blood clot in January 1874. Eng, who was not ill, died a few hours later after what doctors determined to be panic. ■

Lamphun

▲ 212 B2

Visitor information

✉ Tourism Authority of
Thailand, 105/1
Chiang Mai—
Lamphun Rd.,
Chiang Mai

☎ 053-248604 or
053-248605 (fax)

Lamphun

JUST 16 MILES (26 KM) SOUTH OF CHIANG MAI LIES THE
ancient and almost deserted town of Lamphun. The original capital
of the Haripunchai Empire, it is a quiet town of wooden houses in a
river setting, with a handful of remarkable temples that predate
the founding of the Lanna Kingdom.

Lamphun is believed to have been
founded in the eighth century by a
wandering monk, Suthep Reussi,
who invited a Lop Buri princess
named Chama Thewi to be its first
queen. The town, initially called
Haripunchai, formed the
northernmost extremity of the old
Dvaravati Kingdom of Central
Thailand. Within a few years, a
moat, ramparts, and several Mon-
inspired temples were constructed
on the banks of the Kuang River.
Over the next six centuries
Haripunchai held sway over vast
portions of Northern Thailand in
its role as an independent Dvaravati
kingdom. The city fell to King
Mengrai and his Lanna Kingdom in
1281 but revived the following
century when it was transformed
into a major religious center,
becoming the heart of Theravada
Buddhism in Northern Thailand.

**Lamphun National
Museum**

✉ Inthayongyot Rd.,
opposite Wat
Phra That
Haripunchai

🕐 Closed Mon.–Tues.

💲 $

LAMPHUN NATIONAL
MUSEUM

Lamphun's rich history and the
artistic traditions of Haripunchai
are revealed in this small but well-
organized museum in the center of
town, just opposite Wat Phra That
Haripunchai. Exhibits include
examples of early Haripunchai
stucco figurines and relics from the
final rulers of Lamphun.

WAT KUKUT

Lamphun's oldest monument, Wat
Kukut (also known as Wat Chama
Thewi, after the legendary queen),
is the final surviving example in
Thailand of original Dvaravati

architecture. Quite unlike the style
of Sukhothai or Ayutthaya temples,
the pyramidal *chedi* dates from
1218 and is thought to have been
modeled after a similar structure in
Polonarawa, Sri Lanka, or perhaps
the Mahabodhi temple in Bodgaya,
India. No matter the inspiration for
the design, Wat Kukut provides a
direct link between the architecture
of India and the Siamese mainland.

WAT PHRA THAT
HARIPUNCHAI

It is this temple complex in the
center of town that provides the
widest and most intriguing range of
religious structures. Siamese
chronicles date the foundation of
the walled compound to A.D. 897,
when an early Mon king ordered its
construction to house a sacred relic
of the Buddha—believed to be
either a fragment of the sage's skull
or a hair from his head. The
complex has been expanded and
renovated several times over the
centuries and today consists of
almost a dozen buildings reflecting
the Burmese style of architecture.

The main feature of the
spacious temple courtyard is a
massive, bulbous chedi covered
with gleaming copper plates. Older
structures are believed to exist
underneath, but the present
monument dates from the early
20th century. The summit is capped
with a nine-tiered umbrella of solid
gold to signify the supremacy of the
Buddhist order.

Many of the original
Haripunchai- and Lanna-style

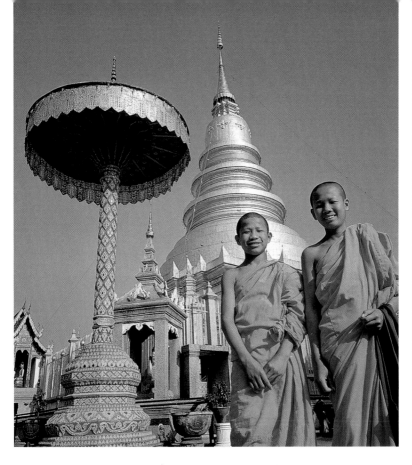

Buddhas once mounted around the temple buildings are now displayed inside the dusty but fascinating **temple museum,** in the southwest corner of the compound. Hidden away in the northwest corner is a classic Mon-style chedi that closely resembles Wat Kukut with its stepped pyramidal outline and arched niches, which would once have held standing Buddhas. The *wihan* behind the golden chedi dates from 1925 and is an excellent example of modern temple architecture, with its gracious proportions, colorful interior murals, and well-crafted Lanna-style bronze Buddha image displayed on the central altar.

Several other minor structures add to the overall appeal, including the 19th-century library, which has been raised on a steep platform to prevent destruction of the manuscripts by ants and termites. There is a Burmese-style bell tower, a bronze gong that is purported to be the largest of its type in the world, and a modern *bot* with a pair of impressive bronze Buddhas.

WAT PHRA YUN

Constructed as a forest monastery for local monks, this temple is notable for its Burmese-style square chedi built on the original site of a *mondop* dating back to 1370. Steps climb to a terrace framed by four smaller chedis. The larger chedi has four standing Buddha icons inside alcoves. To get to the temple, head east first across the moat from Wat Hariphunchai, then across Kuang River for half a mile (1 km). ■

Wat Phra That Hariphunchai, dating back to A.D. 897, contains a dazzling array of religious structures.

Tobacco for Thailand's homegrown cigarette brands is dried in kilns such as these.

More places to visit in Northern Thailand

MRABI HILL TRIBE
(PHI THONG LUANG)

One of Northern Thailand's most reclusive
minority groups is the Mrabi tribe. These
nomadic hunters, believed to number only in
the hundreds, were discovered several decades
ago and have since been heavily proselytized
by U.S. missionaries. The Mrabi—also known
as "spirits of the yellow leaves," after the pale
color of their temporary leaf huts—can be
visited on excursions from Phrae and Nan.
Local tourist offices or your hotel will
arrange a guide.
🔼 Map 212 C1 & C2

NONG BUA

A short ride north of Nan is a small village
inhabited by migrants from Yunnan Province
in southern China, known as Lue, who have
maintained their traditions in weaving,
domestic architecture, and religious shrines, as
highlighted by their famous temple, **Wat
Nong Bua.** The temple features lintels and
carved porticoes of rare design, as well as
murals that were probably painted by the
artists of Wat Phumin (see p. 254). Traditional
Thai-Lue handwoven fabrics are sold locally.
🔼 Map 212 D2

PA SANG

This small town to the south of Lamphun is
the center of the traditional cotton-weaving
industry. The cotton, woven with distinctive
designs, is made up into clothing—mainly
shirts and sarongs—which is sold along the
town's main street. A guide can be arranged by
your hotel or local tourist office.
🔼 Map 212 B2

TOBACCO KILNS

The rich soil and climatic conditions
of Northern Thailand near the Mekong
River make it an ideal environment for
growing temperate vegetables such as
cabbages and tomatoes, and also for the
production and processing of Virginia
tobacco, used in local cigarettes such as
Krung Thep. Several large and unmistakable
tobacco kilns and factories can be spotted
near smaller towns such as Fang and Chiang
Saen, and in the countryside near Phrae
and Phayao. Although there are no organized
tours of the factories, visitors are welcome
to wander through the storage yards and
inspect the primitive kilns. Arrange a
guide through your accommodations or
local tourist office.

Quiet beaches, lively resorts, secluded islands with psychedelic underwater worlds of coral, and mountains blanketed by tropical rain forests characterize the beauty of the South.

Southern Thailand

Angelfish are common among Southern Thailand's corals.

Southern Thailand

SOUTH OF BANGKOK, THE COUNTRY UNDULATES BETWEEN THE GULF OF Thailand and the wild mountains of the Myanmar (Burma) frontier, along a thread of land at some places so thin that barely 7.5 miles (12 km) separates the gulf from Myanmar. Farther south, the Isthmus of Kra marks the narrowest point between the Indian and Pacific Oceans. From there, Thailand widens—not by much—to form the Malay Peninsula, eventually exposing its east and west coasts.

Three centuries ago, when the southern Burmese port of Mergui was part of Siam, towns along this narrow strip enjoyed great importance and influence. Prachuap Khiri Khan was the eastern trade center on the route between Ayutthaya and India. Its markets brimmed with the finest silks, perfumed woods, and rare porcelain. At Phetchaburi, Khmer dynasty temples prove that the town once lay at the southern extremities of the mighty Khmer Empire. Farther south at Chaiya, evidence has been unearthed showing it to have been a significant city of the Srivijaya Empire (8th–13th centuries), which ruled much of what are today Indonesia, Malaysia, and Southern Thailand.

Throughout the 19th and 20th centuries, and up to the present day, the area enjoyed the patronage of Thai royalty. Kings and princes built magnificent palaces as retreats from the pressures of their regal duties. It was at the Royal Hua Hin Golf Course in 1932 that King Prajadhiphok (Rama VII) was informed he had been overthrown in a bloodless coup, ending the 165 years of absolute monarchy of the Chakri Dynasty. The current monarch, King Bhumibol, holidays in the royal palace in Hua Hin, where he used to sail a dinghy he personally built. Three kings (Ramas V, VII, and IX) even made it to isolated Ko Phangan, in the Ko Samui archipelago, to carve their insignia on a rock beside Than Sadet Falls.

Monks' robes drying at a _wat_ in Ranong catch the early morning light.

The first section of Southern Thailand, the finger of land between Phetchaburi (about 100 miles/160 km south of Bangkok) to Chumphon, is little explored by foreign visitors but contains a richness of attractions that belies its limited area. Its string of low-key beach resorts and its surprisingly rugged and verdant interior are mainly the domain of Thai tourists. One exception is Hua Hin, now a nascent international resort steadily gaining in popularity.

At the appropriately named Chumphon (derived from the Thai *chumnumphon,* or meeting place), visitors have a choice. They can follow the arterial Highway 4 as it cuts through the scenic mountains to Ranong and the beautiful, but hardly investigated, west coast and pristine islands. Or they can continue south along the east coast on Highway 401 to Surat Thani, the launching pad for trips to the tropical splendor of the Ko Samui islands. ■

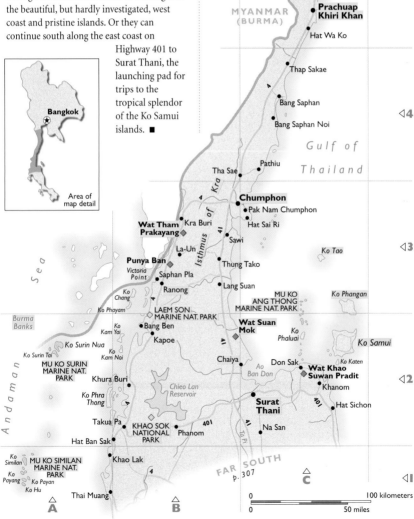

Phetchaburi

🅰 263 C6

Visitor information

✉ Tourism Authority of
Thailand, 500/51
Phetkasem Rd.,
Cha-am

☎ 032-471005

Phetchaburi & around

THAILAND IS KNOWN FOR THE VARIETY OF TRANS-
literations of its place-names into English, and Phetchaburi is an
example of this at its quirky best. The town is known variously as
Phetchaburi, Phetchburi, Petchburi, Petchaburi, Phetburi, and
Petburi—an acknowledged record. But whatever you care to call it,
Phetchaburi has an embarrassment of cultural, historical, and
natural attractions.

Like other locations on this thin
neck of land, Phetchaburi won
favor with Chakri dynasty kings in
the late 19th and early 20th
centuries as a royal hideaway. King
Mongkut built the most dominant
symbol of this patronage in 1859,
Phra Nakhon Khiri. Crowning
the 302-foot (92 m) hill, Maha
Samana, this is now a historical
park. The grand complex includes
a temple (Wat Phra Kaeo), a *chedi*,
and a neoclassic-style mansion.
There is also an observatory (you
can climb the spiral staircase to
the glass-domed roof) where
King Mongkut, an avid
astronomer, could indulge in one
of his favorite pastimes.

Other buildings, including
throne halls, a theater, stables, and
guardhouses, are all done in a
jumble of architectural styles that
blend together delightfully. The
views over the town and lush
landscape are outstanding. You can
get to the palace by negotiating a
strenuous cobblestone path and
dodging gangs of rowdy monkeys,
or by riding a cable car.

On the palace grounds, **Phra
Nakhon Khiri National
Museum** *(closed Mon.–Tues.)*
houses memorabilia, bronze and
brass sculptures, ceramics, and
furnishings of royal households.
The week-long Phra Nakhon
Khiri Fair, featuring a sound

and light show at the palace, is held in early February.

BEYOND TOWN

The vast main cavern at the cave complex of Tham Khao Luang, about 3 miles (5 km) north of town on Highway 3173, seethes with dramatic effect. Shafts of light pour through sinkholes, bathing dozens of Buddha images, minature chedis, and the magnificent arrangement of stalactites in an ethereal glow. Buddha images are placed there by pilgrims, including one from King Chulalongkorn, dedicated to his father, King Mongkut.

Tham Khao Yoi, 14 miles (22 km) north, off Highway 4, is another sensational fusion of nature and spirituality. Large caves are enshrined with crowds of Buddha images, and spectacular stalactites drop from vaulted ceilings. In the main cavern, soft light gently pours over an enormous reclining Buddha.

Thailand's biggest national park, **Kaeng Krachan,** is well worth the day trip from Phetchaburi. The park, 44 miles (70 km) southwest of town, encompasses 1,120 square miles (2,900 sq km) of wild and spectacular scenery as it runs to the Tenasserim Mountains, which separate Thailand from Myanmar (Burma). Dense rain forests, water-falls, limestone peaks, and numerous caves, enlivened by screeching wild-life, offer good trekking. The huge Kaeng Krachan Dam has created a vast reservoir here, a popular stopover for migrating birds.

There are a few beaches interspersing fishing villages along the 25-mile (40 km) route south from Phetchaburi along the coast road to **Cha-am,** but they lack the quality of beaches farther south. Few foreign visitors venture here, but the area is popular with Thai vacationers.

Faded **Hat Chao Samran,** 7.5 miles (12 km) north of Cha-am, was once a seaside resort for the Thai elite. Now it is passed over for nearby **Laem Luang Beach,** 4 miles (7 km) south.

Hat Puk Tian, a sandy, casuarina-lined strip of coast, is packed with locals on weekends, enjoying the water and the food that is dished up by swarms of vendors. Offshore a sizable statue of Phi Seua Samut, a watery female deity from the epic poem *Phra Aphaimani,* is an interesting aberration from an otherwise totally normal local beach scene.

The long, sandy beach lined with casuarinas that fronts

Above: King Mongkut built the magnificent Phra Nakhon Khiri palace as a summer retreat in the mid-19th century. Right: Delicate murals cover the walls at Phetchaburi's Ayutthaya-period Wat Ko Kaew Sutharam.

Cha-am is popular among Thais. The city fathers are busily trying to promote the resort as a quiet alternative to popular Hua Hin (see pp. 268–69). There are a number of luxury resorts at the southern end of town, and Cha-am is part of a green belt of quality golf courses that stretch between the two resorts. ■

Phetchaburi walk

A walking tour of Phetchaburi's temple complexes gives visitors an insight into the pervasive role that Buddhism played, and still plays, in everyday Thai life. It also provides a good introduction to the religious and historical importance of this charming town.

Begin at the eastern end of Chomrut Bridge, in the northern part of the town, and walk away from the bridge along Pongsuriya Road. **Wat Yai Suwannaram** ❶ is on the right. Built during the 17th century, this outstanding *wat* is best known for its large *bot*, with intricately carved wooden doors, octagonal pillars, murals featuring Hindu deities paying homage to Buddha, and flowing decorative art with vivid flora and fauna. The murals date from the end of the Ayutthaya period. A cloister with gilded Buddha images surrounds the bot.

Inside the Ayutthaya-period Wat Ko Kaew Sutharam

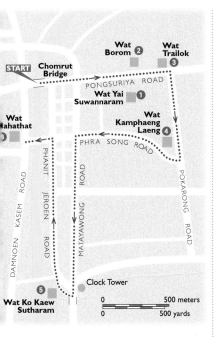

See area map p. 263 C6

► Chomrut Bridge

↔ 3 miles (5 km)

🕐 3 hours

► Wat Mahathat

NOT TO BE MISSED

- Wat Yai Suwannaram
- Wat Kamphaeng Laeng
- Wat Ko Kaew Sutharam
- Wat Mahathat

A splendidly ornate *hor trai,* or library, sits in the middle of a pond next to the bot.

Opposite are the neighboring **Wat Borom ②** and **Wat Trailok ③**. Both appear a little untidy and are overrun with dogs. (People dump their unwanted pets at temple complexes rather than have them put down.) Long, fragile-looking wooden dormitories on stilts contrast with the heavy mortared, ornate Ayutthaya-period buildings in the center of the grounds.

Turn right off Pongsuriya Road and head south along Pokarong Road, opposite Wat

Trailok. After about 10 minutes, **Wat Kamphaeng Laeng ④**, Phetchaburi's oldest temple, appears behind some buildings on the right. The wat houses a 13th-century Khmer monument consisting of a central *prang* framed by three smaller prangs and a *gopura*. The prang nearest the wat entrance contains a Buddha footprint, while the central prang, once dedicated to Hindu deities, now holds a Buddha image. The other two prangs provide refuge for the numerous chickens that roam the grounds of the wat.

Walk west along Phra Song Road, fronting Wat Kamphaeng Laeng, and turn left at Matayawong Road. Walk south for about 15 minutes to the town's clock tower. Turn right just before a small bridge, and follow the road for a minute or so to **Wat Ko Kaew Sutharam ⑤**. The wat is difficult to see from the road, so look for the *sois* (side streets) Wat Ko Kaew I and Wat Ko Kaew II, on the left.

Wat Ko Kaew Sutharam is one of Phetchaburi's best temples. The bot and its adjacent building, both fine timber buildings raised on stilts, were constructed during the Ayutthaya period. The outside of the bot has a pillared porch, whose gables and pediments are decorated with stucco floral art and deity motifs. If the bot is locked, ask a monk to open it. Inside, some of Thailand's finest, oldest, and most originally conceived murals fill the walls. Dating back to the mid-18th century, these murals are a delightful depiction of Phetchaburi life 300 years ago.

One of the walls shows foreigners converting to Buddhism, while another depicts a Jesuit priest in the robes of a Buddhist monk. Another superb mural is a sea of intricately connected scenes depicting Buddha's victory over evil.

Follow the road in front of Wat Ko Kaew Sutharam until it merges with Phanit Jeroen Road. Turn right and head north for 10 minutes back to Phra Song Road, and turn left over the bridge. **Wat Mahathat ⑥** is easy to spot, with its huge, brilliant-white, Ayutthaya-period prang rising from the middle of the temple grounds; you can climb it for some great views. Wat Mahathat is the town's most popular wat and buzzes with activity. ∎

Hua Hin
⛰ 263 C6
Visitor information
✉ Hua Hin Municipal
Office, corner of
Phetkasem Rd. &
Damnoen Kasem
Rd., Hua Hin
☎ 032-511047

Hua Hin & around

THAILAND'S FIRST BEACH RESORT ORIGINALLY ATTRACTED the leisure class from Bangkok in the early 20th century. Its popularity among foreign visitors has been more incipient, but vacationers are drawn to the beach town for its amiable, wholesome atmosphere. With its salubrious feel, Hua Hin adds another dimension to Thailand's wonderful and varied collection of international beach resorts. Unfortunately, ill-conceived 1990s development has sucked some of the charm out of the town.

The resort has long enjoyed the favor of Thai royalty, which has contributed to its status and growth as a premier resort among Thais. Hua Hin has managed to avoid the gaudy excesses of other beach resorts and, on the whole, remains quiet and relaxing. However, there is a feeling that city fathers need to be more judicious in future town planning if Hua Hin's sanguine sobriquet, Queen of Tranquility, is not to end up a sad irony. Foreign visitors, a rare sight just a few years ago, are now well catered for with first-class facilities, including international brand hotels.

In 1910, Rama VI's brother, Prince Chulachakrabongse, visited Hua Hin on a hunting trip. The prince was so delighted with the success of his trip and the location that he built **Klai Kangwon** ("far from worries"), a palace at the northern end of town on Naret-damri Road, one street back from the waterfront, still used by the royal family.

Rama VI followed in the early 1920s. Also enamored with the surroundings, he ordered the construction of a beachfront summer palace in 1924. **Marek Khantayawan Palace,** the "palace of love and hope," was the king's idyllic royal retreat. The renovated palace is a harmonious collection of buildings, constructed of teak and marble, and linked by elevated corridors that lead to *salas* on the beach, all rendered in elegant Thai-Victorian architecture. The center of the palace provided the living quarters of the royal family. Further opulence is found in the throne room and theater. The palace, 9 miles (15 km) north of Hua Hin, is well worth a visit.

Prompted by visiting royalty, a railway from Bangkok was completed in 1922. Two stations were built within a hundred yards—one for commoners and one for royalty. The smaller **Royal Train Station** is a flamboyant gem in Thai-temple style, with a staggered, steeply pitched, four-cornered tiled roof, angled windows, timber slats, and carved timber poles and gables supporting the roof overhangs. The luxurious Eastern & Oriental Express train, which runs from Singapore to Bangkok and on to Chiang Mai, stops here.

King Bhumibol maintains a palace in Hua Hin and occasionally visits to sail his dinghies, adding a century-old continuity to Hua Hin's relationship with royalty.

The **Hua Hin Railway Hotel** *(Dameon Kasem Rd., tel 032-512021)* was built a year after the railway line reached town, as Hua Hin's popularity was growing among the Thai elite. It is now somewhat clumsily renamed the Hotel Sofitel Central Hua Hin, but renovations in 1986 returned it to its former colonial glory. With its breezy open-fronted lobby, leisurely rotating ceiling fans, forests of

potted palms, timber paneling, shiny brass fittings, and imaginative gardens of animal topiary, it is now a trademark Southeast Asian colonial hotel. Before its lavish restoration it was used as the setting for Phnom Penh's Hotel Le Phnom in the 1984 movie *The Killing Fields*.

Hua Hin still retains a little of its fishing village character, albeit in a less emphatic way. The fishing pier, **Tha Thiap Reua Pramong,** along the town's north waterfront, livens up in the late afternoon and early evening, when fisherfolk return with their daily catch piled into multitudes of plastic baskets. Judging by location, the clutch of seafood restaurants nearby should have the freshest seafood. As you might expect, there is a plethora of

seafood restaurants in Hua Hin, from the upscale selections in four- and five-star hotels, to folding-table rudimentary on the beach, along the footpaths, and in the markets. Be aware that price does not always reflect freshness or quality.

In the evening, the colorful and inexpensive **Chatchai Market,** just off Phetkasen Road from the main Dechanuchit Road, is jam-packed with locals enjoying fresh seafood in a boisterous, enjoyable atmosphere. More seafood restaurants can be found side by side on Damneon Kasem Road, between Naep Khehat Road and Punsuk Road.

The Hotel Sofitel Central opens graciously onto the town's hallmark **Hua Hin Beach,** an impressive length of wide, white sand and

Hua Hin's long beach ends at the hilltop Wat Khao Lad, famous for its immense Buddha image.

clean water, with long rows of colorful beach umbrellas. Note the smooth, round boulders just beyond the shoreline. You can hire horses for a ride along the beach. Sailing is a favorite pastime, and hoby cats, along with the scourge of Thailand's beaches—jet skis (water scooters)—can be rented.

3 miles (5 km) south. In between are the resort beaches of **Hat Takiap, Hat Suan Son,** and **Hat Tao.** The turnoff to Khao Takiap is 2.5 miles (4 km) along the coast road south from Hua Hin, or you can walk along the beach, hopping over and around rocks at its southern end.

Thailand's ubiquitous markets purvey all kinds of goods, from dried cuttlefish to batteries to baskets. Beyond this one in Hua Hin stands the Royal Train Station, once used for visiting royalty and now serving as a stopover for the Eastern & Oriental Express.

SOUTH OF TOWN

To the south, the beach edges onto a rocky bluff called **Khao Takiap,** or "chopsticks hill," because of its twin peaks. A golden 66-foot (20 m) Buddha image abuts the cliff face with appropriate prominence at **Wat Khao Lad.** Watch for the army of precocious monkeys roaming the temple's lower grounds—they like to steal eyeglasses and handbags. A staircase leads to the top of the *wat,* from where there are wide views of the coast and mountains, forest-shaded beaches, and the march of high-rise resort development.

Boats can be chartered from a nearby fishing village to these beaches. Khao Takiap frames the northern end of a slightly curving bay before meeting Khao Tao about

Farther south, the road cuts in from the coast to Pran Buri. Head through thick forests to the busy fishing village of **Ban Pak Nam Pran,** which has secluded beaches nearby. This part of the coast has also seen resort development.

In 1932, Rama VII was playing golf at the **Royal Hua Hin Golf Course** *(tel 032-512475)* at the western edge of town, when he was told he had been overthrown in a bloodless coup. Scottish railway engineer A.O. Robins designed the course in 1924, which accounts for its "British" layout. Disturbing this Anglo-centric feel are views of hilltop *chedis* and monkeys that make off with golf balls lying too close to the fairway's jungle fringes.

Nowadays, golf courses are more refined. The **Springfields Royal**

Country Club of Cha-am (*193 Huay-Sai Nua, Petchkasem Rd., Cha-am, tel 032-471303*), was designed by top U.S golfer Jack Nicklaus (1940–) and is one of the finest golf resorts in Thailand.

Pricey green fees in other Asian territories have made less expensive Thai courses very popular among golfers from Singapore, Hong Kong, and Japan, where the sport has always been the domain of the wealthy. Special weekend golf package tours (including green fees, accommodations, and airfare) from these places to Thailand are sometimes less expensive than a round of golf on a local course!

Eight quality courses in Hua Hin and nearby Cha-am make this area one of Asia's premier golf destinations. Fees are reasonable, and you can hire clubs and golf carts. Caddies are provided, and tips are expected. Because of the debilitating tropical heat, there are plenty of refreshment stops around the courses. Hua Hin Golf Tours (*tel 032-530119*) can help with suggestions and arrangements.

About 18 miles (29 km) west of Hua Hin, near the village of **Ban Nong Phlab,** interesting caves are found hidden in the forests that carpet the mountains of Hua Hin's scenic backdrop. Dao, Lablae, and Kailon are caves a few miles apart from each other, near the village of Ban Nong Phlab. They are notable for their profusion of unusually wide, shell-shaped stalactites and contorted stalagmites. The best way to get to the caves is with a half-day tour, booked at your hotel. ■

In addition to meditation and learning, a monk's duties include the maintenance of the temple grounds.

Khao Sam Roi Yot National Park

KHAO SAM ROI YOT ("MOUNTAIN OF THREE HUNDRED peaks") was Thailand's first coastal national park. Its 38 square miles (98 sq km) of land and small offshore area was gazetted in 1966. Steep limestone hills harbor deep caves, rising above rare coastal marshes, lagoons, and secluded beaches. Inland, gentle wooded valleys give way to precipitous cliffs, and extensive marshland shelters rich birdlife. The visitor center at Ban Khao Daeng (approached from Highway 4) has information on all the sites described below.

A royal pavilion, majestically bathed in streams of light from sinkholes (the best time to view is 10:30 a.m), was built inside one of the magnificent caverns at **Tham Phraya Nakhon** in 1890, in honor of a visit by King Chulalongkorn. King Mongkut had visited in 1868, along with a huge entourage of Thai and European dignitaries, to observe a total solar eclipse that he had predicted.

The cave sits high above **Laem Sala Beach,** a deep circular cove hemmed by bare limestone hills on three sides, with bungalows and a restaurant shaded by groves of casaurina (sea pine) trees. A boat brings visitors from the nearby village of Ban Bang Phu for a few dollars, or walkers can take the steep cliff trail, with views of a chain of limestone bluffs rising at the sea's edge and scrolling along the coast. From the beach, a well-maintained trail leads up to the cave and takes about 20 minutes.

There are a couple more caves worth exploring. At **Tham Kaeo,** about a mile from Ban Bang Phu, you climb down a ladder to a number of chambers connected to passageways, passing giant limestone formations, including spectacular petrified waterfalls. Many of the formations are encrusted with calcite crystals, causing them to glitter in the dull light.

To get to **Sai Cave,** take a 1.5-mile (2.5 km) trail from the coastal hamlet of Ban Khung Tanot to the start of the hike. The trail climbs for 920 feet (276 m) up a hillside to the mouth of the cavern, which has all sorts of weird rock formations and unusually shaped stalactites and stalagmites. Ask for a guide at park headquarters.

Ban Khung Tanot overlooks **Sam Phraya Beach,** with its wide, long sands and fringe of trees along the base of a string of hills.

At Ban Khao Daeng, a canal, **Khlong Daeng,** winds past mangrove swamps rich with birdlife. Monkeys hide in the tangles of branches, and the occasional monitor lizard can be

Khao Sam Roi Yot National Park
- 263 C5

National Parks Division
- ✉ Royal Forestry Department, 61 Phahonyothin Rd., Bangkhen, Bangkok
- ☎ 02-561-4292

Visitor information
- ✉ Tourism Authority of Thailand, 500/51 Phetkasem Rd., Cha-am
- ☎ 032-471005

seen basking on the muddy banks. The best times to hire boats for the 90-minute trip are early morning or late afternoon, when wildlife is more active.

A steep, rocky climb starts from close by the park headquarters up to the 523-foot (157 m) summit of **Khao Daeng.** From here, there are dramatic vistas of limestone mountains.

The 12,350 acres (5,000 ha) of freshwater marshes at **Rong Yai Marsh,** combined with an abundance of tidal marshland along the coast, offer one of the largest areas of wetlands in Southeast Asia for migratory birds making their way along the Asia–Australia flyway. About 300 species have been identified in total, of which around 180 are migratory.

Thousands of bird-watchers are drawn to the park between September and November, the best time to view the birds.

Shrimp farmers have encroached into the national park and, at one stage, threatened to destroy the wetlands. Belated action by the authorities finally stemmed and abated this menacing advance (see p. 151).

Visitors can pick up a bird-watching guide at headquarters. You can also take boat rides with rangers through the marshes and get closer views of the magnificent limestone cliffs. Rong Yai Marsh is reached from near the town of Ban Rai Mai, on Highway 4. Cross the railway tracks into the park, and continue for about another 4 miles (7 km). ■

Above: Extensive wetlands and 300 species of birds make Khao Sam Roi Yot National Park a popular bird-watching area. Opposite: Egrets and cormorants share a tree in the national park.

A fishing boat at anchor in Prachuap Khiri Khan's attractive bay. The town is famed for its seafood.

Prachuap Khiri Khan

THIS PEACEFUL TOWN IS VIEWED WITH PASSING INTEREST rather than as a place to stop and look around. Its location, on the slender neck of land attaching Bangkok and the central plains to the Malay Peninsula, has a lot to do with it—tourists tend to ignore Prachuap on their dash along arterial Highway 4. But Prachuap is a pleasant and relaxing fishing town, attractively placed at the edge of a curving bay on the Gulf of Thailand.

Prachuap Khiri Khan

🅰 263 C5

Visitor information

✉ Tourism Authority of Thailand, 500/51 Phetkasem Rd., Cha-am

☎ 032-471005

Buttressing the northern end of this bay is **Khao Chong Gra Jok** ("mirror tunnel mountain"), a limestone cliff named after an arch worn through its side that appears to reflect the sky. From its base, stairs climb to sweeping views. Khao Chong Gra Jok is crowned by a small temple, **Wat Thammikaram,** surrounded by fragrant frangipani trees and inhabited by gangs of pick-pocketing macaque monkeys.

The shores below buzz with the activity of the town's fishing boats. Prachuap Khiri Khan is famous for its seafood; a meal at one of the two night markets (by the seawall on Cha Thelah Road, next to the municipal offices in the town's center) is a lively and tasty way to while away an evening.

Prachuap's best beaches are found along the scenic road that runs past the rocky headland of Khao Mong Lai, which frames the southern end of the bay. **Ao Manao,** a lovely white-sand bay 3 miles (5 km) from town, is where invading Japanese troops landed in 1941. At **Hat Wa Ko,** 5.5 miles (9 km) farther south, is another fine beach with a small museum and monument paying tribute to King Mongkut, who predicted a full solar eclipse in the area in 1868.

About 5 miles (8 km) north of Prachuap, on the road that rings Khao Chong Gra Jok, is **Ban Ao Noi.** Follow the path from the small town's hillside temple to a limestone peak and the temple cave **Tham Khao Khan Kradai,** to view the impressive 53-foot (16 m) reclining Buddha. ∎

Chumphon & beyond

THE TOWN OF CHUMPHON SITS ON THE EASTERN SIDE OF the Isthmus of Kra. From here, the major route south divides, with Highway 4 slicing through the mountains of the Malay Peninsula to Ranong and the Andaman coast, while Highway 41 skirts the Gulf of Thailand to Surat Thani and beyond. A string of good beaches lines the coast, with coral-fringed islands offshore.

A puppet master with the tools of his trade in Chumphon

Forty limestone islands off Chumpon's coast have recently been incorporated into the **Mu Ko Chumphon Marine National Park.** The diving here is excellent but not yet fully explored. About 7.5 miles (12 km) north of town, **Thung Wua Laen Beach** is set in a picturesque bay, backed by forested mountains. Here, dive trips can be organized through Chumpon Cabana Resort *(tel 077-560245)* to the outlying islands of the archipelago.

The colorful reef at **Ko Ngam Yai,** about 75 minutes by boat from Thung Wua Laen, sits just 6 feet (1.8 m) beneath the surface in some places, making it ideal for snorkeling. Good snorkeling can also be had off the northern point of nearby **Ko Ngam Noi,** but the island itself, an accumulation of impossibly balanced boulders and precarious bamboo dwellings, is off-limits. The dwellings belong to gatherers of swiftlets' nests, part of a lucrative bird's-nest concession. An undersea ledge at **Ko Lak Ngam,** south of Ko Ngam Noi, has platform gardens of sea anemones leading to a wall clustered with clams, oysters, and multicolored sponges.

About 17 miles (28 km) southeast of Chumphon on Highway 4001, you pass several attractive stretches of sand and sea before reaching **Hat Sai Ri,** where a torpedo boat rests forever on a bed of concrete. At Pak Nam, and beaches along this stretch, charter boats are available to reach more islands close to the coast. The diving is not so good, but there are accommodations, good beaches, and great opportunities for snorkeling.

Chumphon
🗺 263 B3
Visitor information
✉ Tourism Authority of Thailand, 5 Talat Mai Rd., Surat Thani
☎ 077-288818

Mu Ko Chumphon Marine National Park
✉ National Parks Division, Royal Forestry Department, 61 Phahonyothin Rd., Bangkhen, Bangkok
☎ 02-561-2921

Ranong & around

THIS BORDER TOWN WAS ESTABLISHED IN THE LATE 18TH century as a tin-mining center, settled by Hokkien Chinese. Today, their lingering influence is seen in pockets of architecture and in an industrious spirit among the people. Ranong's proximity to the funky Myanmar (Burmese) trading town of Victoria Point, just across the murky Pak Chan Estuary, and its role as a major regional fishing port give it a bustling feel that belies its relatively small population.

A monument at the former residence of Koh Su Chiang—tin-mining boss, tax collector, and, under Rama V at the turn of the 19th century, Ranong's first governor—is found at **Nai Kai Ranong,** off Ruangrat Road, on the northern edge of town. Inside the compound's ornate Hokkien-style buildings, mementoes trace his ancestral history.

On Highway 4005, about half a mile (1 km) east of town and alongside the small **Wat Tapotaram,** pools in a tropical garden setting are fed with steaming water from nearby hot springs. There are also rooms set aside for bathing in the spring water. At the Jansom Thara Spa Resort hotel (*Phetkasem and Kamlangsap Rds., tel 077-821511*), a giant jacuzzi for the use of guests is kept well supplied with water from the springs.

Longtail boats jostling at the town's large diesel-stained fishing port of **Saphan Pla,** 5 miles (8 km) west of town on Tha Muang Road, take passengers across the estuary to **Victoria Point** (Kawthung). The trip offers a fleeting, if deceptive, glimpse of neighboring Myanmar (Burma). Victoria Point feeds off the prosperity of Southern Thailand and throngs with marketeers, along with an unexpected mix of Buddhist and Muslim inhabitants. A more comfortable way to get to the town is by taking day

excursions with Jansom Travel (*tel 077-835317*), at the Jansom Thara Spa Resort hotel.

A modern casino resort and 18-hole golf course sprawl over a small island only a few minutes from Victoria Point on the Burmese side of the border, attracting a large Thai clientele.

Ko Chang, with bungalows, good beaches, and snorkeling, can be reached by chartered boat from Saphan Pla, or tours can be arranged from Ranong.

LAEM SON MARINE NATIONAL PARK

This important protected area slides down the southern coastline of Ranong and into the neighboring province of Phang-Nga, collecting a string of white-sand beaches and swaths of mangrove forest along the way. The park encompasses 62 miles (100 km) of coastline, one of Thailand's longest stretches of protected seaboard. Its jurisdiction also extends offshore to 20 sparsely populated and deserted islands, pushing out to the edges of the Myanmar maritime border.

A 7.5-mile (12 km) road off scenic Highway 4, 30 miles (50 km) south of Ranong town, snakes its way through tangles of mangrove before arriving at park headquarters on **Bang Ben Beach** (*National Park Co-operation Center, Ranong, tel 077-823255*). Edged with casuarina trees, Bang Ben is

Ranong & around
🗺 263 B3
Visitor information
✉ Tourism Authority of Thailand, 5 Talat Mai Rd., Surat Thani
☎ 077-288818

Laem Son Marine National Park
✉ National Parks Division, Royal Forestry Department, 61 Phahonyothin Rd., Bangkhen, Bangkok
☎ 02-561-2921
🕐 Closed Dec.–March

long, wide, and sandy, and offers views across the water to the islands. It is one of the park's most popular beaches, and as such it can get crowded and litter-strewn on weekends.

For more seclusion, walk 2.5 miles (4 km) north along the coast, past more twisted stands of mangroves teeming with birdlife, deer, and monkeys, through shallow streams that have carved weird designs into the rocks, to **Laem Son Beach,** a superior and usually deserted stretch of sparkling sand (accessible only on foot).

During the area's dry season from November to April (monsoons whip the coast for the rest of the year, closing the park), park rangers can arrange trips to some of the offshore islands. Sister islands **Ko Kam Yai** and **Ko Kam Noi,** southwest of Bang Ben, can be reached in a little over an hour. They share the familiar features of secluded beaches—clear waters and good coral close to the shore for snorkeling.

Ko Kam Noi and the smaller **Ko Kam Tok** have freshwater springs. No accommodations are available on these two islands, and while you can camp, park rangers discourage this because they are not patroled.

The larger **Ko Phayam,** 11 miles (18 km) northwest of Bang Ben, has private accommodations backing some of its beaches. Silt from the mouth of the Pak Chan River can cloud its waters.

There are no other options for accommodations on any of the islands in the group. ■

Longtail boats at Ranong's port of Saphan Pla wait for passengers traveling to Victoria Point in Myanmar (Burma).

Chaiya
🅐 263 C2, 263 B2
Visitor information
✉ Tourism Authority of
Thailand, 5 Talat Mai
Rd., Surat Thani
☎ 077-288818

Chaiya & Wat Suan Mok

HISTORIANS SUGGEST THAT UNTIL THE TENTH CENTURY Chaiya was the capital of the Hindu Srivijaya Empire that ruled over much of Indonesia, Malaysia, and Southern Thailand. They contend its name is derived from Srivichai, the Thai rendering of the Javanese Srivijaya. Others disagree, sticking to the established belief that Srivijaya was ruled from Sumatra.

Replicas of ancient artifacts removed from Wat Phra Boromathat Chaiya can be seen in a museum on the grounds.

Even so, the surfeit of artifacts unearthed at Chaiya, one of Thailand's oldest cities, is more than enough to prove that the city played a significant role in the Srivijaya Empire. Most of the artifacts excavated from Chaiya, now a nondescript town 34 miles (54 km) north of Surat Thani on Highway 4, are in the care of the National Museum in Bangkok (see pp. 80–83).

Phra Boromathat Chaiya, about a mile (1.5 km) southeast of Chaiya on Highway 4191, was abandoned at the end of the Srivijaya Empire. The restored 1,300-year-old stupa is a fine example of Srivijayan art, with its ornate stacked-box architecture reflecting a style similar to the *candis* of Java. The museum on the grounds of the *wat* contains models of artifacts removed to Bangkok's National Museum. At **Wat Kaew,** a worn Srivijaya-period monument with five brick chambers rises from a square terrace.

Wat Suan Mok ("temple of the garden of liberation"), a modern forest monastery on Highway 41 southwest of Chaiya, shines with the unconventional style that characterized its founder, Thailand's most famous monk, Buddhadhasa Bhikkhu (1906–1993). His no-frills approach to Buddhism cut through ritual and superstition, earning him the wrath of the religious hierarchy and adoration among the people.

Wat Suan is Thailand's most popular Buddhist meditation retreat for Westerners, fusing Zen, Taoist, and Christian elements into an unconventional whole. Monks at the wat give meditation lessons (these are conducted in English) during the first ten days of each month. Meditation cells dotted around this beautiful forested setting are perfect for peace and solitude. Reservations for cells should be made at the wat a few days in advance.

Surat Thani

THIS BUSINESSLIKE PORT RECEIVES PLENTY OF VISITORS, but unfortunately most arrive with the intention of leaving again as soon as possible. The role of the city as the major transportation hub for the alluring Ko Samui archipelago, Phuket, and Thailand's far south has determined its fate. But it is also a busy and prosperous commercial center, with enough attractions in its own right to keep visitors entertained while they wait to catch the next ferry, train, or bus out of town.

Surat Thani
🖾 263 C2
Visitor information
✉ Tourism Authority of Thailand, 5 Talat Mai Rd., Surat Thani
☎ 077-288818

The local tourist office can arrange boat trips along the **Ta Pi River Estuary,** which winds in from the Gulf of Thailand to form the city's waterfront. The cruise takes you past areas of mangroves interspersed with rickety fishing docks and shipbuilding and repair yards. It also provides opportunities of viewing surprising populations of birdlife. On the north banks of the river, *khlongs* (canals) lead off into the verdant landscape.

At the cleaner southeast **Tha Thong estuary,** Surat Thani's famously succulent giant *tilam* oysters are farmed. Taste them for yourself at the restaurants along the bustling waterfront.

About 5.5 miles (9 km) southwest of the city on Highway 401, at the **Surat Thani Monkey Training School** *(tel 077-227351),* Somphon Saekaew teaches pig-tailed macaque monkeys to scamper up trees and fetch coconuts. Macaques are traditionally used by plantation owners for coconut harvesting, and it is a delight to watch them at their labors.

Surat Thani is Thailand's most famous monkey school, established in 1985 under royal patronage. Somphon occasionally puts on shows for the public; you should ask at the local tourist office for details of these.

About half a mile (1 km) west of the monkey training school, on the

Highway 4009 turnoff, the tall white and gold stupa of **Si Surat** rises from a hilltop above the forests. The stupa houses Buddhist relics that were donated by the Indian government. It also offers good views down to the meandering Ta Pi River.

Continue along Highway 41 to Highway 4142. The road runs to the coast and **Wat Khao Suwan Pradit,** a tremendous 150-foot (45 m) pagoda commanding a hilltop, with a broad sweep of coastal views. ∎

A pig-tailed macaque gets a lesson in gathering coconuts. Farmers in the South still use monkeys to collect coconuts.

Khao Sok National Park

THE PARK, WITH THE ADJOINING KAENG KRUNG AND Khlong Nakha wildlife sanctuaries, and Sri Phang-Nga National Park, forms the largest area of protected land on the Malay Peninsula, some 1,550 square miles (4,000 sq km). Khao Sok is characterized by precipitous limestone outcrops and mountains carpeted in rain forest.

The major attraction of Khao Sok is the **Chieo Lan Reservoir,** a lake created on the Pasaeng River in 1982, some 40 miles (64 km) from the park's entrance and accessible by road from park headquarters, just off Highway 401. More than 100 craggy limestone monoliths protrude from the immense lake, creating an awesome, primordial wonderland. Visit in the early morning, when these limestone islands are shrouded in a light mist.

The limestone peaks around the reservoir are pockmarked with caves. Subterranean streams, fantastic rock formations, and stalactites and stalagmites make up the **Tham Nam Thalu** cave complex. In the1970s, Communist rebels used the confusing passageways of **Tham Si Ru,** a cave with four converging passageways, as a hideout. The entrance to **Tham Khang Dao,** a haunt for thousands of bats, is high on a cliff.

Maps of the park, marked with a number of trails, can be picked up at the visitor center at park headquarters. Tracks running along the park's major watercourse, the **Klong Sok,** wind past enormous stands of bamboo and tangled tropical rain forests. About 1.5 miles (2.5 km) from the headquarters, the falls at **Wing Hin** ("running rock waterfall") tumble 65 feet (20 m) onto huge rocks worn smooth by the incessant wash. Another 2 miles (3 km) on is **Tang Nam,** where the Klong Sok has worn a dramatic gorge through the mountains. At the gorge is a deep pool of crystal-clear water, perfect for swimming.

Some 2 miles (3 km) beyond Tang Nam is one of the park's most beautiful waterfalls, **Ton Gloy.** Water tumbles into a clear pool fringed by thick jungle. On top of the falls, flat rocks make platforms for panoramic views over the park.

A track behind the park's restaurant leads 2.5 miles (4 km)

past tall bamboo forests, criss-crossing the Bang Laen River six times, to the base of **Sip Et Chan waterfall.** Here, waters cascade over 11 tiers before crashing into a wide pool.

Trails and river crossings are safer and more manageable during the dry season, from December through April. However, to see

Jungle-laden limestone cliffs dominate much of Khao Sok National Park's scenery. Opposite: Elephant trekking, along with pony trekking and river rafting, are some of the activities available in the park.

Wild lotus

Khao Sok is home to one of the world's rarest and largest flowers, the *bua poot,* or wild lotus (*Rafflesia kerri meijer*). The parasitic flower spends most of the year as microscopic threads drawing nutrients from inside the roots of lianas, a common jungle vine. Buds develop inside the bark of the roots, bursting through and swelling to the size of a chicken. When they bloom, in January and February, the reddish-brown flowers grow to an astonishing 32 inches (82 cm) in diameter. The scent is most unpleasant to humans, but insects love it. The flower can be seen along some of the park's trails. Ask the rangers for directions. ■

waterfalls at their surging best, and to have a better chance of spotting the monkeys, gibbons, gaurs and bantengs (both species of ox), langurs, wild boars, elephants, and Malayan sun bears that live in the park, go toward the end of the wet season—August to October.

Longer excursions into the park, including elephant and pony trekking and river rafting, can be arranged at the guesthouses just outside the park's entrance or with rangers. Park-administered accommodations are available, but most visitors opt for the nearby private guesthouses. Tree Tops Jungle Guesthouse (*contact Vieng Travel in Bangkok, tel 02-280-3537 or Greenwood Travel Phuket, tel 076-331018*) has tree houses, cave lodges, and raft houses. ■

Mu Ko Surin
Marine National Park

THIS SPECTACULAR PROTECTED AREA OF MARINE PARK presents an ideal opportunity to explore some of Thailand's most pristine environments, both above and below the water, in agreeable isolation. While this group of five islands in the Andaman Sea, 62 miles (100 km) north of the Similan Islands and 37 miles (60 km) from the mainland, is known for its diving, the archipelago has dimensions that also make it appealing to nondivers.

Some excellent hiking trails cut across the two major islands of **Ko Surin Nua** and **Ko Surin Tai,** separated by a narrow channel that can be crossed on foot at low tide. These trails climb through rain forest, with quantities of wildlife (monkeys, lemurs, mouse deer, squirrels, and birds) sheltering in a canopy of green that averages 106 feet (32 m) in height. The islands are indented with shimmering white-sand bays, protected by rocky headlands.

Easily accessible reefs just off the coast and in shallow waters around the islands, together with vivid coral and teeming marine life, make the five Surin islands Thailand's premier snorkeling location. The park headquarters near **Ao Mae Yai,** a deep, tranquil bay on the southeast side of Ko Surin Nua, rents snorkeling gear, although the quality is variable. They also run longtail boat charters to snorkeling sites and beaches, and operate a restaurant and small bar.

Inexpensive, basic dormitory-style bungalows on Ko Surin Nua are available but must be reserved at the park's mainland office in Ban Hin Lat (*tel 076-491378*), north of Kura Buri, which is 100 miles (160 km) north of Phuket. They can also be booked at the Marine National Park Division of the Royal Forestry Department in Bangkok.

Distance from the mainland, deep water, and strong north–south ocean currents keep the waters clean around the islands, stimulating the growth of coral, especially in the sheltered bays on the eastern seaboard.

Visibility of up to 66 feet (20 m) is not uncommon during the dry season, from November to April. **Ao Mae Yai** is the best site for snorkeling, where shallow, clear waters drop into abundant and beautiful corals, with colorfully attendant parrot fish, clownfish, lionfish, and angelfish.

Ko Chi, a large rocky outcrop north of Ko Surin Nua, is also suitable for snorkeling. It is notable for its large visiting pelagics, and it is one of the best places on the islands to see sea turtles, including the occasional giant leatherback. **Turtle Ledge,** a shallow platform off the east side of Ko Surin Tai, is also a good place to spot turtles swimming around the sloping reef. Thick schools of darting batfish are also found among the staghorn and spiny acropora corals.

Just east of Turtle Ledge, **Hin Kong** is a spectacular undersea muddle of boulders, cliffs, caves, and arches.

The premier dive site is **Richelieu Rock,** southeast of Ko Surin Nua and Ko Surin Tai. The reef here is covered with a

Mu Ko Surin Marine National Park
🅐 263 A2
Marine National Parks Division
✉ Royal Forestry Department, 61 Phahonyothin Rd., Bangkhen, Bangkok
☎ 02-561-2921

Visitor information
✉ Tourism Authority of Thailand, 5 Talat Mai Rd., Surat Thani
☎ 077-288818

One of Ko Surin's glorious beaches

profusion of purple and pink gorgonian coral. Divers are presented with a rare pleasure—the chance to swim with magnificent whale sharks, the largest fish in the world. Richelieu Rock is one of the few dive sites in the world where these creatures are seen regularly.

At **Ko Torinla,** half a mile from Ko Surin Tai, a sloping reef takes you past vivid gardens of sea anemones. Grouper and red coral trout hide in the corals. A shallow section is a carpet of staghorns. There are many shelves along the reef—the shallower ones harbor hermit crabs, urchins, and shrimp.

A community of sea gypsies (*chao lae,* see pp. 284–85) lives on a beach in Ko Surin Tai. Visit their village for an insight into the subsistence lifestyle of these mostly nomadic people. The chao lae on Ko Surin are paid to collect turtle eggs for a hatchery on Ko Surin Nua. In April, Surin's chao lae honor their ancestors by launching colorfully decorated minature boats from the beach. The boats represent the fortunes of their clans, and if they return to the same beach, the tradition holds the community must move to a new location.

Trips from the mainland aboard marine park boats run daily, from mid-November to April (the park is closed other times), from **Ban Hit Lit.** Rangers will also help arrange private charters. Live-aboard dive boats will take nondiving visitors (see Ko Similan, pp. 287–88). Several companies also offer excursions from Phuket. ■

People of the sea

Thailand's sea gypsies come in three groups—Moken, Urak Lawoi, and Moklen—but are collectively called *chao lae* (people of the sea) by the Thais. Their dusky complexions, thick mops of black hair, and small but sturdy frames distinguish them from Thais.

Many sea gypsies earn a meager living selling fish at small markets.

Their beliefs are strongly rooted in animist ritual, and they have no interest in becoming either Buddhist or Muslim. The chao lae forsake material possessions. They are shy, coy, and vulnerable, and avoid confrontation. They are egalitarian; any central authority is anathema, and they cannot countenance officialdom. The chao lae, therefore, present all the credentials needed to push them beyond the margins of mainstream society: they look different, they think differently, and they worship different gods.

Thailand's estimated 4,000 chao lae mostly live as ocean itinerants, sailing, fishing, diving for oysters, and camping from island to island. Others are packed into ramshackle villages of corrugated iron and cardboard on Andaman Sea islands to fish in ever decreasing areas or to sell trinkets to tourists.

Thailand accepts the chao lae as long-term guests, not citizens. They have no political rights and no security of tenure. This, and their refusal to deal with anything outside their own belief systems, has made the sea gypsies outcasts.

The chao lae have a hidden history. There is no written language, and the eschewing of material possessions has left them with few heirlooms with which to trace their past. A nomadic existence has left no monumental legacies, and their taciturn nature precludes an oral history. Colonial tales cast them as pirates who terrorized maritime traffic in the Straits of Malacca.

The chao lae choose to live within confined geographical boundaries, from the islands in Myanmar to Langkawi, just south of the Thai–Malaysia sea border.

The 400 Moken most exemplify the romantic notion of the sea gypsy: families live aboard boats and fish, with no terrestrial roots. The thousand or so Moklen live in beach shacks on islands from the Surins to the northern tip of Phuket, using longtail boats for fishing. The Urak Lawoi are the largest group and the most settled, numbering about 2,500. They are mainly found in Phuket, in villages on Ko Sirey near Phuket town, and at the northern end of Rawai Beach. Other settlements are found on the Phi Phi islands, Ko Lanta, and the Tarutao archipelago. The three groups have different but not dissimilar languages. They intermarry and share the same strong sense of community and solidarity.

The chao lae continue to fish to survive, but they can't compete with the huge trawlers that have depleted their traditional fishing grounds. Large areas of these have been taken away from them in the cynical and uncompromising name of environmentalism. In frustration they have resorted to explosives and poisons to increase their catch, and end up in jail. They are now—again because of depletion—prohibited from collecting the shells and corals they used to sell to visitors. Their future is bleak. ∎

Above right: Sea gypsies have their own beliefs and rituals and, with no political rights, are often marginalized from Thai society. Below right: Because of the sea gypsies' poverty and their transitory way of life, their dwellings are frequently ramshackle.

Mu Ko Similan Marine National Park

THE NINE ISLANDS OF THE MU KO SIMILAN MARINE National Park present a combination of beauty above and below the sea that few places can match. The archipelago, basking in the Andaman Sea about 25 miles (40 km) from Thailand's southwest coast, is rated as one of Asia's top dive sites. Similan is derived from the Malay word for "nine," *sembilan*—a prosaic name for such a stunning place.

The huge granite boulders that form the Similan islands slide into crystalline waters to create an underwater theme park of extreme and bizarre beauty. Under the water, the boulders form canyons, caves, tunnels, and twisted overhangs garnished with vivid coral. Reef walls slope steeply downward for 133 feet (40 m) to the seabed, with huge bommies (coral heads), riotously colored soft corals, and sea fans waving in the surging current.

Above the water's surface the beauty continues. Sweeps of brilliant white sand touch azure waters, while inland thick green foliage creeps over steep, craggy hills and hangs from the cliffs.

Fantasy Reef, on the west coast of Ko Similan (Island #8), is one of the most popular dives. Rock formations cover a huge expanse, delivering an imagination-stretching array of caves, arches, boulders, and nooks flush with iridescent corals and giant fans, in depths ranging from 45 to 133 feet (15 to 40 m). **Beacon Reef (South),** at the southern end of Ko Similan, has a steep dropoff with a remarkable diversity of hard corals from near the surface to the seabed, 116 feet (35 m) below.

Three giant rocks rear from the sea at **Elephant Head,** between Ko Similan and Ko Payu (Island #7), and fall 100 feet (30 m) to the seabed to form a natural amphitheater that gives the impression of swimming in a giant aquarium. Yellowtails, snapper, lionfish, coral trout, yellowed and black Moorish idols, and angelfish are found in abundance.

And so it goes on, from the inquisitive batfish escorting divers at **BatFish Bend** near Ko Miang Sang (Island #6), to the sheer 130-foot (40 m) coral wall and leopard sharks at **Ko Miang** (Island #4). There are more incredible dive sites at **Ko Payan** and **Ko Payang.** At **Ko Huyong** (Island #1), at the southern end of the island group, boulders create a deranged jumble of underwater ledges, caves, and archways.

VISITING THE ISLANDS
National park offices are on Ko Miang and Ko Similan. Ko Miang has a camping area and bungalows. Reservations for the bungalows must be made at least a month in advance through the Marine National Park Division of the Royal Forestry Department in Bangkok, or at its office in Thap Lamu *(tel 077-411914).* Longtail boats can be hired at Ko Similan or Ko Miang

On the west coast, which takes the brunt of the southwesterly monsoons from May to October, are rugged coastlines where weathered boulders on the shoreline roll down into the sea.

Around Ko Similan's nine islands—each of which carries a number as well as a name—are 19 recognized dive sites, all claiming special characteristics. On the northern edge of the group, **Christmas Point,** at Ko Bangru (Island #9), has a drift taking you through a maze of giant arches. Abundant radiant soft coral growth mingles with huge sea fans and hordes of small fish. **Breakfast Bend,** also on Ko Bangru, is best tackled early morning, when light filters through the water, enhancing multicolored coral gardens.

Mu Ko Similan Marine National Park
🅰 263 A1
Marine National Parks Division
✉ Royal Forestry Department, 61 Phahonyothin Rd., Bangkhen, Bangkok
☎ 02-561-2921

Visitor information
✉ Tourism Authority of Thailand, 5 Talat Mai Rd., Surat Thani
☎ 077-288818

Low tide exposes some of Mu Ko Similan's rich variety of corals.

for trips to other islands. A good beach on Ko Similan is Campbell's Bay; climb the huge boulder at the north end for wide views.

Most visitors arrive on live-aboard dive boats from Phuket, 62 miles (100 km) south (see pp. 324–28), for three- to five-day diving expeditions. Others come via Thap Lamu, 25 miles (40 km) east, near the resort town of Khao Lak, in Ranong. Reputable operators in Phuket include: Fantasea Divers *(tel 076-340088)*, Siam Diving Center *(tel 076-330936)*, Marina Divers *(tel 076-330272)*, Scuba Cat Diving *(tel 076-293120)*, and Dive Asia *(tel 076-330598)*. ■

Longtail boats

Originally used as fishing and trading vessels, these sleek, speedy, but noisy boats are now more likely to be found ferrying tourists and locals across rivers and lakes and to and from islands. They were designed as sailboats but now come with 10-foot (3 m) rods attached to a huge diesel motor at the stern. The rod or "tail" has a propellor affixed to it and works as a rudder. One crew member has the arduous task of steering the boat by pushing and pulling the end of the tail. ■

More places to visit in Southern Thailand

BURMA BANKS

About 81 miles (130 km) off the coast, past the Surin islands, is one of the world's fabled diving sites, the Burma Banks, with riotous underwater fields of colored coral. Farther north, the **Meguri Islands,** an archipelago laced with hundreds of uninhabited islands and multitudinous coral reefs running for hundreds of miles off the coast of Myanmar (Burma), are yet another Andaman Sea diving wonderland.

Diving tours to the Burma Banks, and diving and ecotours to the Meguris, can be arranged through the numerous dive shops in Phuket.

🄰 263 A2

ISTHMUS OF KRA

From Chumphon on the Gulf of Thailand, Highway 4 slices through the luxuriant mountainous spine of the Malay Peninsula before edging the Myanmar (Burma) border and swinging south to Ranong. From there it rolls down the scenic Andaman Sea coast toward Phuket. The narrowest point of the peninsula, the Isthmus of Kra, is signposted north of Ranong, near the town of Kra Buri. Here, a scant 14 miles (22 km) of land separate the Pacific Ocean from the Pak Chan Estuary, which opens into the Indian Ocean.

Plans to carve a canal across the isthmus are pulled off the shelf every now and again. Such a waterway would allow shipping a short cut between the Andaman and South China Seas, cutting days off the journey from Europe and the Middle East, via the Straits of Malacca and Singapore, to East Asia.

🄰 263 B3

KHAO LAK

One of the south's best-kept secrets is the 15-mile (25 km) string of delightful beaches paralleling Highway 4 between Takua Pa (midway between Ranong and Phuket) and the sleepy village of Khao Lak.

There are numerous understated resorts along this stretch, a favorite place for European visitors. Khao Lak's long white-sand beach is one of the most popular, but never crowded, even during the November–March

Giant gorgonians are one of the natural treasures divers find at the Burma Banks.

peak holiday season. You can charter longtail boats at the resorts, for snorkeling trips to a large coral reef about 45 minutes offshore. The beach runs nearly as far as **Hat Ban Sak,** 8.5 miles (14 km) north, a beach fringed with casuarina (sea pine trees) on a wide, scenic bay that is a great spot for picnics on weekends.

🄰 263 A1, 263 B2

WAT THAM PRAKAYANG

About 7.5 miles (12 km) south of Kra Buri, turn left at the Kilometer 504 road marker to the cave temple of Wat Tham Prakayang. Borrow a flashlight from the monks to explore this deep cave, which leads to an image-filled cavern. The highlight is an unusual jet-black Buddha image, with eyes fixed in mother-of-pearl.

Farther south on Highway 4, **Punya Ban Falls** can be seen tumbling from a high cliff to the left of the road, about 10 miles (16 km) north of Ranong. A little farther south, the road opens up expansive views of the Pak Chan Estuary—the border with Myanmar (Burma) and the islands dotting the Andaman Sea beyond.

🄰 263 B3 ∎

Ko Samui archipelago

Off the coast of Surat Thani, in the Gulf of Thailand, is a tousled array of 80 islands—only five populated—with myriad shapes, sizes, and persuasions. The Ko Samui archipelago has a swashbuckling history of seafarers, shipwrecks, pioneers, and trailblazing travelers. The archetypal tropical island of Ko Samui, the group's largest, is one of Southeast Asia's favorite holiday getaways, but these days visitors are also attracted to the "Big Island's" idyllic satellites.

About 150 years ago, Hainanese explorers sailed south from China to settle on Ko Samui and began harvesting coconuts. Apart from earning a reputation as a prolific coconut exporter, Ko Samui was known for little else. The island and its people—the industrious Hainanese, independent *chao Samui* (people of Samui), and a scattering of Muslim Thai-Malay settlers—basked more or less anonymously under the Gulf of Thailand sun for the next 125 years. As backpacker legend has it, the second major wave of international travelers began arriving in the mid-1970s and were instantly overwhelmed by the island's deserted, palm-packed beaches and friendly, unaffected people.

Those idyllic times are long gone. Samui now bursts at the seams with 500,000 visitors a year. More than 250 hotels and bungalow "resorts" line the beaches, ranging from mosquito-net basic to five-star cabana. Nightlife covers the gamut, from rowdy down-to-earth to nascent sophistication. The tourist infrastructure is first class, and access to water

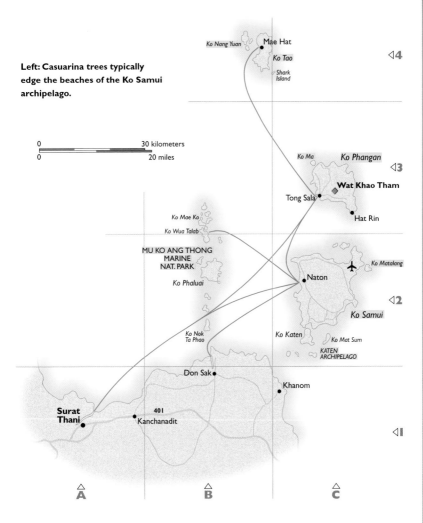

Left: Casuarina trees typically edge the beaches of the Ko Samui archipelago.

sports and other activities is unhindered. Nonetheless, after all these years and all these changes, Ko Samui, with its unshakable carefree nature and honest island feel, is still a great place to visit.

Ko Samui's popularity has awoken its neighboring islands. People wanting to escape the crowds have sometimes found other, more tranquil gems. Frequent inter-island boat services, organized day trips, and diving and snorkeling tours to islands around the archipelago smooth the rough edges of adventure. Ko Phangan, the second largest island of the group, best known for its raucous Full Moon parties, has dozens of isolated, tranquil coves decked with shimmering sands hiding along its rugged coastline. Lonely Ko

Tao, on the outskirts of the archipelago, has become a scuba diver's paradise, with a plethora of excellent dive sites just off its coastline.

And there is the magnificent Ang Thong group. Wrapped in a blanket of national park protection, this beautiful group of over 40 islands is swamped with idyllic bays, indented hills of deep green jungle, and clear waters. Add to this the dozens of other uninhabited islands, and the archipelago becomes a tropical paradise.

The archipelago is best visited during the dry season, from January to June. Rains begin in early July and continue to build until the end of the year. Torrential rains often lash the islands in November and December. ■

Ko Samui

NO MATTER WHAT THEIR BUDGET, INCLINATION, OR pleasure, visitors to 95-square-mile (247 sq km) Ko Samui usually find what they are looking for. Ko Samui is that sort of place—easy-going and hedonistic. There are $3-a-night thatched bungalows in the shadows of gleaming new hotels. Crowded, lively beaches lie a rocky headland away from sweeping, near-deserted bays. Luxury resorts in secluded coves front modest jungle-spa hideaways. The miscellaneous nightlife disappoints few. And all this is built on the solid foundation of excellent tourist facilities and services.

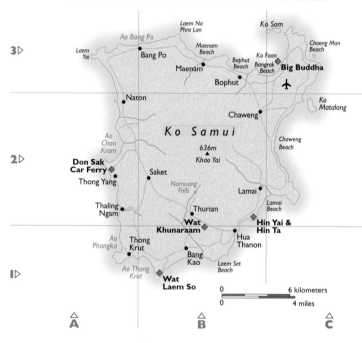

Ko Samui
- 263 C2 & 291 C2

Visitor information
- Tourism Authority of Thailand, 5 Talad Mai Rd., Surat Thani
- 077-288818

- Tourism Authority of Thailand, Northern end of Naton, Ko Samui
- 077-420504

Only a few minutes from Samui's airport (one of the most delightful anywhere in the world, with open-sided palm-thatched halls and landscaped gardens blazing with tropical flowers) is **Chaweng Beach,** the island's most popular and longest beach. A 4.5-mile-long (7 km) sweep of fine white sand on the east coast of the island gently inclines to clear waters. Generous groves of coconut palms edge the beach, and a backdrop of Samui's green and rugged interior completes the tropical island scene. Despite a concentration of development, Chaweng Beach manages to maintain its tropical charm and is an agreeable place to spend some time.

Among the rows of palms, inexpensive bungalows sit beside luxury hotels. Although not completely hidden, most of these places are unobtrusive, and in some areas the more attractive timber bungalows and open,

timber-decked restaurants add to the beach's resort appeal.

The crowded middle reaches of the beach are also the most attractive and the best sector for water sports. Windsurfers, hoby cats (instructors are available), and jet skis can be hired. Visitors attached to billowing parachutes are towed along by speedboats, to float high above the coconut palms.

The shallow waters here at the northern end of the island are sheltered inside a coral reef running parallel to the beach, which creates a lagoon at low tide. The southern end of Chaweng is more open to the ocean and less crowded.

The laid-back tropical ambience of Chaweng Beach dissipates with a thud about 100 yards (90 m) back from the shore. A road parallel to the beach runs nearly its entire length, lined with bars, restaurants, mini-marts, tailor shops, video parlors, tour agencies, banks, and dive shops. Midway along this route is Chaweng's

Longtail boats stand by to ferry passengers to other islands.

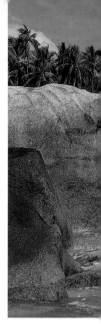

entertainment epicenter: a chaotic, thumping collection of bars, nightclubs, and discos blasting away into the night and reverberating onto the nearby sands.

South of Chaweng, just off Samui's ring road, Highway 4169, is **Lamai Beach,** the island's second most popular beach. It's about half the length of Chaweng but shares many of its characteristics—a long, wide, fabulous stretch of white sand and clean water, fringed by bending coconut palms under which sit bungalows and hotels. However, the water here is deeper, there are fewer visitors, and the beach has fewer pretensions than its neighbor. A less frenetic, although in some places seedier, nightlife erupts along the road on the far side of the coconut palms. Lamai has a more down-market feel, escaping—for better or worse—much of the newer resort development found on Chaweng.

At the rocky outcrop that defines the southern end of Lamai are a pair of conspicuous formations known as **Hin Yai** and **Hin Ta,** or "grandfather rock" and "grandmother rock," weathered into the suggestive shapes of male and female genitalia. Legend has it that the bodies of an elderly couple were washed up on the shore after a shipwreck to create the rocks.

Heading north from Lamai, past Chaweng Beach, the secondary route, Highway 4171, skirts a headland through rugged scenery, past isolated coves to the quiet and curving **Choeng Mon Beach.** Here, abandoned rice barges have been converted into upscale accommodations, adding an idiosyncratic touch to one of the island's most attractive bays. Toward the tip of the headland, off a dirt road, is **Laem Samrong,** a cape indented with rocky coves and patches of brilliant-white sand that are to be found at the end of narrow paths.

From Laem Samrong, the road continues, passing the landmark 38-foot (12 m) golden **Big Buddha** statue, which is set on an islet attached to a short causeway, at the top of a brightly painted *naga* staircase. The image dominates **Bangrak,** or "Big Buddha" Beach, a narrow 2-mile (3 km) strip of coarse brownish sand with shallow and cloudy water—not the most appealing of Samui's beaches.

Beyond the rocky headland Bangrak gives way to **Bophut Beach,** more notable for its charming, unaffected village (believed to be Samui's first settlement) than the quality of its sand or sea; thickets of leaning coconut palms and a verdant hilly backdrop add to its character and appeal. The beach is favored by visitors who seek peace and quiet, and a friendly community feel. Quaint timber buildings at Bophut village—a short walk from the beach—have been dressed up as European restaurants.

From Bophut and Bangrak, speedboats can be chartered to Ko Phangan, Ko Tao, and other islands in the archipelago.

To the west of Bophut, past a jutting cape, a right turn at the village of Maenam leads to **Maenam Beach,** an isolated, 3-mile (5 km) gentle curve of narrow white sand and clear water. The water is calm and deep, offering good conditions for the hoby cats and windsurfers on hire here. There are good, clear views of Ko Phangan from restaurants along the beach.

Scenic Highway 4169 follows the island's rocky northern coastline, passing villages and coral-fringed bays, before turning down to Ko Samui's bustling port and commercial center, **Naton.**

The majority of visitors arrive here by ferry from Surat Thani. (There is also a car-ferry port south of Ataon at Thong Yang.) There is little reason to stay around Naton, but it's worth calling in at the Tourism Authority of Thailand's office *(tel 077-420504)* at the northern end of the town.

Ko Samui's western and southern coastlines are more noted for their solitude than their sandy bays. Highway 4169 cuts a hilly and scenic course inland from Naton, through plantations of coconut palms, before joining the east coast at the Muslim village of **Hua Thanon,** near Lamai.

To visit the south coast, take Highway 4170 just before the village of Ban Saket. A handful of luxury resorts nestle along the rocky shoreline. On the tip of a cape at one end of Ao Thong Krut, waves wash the striking **Wat Laem So,** a Srivijaya-style *chedi* embellished with hundreds of bright yellow tiles. Towering coconut palms just yards from clear waters set an idyllic scene at **Laem Set Beach,** which can be found on the southeastern corner of the island.

Just a mile (1.5 km) north of the junction where Highway 4169 meets the ring road is **Wat Khunaraam,** famous for the macabre sight of Luang Pordeang, a monk who died while meditating 25 years ago and was "mysteriously" mummified. The venerated monk still sits in the lotus position.

Samui's rugged hinterland rises to a peak of 2,087 feet (636 m) at **Khao Yai** near the center of the island. Trails crisscross the island, climbing through thick jungle, past streams and waterfalls. You can hike to viewpoints offering fabulous panoramas or take elephant treks to tumbling waterfalls. One of the best of these, **Namuang,** pours over a sheer cliff for 250 feet (80 m) and thunders into a cool emerald pool. The falls are at their best toward the end of the rainy season, in November and December.

The best way to travel around the island is by car or motorbike, both of which can be hired from operators in Naton, Chaweng, Lamai, and other beaches. ■

Rocks frame Lamai Beach. After Chaweng, this is Ko Samui's second most popular stretch of sand.

Marine national parks of the South

Only about 5 percent of visitors to Thailand's 80 national parks are foreigners, and most of those crowd into only a few of the 17 marine national parks in the South.

The country's ongoing environmental abuse and the delays in starting to preserve its coastal and marine heritage have taken their toll, but the marine national parks still offer some of the most gorgeous scenery and pristine environments in Thailand—both above and below the water.

The first marine national park, Khao Sam Roi Yot, was not set up until 1966, and the second, Mu Ko Tarutao, an archipelago spreading down the southwest coast to the Malaysian border, was not declared until 1974.

Many more marine national parks have been added to the list since then, but much of the environment had already been badly damaged through carelessness and greed: overfishing, dynamite fishing, and anchor drag have depleted marine life and destroyed coral reefs. Wetlands and mangrove forests have been turned into shrimp farms, destroying the habitats of wildlife. Unfortunately, all this is still happening.

The advent of mass tourism in Southern Thailand since the early 1990s has compounded the problem, as pressure increases to develop tourist resorts inside marine national parks. This is especially evident in the Phi Phi–Hat Nopparat Thara Marine National Park, where some of the beaches and islands have been burdened with ill-considered (and frequently illegal) development.

While legislation is in place to protect the national parks, at times it is flagrantly abused, often by high-ranking politicians and prominent businessmen. However, a small, vocal environmental lobby and a sympathetic media are slowly turning the tide. Growing numbers of people are speaking out against encroachment and other abuses.

Despite these difficulties, Southern Thailand's marine national parks, in general, are well managed and still have plenty to offer. Some of the more isolated parks are sparkling, untouched gems rarely visited by foreigners. Here you find the special solitude that gives tropical islands their enchanting edge. Such islands are not very difficult or prohibitively expensive to get to—try Ko Surin, Ko Tarutao, Ko Phetra, or Hat Chao Mai.

On most marine park islands, rangers operate clean and comfortable bungalows (mainly dormitory style), which can be rented as complete units. Many parks also have privately run accommodations.

Rangers hand out maps, offer advice, help visitors arrange boat trips to other islands or coral reefs, and often act as guides. At the more isolated islands, there are park-run restaurants and small provision stores.

Southern Thailand's marine parks can get irritatingly busy on weekends, public holidays, and school vacations, but at other times they remain almost deserted. It is safest to book accommodations in advance at the Marine National Parks Division of the Forestry Department head office in Bangkok *(61 Phahonyothin Rd., Bangkhen, Bangkok 10900, tel 02-561-2921)*. The Tourism Authority of Thailand (TAT) offices in provincial capitals or major tourist centers also book accommodations.

For scuba divers, marine national parks offer some of the best dive sites in Asia. Like many other tourism sectors in Thailand, the infrastructure is first class. There are numerous dive shops in Southern Thailand that supply training, equipment, and transportation—and they are inexpensive. ∎

Opposite and above: The overdevelopment of tourism in the South threatens the beaches and waters of Ko Phi Phi Don. Below: Longtail boats are often the main means of transportation between marine parks.

Ko Phangan

THIS, THE SAMUI ARCHIPELAGO'S SECOND LARGEST island, is hardly a convenient paradise. A rugged coastline and mountainous interior put up intimidating barriers against infrastructure, so that much of the island remains undeveloped and, apart from the riotous monthly full moon bashes, tranquil and laid-back. For many, Ko Phangan is a pleasing throwback to the Samui and Phuket of the 1970s.

Ferries from Naton, Surat Thani, and Ko Tao arrive at **Tong Sala,** Phangan's jumbled port town and service center. Speedboats and longtail boats from Ko Samui's Bophut and Bangrak Beaches deposit visitors at the beach of Hat Rin, in the south of the island.

The roads are poor, and transportation around the island can be treacherous. Motorbikes may be rented but are not recommended unless you are an experienced rider. Mostly, the best option for visiting the island's glorious string of east coast beaches is by chartering longtail boats.

Hat Rin, Phangan's most popular beach, runs along a stubby tail of land on the island's southern tip. It can be reached from Tong Sala by boat or along a winding and very hilly road with spectacular coastal views. There are beaches on both sides of this wide verdant cape, although **Hat Rin Nok** on the eastward side, with its fringe of palm trees, wider stretches of sand, and cleaner and deeper water, is the preferable side of the cape. On the full moon each month, up to 6,000 people descend on Hat Rin for the full moon party, a recent tradition that has quickly become an institution, attracting international attention. It is a wild, dusk-till-dawn, cacophonous affair of blasting music and frantic, wide-eyed mob dancing.

An irritatingly pretentious "backbacker chic" can pervade the atmosphere along Hat Rin's beaches, and a messy collection of bungalows, restaurants, tacky souvenir shops, and bars have grown up along parts of the cape. Visitors who prefer peace and quiet to attitude and posturing would do better to look elsewhere.

Boats or chartered longtails from Hat Rin (between February and November) travel up the east coast past beautiful beaches with palms, jungle-clad cliff ridges, and milk-white sand following the contours of coves and bays. Some of these remote beaches have a few modest bungalows for hire.

A two-hour hike to the north along a well-marked trail from Hat Rin leads to the first beach, the deserted and beautiful **Hat Yuan.** Farther along the trail is **Hat Tien,** tucked into a crescent-shaped bay, with bungalows shaded by coconut palms. North of Hat Sadet is magnificent **Ao Tong Nai Pan,** a twin-horseshoe bay chiseled out of the rugged coast. Here, a few basic bungalows face the beaches under the palm trees.

It is possible to follow the coastal trail all the way from Hat Rin to Ao Tong Nai Pan, staying at bungalows or camping along the way—it's about 9 miles (15 km), and guides, who can be arranged for at the bungalows or through travel agents, are required.

Other hiking trails offer an excellent chance to explore the island's interior, with the benefit of

an experienced guide. Trails climb rugged limestone slopes through luxuriant jungle, past streams to tumbling waterfalls.

From Ao Tong Nai Pan, a rough dirt road tapering into a trail leads to Hat Khuat, or **Bottle Beach**—one of the most attractive on the northeastern corner of island. Continuing west, around the imposing cliffs of Laem Kung Yai, you come to **Hat Khom,** yet another splendid beach, curving at the edge of rugged, forested hills. Both Hat Khuat and Hat Khom beaches have basic accommodations, and are joined by a steep trail over the ridge. You can also get there, and to Ao Tong Nai Pan (depending on the weather), by chartering a longtail boat from the pleasant fishing village of **Ban Chaloklam,** set on a deep bay. To get to Ban Chaloklam, an adventurous *songthaew* ride from Tong Sala is required.

On the road from Tong Sala to Hat Rin, and just before the village of Ban Tai, a dirt road leads inland to **Wat Khao Tham,** a Buddhist meditation retreat at the top of a forested peak. The retreat holds meditation classes for foreigners but is strictly regimented. ■

Uncrowded Ko Phangan reminds many people of Ko Samui and Phuket in the 1970s.

RETREATING
You can register for the retreats at Wat Khao Tham, or write in advance (P. O. Box 18, Ko Pha Ngan, Surat Thani, 84280).

Ko Tao

NAMED TURTLE ISLAND AFTER ITS MOUNTAINOUS HUMP-
backed, turtle-shell shape, Ko Tao is a green and white speck of an
island lulling in the Gulf of Thailand, 26 miles (45 km) north of Ko
Samui and 25 miles (40 km) from the mainland, and is easily missed.
Its lucid waters, abundant coral, and swarming marine life have made
it a haven for increasing numbers of scuba divers.

**Barracuda cruise off Ko Tao, a
favorite spot for divers.**

Sandy bays defined by rocky
headlands dot the south and west
coasts of Ko Tao. On the north and
east coasts, huge smooth granite
boulders run from the shore, and
climb and lodge on jungled hills in
a quirky display. The island's lush
and hilly hinterland squeezes into
an area of just 8 square miles
(21 sq km) and peaks at a
respectable 1,027 feet (313 m).
Although there are plenty of
beaches on Ko Tao, shallow waters
preclude serious swimming.

Ko Tao's waters, and those of
nearby islets, are well away from
coastal runoffs, allowing coral to
thrive in exceptionally clear water.
The abundance of coral has lured
large numbers of reef fish, giving
the area the best dive sites in the
Gulf of Thailand.

Despite its relative isolation, Ko
Tao is easy to reach. Regular ferries
and charter boats ply from Ko
Samui, Ko Pha Ngan, and
Chumphon to Ban Mae Hat, the
island's service town, where there
are a number of dive shops. Expect
to be accosted by touts offering dive
trips; ignore them and head to the
dive shops in Ban Mae Hat to find a
trip that suits your itinerary.

One of the great advantages of
diving around Ko Tao is the
proximity of the dive sites to the
island and to each other. Virtually
all are within 30–45 minutes of the
island, allowing for several dives per
day. Dive tours can be booked from
Ko Samui or from any one of the
20 or so dive shops on Ko Tao.
Competition and convenience have
kept prices down, and made the
island the least expensive place in
Thailand to earn or improve scuba-
diving certification.

About a half-mile (1 km) south
lies Hin Khao, or **White Rock,**
so called because the sunlight
refracting through the water makes
the two coral-dressed submerged
pinnacles appear ghostly white. The
dive drops about 65 feet (20 m)
among varied coral and marine life,
including feisty triggerfish. The
spot is popular for night dives,
when the abundant small marine
life attracts turtles and barracuda.

Eastward, the four **Chumphon
Pinnacles** rise high above the sea,

Ko Tao

⚑ 263 C3 &
291 B4

Visitor information

✉ Tourism Authority of
Thailand, 5 Talad
Mai Rd., Surat Thani
84000

☎ 077-288818

the tallest reaching 52 feet (16 m) above the surface. The dive averages 65 feet (20 m) and features ledges, overhangs, and gorges. This is a favorite haunt for pelagics, including schools of barracuda, tuna, mackerel, and giant trevalley.

At dorsal-shaped **Shark Island,** just off the southeastern tip of Ko Tao, gorgonian fans wave in the tidal surges. An underwater tunnel and cruising pelagics add drama to the site.

Closer to shore, coral reefs growing in shallow waters off the headlands and beaches are ideal for snorkeling. The best spot is off the beach at **Ao Leuk,** on Ko Tao's southeast coast.

Sai Ree Beach dominates the west coast with its long stretch of palm-backed sand. It is just north of Ban Mae Hat and easily accessible by *songthaew* or on foot. A mile (1.5 km) southeast of Ban Mae Hat, arching **Chalok Ban Kao Bay** sits beneath steep cliffs.

As the popularity of Ko Tao grows with divers, its allure as a quiet tropical getaway for those who don't dive continues to diminish. The island is becoming a "scuba divers only" zone. During peak season, between January and September, most accommodations, many of which are associated with dive operations, will not rent bungalows unless guests sign up for a scuba course or take some dive trips. And its distance from other islands puts day trips out of reach. If you don't dive, there are plenty of other beaches and many other islands on which to lay your towel. ■

Chalok Ban Lao Bay at sunset

Mu Ko Ang Thong
Marine National
Park
⚠ 263 C3 &
291 B2
**Marine National
Parks Division**
✉ Royal Forestry
Department, 61
Phahonyothin Rd.,
Bangkhen, Bangkok
☎ 02-561-2129

Visitor information
✉ Mu Ko Ang Thong
Marine National
Park Office, 26/1
Mu 5 Talad Lang
Rd., Surat Thani
☎ 077-283025

Mu Ko Ang Thong Marine National Park

THE 42 ISLAND WONDERS OF THE MU KO ANG THONG
Marine National Park line up in formation along a north–south axis
between the mainland and Ko Samui, reaching as far north as Ko
Phangan and south to within 6 miles (10 km) of Surat Thani
Province. They come in a multitude of shapes and sizes, but all share
one attribute—remarkable natural beauty.

Mu Ko Ang Thong was declared a
national park in 1980. Previously it
had been under the administration
of the Royal Thai Navy, which used
its maze of sea corridors, channels,
and bays for training. As a result,
the islands remained safe from
encroachment.

This unspoiled environment
meets all the preconceptions of a
tropical paradise. The rocky
limestone islands are invariably
carpeted with thick, deep-green
forest. Brilliant white sands hide in
idyllic coves and spread generously
along bays that slope gently to the
water's calm edge. When outlined
against a deep blue sky and the
sparkling waters of the Gulf of
Thailand, they present a majestic
spectacle.

The Ang Thong islands come in
a variety of shapes that have
inspired whimsical appellations:

Sleeping Cow Island, Rhinoceros
Island, Camera Head Island, and
Tree Sorrow Island.

The islands vary in size, from
awesome craggy cliffs towering
above ribbons of white sand on the
biggest island, Ko Wua Talab, to
small, understated mounds no
bigger than a tennis court. On the
bigger islands, the beaches are
wider and shaded by forest, while
mangroves thrive in sheltered areas
where sandbars and mudflats have
developed. Lush evergreens are
dominant inland, and limestone
forest clings tenaciously to
exposed cliff faces.

Each of these 42 islands could
stand proudly against the beauty of
most other tropical islands, but the
effect of having so many jewels
encrusted into one crown in an area
of just 39 square miles (102 sq km)
is almost overwhelming. Ang

The Beach

**Opposite: The
unusual shapes of
Ang Thong's
islands have
inspired quirky
names with
meanings such as
Cow, Rhinoceros,
and Tree Sorrow.**

Ko Ang Thong was the setting
for the cult novel by the
English author Alex Garland, *The
Beach* (1996). The book was made
into the Hollywood blockbuster
movie of the same name, released
in 2000, produced by and starring
Leonardo Di Caprio. The main
protagonist in both the book and
the movie finds a map in the room
of a junkie who commits suicide in
a flophouse in Bangkok. The map

eventually leads him to a small
community of foreigners who are
living in secrecy on an island of
profound majesty. However, while
Garland settled for a backdrop
of Ang Thong for his novel,
Hollywood, for its version, moved
across the Malaysia Peninsula to
the Andaman Sea and the
stunning Maya Bay on Ko Phi Phi
Ley (see p. 331), another marine
national park. ■

Thong is reminiscent of the limestone islands and monoliths that crowd into Phangnga Bay near Phuket (see pp. 332–35), although it lacks the haunting drama of that place.

Nevertheless, you should not miss the experiences of sailing or kayaking among these lovely islands, exploring the caves, shimmering lagoons, and bounty of beaches, or climbing to breathtaking panoramas.

The islands at the northern end of Ang Thong are the best for snorkeling.

Excursions to Ang Thong are made from Ko Samui. Many operators run daily trips to the islands, which lie about 19 miles (30 km) east. Boats depart at 8:30 a.m. and return at 5 p.m. Ask your hotel or TAT office to recommend a reputable operator. Other organized tours can be arranged with travel agents on Samui or from your hotel's travel desk; these, however, tend to ply a well-worn route to the islands' attractions and generally haul mobs of other visitors along, taking the edge off the experience. It is better to take a private or small group charter organized through the larger hotels and resorts if you can. At least one tour company, Blue Stars Kayaks *(tel 077-413231)*, on Chaweng Beach, offers kayaking

trips around Ang Thong, a recommended way to explore the nooks and crannies of the islands.

Dive trips around Ang Thong are available but not recommended because of generally poor visibility, caused by the sediment washed out from the Ta Pi River Estuary. However, there is good snorkeling to be had at **Hin Nippon** and **Ko Wao,** at the northern outreaches of the archipelago, well away from the estuary.

For those who want to extend their stay, the national park administers accommodations, which must be booked and paid in person at the office in Surat Thani on the mainland. Camping is allowed on certain islands, but permission must be obtained from park rangers.

The accommodations on **Ko Wua Talab,** where the ranger station is located, are basic but comfortable dormitories, and can be rented as complete units. It is worth staying here for a day for the unrivaled panoramas and the unusual opportunity to catch both the sunrise and sunset from the same viewpoint, atop a 1,300-foot (400 m) peak.

Around the park headquarters is a good place to spot birdlife; kingfishers, Brahminy kites, white-bellied sea eagles, and sandpipers frequent the area. Swiftlets, whose nests form the ingredients of the Chinese delicacy bird's-nests soup, inhabit caves around the island.

From the park headquarters, a tough 656-foot (200 m) climb brings you to **Tham Bua Bok,** or "waving lotus cave," a name that describes the unusually shaped rock formations that fill the cavern.

The abiding beauty of **Thale Nai** waits at the top of **Ko Mae Ko,** a 790-foot (240 m) climb from the shoreline. Here, limestone peaks tower over and encircle an emerald saltwater lake, fed from a stream that cuts through the mountains. From the rim of the lake, magnificent views take in the archipelago, and the site gives the island group its name—Ang Thong means "golden bowl."

Nearby **Ko Thai Phlao** and **Ko Wua Kan Tang** are noted for their particularly dazzling beaches.

Hiking on most islands is limited by a lack of trails, but the bigger islands of Ko Wua Talab and Sam Sap have some tracks. ∎

A young boy sits in a longtail boat near Ang Thong beach. Local fishermen will take visitors on excursions around the island.

More places to visit in the Ko Samui archipelago

KATEN ARCHIPELAGO

The seven islands of the Mu Katen archipelago are scattered across the strait between the port of Don Sak, in Surat Thani, and Ko Samui. The islands are popular day trip destinations from Ko Samui; book your trip through your hotel or a travel agent on the island. Minibuses pick visitors up from their hotels and deliver them to the small fishing village of Ban Throng Kruk. Tours pass a fleet of colorful fishing boats before heading to the islands.

The 3-square-mile (7.5 sq km) **Ko Katen** is the largest island in the group and the only one populated (population 70). A number of good nature trails cut through the island's forested interior.

Ko Katen is unusual in that no dogs— domesticated or stray— live there. Mostly docile, stray dogs are found throughout Thailand. Buddhism dictates that all life is sacred, and dogs seem to be the major beneficiary of this precept. On Ko Katen, locals say dogs cannot survive because of the supernatural powers of the island's thriving cat population: The cats place a curse on any canine that has the misfortune to be washed up on the island. Ill fortune also befalls people who might bring dogs onto the island—or so legend has it.

A coral reef offers good snorkeling at **Laem Hua Sai** on the northern tip of Ko Katen. The Katen archipelago lacks good beaches, but the best are on the attractive island of **Ko Mat Sum,** where white stretches of sand incline to crystal-clear water. **Ko Daeng** is also worth a visit for its clear waters, white beaches, coral, and lack of inhabitants. Basic—in some cases primitive— accommodations are available on Ko Katen, Ko Mat Sum, and Ko Rab.
▲ Map p. 291

KO MA

About 550 yards (500 m) to the northwest off Ko Phangan, hilly and verdant Ko Ma ("dog island") is an excellent snorkeling site. Here, you'll find a wealth of marine life (angelfish, cuttlefish, red snapper, parrot fish, and wrasse) cruising and darting around the anemones and sponges that encrust the reef just offshore. A long sandy beach edges the steep, heavily forested hills.

To reach Ko Ma, charter a longtail boat from Phangan's port town of Tong Sala or from the popular Hat Rin. Boats can also be hired from the remote village of Hat Mae, opposite Ko Ma. Accommodations are available on the island.
▲ Map p. 291

KO MATALANG

Just off the northern end of Chaweng Beach (see p. 292), easily accessible Ko Matalang is rated as the best snorkeling site in the area. Sunlight penetrates the shallow reef that fringes the southern coastline of the island, accentuating the kaleidoscopic colors of the coral. Gardens of sea anemones, staghorns, gorgonians, and foliaceous coral are found here, along with the occasional cruising black-tip reef shark. You may see people wade out and swim to the island, but chartering a longtail boat is safer as currents can be unpredictable.
▲ Map p. 291

KO NANG YUAN

If you are looking for a dose of upscale isolation in an incredible setting, then Ko Nang Yuan is highly recommended. Just off the northwest tip of Ko Tao, it is a trio of small islands strung together by wide crescent-shaped, perfect-white sandbars that form two shallow, clear bays filled with coral. The middle island, a squat jumble of boulders and jungle, has a solitary upscale resort (Ko Nang Yuan Dive Resort, tel 077-437398). The two larger islands are giant mounds of granite covered with thick foliage and strewn with huge boulders, both at the shoreline and on the steep hills.

The bays are perfect for snorkeling and dive-school courses. For experienced divers there are a number of small wall dives and swimarounds. Fish, in places, are prolific. You pick up a longtail boat and make reservations for the resort from Ban Mae Hat, the main town on Kao Tao.
▲ Map p. 291 ■

Home to some of Asia's best beaches, islands, and international resorts, the most southerly part of Thailand is a tropical paradise, but with the bonus of quaint villages, bustling towns, and an intriguing mix of Buddhist and Muslim ways.

Far South

Shadow puppet, or *nang,*
figure

Far South

THAILAND'S SOUTHERN PROVINCES DOWN THE NARROW MALAY Peninsula have a distinctive and appealing topography. Rugged hinterlands are littered with forest and laced with waterfalls. Limestone monoliths, pockmarked with sanctified grottoes, jut from both land and sea. Rubber and coconut plantations buffer quaint villages and bustling tourist towns. Along the region's extensive coastlines glorious beaches shimmer and, offshore, coral-ringed islands captivate with their tropical beauty.

Distinctive, too, are the people, known as *khon pak tai*. The far south's long and colorful history has forged a hardy, polyglot race. Chinese, Muslim-Malay, and Thai cultures and traditions coexist and sometimes intermingle. Customs, dialects, festivals, cuisine, architecture, and entertainment are often co-opted and shared.

The far south is linked with the Sumatra-based Srivijaya Empire, which dominated much of what is today Indonesia, Malaysia, and Southern Thailand between the 7th and 13th centuries. With the disintegration of Srivijaya, the region, pinned to the authority of Nakhon Si Thammarat, fell under the respective rule of the Sukhothai and Ayutthaya Kingdoms, but still managed to retain a high degree of autonomy. When Ayutthaya fell in 1767, the southern provinces were controlled by the Bangkok government but remained semi-independent before being gradually absorbed into the Thai nation.

Most of Thailand's three million Muslims live in the far south.

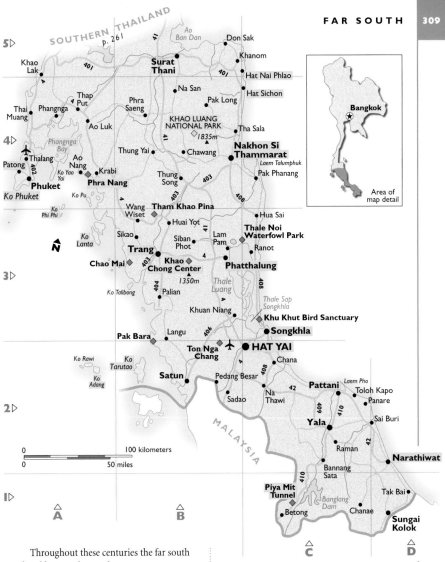

p. 261

SOUTHERN THAILAND

Ao Ban Dan
Don Sak
Khanom
Khao Lak
Surat Thani
Hat Nai Phlao
Na San
Hat Sichon
Thap Put
Phra Saeng
Pak Long
Phangnga
Thai Muang
Ao Luk
Tha Sala
KHAO LUANG NATIONAL PARK 1835m
Thalang
Ao Nang
Thung Yai
Chawang
Nakhon Si Thammarat
Patong
Ko Yao Yai
Krabi
Laem Talumphuk
Phuket
Phra Nang
Ko Pu
Thung Song
Pak Phanang
Ko Phuket
Ko Phi Phi
Wang Wiset
Tham Khao Pina
Hua Sai
Huai Yot
Thale Noi Waterfowl Park
Sikao
Siban Phot
Lam Pam
Ranot
Ko Lanta
Trang
Khao Chong Center
Phatthalung
Chao Mai
1350m
Palian
Thale Luang
Ko Talibong
Thale Sap Songkhla
Khuan Niang
Khu Khut Bird Sanctuary
Pak Bara
Langu
Songkhla
Ko Rawi
Ko Tarutao
Ton Nga Chang
HAT YAI
Chana
Ko Adang
Satun
Pedang Besar
Na Thawi
Pattani
Laem Pho
Toloh Kapo
Sadao
Panare
MALAYSIA
Yala
Sai Buri
Raman
100 kilometers
Bannang Sata
Narathiwat
50 miles
Piya Mit Tunnel
Tak Bai
Banglang Dam
Chanae
Betong
Sungai Kolok

Area of map detail
Bangkok

Throughout these centuries the far south played host—often a reluctant one—to streams of foreigners intent on trade, exploitation, and colonization. Early settlers arrived from the Indian subcontinent and from across the loosely defined southern borders of the Malay states. Trang and Phuket, with their strategic positions along the Straits of Malacca, became Thai centers of world trade and entry points for foreign merchants moving farther into Thailand. The influence of seafaring Portuguese and Chinese immigrants (many of whom arrived in the 19th century to work the tin mines) is seen in the ornate Sino-Portuguese architecture still standing in some towns. The British, who controlled Malaysia and, at various times, parts of southernmost Thailand, were a constant presence.

This centuries-long cultural mixture exerts itself in engaging ways. Malaysian-Islamic domed mosques share the landscape with elaborate Buddhist *wats*; semi-nomadic sea gypsies sail from island to island eking out a livelihood from fishing; attractive fishing villages and towns dot the coast; and vibrant commercial centers testify to the region's prosperity. ■

Nakhon Si Thammarat

NAKHON SI THAMMARAT IS BUSILY SHAKING OFF ITS rough and ready reputation as the breeding place of some of Thailand's most notorious gangsters. These days it is being promoted heavily by tourism officials for its many historic and cultural attractions. The city, one of the oldest in the country, proudly hangs on to its past through its revered temples, excellent museum, and thriving, high-quality handicraft industry.

At the beginning of the Christian era, Nakhon (then known as Ligor) was the capital of the Tambralinga Empire, one of a number of kingdoms in Southeast Asia that were set up by Hindu colonists from India. Sometime in the seventh century, Nakhon fell under control of the Srivijaya Empire, the then dominant force in Malaysia and Indonesia, and was renamed Nagara Sri Dhammaraja.

After 200 years of Srivijaya power, the Tambralinga won back Ligor, first conquering the Mon Kingdom of Lop Buri and placing Prince Suryavarman I (R.1011–1050) on the Khmer throne at Angkor. The city remained part of the Khmer Empire until the rise of the Sukhothai Kingdom in 1292.

Under Sukhothai rule, Nakhon thrived as an economic power and influential spiritual center. Its enduring legacy of this period is the promotion of the Sri Lankan-based Hinayana (Theravada) Buddhism, which was to become Thailand's major religion.

Nakhon's part in helping define religion in Thailand presents itself at **Wat Mahathat,** also called Wat Phra Boromothat (on Rachadamnoen Rd., about a mile/1.5 km south of the city center). The temple is Nakhon's founding monument, built about a thousand years ago by King Sri Thammaso-karaj when he moved his capital south from Chaiya.

Wat Mahathat is one the oldest and most important places of worship for Buddhists in Thailand. Its centerpiece, an imposing 255-foot (77 m) chedi with a spire topped with 600 pounds (272 kg) of solid gold, towers over an expansive cloister teeming with Buddha icons and elephant-head statues. South of the chedi in the Wihan Luang, the prominent Buddha image smiles below a fantastically ornate red ceiling that is propped up by inward-angled pillars, the mainstays of Ayutthayan architecture.

A short distance beyond Wat Mahathat, also on Rachadamnoen Road, is the city's prestigious **National Museum** (open Wed.–Sun., tel 075-341075). It traces the history of the region from prehistoric times through art, archaeological, and ethnological objects, including Buddha, Vishnu, and Siva images, ceramics, and handicrafts such as basketry, textiles, and the province's famed shadow puppets.

Shadow puppetry (nang thalung), introduced to Thailand during the Ayutthaya period, was once tremendously popular in Nakhon and nearby Phatthalung (see pp. 314–15). Sadly, master practitioners are thin on the ground these days, and shows rare. One such master and living treasure is Suchart Subsin. "Uncle" Suchart, who has received accolades from

Shadow puppetry

Shadow-puppet theater found its way to Southeast Asia about 500 years ago, introduced by traders from the Middle East. It slowly made its way up the Malay Peninsula, where it was modified to suit Thai legend and tradition. During the Ayutthaya period, shadow puppetry was an important form of entertainment. Shows would begin at midnight and last until dawn, when the puppets' silhouettes could no longer be seen through the screen. Today, shadow puppetry is mainly found in the southern provinces of Nakhon Si Thammarat, Songkhla, and Phattalung. Performances are rare, usually given only for the benefit of privileged tour groups or visiting dignitaries from Bangkok.

Thailand has two forms of shadow puppetry: *nang thalung* and *nang yai*, the difference being in the size of the puppets. In both forms, puppets are viewed by the audience through a screen illuminated from behind. Only the silhouette, or shadow, of the puppet is visible. Dramatic effects are achieved by varying the puppets' distance from the screen. Nang thalung figures, cut in intricate, sometimes lacy, patterns from buffalo hide, are similar in size to the shadow puppets of Malaysia and Indonesia. Nang yai, however, is unique to Thailand. This form uses much larger, almost life-size, buffalo hide cutouts. In nang yai, each figure is bound to two wooden poles held by a puppet master. Several masters may participate in a single performance because of the puppets' size. In nang thalung, buffalo horns may be used as the handles for the puppets.

Nang yai is rarely performed nowadays because of the lack of trained masters and the expense involved in making the shadow puppets. Most nang yai made today are sold as decoration. Shadow puppets represent an array of characters from classical and folk drama, principally the *Ramakien*. ■

Besides mastering the manipulation of the puppets, a *nang,* or master (exclusively male), must memorize hundreds of pages of traditional prose and verse. He is expected to add his own improvisations and to use a different voice for each character.

Buddha images at Nakhon's Wat Mahathat: The 1,000-year-old temple is one of the most important in Thailand.

the king for his work, keeps the spirit of nang thalung alive at his small workshop, **Suchart House** (110/18 Si Thammasok Rd., Soi 3, tel 075-346394). Suchart handcrafts leather puppets to sell, offers information on upcoming shows, and puts on private performances—involving voice characterizations, singing, and live music—and occasional impromptu demonstrations for customers.

After its leather shadow puppets, Nakhon is known throughout Thailand for its intricate nielloware (krueang tom) and colorful baskets woven from superfine grass (yan lipao). A number of centers selling these and other handicrafts have sprung up in town in recent years as part of the Tourism Authority of Thailand's

campaign to promote the province. The central **Bovorn Bazaar** (1106 Rachadamnoen Rd.,) has a grand collection of handicraft stalls and appealing cafés.

There are more well-presented handicraft shops edging Tha Chang Road, near the local tourism office and sports field.

Close to Bovorn Bazaar is **The Book Garden** (1116 Rachadamnoen Rd.), an attractive, Southern Thai-style wooden house containing a nonprofit bookstore that specializes in local history, national politics, fine arts, and religion. Like so much of Nakhon, the store has had a colorful past. Since being constructed in 1888, it has successively served as a Chinese medical clinic, an opium den, and a brothel. ■

Khao Luang National Park

LYING AT THE HEART OF NAKHON SI THAMMARAT Province, this park covers 220 square miles (571 sq km) and encompasses numerous splendid waterfalls lacing the slopes of Khao Luang, the far south's highest mountain. The arduous climb to the mountain's 6,020-foot (1,835 m) summit is a challenge taken on by avid trekkers every year.

The village of **Khiriwong,** 17.5 miles (28 km) west of Nakhon Si Thammarat off Highway 4015, is the starting point for treks to the summit, and the Nature Education Center there can provide guides and porters. The Tourism Authority of Thailand office in Nakhon Si Thammarat can also help with arrangements.

The first stage of the 14-hour climb follows a slope to 1,968 feet (600 m), passing rocks, streams, and waterfalls. Villagers have planted fruit trees amid the lowland areas and hill forests. At one set of falls, **Wang Ai Yang Bon,** vibrant orchids grow near the rocks. After a six-hour climb, the first night is spent in a simple hut hidden by thick jungle at **Kratom Suan** rest stop.

Next morning, the climb continues up a steep trail through virgin rain forest to a stop at **Laan Sai.** Stands of tree ferns and an incredible variety of orchids grow beside a watercourse. The trail then becomes extremely steep, passing through tangles of jungle dangling with beautifully colored orchids. At Laan Hor, a side trail leads to **Hubpha Sadan,** an amazing valley thick with ancient tree ferns.

Back on the main trail, the steep climb continues as the forest grows thick with rattan and blossoming begonia. During the final stage of the climb (three hours), from Laan Dr Chavalit to the summit, the incline eases off slightly as it passes through thick montane forests.

A less time-consuming trek of 2.5 miles (4 km) leads to the magnificent **Krung Ching waterfall.** It starts from a paved trail at the Krung Ching Park Office at the park's northwestern end *(off Hwy. 4016, 53 miles/85 km) from Nakhon Si Thammarat).* The trail—steep in places—climbs past ancient ferns and extensive stands of palms, to a difficult final ascent over rocks and boulders. Krung Ching falls is a justifiable reward for the climb. Water pours, pauses, and pours again over seven tiers to settle eventually in an expansive pool so clear you can see the granite bedrock many feet below. ∎

Khao Luang National Park
🅰 309 B4
National Parks Division
✉ Royal Forestry Department, 1 Phahonyothin Rd., Bangkhen, Bangkok
☎ 02-561-4292

Visitor information
✉ Tourism Authority of Thailand, Sanam Na Muang, Ratchadamnoen Rd., Nakhon Si Thammarat
☎ 075-346515

Spectacular Krung Ching, "waterfall of a hundred thousand raindrops"

Phatthalung & around

Phatthalung

🅰 309 B3

Visitor information

✉ Tourism Authority of Thailand, Sanam Na Muang, Ratchadamnoen Rd., Nakhon Si Thammarat

☎ 075-346515

PATCHWORKS OF RICE FIELDS SHADED BY GIANT LIMESTONE cliffs, temple grottoes, and teeming birdlife along the shore of the vast Thale Luang lake distinguish the peaceful province of Phatthalung. It is a region rarely visited by foreign tourists but makes a fascinating diversion from the well-established attractions of the far south, especially if you are interested in observing the birds that make their home in the marshy Thale Noi reserve.

Other than the lively **Morning Market,** north of the Hoa Fah hotel on Kuha Sawan Road, there is not much to see in Phatthalung's capital, but there are interesting attractions nearby. **Wat Kuha Sawan** is sheltered inside a limestone cliff, just to the west of town on Kuha Sawan Road. In the lower, vaulted cave of this Ayutthaya-period grotto are dozens of highly stylized (some say ugly) statues of monks and Buddhas. A steep trail leads to another cave filled with more Buddha statues, giving excellent views over Phatthalung, rice fields, and mountains to the west.

The province's two famous limestone peaks, Broken-Chest Mountain and Broken-Head Mountain, flank the main grotto of **Tham Malai,** 2 miles (3 km) north of town on Nivas Road, or you can catch a boat (about 15 minutes' ride) from behind the railway station. Legend has it that these mountains represent two jealous women, turned to stone after fighting over a man. The cave is illuminated and filled with stalagmites and stalactites.

Phatthalung's oldest temple is **Wat Wang,** 5 miles (8 km) northeast of town following Ramat Road. Built to celebrate the establishment of Phatthalung during the reign of Rama III (*R.*1824–51), its major feature is a refurbished chapel with murals

Up to 187 bird species hide among the vibrantly colored flowering plants at Thale Noi Waterfowl Park.

dating from the 18th century. Along the same road, another 2.5 miles (4 km) beyond Wat Wang, is the fishing village of **Lam Pam,** on the banks of Thale Luang lake. This lagoon forms the northern end of Thale Sap (Songkhla Lake). The village beach, Hat Sansuk, is pleasant enough, especially for sitting in the shade and tucking into the local seafood. If the urge for activity takes hold, hire a boat for short trips to the limestone islands of **Ko Si** and **Ko Ha.** Here, in crevices on the cliff faces, swiftlets build nests that make the main ingredient in bird's-nest soup.

KHAO CHONG CENTER OF WILDLIFE AND NATURE STUDY

Some 22 miles (35 km) west of Phatthalung on Highway 404, this area of natural rain forest has a small conservation and botany museum. Hiking trails leading to mountains and waterfalls start from park headquarters. ∎

WATERFOWL PARK

About 20 miles (32 km) northeast of Phatthalung's capital on Highway 4048 is Thailand's version of the Everglades—without the alligators. Declared a protected area in 1975, **Thale Noi Waterfowl Park,** the most inland part of Thale Sap, is the country's largest waterbird sanctuary, encompassing 180 square miles (450 sq km) of rice paddies, peat swamp forest, grassland, tropical evergreen forest, and wetlands. Park officials estimate 187 species of birds, both native and migratory, shelter at the sanctuary, including various species of herons, ducks and geese, rails, jacanas, cormorants, and stilts.

From October to March, when migratory birds come to escape the winter in Siberia, numbers swell to nearly 50,000, and the park becomes a thunderous celebration of wildlife. Birds hiding among the lake's multitudinous purple lilies and thick grasses erupt at dawn in a cacophony of song and color. The purple swamp hens are masters at utilizing the grasses that grow in this shallow lake, pulling off shoots to construct platforms on the water, where they can perch and walk during feeding. The grasses are also used by locals, who weave them into mats, hats, and bags. Boat tours stop at a village where you can see items being woven.

There are four large shelters around the park for visitors and an observation platform in the middle of the lake. A guided loop of the park by boat takes 90 minutes. ∎

Songkhla & beyond

THIS BREEZY AND AFFABLE SEASIDE TOWN LIES ON THE spit of land that divides the Gulf of Thailand from the huge area of Thale Sap (Songkhla Lake). It is a picturesque place, all but ignored on foreign tourist maps. Instead, it remains a favorite holiday spot among southern Thais, who come to enjoy its beaches, lake, and seafood, as well as cultural displays housed in two of the far south's best museums.

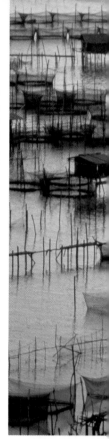

On the town's seaward shore is the lively 5-mile-long (8 km) **Samila Beach,** lined with all the essentials of Thai beach life: seafood restaurants, food vendors dishing up everything from watermelon to spicy noodles, and plenty of shady casuarina trees. Samila may not match the quality of beaches on Samui and the southwest coast, but it is still an agreeable stretch of sand. To the south of Samila, the small Muslim fishing village of **Kao Seng** stands on a headland. This is a good place to photograph the fleets of brilliantly colored and patterned traditional boats (*kolae*), and enjoy tasty seafood from waterside restaurants.

The centrally located **Songkhla National Museum** (*Rong Muang and Jana Rds., tel*

074-311728; closed Mon.–Tues.), houses some interesting and quirky treasures of Thailand's southern provinces. The museum is in an elegant 19th-century Sino-Portuguese mansion, once the grand home of a wealthy Chinese merchant. Highlights of the collection include Thai and Chinese ceramics, Ayutthaya-period Buddhas, Chinese furniture, Thai furnishings, and shadow puppets. There are also aerial photographs of the province and a useful topographical map. Farther south on Saiburi Road rises **Wat Machimawat,** a 17th-century temple with intriguing murals of 19th-century life.

The lake waterfront at **Thale Sap,** on the opposite side of town to Samila Beach, is another colorful place. Walk along **Nakhon Noak Road** for an authentic encounter with the sights, sounds, and (often overpowering) smells of the province's bountiful fishing industry. Part of Songkhla's old town, this area contains remnants of Sino-Portuguese architecture.

In the middle of the channel that connects Thale Sap to the Gulf of Thailand is the thickly wooded island of **Ko Yo,** noted for its seafood restaurants, traditional cotton weaving, and **Folklore Museum** at the Institute of Southern Thai Studies (*Ban Ao Sai, tel 074-331185*). It can be reached from Highway 4146, about 8 miles (13 km) from downtown Songkhla.

Songkhla
⚐ 309 C3
Visitor information
✉ Tourism Authority of Thailand, 1/1 Soi 2 Niphat Uthit 3 Rd., Hat Yai, Songkhla
☎ 074-231055

This is the largest museum in Southern Thailand, with an impressive collection of regional artifacts displayed in 17 traditional pavilion houses, overlooking the lake and the island's forests. Exhibits are grouped into pottery, beads, shadow puppets, basketry, textiles, musical instruments, boats, religious arts, and weapons, with further displays of household, fishing, and agricultural implements. In addition, the grounds contain a cultural park, an outdoor performance area, and an audiovisual center.

Ko Yo is also home to a thriving cotton-weaving industry. Excellent deals in quality fabrics and clothes can be picked up from the weaving center to the south along Highway 4146. The clattering sound of cotton being woven on hand looms emanates from houses behind the market. A meal at the famous Porntip II seafood restaurant *(at the southern end of the island on Hwy. 4146)* is another of Ko Yo's popular attractions.

On Thale Sap's eastern shores, about 34 miles (55 km) north of Songkhla town on Highway 4083, is the wetlands reserve of **Khu Khut Bird Sanctuary** *(Tambon Khukhut, Amphur Sathing Phra, tel 074-397042)*. There are more than 200 resident and migratory species, including egrets, herons, storks, kites, sandpipers, and kingfishers. The best times to view the birds are morning and late afternoon, from December to early January. Park rangers organize inexpensive boat trips for keen bird-watchers. ■

Fish farms are a familiar sight on the enormous Songkhla Lake. Opposite: Fishermen repair their nets.

Hat Yai & environs

THIS BRASH CITY OF 200,000 INHABITANTS—MAINLY Chinese—is the closest thing to a metropolis in Southern Thailand. One of Thailand's largest cities, it is the region's thriving transportation hub and its commercial, shopping, and entertainment center. The Malaysian border is just 34 miles (55 km) to the south, making this a favorite holiday spot for Malaysians.

Hat Yai

🗺 309 C2

Visitor information

✉ Tourism Authority of Thailand, 1/1 2 Soi Niphat Uthit 3 Rd., Hat Yai, Songkhla

☎ 074-231055

After sundown, vendors erect stalls along the already narrow footpaths of **Niphat Uthit No. 2 and 3 Roads,** in the middle of the city, and **Sanehanuson Road** and the **Plaza Market,** stacking them with everything from canned food to ghetto blasters. Good buys at these lively night markets include ready-made leisure and sportswear, preserved Thai fruits, imported Asian foodstuffs, batiks, cheap

electrical goods, watches, and Thai handicrafts. This is a good city for shopping generally, and there are a number of department stores, including Diana, Ocean, and Expo on Niphat Uthit No. 3 Road, and World and Robinson on Thamnoonvithi Road, where the shopping experience is calmer.

With its Chinese, Muslim, and Thai culinary influences, Hat Yai offers plenty of good opportunities for dining, but none so bizarre as the fare served along **Thanon Ngu** ("snake street"), on Chaniwat Road Soi 2. Along this bustling side street, the term *dining experience* takes on a whole new meaning. Snakes are taken from cages, strangled with wire, and sliced open. Visiting Singaporean and Malaysian Chinese drink the snake's blood (mixed with rice wine) and eat the gallbladder, before settling down to a more substantial meal of snake soup cooked with herbs and spices. The snake handlers like to show off the reptiles before killing them, so it is best to keep your distance.

Hat Yai's nightlife is engineered to please Malaysian male clientele escaping the strict moral Muslim codes of their country, so there are plenty of massage parlors and seedy nightclubs. More tempered nightspots are found mainly in the hotels and include the Diana Club *(Lee Gardens Hotel, 1 Lee Pattana Rd., tel 074-234422)* and the Metropolis Club *(JB Hotel, 99 Chuti Anuson Rd., tel 074-234300).*

The city holds monthly bullfights—rowdy spectacles unique to the far south (see p. 321)—at **Nurn Khun Thong** arena, on Highway 4, near the airport. Check venues and dates with the local tourist office.

Several attractions close to Hat Yai can be included in day excursions. About 15 miles (24 km) west of the city along Highway 4 is **Ton Nga Chang** ("elephant tusk falls"), where water cascades spectacularly over seven tiers and splits into two streams, in a formation resembling elephant tusks. At **Tham Khao Rup Chang** ("cave of the elephant fountain"), some 6 miles (10 km)

Locals ward off a heavy downpour.

from the large border town of Padang Besar, three large grottoes are garnished with stalagmite and stalactite formations, and with Buddha images.

A visit to **Chana** is well worth the effort between January and June to experience the delightful dove-cooing contests (see below). ∎

Dove cooing

Dove-cooing contests are a popular pastime among southern Muslim Thais, notably in Narathiwat, Yala, Pattani, Satun, and Songkhla. Farms in Chana, about 25 miles (40 km) southeast from Hat Yai on Highway 407, breed the most sought-after birds. The town hosts contests on weekends from January to June. Hundreds of caged doves are raised on tall poles in open fields and begin choruses of cooing. Their songs are judged on pitch, melody, and volume. It's all taken very seriously, with champion doves valued at as much as $12,000. ∎

Pattani

 309 C2

Visitor information

✉ Tourism Authority
of Thailand,102/3
Mu 3 Narathiwat-
Takbai Rd.,
Narathiwat

☎ 073-516144

Pattani

PATTANI IS ONE OF PROVINCES OF THE FAR SOUTH (ALONG
with Narathiwat, Yala, and Satun) where the spiritual borders of the
predominant Buddhist beliefs meet and merge with the Islamic
faith of Malaysia, the southern Philippines, and Indonesia.
Mosques replace Buddhist temples, architecture is more Malay
than Thai in style, and the language spoken on the streets is the
Malay dialect of Yawi.

**The imposing
minaret at
Pattani Mosque
reflects the
town's strong
commitment to
Islam.**

At local markets—which resemble
those found in the towns of
northern Malaysia—men wear
Muslim *haji* caps, and women
wrap themselves in brightly
colored shawls.

Nearly 80 percent of Pattani's
population is Muslim, and as one of
the centers of Islamic studies in the

17th century, the province
accommodates some of the most
impressive and important mosques
in Thailand. The oldest is **Masajid
Kru Se,** 4.5 miles (7 km) east of
the provincial capital, on Highway
42. Chinese immigrant Lim To
Khieng began constructing the
mosque in 1578, after his marriage
to a Pattani woman and conversion
to Islam. His sister, Lim Ko Niaw,
upset at Lim To Khieng's change of
faith, traveled from China to try to
change her brother's mind. When
he refused, Lim Ko Niaw placed a
curse on the mosque and hanged
herself from a nearby cashew tree.
A replica of the tree is enshrined at
Leng Chu Khiang temple, on
Arnoaru Road. The shrine is the
focus of the annual Chao Mae Lim
Ko Niaw festival, held on the full
moon of the third lunar month
(February or March), when
devotees walk across red-hot coals
and pierce their bodies with swords
and spears.

The striking **Matsayit Klang,**
or Pattani Mosque, with its twin
minarets, arched stained-glass
windows, orange-hued facade, and
domes inlaid with green stone, is
one of the most beautiful in
Thailand. This grand building,
dating from the early 1960s, is on
Yarang Road.

For a taste of southern Thai
beach life, head to **Toloh Kapo,**
about 10 miles (16 km) south of
the capital, off Highway 42. Locals
flock here on weekends. ∎

Narathiwat

Narathiwat
🗺 309 D2
Visitor information
✉ Tourism Authority of Thailand, 102/3 Mu 3 Narathiwat-Takbai Rd., Narathiwat
☎ 073-516144

IT MAY CARRY THE RESPONSIBILITIES OF A PROVINCIAL capital, but Narathiwat ("the residence of good people") prefers to maintain its character as a laid-back fishing village. Hugging the gentle curves of the Bang Nara River, which flows into the Gulf of Thailand, the town is a delightful escape from the more rambunctious concrete provincial capitals and thronging tourist resorts of Thailand's far south.

Thailand's royal family also consider it a relaxing place, making their way to Narathiwat for about two months a year between August and October and staying at **Taskin Palace,** 7.5 miles (12 km) south of town. The summer palace is open to the public at other times. The palace stands on **Ao Mano,** an attractive curving bay lined with casuarina (sea pines) and food vendors. The royal vacation is celebrated each September with parades, dove-cooing contests, and races in the traditional, intricately painted fishing boats *(korlae).*

About 9.5 miles (15 km) north of Narathiwat is **Wadin Husen.** Built in 1769, this timber mosque is one of the oldest in Thailand. In an intriguing deviation from the norm, it abandons traditional mosque styles and mixes Thai, Chinese, and Malay architectural elements. King Chulalongkorn

built the mosque's Buddhist equivalent, **Wat Chonthara Sing He,** in 1873, also in local style. A peaceful, reflective place, the temple is idyllically set on the waterfront in Tak Bai village. ∎

Muslim fishermen along the far south coast favor traditional multicolored fishing boats (korlae).

Bullfighting

Bullfighting in Thailand's far south has no call for matadors or bloody ritual. It is a far more equal contest: a 2,000-pound (4,410 kg) bull versus another of the same weight, in a thunderous and dusty rumble. Before the fight begins, the specially trained bulls—worth as much as $25,000—are led out into the arena and paraded before spectators. Guided together by handlers, they dip their heads, lock horns, and shove each other like snorting, four-legged sumo wrestlers, until one falls or gives up and takes flight. Fights can last from a few seconds to 30 minutes. During longer battles it is more entertaining to watch the crowd than the bulls: Betting is the big attraction, and the frenzy depends on how much was gambled, rather than appreciation of the finer details of the sport. ∎

Islands of the Southwest

If you can't find your own version of tropical paradise in the generous sprinkle of islands off Thailand's southwest coast, then you are probably not looking hard enough. From Phuket—Thailand's largest island and favorite beach resort—and the limestone outcrops crowded into Phangnga Bay, down to the deserted coral-fringed gems near the Malaysian border, the beauty of the hundreds of islands that sparkle in the Andaman Sea is astounding.

The islands, many of which enjoy some degree of sanctuary within marine national parks, throw up a wealth of recreational activities, made easy by a solid tourist infrastructure. Visitors can enjoy diving, snorkeling, hiking, beachcombing, mountain biking, water sports, camping, sea kayaking, rock climbing, golf, island hopping, and the more somnolent pursuit of sunbathing—all with minimum fuss. It generally takes no more than a stroll to the tour operator's desk at your hotel to organize an itinerary. As in most of Thailand, public transportation is plentiful, and rental cars and drivers are

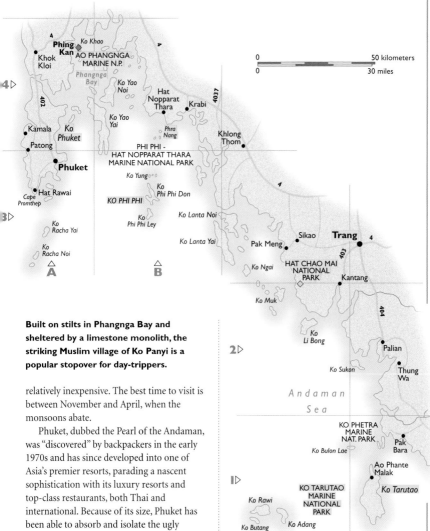

Built on stilts in Phangnga Bay and sheltered by a limestone monolith, the striking Muslim village of Ko Panyi is a popular stopover for day-trippers.

relatively inexpensive. The best time to visit is between November and April, when the monsoons abate.

Phuket, dubbed the Pearl of the Andaman, was "discovered" by backpackers in the early 1970s and has since developed into one of Asia's premier resorts, parading a nascent sophistication with its luxury resorts and top-class restaurants, both Thai and international. Because of its size, Phuket has been able to absorb and isolate the ugly excesses of tourist development, and today developers tend to take a long-term view. Sadly, the same cannot be said for the miraculous island of Ko Phi Phi Don, whose national park status has done little to protect it from environmental abuse.

From the scenic treasures hidden among the steep limestone islands of Phangnga Bay, the coast sweeps southwest down to Krabi, another favored spot for international vacationers. The sheer cliffs that form Krabi's spectacular coast make it one of the world's rock-climbing hot spots and a great place to learn the sport. Beyond these cliffs, some 200 islands lie basking in the Andaman Sea.

Past Krabi, in the provinces of Trang and Satun, foreign visitors are thin on the ground. The pristine islands that make up the Hat Chao Mai National Park and Tarutao Marine National Park revel in their isolation. It is a place where perceptions of tropical paradise sharpen into focus. ■

Ko Phuket

Ko Phuket

🗺 309 A4 &
323 A4

Visitor information

✉ Tourism Authority of
Thailand, 73–75
Phuket Rd., Amphur
Muang, Phuket

☎ 076-211036 or
076-212213 or
076-217138

PHUKET PLAYS HOST TO OVER 1.2 MILLION INTERNATIONAL tourists each year, making it one of Asia's most popular resorts. The island has always been a favorite with visitors. Over the centuries, motley crews of Malay pirates, Tamil settlers, Burmese warriors, Chinese tin miners, Portuguese pioneers, and European traders have washed up on its shores in search of trade, war, colonization, and their inherent spoils. Today, visitors settle for its upscale resorts, varied nightlife, diverse scenery, and easy-going tropical lifestyle.

The growth of tourism since the mid-1970s, along with tin mining and rubber production, has made Phuket the richest province in

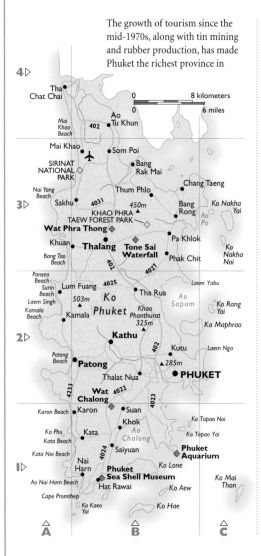

Thailand after Bangkok. The island, at 324 square miles (810 sq km), is Thailand's largest and most geographically diverse. Beaches vary from broad sweeps of white sand fringed by casuarina and palm trees, to rocky, isolated bays. The interior is a pleasing mixture of forested hills, limestone cliffs, tropical vegetation, and rubber, coconut, and cashew plantations. Scattered over this appealing landscape are quiet Muslim hamlets, laid-back holiday towns, and raucous tourist centers.

Snippets of the island's multicultural past can be found in the compact capital town of **Phuket.** It has some of the best remaining examples of Sino-Portuguese architecture in the South—mainly long, narrow Chinese shop-houses with splendid 19th-century European ornamentation. The 19th-century colonial mansions of Chinese tin-mine bosses (some of which are now used as government buildings) skirt the town center. Good examples of Sino-Portuguese architecture include the **Standard Chartered Bank Building** on Phangnga Road, the **Thai Airways office** on Ranong Road, and the **Provincial Hall** on Damrong Road. More can be found among the buildings on Yaowarat, Thalang, Dubik, and Krabi Roads.

Chinese heritage is also evident in the dozen or so shrines that

punctuate the town with splashes of red and gold. The shrines are the focal points for the annual nine-day Vegetarian Festival, held in October, when young men pierce themselves with spears and swords in rituals of atonement and purification.

Tin mining has brought Phuket much of its wealth and a fair share of conflict. In 1876 the Chinese mine laborers *(angyee)* went on a bloody rampage throughout the island, first battling with each other, then turning on the local people. Many folk sought shelter at the Buddist compound of

Wat Chalong, 5 miles (8 km) south of Phuket Town, on Highway 4022. Here, inspired by the head monk, Luang Por Chaem, they fought off the marauding Chinese. Luang Por Chaem's statue holds an honored place in the colorful, ornate *wat.*

At the southern end of Highway 4129, at Cape Phanwa, is **Phuket Aquarium** *(tel 076-391126)*, part of the Marine Research Center. The aquarium aids in the repopulation of the island's depleted turtles. With the help of the Royal Thai Navy, staff collect turtle eggs from nesting

Phuket's traditional way of life carries on regardless of the island's status as an international resort.

Tin mining

In 1518 the Portuguese won a concession to set up a tin-trading station in Phuket. The tin ore was mined from pits, smelted in crude furnaces, and fashioned into spear tips, swords, body armor, muskets, and bullets. As mining and smelting procedures improved, so did the quality of the tin. Bangkok needed it for coins and roof tiles, and it was also in demand in Europe. Droves of Chinese migrated to Phuket in the mid-1800s to work the industry. Huge areas of land were stripped in the search for the ore. The first offshore dredger arrived in 1906, and hydraulic pumps, excavators, and vast furnaces were introduced. But demand for tin started to decline in the following decades, and today tin mining in Phuket has all but ceased. ∎

ELEPHANT TREKKING

Animals at some elephant-trekking camps are overworked and mistreated. If you want to try this activity, use one of the more reputable camps, such as Siam Safari Nature Tours (tel 076-280116), half a mile (1 km) north of Chalong Circle on the island's Highway 4024. ■

Opposite: Tourists rarely visit expansive Mai Khao Beach in Sirinat National Park, on Phuket's northwest coast.

sites on Phuket and nearby islands. The eggs—including those of the giant leatherback turtle—are hatched, and the young nurtured here and later released.

The privately run **Phuket Sea Shell Museum** (tel 076-381266), at the southern end of the island on Highway 4024, has one the world's most valuable collections of seashells—some are for sale. Its gigantic golden pearl, weighing 140 carats, is a world-beater. A massive shell that tips the scales at 550 pounds (250 kg) is one of the museum's weightier exhibits.

Rawai Beach, a few hundred yards beyond the Sea Shell Museum, is a good place to begin a tour of Phuket's west coast. Rawai was, in fact, Phuket's first beach resort. This had nothing to do with its beauty (it is drab and rocky)—it was the first beach to be connected by paved road to Phuket Town, 10.5 miles (17 km) north. A host of inexpensive seafood restaurants line Rawai's foreshore, and you can hire longtail boats or speedboats to the nearby islands of Ko Lone, Ko Hae, and Ko Aew for swimming, snorkeling, and sunbathing.

At the beach's northern end is a sad-looking *chao lae* (sea gypsy) village, only worth a stop if you enjoy watching tourists haggle for tacky souvenirs from one of Thailand's marginalized minorities (see p. 284). Follow Rawai's beachfront south to **Cape Promthep,** a headland at the very south of the island, to join the crowds watching the sunset.

More than a dozen main beaches, and many coves and small bays, line the island's west coast. A good coastal road, Highway 4233, makes access easy and traverses some of Phuket's most attractive countryside, climbing and winding in and out of forests, and coconut and rubber plantations, up to ridges

with stunning panoramas of the Andaman Sea. The route also passes a number of elephant-trekking camps, where handlers take visitors on hour-long rides into the jungle. This has proved so popular that Phuket suffers from overpopulation of the beasts, and food and water have to be trucked in.

At the southern tip of the island, near Cape Promthep and about 12.5 miles (20 km) from Phuket Town, is **Nai Harn,** an attractive beach locked between high, verdant headlands and bordered by casuarina trees. It is popular during the high season but has escaped major development because the beachfront is owned by a monastic group, which prefers peace and quiet to high rises.

Some 6 miles (10 km) north of Nai Harn is **Kata.** Its beach is on the lip of the island's third largest tourist center—a jumble of guesthouses, souvenir shops, tour operators, and restaurants—which tends to add to rather than detract from the holiday village character. Like Nai Harn, it is a pleasant sweep of beach, trapped between green headlands and backed by hills. A small island close by, Ko Phu, completes the picture; you can hire a longtail boat from Kata Beach to take you there for snorkeling.

Just north of Kata is the long beach of **Karon.** A busy road separates sand and water from hotels, and with its lack of trees, and a backdrop of isolated high-rise hotels and condos, shoddily built restaurants. and disused rice paddies, the town's search for an identity continues. The town center is an uninspiring avenue of hotels, shops, bars, and restaurants at the northern end of the beach.

North of bustling Patong (see p. 329), beach life gets a bit quieter. **Kamala,** 5 miles (8 km) from Patong and 15 miles (24 km) from

During Phuket's October Vegetarian Festival hundreds of young men pierce their cheeks with swords and spears in a bizarre and bloody parade of purification and atonement.

Phuket Town, is a Muslim fishing village with a long sandy beach. The best spot is its northern end, where you can enjoy the shade of casuarina trees—that is, if you don't mind laying down your towel over an old Muslim graveyard. Kamala's most famous sight is the parade of water buffalos wandering down to the beach each afternoon to cool off. FantaSea is a sprawling entertainment complex at Kamala, with nightly glitzy, Las Vegas-style Thai cultural shows (complete with disappearing elephants), and a buffet dinner for up to 2,000 people.

Surin Beach, below the hills to the north of Kamala, is a favorite weekend picnic spot for locals. Just south of Surin, **Laem Singh** is a gem—a small, curving bay with rocky headlands at the foot of sheer, forest-fringed cliffs. Look for signs to a path down to the beach.

North of Surin, around a small headland, is **Pansea Beach,** backed by steep hills and luxury resorts, which give the impression that this is a private beach. It is not—all beaches in Phuket are public.

Surin, Pansea, and **Bang Tao** are all beaches within walking

distance of the attractive Muslim village of **Sope Sali.** Bang Tao is a large open bay, with one of Phuket's longest beaches. Its hinterland was all but destroyed by tin mining, but in the late 1980s and early 1990s it was transformed into the island's largest resort, the surprisingly unobtrusive Laguna Phuket.

Set next to Phuket International Airport, **Sirinat National Park** covers 36 square miles (90 sq km) of the northern coast of the island, with tropical evergreens, casuarina-dominated forests, and isolated beaches—perfect for dedicated beachcombers. Here, too, are Phuket's only mangrove forests.

The island's other national park is **Khao Phra Taew Forest Park,** rain forest taking in 9 square miles (22 sq km) of the island's northern interior. Vegetation is striking—majestic trees buttressed with tangles of undergrowth.

At the entrance to the park, off Highway 4027, is the **Gibbon Rehabilitation Center** *(tel 076-260492).* Volunteers from around the world nurture gibbons that have been held illegally as pets, then reintroduce them into the wild. ∎

Patong

SINCE THE EARLY 1970s PATONG HAS GROWN FROM A sleepy fishing village into Phuket's boisterous tourist center—an energetic accumulation of high-rise hotels and condos, restaurants, guesthouses, tourist shops, beer bars, and discos. Most times of the year, and particularly during the high season between November and March, sidewalks overflow with visitors from around the world. The town sits attractively on an expansive beach, hemmed in on three sides by verdant hills.

Patong is not a place to go for peace and quiet; but for bargain shopping, restaurants, and entertainment it is the island's epicenter. Most of Patong's attractions lie along **Thawiwong Road,** or Beach Road, the town's animated thoroughfare that runs north–south along the seafront and off its narrow side streets. **Patong Beach,** with its stretch of sand and clean waters, gets crowded, but you can always find an umbrella and a beach chair to settle in to soak up the sun and atmosphere. There is plenty of opportunity for water sports, including snorkeling, boogie boarding, jet-skiing, windsurfing, waterskiing and sailing. Paragliding is a pulse-quickening way to get great views: Harnessed to a parachute, you're pulled up high behind a speedboat.

After sunset draws a veil over the beach, the action shifts across the street. Vendors erect makeshift stalls, bars turn up their stereos, and cavernous discos open their doors. Patong is the best place in Phuket to shop for cheap clothes (including fake designer clothing), souvenirs, novelties, watches, and electrical appliances, especially along Thawiwong Road. Hundreds of restaurants offer food for differing palates, including excellent local lobster and king prawns. ■

Ko Phi Phi
309 A3 &
323 B3
Visitor information
✉ Tourism Authority of
Thailand, Uttarakit
Rd., Krabi
☎ 075-612740

✉ Tourism Authority of
Thailand, 73–75
Phuket Rd., Amphur
Muang, Phuket
☎ 076-211036 or
076-212213 or
076-217138

Ko Phi Phi

IT'S A CREDIT TO THE RESILIENCE OF THE PHI PHI ISLAND group that it has absorbed some of the worst excesses of tourist development in Thailand but still manages to stun visitors with its extraordinary beauty. And there is no shortage of visitors. The largest island, a warped miracle of nature, Ko Phi Phi Don, nearly sinks under the weight of 400,000 tourists a year.

Large ferries from Phuket and Krabi regularly tie up at **Ton Sai** pier on Ko Phi Phi Don, disgorging thousands of day-trippers. Once a small sea-gypsy village, Ton Sai, on the slender isthmus connecting the bays of Ao Ton Sai and Lo Dalam, has become a shoulder-to-shoulder shantytown of narrow alleyways winding past shops, restaurants, bars, souvenir stalls, and piled-up garbage.

It is not easy to find a bay or cove on Ko Phi Phi where the solitude and scenery are not broken by the loud cracking motor of a longtail boat jammed with vacationers or spoiled by plastic bags, water bottles, and other garbage. But for the most part the extraordinary beauty of the six Phi Phi islands—part of the Phi Phi–Hat Nopparat Thara Marine National Park—endures.

Trips to Phi Phi are easily booked from hotels in Krabi and Phuket. Early morning minivans pick up from hotels and shuttle visitors to ferries, which take less than two hours to reach the islands (during the monsoon season, from May to October, the passage can sometimes get rough and scary). Phi Phi Don has accommodations (reserve rooms in advance).

Typically, packaged day trips include visits to other islands in the group, with lunch and an afternoon of snorkeling. To tailor your trip, buy return fares without the frills, and ask tour agents in Ton Sai to organize full-day tours around the island or overnight camping on the deserted beaches of **Ko Phai** (Bamboo Island) and **Ko Yung** (Mosquito Island).

BOAT TOURS

Tours can begin with snorkeling over coral beds to the east of Phi Phi Don, followed by a stop at Ko Phai. The boat then sweeps down to **Ko Phi Phi Ley,** the second largest island of the group. The first stop at Phi Phi Ley is **Viking Cave,** a vast cavern with a series of paintings of ships generously described as pictographs of Viking longboats. They are more likely to be images of Chinese junks.

Like so many places in this island group, **Maya Bay,** the next stop, is blessed with beauty. It became Hollywood's version of tropical paradise in 1999, when scenes from the movie *The Beach* (see p. 302) were filmed here. Just when you think that it couldn't get much better, the boat channels into **Lo Samah,** bitten out of the cliffs at the southern end of the island. This finger of seawater is hemmed in by imposing cliffs.

Most tours provide snorkeling gear, or you can rent from dive shops in Ton Sai. Tailor day trips to include snorkeling at Hin Pae on Phi Phi Don's east coast or in Phi Phi Ley's bays of clear water. Ask to visit the many beautiful, relatively isolated beaches, capes, and bays around Phi Phi Don, such as Lo Bakao, Hat Laem Thong, Hat Pak Nam, Hat Runtee, and Lo Loma. **Ko Bida Nok,** a small island half a mile (1 km) south of Ko Phi Phi Ley, is the best dive site. ∎

The coves and bays of amazing Ko Phi Phi Ley shelter shimmering, white-sanded beaches and crystal waters. Even so, the onslaught of tourism threatens. Right: Young men clamber up bamboo poles to gather swiflets' nests in the crevices of Ko Phi Phi's caves.

Bird's-nest soup

Swiftlets build their nests in crevices high up in the caves that pockmark the limestone crags found in the coastal areas of Southern Thailand. Their handicraft, once softened and separated into vermicelli-like threads, ends up on the tables of Chinese restaurants around the world as the expensive delicacy bird's-nest soup. It is the sea gypsies *(chao lae)* who have the dangerous job of scampering up rickety scaffolding to dislodge the nests from the rocks. The government awards much sought-after concessions to local groups to harvest the nests. So lucrative is the trade that armed guards are often found in front of caves. ∎

Phangnga Bay
🅜 309 A4 &
   323 A4–B4
Visitor information
✉ Tourism Authority of
   Thailand, Uttarakit
   Rd., Krabi
☎ 075-612740

Ao Phangnga Marine National Park
🅜 323 A4–B4
✉ Royal Forestry
   Department, 61
   Phahonyothin Rd.,
   Bangkhen, Bangkok
☎ 02-561-2129

SeaCanoe International
✉ 367/4 Yaowarat Rd.,
   Phuket
☎ 076-212252 or
   076-212172 (fax)

Phangnga Bay

AN UNFORGETTABLE PLACE, WITH HUNDREDS OF CRAGGY little islands jutting out of emerald-green waters, Phangnga Bay is one of the great natural wonders of Southeast Asia. The main prize of this remarkable spot is hidden inside those imposing craggy sea cliffs: It is the *hongs*, or sea caves, that provide visitors with the most abiding memories.

The hongs (the Thai word for "rooms") are ancient caves of limestone inside large coral formations. They were formed underwater some 130 million years ago and forced upward above sea level as the Earth's continental plates shifted. The subsequent millions of years of erosion by rain, wind, and sea have opened the tops of some of these caves.

The stunning result of nature's handiwork is a bay full of rocky, foliage-laden islets, with enclosed lagoons and sandy beaches, as well as self-contained ecosystems, multi-chambered grottoes, and giant rock archways and passageways, a paradise that can be explored by canoe. Some 20 companies in nearby Phuket offer sea-canoeing trips in and around the hongs and islands, lasting from one to six days; they can generally be booked from your hotel tour desk. The trips include pick-up and drop-off at the hotels. Canoeing is made easy by the accompanying "mother" ships, which anchor near the hongs to off-load canoes.

The popularity of the tours has given rise to logjams at many of the cave entrances—and too many people can spoil the experience. SeaCanoe International was the first company to lead people into the hongs in the early 1990s, and the company tries to avoid the crowds by offering overnight trips and tours of the caves at less popular times. It also limits the number of its tours, and its guides

enliven the trip with lessons in the natural history of the bay.

Most of the hongs can be entered only at low tide, when the ebb reveals the narrow, craggy entrances. The dark tunnels are illuminated by streams of light pouring down giant shafts in the limestone. The hongs vary in size, but not in impact, with the smallest just 65.5 feet (20 m) in diameter. Some of the caverns are linked by tunnels in the rock.

The bay is part of the **Ao Phangnga Marine National Park,** but some areas are given away as lucrative government concessions to companies collecting the nests of swiftlets, used in the Chinese delicacy bird's-nest soup. In the past, concessionaires have had disputes with sea-canoe operators, claiming that visitors were scaring off the birds. Concessionaires now collect a percentage of the canoe companies' earnings, as "entrance fees" to what they claim as their caves. The disagreements reached a head in 1998, when the concessionaires barred entry to canoe companies who had not paid entrance fees, but the situation now seems to have settled down again.

One of the focal attractions of Phangnga Bay is **James Bond Island**, or Ko Khao Phing Kan ("leaning island"), the much-visited rocky cleft that served as an imposing setting for the 1974 James Bond movie, *The Man with the Golden Gun*, starring Roger Moore.

Opposite: Phangnga Bay, with its hundreds of soaring limestone crags, is one of the wonders of Southeast Asia.

(James Bond returned to Phangnga Bay in 1997, this time in the guise of Pierce Brosnan, for *Tomorrow Never Dies*.) Avoid the hawkers and touristy souvenir stalls around the beach, and hike up the network of trails that leads to spectacular viewpoints overlooking this hauntingly beautiful bay.

Ko Panyi, built on mangrove stilts over the water and tailing out from a huge hunk of limestone, is a self-contained Muslim fishing village connected by a labyrinth of walkways. It is a hostage to tourism during the day, but when the last of the visitors flee in late afternoon it resumes its own delightful character. It is possible, and worthwhile, to stay overnight. Cruise tours that incorporate James Bond Island, Ko Panyi, and a number of other incredible islands that dot the bay can be taken from Phuket, but it is quicker and less expensive from Phangnga Town. Sayan Tours *(tel 076-430348)* at the Phangnga bus station is the best. ∎

Local companies conduct tours of the caverns, formed when the roof of an island's cave collapsed.

Gap eroded to form a cave

Water enters through fissures and erodes the limestone, forming internal passageways and caves, or *hongs*.

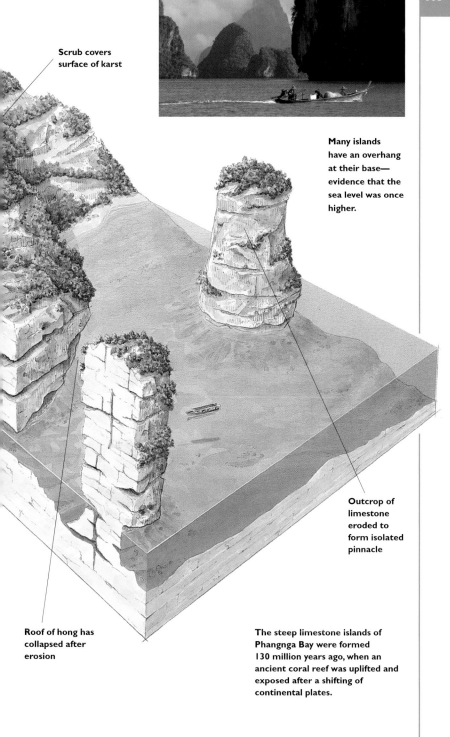

Scrub covers surface of karst

Many islands have an overhang at their base—evidence that the sea level was once higher.

Outcrop of limestone eroded to form isolated pinnacle

Roof of hong has collapsed after erosion

The steep limestone islands of Phangnga Bay were formed 130 million years ago, when an ancient coral reef was uplifted and exposed after a shifting of continental plates.

Phra Nang

THE MAJESTIC CAPE OF PHRA NANG TAKES YOUR BREATH away. Like Ko Phi Phi and Phangnga, the cape's overwhelming grandeur lies in its towering limestone cliffs, flush with vegetation and looming above sandy beaches and crystal-clear waters. Phra Nang exists amid a cluster of other beaches and scenic wonders in Krabi Province, but is outstanding for its beauty. The cape is part of the 150-square-mile (390 sq km) Ko Phi Phi–Hat Nopparat Thara Marine National Park, west of Krabi Town.

Phra Nang can be reached in spectacular fashion along the province's rugged coastline, in 45 minutes by longtail boat from Krabi Town's Chao Fa pier, or 15 minutes from Ao Nang Beach.

Phra Nang Beach is the cape's best—a fine, bright sweep of sand offset by sparkling blue waters and awesome green cliffs. It is also the most upscale. While Phra Nang's other two beaches—Railae Beach East and Railae Beach West (the longest and most popular)—swarm with cheap guesthouses and restaurants, Phra Nang itself remains the almost exclusive domain of an unobtrusive luxury resort. A dominating limestone headland reaches out to the tip of the cape at the southern end of Phra Nang Beach. At the bottom is

Tham Phra Nang Nok ("outer princess cave"), legendary home of a sea princess who bore a child who was later to become her lover. Wooden phalluses, carved by local fishermen, are placed inside the cave to guarantee successful fishing and protect against bad weather.

A steep, rope-aided cave trail from behind Tham Phra Nang Nok leads up to some stunning views over the cape, before dropping down to an immense seawater lagoon, **Sa Phra Nang** ("princess lake"). You'll need a guide, easily hired from the plethora of guesthouses on Railae Beach West and Railae Beach East. Experienced rock climbers can reach the top of the cliff and enjoy magnificent sweeping views over the entire cape, and to the islands of Ko Poda and Ko Hua Khwan.

Up a hill behind the disappointing Railae Beach East (mudflats and mangroves) is **Tham Phra Nang Nai** ("inner princess cave"). This beautiful cavern, acclaimed as the best in Southern Thailand, has three main chambers with some wondrous and weird stone formations. Tham Phra Nang Nai was the "grand palace" of the legendary sea princess, while Sa Phra Nang was her summer palace.

The cliffs around Tham Phra Nang Nai, and all along the giant headland that dominates Phra Nang, have made the area an

Phra Nang
- 309 A4 & 323 B4

Visitor information
- Tourism Authority of Thailand, Uttarakit Rd., Krabi
- 075-612740

Left: Streamlined longtail boats are the major means of transportation around Phra Nang and nearby islands. Above: Inexpensive bungalows, like these at Railae Beach, are plentiful (you may need to book ahead during high season).

international destination for rock climbers. The sport's popularity has spawned numerous rock-climbing schools around the cape, making it an ideal (and inexpensive) place to learn the sport. Companies offer courses ranging from half-day basic introductions to three-day certificate courses. The latter, designed to teach techniques and theory, includes self-rescue, rappelling, and lead and multi-pitch climbing. Climbers have identified over 160 routes, most at the mid-to-high difficulty level, as well as a few ranked as extremely difficult. Any hotel or guesthouse will put you touch with a school, and experienced climbers can rent gear from these places.

Just off Phra Nang Beach lies **Ko Rang Nok** ("bird's-nest island"), easily accessible by longtail boat from the shore, and yet another excellent spot for swimming and sunbathing. Snorkelers can explore an underwater cave and a sunken boat on the south side of the island. Farther afield, but still accessible by longtail from Phra Nang, **Ko Hua Khwan** is also known as Chicken Island for its strange rock formations at the northern end. Aside from occasional sea gypsies camping on the beach for a night or two, the island is deserted. It has some splendid beaches, coves, and coral reefs, ideal for sunbathing, swimming, and snorkeling. To escape the crowds in a more comfortable way, the picturesque **Ko Poda,** just south of Ko Hua Khwan, has bungalows for rent. ∎

Krabi

WHEN COMPARED WITH PHUKET AND KO SAMUI, KRABI
Province seems relatively undeveloped, but it maintains an efficient
tourism service that allows visitors to get the most out of its
attractions. And there is no shortage of things to see and do when you
get there. The province is famed for its coastline of limestone cliffs
and an overabundance of perfect deserted islands.

Krabi

309 A4 &
323 B4

Visitor information

Tourism Authority of
Thailand, Uttarakit
Rd., Krabi

075-612740

Krabi Town, the small, affable
provincial capital on the Krabi
River, has very little in the way of
attractions, functioning instead as a
conduit for getting visitors out to
the beaches and islands. It is full of
tour agents that organize camping,
snorkeling, diving, and sea-
canoeing trips (see panel opposite).

Most new arrivals head straight
for the beaches, but a trip to the
Krabi River mangrove swamps

opposite the town makes an interesting diversion. Longtail boats leave
Chao Fa pier (also the departure
point to the province's beaches and
islands) to explore the numerous
channels winding through the mangroves. These harbor a wealth of
wildlife. Birds include brown-winged
longer kingfishers, Pacific reef
egrets, Asian dowitchers, and white-
bellied sea eagles. You may also spot
otters, mudskippers, fiddler crabs,

and formidable monitor lizards basking on the muddy banks.

A large slice of Krabi's coast and islands comes under the jurisdiction of the 156-square-mile (390 sq km) Ko Phi Phi–Hat Nopparat Thara Marine National Park. At the southeastern edge of the park, near the mouth of the Krabi River, is a most curious attraction, the **Su San Hoi Shell Cemetery.** This geological oddity consists of fossil beds formed from petrified seashells. The beds, which resemble giant concrete slabs, date back 40 million years.

The park also includes a magnificent jagged coastline running southwest from the mouth of the Krabi River and a profusion of Andaman Sea islands. Park headquarters are at the southern

end of **Nopparat Thara Beach,** 11.5 miles (18 km) west of Krabi Town on Highway 4202. Nopparat Thara is a broad sandy beach lined with casuarina trees and food stalls. Quieter and more conservative than other beaches in Krabi, it draws local families on weekends, but at other times offers a fine solitude. The national park's visitor center, next to the parking lot at the end of the road, has photographs, display maps, and samples of local marine fossils. Rangers rent out basic and inexpensive bungalows. Several rocky islets lying just offshore can be reached on foot at low tide.

To the south of Nopparat Thara, past sheer cliffs dropping into the sea, is **Ao Nang Beach,** which can be reached by either road or boat from Krabi Town. The beach's inferior tract of sand and cloudy water is made up for by a spectacular bay setting. Developers have built huddles of bungalows, restaurants, and bars along the front and behind the beach. Consequently, Ao Nang has become a boisterous beach center and the best place to organize activities such as sea canoeing, diving, cycling, and island-hopping.

Trips to the islands can be organized via tour operators at Ao Nang or by negotiating with the longtail boat owners on the beach. Take water and some food when visiting these idyllic and deserted places. The best and most convenient islands to explore are **Ko Hong, Ko Dang, Ko Lading, Ko Pakbia,** and **Ko Rai.** Camping is permitted for those who want to stay on for a day or two. Rather than just hire a boat for a two-way trip, opt for a guided tour that takes you to a number of the islands. Many of the guides are sea gypsies, with a good knowledge of the islands and their secret coves and bays. ■

TOUR AGENTS

Recommended tour agents in Krabi are Jungle Book Tours *(141 Uttarakit Rd., Krabi, tel 075-611148).* ■

Impact of tourism

Tourists gather in villages near the Myanmar (Burma) border in the Northern Thai province of Mae Hong Son to gawk at the "long-neck" women and girls of the Paduang tribe. The women, their necks manacled with a brace of brass coils that deforms the bones so severely that their necks are stretched to freakish proportions, don't seem to mind. With seemingly good humor they pose for photographs, bargain with visitors wanting to buy tacky souvenirs, and get on with life under unrelenting stares.

The traditional reasons why these women have had their necks shackled (to protect against tigers and to stop them being kidnapped by other tribes, to name a couple) are no longer relevant. These days their necks are stretched with the coils—starting with girls as young as five—to make money. These glinting necklaces have become a status of wealth. To keep the money rolling in, parents insist their daughters should carry on the "tradition."

The long-neck, or "giraffe-neck," Paduang women and their husbands—refugees from intermittent fighting between government troops and ethnic tribes over the border in Myanmar—have become the beneficiaries of a slick marketing campaign by sectors of Thailand's tourism industry. Their faces and

necks often appear on tourist brochures, and visits to villages are included on organized tours to the north of the country. The villages have been decried as human zoos by some (many tour operators charge entrance fees), but officials, investors, and guides—usually with vested interests—say it is an example of how impoverished refugees can sustain themselves through tourism.

The Paduang "long necks" represent, if only in a small part, the dilemma Thailand faces in its mad rush to cash in on tourism and the billions of dollars that it generates every year—a rush that opens up a store of moral and environmental issues. On a much larger scale than the exploitation of the Paduang women is sex tourism, a sector of the tourism industry that brings huge volumes of cash into the country. Although Thai tourism and government authorities naturally play down the impact of the sex trade on tourist numbers, few doubt that many men come to Thailand for the purpose of having sex with Thai women. Many also believe prostitution is

Growing concerns about the tourism industry in Thailand range from the notorious sex trade (above) to the exploitation of minority groups such as the Paduang "long necks" (right).

tolerated by the authorities because of its ability to generate substantial amounts of income from tourists.

Another ongoing concern is widespread environmental degradation. Ko Phi Phi Don, an island midway between Krabi and Phuket in the Andaman Sea (see pp. 330–31), once recognized as one of the most beautiful islands in the world, shows what the most savage excesses of tourist development can do. The island is littered with piles of garbage that, when finally collected, are simply taken a few miles out to sea and dumped.

However, the tide is turning, for while the authorities have taken their time, they are now showing increasing concern about such places. Many local governments have introduced zoning laws at tourist resorts. On Ko Samui, for example, no hotel can be built higher than the canopy of coconut palms. And resort developments are becoming more stylish, blending in with the local environment rather than altering it. The gathering of seashells and coral has been banned, and many offshore areas have been declared no-fishing zones. Stronger policing of national parks, where much illegal logging and poaching takes place, has been instituted.

The rise of ecotourism in the country has instilled the notion that you can make money out of tourism without bulldozing a rain forest to build an ugly hotel. ■

Endangered elephants are playing their part in Thailand's tourism boom.

Ko Lanta

Often buffalo will be your only company on Ko Lanta's deserted beaches.

THE EXTENSIVE ISLAND GROUP OF KO LANTA DISHES UP A lovely spread of deserted beaches and verdant hinterlands, spiced with an agreeable tinge of isolation, bred from the popularity of other beaches rather than inaccessibility. Regular ferry services from Ao Nang and Ko Phi Phi ply to Ko Lanta, and the main islands are some of the very few in the far south that can be reached by car.

The Ko Lanta archipelago consists of 52 islands, but only banana-shaped **Ko Lanta Yai, Ko Lanta Noi,** and a few of the smaller islands have accommodations. Ko Lanta Yai and Ko Lanta Noi can be reached by a slow and spluttering car ferry from the town of Hua Hin, at the end of Highway 406 in Krabi Province.

A 12.5-mile (20 km) road runs the length of Ko Lanta Yai's west coast. Here, wide white beaches, views of offshore islands, and fabulous sunsets prevail. From **Sala Dan,** at the northern tip of the island, beaches come into view almost immediately. (Motorbikes to explore can be hired here.)

Beyond the main resort area of Khlong Dao is the beautiful 2.5-mile (4 km) stretch of sand at **Palm Beach. Khlong Kong Beach,** 5.5 miles (9km) from Sala Dan, is set amid palm trees, with plenty of coral just offshore. Farther south is the long and deserted **Khlong Nin Beach.** From there, the road winds around cliffs and over hills down to the isolated **Khlong Chak Beach.**

Just before Khlong Nin, a road cuts across the center of the island toward the east coast village of Jeh Lee. Midway, a sign marks a track through the forest to **Tham Mai Keio** cave. The seven connecting chambers here can be explored with the aid of fitted ropes and ladders.

Diving trips (including overnight packages) and instruction can be organized in Ban Sala Dan. Off the five islets of **Ko Ha** are sea caves, walls, and a variety of corals. The two islands of **Ko Rok** have sparkling beaches, clear waters, and plenty of interesting marine life. At **Hin Daeng,** a rock wall plunges 148 feet (45 m) to the seabed, home to barracudas and manta rays. ∎

Ko Lanta Yai

⚑ 309 A3

Visitor information

✉ Tourism Authority of Thailand, Uttarakit Rd., Krabi

☎ 075-612740

Huge limestone cliffs are a prominent feature of Trang's beaches and islands.

Trang & around
🗺 309 B3 & 323 D3
Visitor information
✉ Tourism Authority of Thailand, Sanam Na Muang, Rachadamnoen Rd., Nakhon Si Thammarat
☎ 075-346515

Hat Chao Mai National Park
🗺 323 C3
✉ Ao Chang Lang, Amphur Sikao, Trang
☎ 075-210099

Trang & around

TRANG IS AN UNCROWDED PLACE THAT GREETS VISITORS with a bounty of natural attractions, including lofty limestone cliffs, sparkling beaches, and exquisite tropical islands. Many of the best sights are found within Hat Chao Mai National Park, a protected area that stretches for 75 miles (120 km) along the coast and encompasses nine of the province's 47 shimmering Andaman Sea islands.

To reach the park, take Highway 403 from Trang Town to nearby Katang. A turnoff to the west winds along the coast. The road then splits: The northern arm leads to Pak Meng Beach, 24 miles (38 km) from Trang, and park headquarters at Ao Chang Lang. **Chao Mai Beach,** on the southern road, is a long stretch of white sand backed by pine trees and cliffs with caves.

Pak Meng and Kantang are the ferry points for the park's islands. The tours organized by agents in Trang Town are recommended. (Accommodations can be booked on some islands.) Trang Scuba Dive Center *(59 Hauy Yot Rd., tel 075-222192)* provides entry-level courses for divers, as well as tours for certified divers. Day trips go to the islands, while dive and camp tours take in the wrecks of two Japanese World War II ships sunk off **Ko Kradan.** At **Ko Muk,**

35 minutes south of Pak Meng, is **Emerald Cave** (Tham Morakot). Enter at low tide and follow a long, dark, silent passage to reach a lagoon enclosed by towering, jungle-dressed limestone walls. ∎

Dugongs

These delightful sea mammals come with sad faces, hairless plump bodies, and long forelimbs ending with hands and fingers. A scallop-shaped tail works as a rudder. Sexual organs similar in appearance to those of humans is thought to have given rise to the mermaid myth. Dugongs, in Thailand found only near Trang, have diminished greatly in number since trawling began to destroy much of the sea grasses on which they feed. Conservation programs have now been instituted. ∎

Ko Tarutao

KO TARUTAO AND THE GROUP OF ISLANDS AROUND IT form one of the far south's last backwoods of tourism. This stunning archipelago scattered off the country's southwest coast delivers everything you could wish for in a tropical paradise. The deserted beaches, multicolored coral, roaring waterfalls, deep limestone caves, and thick jungles greet fewer than 20,000 tourists a year.

Ko Tarutao, at 60 square miles (151 sq km), is the largest island in this marine national park. Tourist boats run daily from Pak Bara, in Satun Province, from November to April (a 90-minute trip). After this, battering monsoons dissuade most people from visiting .

Boats arrive at **Ao Phante Malak,** on the northwest tip of the island, where the visitor center provides insights into local geography and history. Most of the island's basic accommodations are at Phante and are best booked ahead from Pak Bara.

Ko Tarutao's isolation made it a dumping ground for political dissidents and criminals during World War II. Evidence of the penal colony (concrete fermentation tanks, charcoal furnaces, and graveyards) is seen at **Talo Udan Bay,** at the southern end of the island, and at windswept **Talo Wao Bay** on the east coast. A narrow convict-built road between the two now serves as an 8-mile (12 km) hiking trail. The trail continues from Talo Wao another 8 miles (12 km) back to Phante.

Ko Tarutao's west coast is lined with sweeping bays and isolated coves that harbor glorious beaches, reached by more well-maintained hiking trails from Phante. A 30-minute walk from Phante leads you to **Ao Chak,** a beautiful twin-arced bay with powdery sands and swaying palms. The trail then snakes through thick rain forest, past a number of waterfalls, to **Ao San,** a four-hour hike from Phante. This bay is a long sweep of glistening sand, with excellent coral for snorkeling just offshore.

Longtail boats hired at park headquarters can drop you at the beaches, from where you can hike back to Ao Phante. ∎

Isolated and beautiful, Ko Tarutao plays host to fewer than 20,000 tourists a year—mostly Thais.

Ko Tarutao
- 309 B2 & 323 D1

Visitor information
- Tourism Authority of Thailand, 1/1 Soi 2 Niphat Uthit 3 Rd., Hat Yai, Songkhla
- 074-231055 or 074-238518

Ko Tarutao Marine National Park Office
- Pak Bara, Ko Tarutao
- 074-711383

More places to visit in the Far South

HAT NAI PHLAO & HAT SICHON

The small beach resort of Hat Nai Phlao, about 44 miles (70 km) north of Nakhon Si Thammarat, commands a prime position on a string of beaches along one of the most attractive coastal stretches on the Gulf of Thailand. The masses of coconut palms that spread along the white-sand bay give it an island feel. The bay sweeps 3 miles (5 km) north to **Khanom Beach** and south to a tall rocky headland.

From there, the coastline weaves past the deserted twin bays of **Thong Yee** and **Thong Yang,** where patches of white sand are interspersed with rocky coves. About 3 miles (5 km) farther south, another low-key resort, **Hat Sichon,** has beach vendors and more groves of coconut palms.

🗺 309 C5, 309 C4

MORE ISLANDS OFF TARUTAO

West of the beautiful island of Tarutao, and part of the marine national park, are a number of other beautiful and isolated islands. On the forested **Ko Adang** and its smaller neighbors, you'll find some of the most pristine environment in Thailand. The rugged hills of Ko Adang are laced with freshwater streams and hooded with jungles of rain forest that give way to narrow beaches on the south coast.

Ko Lipe, by comparison, is flat and clad with coconut plantations. It is home to a large community of *chao lae* (sea gypsies), who settled here for the freshwater springs. Longtail boats can be chartered for trips to nearby islets.

About 12 miles (20 km) off Pak Bara is **Ko Bulon Lae,** part of the Ko Phetra Marine National Park. It is a laid-back island with a few small villages, long strips of excellent beaches, and shallow coral reefs offshore that are ideal for snorkeling.

While waiting at Pak Bara for boats to take you to the islands mentioned above, a visit to **Ko Kebang** is an interesting diversion. Catch a water-taxi for the 15-minute ride past the towering cliffs of **Laem Tanyong Du Ri,** north of the port, and along the jungle-fringed channel, **Pi Yai Klong,** to the main

village of **Ban Bor Jet Lok.** Here, negotiate with the boatmen at the pier for a 30-minute trip up the mangrove-choked channel, **Langu Khlong,** where you will have close-up views of the birdlife.

🗺 309 B2 & 323 D1

PIYA MIT TUNNEL

Hidden in the jungle in Khao Nam Khang National Park, on the Thai–Malaysian border, off Highway 4113 and south from the town of Na Thawi, is the amazing Piya Mit Tunnel. Malaysian Communists, in their long struggle to overthrow the Malaysian government, used this hillside bunker as a guerrilla base and hideout between the 1940s and 1980s.

The immense tunnel, which could hold up to 200 rebels at any one time, has more than 100 rooms. There are sleeping quarters, kitchens, meeting rooms, a medical center, communication rooms—and even a shooting range and a motorcycle training area!

The rebels were granted citizenship and given land nearby as part of a peace deal brokered with the Thai government in 1990. What makes the visit to this remarkable place most memorable are the first-hand accounts of the ex-guerrillas who now act as guides.

🗺 309 C1

TEMPLE CAVES AT TRANG

A number of important temple caves hide among Trang's limestone cliffs. Head north of Trang Town to Huai Yot, and continue west on Highway 4 to **Tham Khao Pina,** an expansive limestone cave on six levels, its caverns filled with Buddha images.

North of Huai Yot on Highway 403, turn right before the town of Khlong Pang to **Wat Tham Phra Phut.** When archaeologists discovered this cave in the early 20th century they found a large Ayutthaya-period Buddha reclining over a collection of royal regalia and upper-class household items, including talismans, fine pottery, silverware, and lacquerware. The collection is thought to have been stashed in the cavern at some time before the fall of Ayutthaya.

🗺 309 B3 ■

Travelwise

**One of Bangkok's ubiquitous
three-wheeled *tuk tuks***

TRAVELWISE INFORMATION

PLANNING YOUR TRIP

WHEN TO GO

Most visitors head to Thailand during the relatively cool and dry season from December to February, when rainfall is scarce and the temperature around a tolerable 84–90°F (28–32°C). (If you're traveling in the hills, temperatures can drop sharply in the evenings, so take a sweater.) The drawback is that popular destinations are crowded and hotel rooms can be in short supply. Prices tend to be higher during the tourist season and internal transportation can be difficult to secure. March to May or June is the hottest time to visit—temperatures may reach 100°F (38°C), particularly in the plains of the Northeast, and the high level of humidity (around 80 percent) can make travel uncomfortable and oppressive.

The wet season runs from June to November, and this may be the finest period to enjoy the charms of the country without the hordes of tourists. These months constitute the "rainy" season, when a dose of precipitation is almost guaranteed most afternoons. The remainder of the day will generally be dry, if overcast. Major monsoons, which can last several days, are relatively rare. Another advantage of travel at this time of year is that the countryside is vibrantly green with flooded rice fields and blooming trees. Vacancy rates are high at most hotels, and it is easier to make reservations with local transportation.

CLIMATE

Thailand has three seasons, although the differences between them are barely distinguishable. The classic divisions are the dry and relatively cool months

(December–February), the extremely hot summer months (March–June), and the rainy season (June–November).

Even in the coolest months, Thailand remains a scorching country with a brutal equatorial climate that punishes even the hardiest of international travelers. Maximum temperatures throughout the year in Bangkok generally reach 90°F (32°C), and humidity rarely drops below 50 percent. While the temperature drops slightly over the Christmas holiday season, humidity remains at sky-high levels to the point where most visitors feel compelled to take several showers daily. During the so-called rainy season it might be bone dry for several weeks, while the supposedly "dry" Christmas season may be flooded out with an unexpected monsoon.

The climate is dominated by seasonal monsoons that sweep across the country. Monsoons are somewhat predictable throughout most of Thailand, although they do vary when you move south down the Thai peninsula toward Malaysia. Ko Samui and the southeast coast can be hit by monsoon winds and rain in November and December, but this area is usually drier than elsewhere during the rainy season.

WHAT TO TAKE

Thailand is a modern country where almost every conceivable item can be purchased—and often at lower costs than you find back home. Shopping emporiums are located in almost every urban center and smaller town in the kingdom.

Thailand is a perpetually hot country where jackets and sweaters are rarely needed.

Coats, ties, and formal dresses may be necessary in a few exclusive restaurants in Bangkok but are otherwise little more than an additional packing burden.

Clothes should be a light cotton or other natural fiber rather than synthetics or heavy materials. Bring the barest possible items of clothing and expand your wardrobe in Thailand, where the clothing selection is excellent and of international quality. A pair of comfortable walking shoes is essential, and sandals will prove useful when visiting temples, where shoes must always be removed prior to entry.

Other items to consider are a small medical kit, sewing kit, mini umbrella, insect repellent, drug prescriptions, an extra pair of glasses, spare passport photos, and photocopies of essential documents.

Electricity in Thailand is 220V, 50Hz, and plugs are generally the flat, two-pin type. If you bring electrical equipment you will need a plug adaptor plus a transformer for U.S. appliances.

INSURANCE

Make sure you have adequate travel and medical coverage for treatment and expenses, including repatriation and baggage and money loss. Keep all receipts for expenses. Report loss or thefts to the tourist police (see pp. 353–54), and obtain a signed statement to help with insurance claims.

FURTHER READING

Thailand has inspired a surprisingly large amount of literature, from casual adventures to serious works on art and culture. The following works are widely available.

Thailand: A Short History, David Wyatt (Yale University Press,

984), is an academic work, unquestionably the finest history available on the country. A lighter and more entertaining read is *The Legendary American,* William Warren (Houghton Mifflin, 1970), which relates the fascinating story of Jim Thompson's revival of the silk-weaving industry and of his mysterious disappearance. *Travelers' Tales Thailand* (O'Reilly & Associates, 1993) is a collection of descriptive writings gathered from 46 talented writers and provides valuable insight into the culture, people, and eccentricities of Thailand.

Arts of Thailand, Steve Van Beek (Thames and Hudson, 1991), is a beautiful coffee-table book with superb photographs; William Warren's *Legendary Thailand* and *Thai Style* (both Asia Books, 1988) are also recommended.

Thai cooking is well served by the persistently popular *Thai Cooking,* Jennifer Brennan (Futura Publications, 1984), and *The Food of Thailand,* Wendy Hutton (Periplus, 1995).

Humor and adventure are the themes of books such as *Waylaid by the Bimbos,* James Eckardt (Post Publishing, 1991), and *Asian Portraits,* Harold Stephens (Travel Publishing Asia, 1983). *Mai Pen Rai,* Carol Hollinger (Houghton Mifflin, 1965), is perhaps the single best book to read prior to departure, to understand something about the essential nature of the Thai personality.

The best written account and photographic coverage of the colorful hill tribes of Northern Thailand is the lavishly illustrated *Peoples of the Golden Triangle,* Paul and Elaine Lewis (Thames and Hudson, 1984). A superbly sensitive explanation of Buddhism is given in *Three Ways of Asian Wisdom,* Nancy Ross (Simon and Schuster, 1966). Novels set in and around Thailand include *Lord Jim,* Joseph Conrad (Penguin, 1900), The

Gentleman in the Parlour, W. Somerset Maugham (Heinemann, 1930), and more contemporary titles such as *Crossing the Shadow Line,* Andrew Eames (Hodder and Stoughton, 1986), and *In Search of Conrad,* Gavin Young (Hutchinson, 1991).

HOW TO GET TO THAILAND

ENTRY FORMALITIES

All visitors must possess a passport that is valid for a minimum of six months from the day of entry. Nationals from 56 favored nations, including the U.S. and most European countries, are given a 30-day permit upon arrival. This permit can easily be extended for another 10 days at immigration offices throughout the country. Take along a passport photograph and photocopies of the inside page of your passport and the page on which the entry permit is stamped.

Visitors who intend to stay longer than 30 days should obtain in advance a visa from a Thai embassy or consulate. This 60-day tourist visa can be extended once for an additional 30 days. Longer visas for qualified individuals are also available at Thai diplomatic offices.

AIRLINES

Bangkok is served by over 50 international airlines, representing almost every major carrier in the world. Most flights arrive at Bangkok International Airport (Don Muang), some 30 minutes northeast of the city center, although future flights will arrive at a new airport now under construction to the southeast of Bangkok. It is expected to be fully functional by 2005, after which Don Muang will be converted into a domestic airport. Both airports are expected to welcome international flights for a few years, until the transition is completed.

International flights also serve Phuket, while airports such as Chiang Mai occasionally welcome international flights, generally from neighboring Southeast Asian countries.

Travel times to Bangkok, including layovers and the necessary refueling stop, are San Francisco, Los Angeles, and Seattle (16–20 hours); Chicago (20–24 hours); and New York via the West Coast (22–26 hours). To reach Bangkok from most European cities takes 12–16 hours on a direct flight.

ARRIVING

Don Muang International Airport is in a northeastern suburb of Bangkok, some 16 miles (25 km) from the city center. After arrival, you pass through immigration to pick up your entry permit or have your visa stamped, then pick up your luggage and go through customs. After these legal formalities, you enter a claustrophobic arrivals lounge, which, nevertheless, has a number of useful services. A small tourist office can help with general brochures and a simple map of the city, while traveler's checks and cash can be exchanged at fair rates into Thai baht at several bank kiosks. The Thai Hotel Association counter can check on vacancies at member hotels and make reservations, though only middle to superior properties are represented by the organization. The airport also has an emergency medical clinic, phones for domestic and international calls, and several restaurants on the upper floors.

There are booths offering inexpensive limousine services (usually Mercedes-Benz cars) inside the arrivals lounge. A trip to your downtown hotel will cost about $15, and the ride will be comfortable and your driver courteous. Alternatively, just outside the arrivals lounge is a taxi stand. When you get to the top of the stand, tell the person inside the booth your destination; he or she will mark it on a coupon, which you then hand to the taxi driver once inside the taxi. Check if the meter is turned on. The fare to the hotel will be the sum of the meter, plus an airport pickup surcharge (about $1.25), plus tolls collected along the highway into town. In most cases, to hotels along Sukhumvit Road, the Silom area, and near the river (such as the Oriental), two tolls will be paid, the total cost of which is less than $2. All up, the fare will be $7–$8. It takes 30–45 minutes to reach hotels in town. Do not accept offers for taxis by touts at the airport.

Solo travelers or those simply watching their baht may want to use the special bus service from the airport to their hotel. The airport bus counter is also left from the exit door, a short walk past the taxi stand. Buses follow various routes. Bus drivers and other attendants working at the bus counter can help with directions and point you in the right direction. Airport Bus A1 goes to the hotels near Pratunam and Siam Square, and those along Silom Road. The bus terminates near the Oriental and Shangri-La hotels. Airport Bus A2 reaches the budget guesthouses near Khao San Road in the Banglamphu district. Airport Bus A3 serves the hotels along Sukhumvit Road. These bus services are quick and inexpensive, but can be crowded.

The least expensive option into town is the train, which departs about every 30 minutes from the railway station just across the highway from the airport. You can use the elevated walkway that crosses the highway and walk to the station in about 10 minutes. The train makes several stops and terminates at Hua Lamphong station, near Chinatown and the hotels on Silom Road. The journey takes about 40 minutes.

When departing, remember to keep 500 baht aside for the airport departure tax. Airport flight inquiries, tel 02-535-1111.

GETTING AROUND

TRAVELING IN THAILAND

BY AIRPLANE

Several airlines serve over 20 domestic airports within Thailand. Most routes are handled by Thai Airways International (THAI), with a handful of smaller destinations served by Bangkok Airways. Bangkok is the hub from which planes fan out to towns including Chiang Mai, Chiang Rai, Nakhon Ratchasima, and Ubon Ratchathani in the Northeast, and several major stops in the South such as Phuket and Hat Yai.

Thai Airways flies from Bangkok to Chiang Mai several times daily, although the night train is a very comfortable alternative and preferred by many experienced travelers. A sensible flight that saves a great deal of time is the daily flight from Chiang Mai down to Phuket with a stop in Bangkok. Another useful service to consider is the shuttle from Bangkok down to Phuket (several daily), chiefly since Phuket lacks a direct train service and the bus journey is a marathon affair best left to hardy backpackers.

Thai Airways has offices in Bangkok and outlets in all towns served by the company. Thailand's other major domestic airline is Bangkok Airways, which uses Sukhothai rather than Bangkok as its hub. Its most important connection is the daily flight from Bangkok to Ko Samui. Bangkok Airways also flies daily between Phuket and Samui, and provides a limited number of international connections such as a flight from Bangkok to Siem Reap, the Cambodian town near Angkor Wat. Another very

useful route is the daily flight from Bangkok to Krabi, a small town in the South near dozens of superb islands and beaches.

BY TRAIN

Trains provide the most comfortable and enjoyable method of traveling around the country, with limited destinations more than compensated by reasonable fares. There are three carriage classes. Third class has seats only and is crowded and uncomfortable—best avoided. Second class has air-conditioned and non air-conditioned sleepers, the latter slightly cheaper. First class is about 40 percent more expensive than second class but is still excellent value and provides you with your own two-berth cabin.

The State Railway of Thailand (S.R.T.) operates four main train routes in the country and a handful of auxiliary spurs that serve smaller towns. The northern line starts at Hua Lamphong train station in Bangkok and heads north to Chiang Mai, passing through Ayutthaya, Lop Buri, Nakhon Sawan, Phitsanulok, Uttaradit, and Lampang. Plans have been announced to construct a spur from Den Chai to Chiang Rai, although economic problems seem to have put train route expansion on hold.

The northeastern line also starts at Hua Lamphong and heads north to Ayutthaya and then northeast to Nakhon Ratchasima (Khorat), where it splits into two lines. The route most commonly used by visitors goes almost due north through Khon Kaen and Udon Thani to Nong Khai on the Mekong River, just opposite Laos. The Bangkok–Nong Khai train journey on an overnight sleeper express is recommended for travelers heading to Laos. The other northeastern line heads east from Khorat to Ubon Ratchathani, passing through Buriram, Surin, and Sisaket.

A rarely used train route heads east from Bangkok to Chachoengsao and Prachin Buri, near the Cambodian border. The opening of Cambodia and the increasing popularity of Angkor Wat have raised the profile of this obscure route, and you can now travel overland from Bangkok to Siem Reap (Angkor) in one day.

Trains also run southward to the beaches and islands. The southern train departs Hua Lamphong and slowly ambles down the tracks to Phetchaburi, Hua Hin, Prachuap Khiri Khan, Chumphon, Surat Thani, Phatthalung, and Hat Yai before continuing across the border into Malaysia. The train track splits at Hat Yai: One spur goes southeast across the Malaysian border to Kota Baru (Bharu), and the other southwest to Penang and Kuala Lumpur.

The chief disadvantage to the southern line is that trains do not go directly to Ko Samui, Phuket, Krabi, and other beach resort towns. However, S.R.T. offers package deals to the more popular resorts and islands such as Phuket and Samui. The packages are similar: Purchase your ticket several days in advance, and catch one of the early evening departures south. The ticket includes a comfortable sleeper, and you arrive at a connection point the following morning, from where buses and, when necessary, boats continue to Phuket and Samui. These packages are reasonably priced and perhaps just as convenient as making your way out to the airport.

Complimentary train schedules for the four major routes can be picked up at the information counter in Hua Lamphong train station. The red train brochure has abbreviated train schedules for the southern line, while the green brochure provides summary details for the north, northeastern, and eastern routes. These immensely useful

brochures also include tips on refunds, fees for classes and upgrades, and other details.

BY BUS

Most small towns can only be reached by bus. Buses are quick and relatively comfortable for short journeys, although longer trips are best accomplished, whenever possible, by either train or plane. Thailand has a government bus service known as Bor Kor Sor (B.K.S.), and dozens of private bus companies provide competitive services on identical routes.

B.K.S. buses come in several classes, including ordinary non-air-conditioned buses for shorter trips and comfortable air-conditioned buses for longer journeys. Ordinary buses are often the only means of reaching smaller towns, but travel this way tends to be very crowded and time consuming as many stops are made en route to the final destination. Superior buses range from the simple air-conditioned option to top-of-the-line "tour buses" with reclining seats and hostesses who serve drinks. The superior classes of B.K.S. buses are comfortable and priced substantially lower than buses owned and operated by private companies.

B.K.S. has steadily introduced new superior bus classes over the years, as seats are removed from the cabins to increase leg room and provide enough space for reclining seats. Many of the buses now include toilets and have a refreshment station for cold drinks and snacks. Prices are higher on these upgraded lines, but they are excellent for overnight journeys as the seats can be reclined to near horizontal positions.

B.K.S. bus terminals in very small towns are often situated right in the center near the market, while terminals in larger towns are almost always outside city limits to minimize traffic jams in

the urban core. Some form of public transportation, a local bus or three-wheeler, will be necessary to reach terminals on the outskirts of town. Larger towns generally have separate terminals for ordinary and air-conditioned buses, but these terminals are usually next to each other. Ordinary bus tickets are sold directly on the bus, while tickets for superior services can be purchased on the same day or in advance at ticket counters at the terminal. Ordinary buses tend to leave constantly during the day at unfixed schedules, while superior buses for longer journeys generally depart in the early morning or early evening.

Private bus companies operate between major tourist destinations, serving Chiang Mai, Phuket, and Ko Samui from Bangkok, with smaller minivans used for newer tourist destinations such as Ko Si Chang and Krabi. Private companies provide several superior options, reducing the number of seats per vehicle. Prices, of course, rise as the number of seats falls.

Most private bus companies schedule departures from their own terminals, next to the B.K.S. stations on the outskirts of town. The chief advantage to private bus companies at first appears to be complimentary transportation from your hotel to the bus terminal, but this is frustratingly time-consuming as passengers are picked up from widely scattered hotels. The best strategy is to take a taxi or other form of transportation out to the bus terminal, where you can then choose between a B.K.S. or a private bus service.

A final matter to consider is that of bus safety. In Thailand, the accident rate is very high. Choose a seat near the rear of the bus to avoid danger in case of a head-on collision. B.K.S. buses tend to be driven with more care than private buses, whose drivers seem to speed with little concern for their passengers' safety.

Do not accept food or drink from strangers and be wary of food or drink offered by seemingly official bus representatives. There have been rare cases in which the food or drink has been spiked by thieves with sleep-inducing drugs.

BY CAR OR MOTORCYCLE

With the exception of chaotic Bangkok and to a lesser degree Chiang Mai, Thailand is an excellent country to tour with a rented car or motorcycle. Outside the major urban centers the traffic tends to very light, roads are in excellent condition, and signs are often in English. Exploring with a private vehicle allows you to get off the beaten track and escape the tourist hordes.

International car rental agencies such as Avis and Hertz are represented in all major tourist destinations such as Bangkok, Chiang Mai, Phuket, and Ko Samui. Local car rental agencies tend to be substantially less expensive and often rent cars for extended periods at large discounts to the daily rate. Daily rental rates are lowest for open-air jeeps and compacts and increase for mid-size sedans and larger cars. Vans suitable for larger groups are also available at reasonable rates. The majority of visitors have few problems driving around most places, but Thai drivers can be hired at very modest rates, and this service may be appropriate for those who wish to relax.

If you rent a motorbike, check it very carefully for signs of wear and damage, particularly to brakes, lights, and tires, and make sure you wear a crash helmet and protective clothing. Driving, or riding on a motorbike can be a harrowing experience in Thailand. To prepare yourself,

first travel with an experienced rider until you get a feel for the local traffic situation.

An International Driver's License is necessary if you plan on renting a car in Thailand. Such a license can be picked up at any local office of the American Automobile Association (AAA) or the Canadian Automobile Association (CAA).

Insurance is highly recommended whenever you rent a vehicle, and foreigners are always assumed the responsible party in the event of an accident. Insurance is sometimes provided with your car insurance policy back home or with the use of a major credit card for the vehicle rental, though this should be confirmed prior to your departure for Thailand. Major car rental agencies include comprehensive insurance with each rental, but this may not be the case with small, locally owned rental firms, which sometimes rent cars without adequate insurance. Be sure to inspect all contracts to determine that adequate insurance is included with your rental.

Drive on the left. The city speed limit is 35 mph (60 kph), unless signed otherwise. Outside the cities, the limit is 50 mph (80 kph). Be warned—although traffic rules and regulations do exist, they are often ignored by local drivers. Gas stations are commonplace on all main roads.

TRANSPORTATION IN TOWNS & CITIES

BY TAXI

Transportation around the cities and towns of Thailand is unusual. Taxis operate in major tourist destinations such as Bangkok, Chiang Mai, and Phuket, but are rarely found elsewhere. Taxis are legally required to be metered in Bangkok. However, taxis found waiting outside superior hotels may refuse to use their meter and instead quote fixed prices, which tend to be about double

the metered rate. Avoid these illegal fixed-rate taxis by walking down to the street and hailing an ordinary taxi.

Taxis in Chiang Mai, Phuket, and Ko Samui do not use meters but quote fixed rates for all destinations. It's best to ask for advice at your hotel front desk or check with several taxi drivers before committing to any lengthy taxi ride. Make sure you agree on the price in advance. Taxis are also available for hire on an hourly or full-day basis.

BY LOCAL TRANSPORTATION

Bangkok is the only city in Thailand with a fully developed bus system, although Chiang Mai and Phuket have public buses on a very limited number of routes. The local bus system is so confusing that most visitors take taxis or another form of private transportation to reach their destination. Minivans may double as shared taxis on popular tourist routes—such as from the local airport to city center—but the most common local conveyances are three-wheeled vehicles known as tuk tuks if powered with a gasoline engine, or samlors if peddled by a person. Samlors are disappearing from most towns but can still be found in a few places.

Tuk tuks are noisy, smelly vehicles that race around at frightening speeds but provide easy transportation at reasonable cost. Tuk tuks are hardly necessary in Bangkok, which has an overabundance of metered taxis but are useful in places such as Chiang Mai, Ayutthaya, and Sukhothai. Tuk tuks are unmetered, and the drivers are quite happy to overcharge unwary visitors, so bargaining is in order on all journeys.

Local transportation may also be in minibuses known as songthaews—small trucks with hard benches at the back— which can be very crowded.

BY SKYTRAIN

Bangkok opened its elevated Skytrain service several years ago to great acclaim. The two lines reach a surprising number of hotels, sights, and shopping districts in the city, as if the Skytrain was constructed to serve the needs of the tourist rather than the locals who continue to favor the much cheaper buses. Skytrain maps are available all over town. The main routes and destinations are the river, hotels along Silom Road, the Patpong entertainment district, hotels along Sukhumvit Road, the shopping centers near Siam Square, and the Chatuchat Weekend Market. You can either buy stored-value tickets (minimum 200BHT) or purchase a per-ride ticket from vending machines. Stored-value tickets and change for the vending machines are available at the station booths. Plans are now in place to extend the Skytrain service in future years.

PRACTICAL ADVICE

COMMUNICATIONS

POST OFFICES

Thailand has an improving postal service with post offices in almost every town. Most visitors find it convenient to leave their postcards and letters with the front desk at their hotel. Airmail to the U.S. takes about 7–10 days. Only nonessential items such as postcards should be sent with ordinary mail service, while important letters and packages should always be sent registered mail—a small percentage of packages seem to disappear on their way into and out of Thailand.

Letters can be mailed to any post office in Thailand, where they will be held for customer pickup for at least 30 days. Letters and packages sent should be clearly marked as "poste restante" (general delivery), and family names should be printed in capitals and underlined. If you are expecting a package and it has not been filed under your last name, be sure to check the folder for your first name.

The Bangkok G.P.O. on Charoen Krung Road near the Royal Orchid Sheraton hotel is open weekdays until 6 p.m. and weekends and holidays until 1 p.m. Post offices elsewhere close on weekdays at 4 p.m. and Saturdays at noon. All packages sent from Thailand must first be inspected at the post office prior to boxing. The procedure is to bring all unboxed items to the post office for inspection, after which you may purchase a box and wrapping materials for your package. Private mailing firms such as Mailboxes Inc. provide an alternative to the rather lengthy mailing procedure required by public post offices. D.H.L. and Federal Express have offices in most tourist destinations in the country.

TELEPHONES

The telephone system in Thailand is very modern and efficient for both local and international calls, which can be made from hotels, public phone kiosks, and international phone offices in G.P.O.s in most provincial capitals. To call the U.S. or Canada from Thailand, dial the international access code (00), the country code (1), the area code, and finally the local telephone number. For the U.K. dial 00 144, followed by the area code (without the initial 0) and local number. The international access code for Australia is 00 61. To call Thailand from the U.S., dial 00 66, the area code for the particular city, then the local phone number.

Domestic phone calls can be tricky as all telephone area codes within the country begin with a zero. International calls do not require the use of this zero in the local area code, but you must add a zero to domestic calls. For example, to call Bangkok from the United States you just use 2 as the area code, but to call Bangkok from Chiang Mai you must use 02 as the area code. Many local phone lines use a variety of final digits to handle incoming calls. A phone number such as 344-9901-09 means you may use 01-09 to reach the central operator.

E-MAIL & THE INTERNET

Internet cafés are now found in almost every town and city, providing excellent service at very low prices. Internet cafés in Bangkok are concentrated in the backpacker's enclave around Khao San Road but are also found in major shopping centers and near the tourist hotels along Silom and Sukhumvit Roads. Internet cafés are also abundant in other tourist destinations, such as Chiang Mai, Phuket, and Ko Samui. Most computers automatically dial up Hotmail.com, from where you can access your messages from your home I.S.P.

EMERGENCIES

EMBASSIES IN BANGKOK

Australian Embassy
37 Sathorn Tai Rd., Bangkok, tel 02-287-2680
Canadian Embassy
Abdulrahim Bldg., 15th floor, 990 Rama IV Rd., Bangkok, tel 02-636-0540
United Kingdom Embassy
1031 Witthayu Rd., Bangkok, tel 02-253-0191/9
United States Embassy
120–122 Witthayu Rd., Bangkok, tel 02-205-4000

EMERGENCY PHONE NUMBERS

Tourist police tel 1155
Ambulance/English-speaking doctors (Bangkok) Bangkok Adventist Hospital, 430 Phitsanulok Rd., Bangkok, tel 02-281-1422 or 02-282-1100
Immigration tel 02-287-3101
International calls tel 100

EMERGENCIES/OTHER INFORMATION

POLICE

Brown-uniformed police are commonly seen, and many speak a little English. However, try to contact the tourist police as they all speak English and are better trained at dealing with any problems tourists may face. They may also provide guidance and escort in remote or dangerous areas. The tourist police have offices in all major tourist areas in Thailand, as well as a hotline (tel 1155) that puts you in touch with them directly from any pay phone in the country.

OTHER INFORMATION

ALCOHOL/DRINKING

The legal drinking age is 18. Alcohol cannot be bought on days celebrating the king's or queen's birthdays, special religious holidays, or election days.

CONVERSIONS

1 kilo = 2.2 pounds
1 liter = 0.2 U.S. gallons
1 kilometer = 0.6 miles
1 meter = 1.1 yards

HEALTH

Thailand is a surprisingly healthy country for foreigners, with generally high standards of hygiene. The country has excellent medical facilities, from pharmacies in almost every town to state-of-the-art hospitals in Bangkok, Chiang Mai, and other cities.

Full health insurance should be purchased prior to travel, and visitors should be sure their vaccinations are current and should check with their doctor regarding any special requirements. Medical prescriptions can easily be filled at local pharmacies, but bring along your prescription from home or you'll need to make an appointment to see a doctor. Malaria is a threat only in isolated regions such as the

border districts with Myanmar (Burma) and Cambodia. Elsewhere, there is little likelihood of contracting the disease, and malaria pills are no longer recommended for most casual visitors.

The most common medical complaints are stomach upsets and heat exhaustion, and simple precautions will help. Peel all fruit and avoid eating raw, unwashed vegetables. Don't overdo things in the first few days, and allow yourself time to acclimatize to the temperature and humidity. Drink plenty of fluids, use a high-factor sunblock, and wear a hat in the sun.

Tap water is not safe to drink in most parts of the country, and even the locals stick to bottled water, soft drinks, or beer.

HOLIDAYS

Banks, government offices, schools, and most stores close on the following national holidays. For a full list of festivals, see pp. 385–86.

Jan. 1 New Year's Day
Feb. (full moon) Makha Puja
April 6 Chakri Day
Mid-April Songkran
May 1 Labor Day
May 5 Coronation Day
Early May Royal Ploughing Ceremony
May (full moon) Visakha Puja
July (full moon) Asanha Puja
Aug. 12 Queen's Birthday
Oct. 23 Chulalongkorn Day
Dec. 5 King's Birthday
Dec. 10 Constitution Day

LOCAL CUSTOMS

The Thais favor a cool heart, or *jai yen*, so displays of anger and raised voices are out, and even kissing and hugging in public are frowned upon. On the other hand, formality is not required in naming people—first names and nicknames are the norm.

The head is the most honored

part of the body and the feet despised, so don't sit with your feet pointing at someone or you may unwittingly be insulting them. Do not touch people (even children) on the head.

For temple etiquette, see p. 19.

MEDIA

NEWSPAPERS

The Thai press is one of the freest in Southeast Asia and is an excellent source of information . Two major English-language newspapers are published in Bangkok: the excellent *Bangkok Post* and the more opinionated *The Nation*. Both are morning newspapers and include special weekly supplements on tourism activities, tours, and special promotional events for visitors.

MAGAZINES

Nearly all the big Western magazines are sold in Bangkok, along with specialized publications such as the *Far Eastern Economic Review, Asiaweek*, and *Time Asia*. Several of the major tourist destinations have local English-language newspapers and weekly magazines that provide insight and information such as promotions at neighborhood restaurants. They include the *Pattaya Mail*, the *Phuket Gazette*, and the *Chiang Mai News*. An excellent resource for Bangkok is the witty and entertaining *Metro* magazine.

MONEY MATTERS

LOCAL CURRENCY

The unit of currency is the baht (BHT), which is issued in a variety of coinage and paper units. Coins have been minted in several sizes over the last decade, often without any English labeling on the coin, and so can be confusing. The most commonly circulated coins are small, thin 1BHT coins, middle-size 5BHT coins, and slightly larger 10BHT coins. Paper currency comes in different sizes and colors, including the 10BHT (brown), 20BHT (green), 50BHT (blue), 100BHT (red), 500BHT (purple), and 1,000BHT (beige). The larger the note, the higher its value.

EXCHANGE RATES

The baht floats in the 36–42BHT per dollar range. The airport money exchange desk is open 24 hours. Traveler's checks bring a slightly higher exchange rate than cash. Exchanges can be made at banks, hotels, guesthouses, and exchange booths (found in tourist areas). Banks and guesthouses give a lower rate of exchange.

Many ATMs accept major credit cards (they will be marked as such) and international ATM card networks such as Cirrus and Magellan. Banks will give cash advances on major credit cards. You will need your passport to receive cash advances and to change traveler's checks.

SECURITY

As in any country, visitors should watch their valuables and use sensible precautions such as money belts and hotel safes to guard their possessions.

TIPPING

A 10 percent service charge and 7 percent value added tax (VAT) is automatically added to all luxury hotel rooms and to most of the upscale restaurants that cater to the tourist industry. The service charge makes it unnecessary to offer a tip in most restaurants. However, it still remains thoughtful to offer a small gratuity to porters and chambermaids and small change as an additional tip to most other service personnel (10–20BHT). Leftover change is also appreciated in cafés, by helpful taxi drivers, and by anyone else who provides a useful service.

OPENING TIMES

Most private businesses keep similar hours to those in the West, while government offices open and close at more erratic hours (see below).

Banks Mon.–Fri. 8:30 a.m.–3:30 p.m. Some banks open on Sat. morning, while others have a mobile exchange trailer near the front door to provide exchange services for extended hours.

Museums State-run national museums are open Wed.–Sun. 8:30 a.m.–noon and 1 p.m.–4:30 p.m. Museums close Mon., Tues., and national holidays.

Government offices Most government offices (such as immigration) are open Mon.–Fri. 8:30 a.m.–noon and 1 p.m–4:30 p.m., and close on weekends and national holidays. The exception are tourist offices, which open daily except holidays 8:30 a.m.–4:30 p.m.

Shopping centers Large shopping emporiums are open daily 10/11 a.m.–9 p.m. year round, and many stay open on national holidays.

REST ROOMS

Few public buildings—aside from government facilities such as national museums and tourist offices—have rest rooms. They are most easily found in large hotels and restaurants, as well as in nightclubs and other entertainment venues. Outside these places, the Thai-style facilities may seem primitive—usually a floor-level basin over which you squat. Toilet paper is available in establishments frequented by foreign visitors but not always in smaller restaurants and bars. Most shopping centers have clean toilets, but they often take a bit of finding.

TIME DIFFERENCES

There is only one time zone in Thailand. Thailand is seven hours ahead of Greenwich Mean Time (GMT +7). It is 15 hours ahead of the West Coast of the United States, 13 hours ahead of

Chicago, 12 hours ahead of New York, 7 hours ahead of London, and 3 hours behind Sydney. Add one hour to these figures during summer daylight saving time. Thailand uses the 24-hour, or military, clock.

TOURIST OFFICES

The Tourism Authority of Thailand (TAT) website (www.tat.or.th) is easy to use and has information on many tourist areas.

AUSTRALIA

Sydney National Australia Bank, 2nd Floor, 255 George St., Sydney, NSW 20000, tel 02-247-7549, fax 02-251-2465

CANADA

Contact any Tourism Authority of Thailand office in the United States (see below).

THAILAND

(Head Office) 4–372 Bamrung Muang Rd., Bangkok 10100, tel 02-694-1222

UNITED KINGDOM

London 49 Albemarle St., London W1X 3FE, tel 020-7499-7679, fax 020-7629-5519

UNITED STATES

New York 1 World Trade Center, Suite 37293, New York, NY 10048, tel 212/432-0433, fax 212/912-0920
Chicago 303 East Wacker Dr., Suite 400, Chicago, IL 60602, tel 312/819-3990, fax 312/565-0359
Los Angeles 611 North Larchmont Blvd., Los Angeles, CA 90004, tel 213/461-9814, fax 213/461-9834

VISITORS WITH DISABILITIES

Thailand is only just beginning to install special facilities for visitors with disabilities. While public rest rooms with wheelchair access have yet to make an appearance, limited numbers of public phones for disabled users have been installed in Bangkok.

HOTELS & RESTAURANTS

Thailand has a superb range of hotels to suit all styles and budgets, from backpacker lodges with rooms for just a few dollars a night to five-star hotels offering world-class rooms and service with rates to match. Restaurants are also numerous, and you will never have to go far to find one that caters to your tastes and pocket.

HOTELS

In fact, it is the top-end hotels and resorts, with their innovative architecture, memorable atmosphere, and high levels of service, that push Thailand consistently to the top of reader polls on magazines such as *Condé Nast Traveler* and *Travel & Leisure*. The real strength of Thai accommodations is that, no matter your budget, the country is prepared to welcome you with clean, comfortable, and well-designed facilities.

Grading system

Thailand has no formal hotel grading system, but rather lists hotels in general price ranges. Most of the finer hotels and resorts in the upper price ranges are comparable to those in the United States. They offer similar facilities and amenities, such as a swimming pool, several restaurants, a business center, and comfortable rooms with all the facilities you might expect.

Hotels in the middle price ranges generally have clean rooms with fresh sheets, private bath, clean towels, maid and room service, and other amenities such as color TV, a stereo system, and mini-refrigerator. These hotels often have a small swimming pool and a single restaurant or café. For travelers who intend to spend most of their time at the beach or exploring, these moderately priced hotels will be adequate.

Small guesthouses are found in almost every city and town in the kingdom. Most backpackers arriving in Thailand tend to congregate in the Banglamphu area of Bangkok, where guesthouses, Western cafés, and tour operators have taken over

whole streets. In Chiang Mai, budget accommodations are easily found in the Tha Phae Gate area. In other towns frequented by tourists, guesthouses tend to be more spread out but can easily be located by asking at the local tourist office or by referring to a backpacker's guidebook.

Location

Hotels are generally in the middle of town near the central market and many of the sightseeing attractions, while those at beach resorts such as Phuket and Ko Samui will invariably be situated directly on the beach. Bangkok has a large number of hotels out in the suburbs that attract local business people on a budget; these are not generally listed in this guide. Hotels in central Bangkok are often accessible by Skytrain, while those farther out are best reached by taxi. Many of the better hotels in Chiang Mai lie a few miles outside the city center, but an efficient taxi service makes them an acceptable option for most visitors.

Thailand also has a small number of remote but extremely luxurious hotels and resorts that are destinations in their own right. These are described below, with contact information and a description of their unique charms and character. Most of these resorts provide private transportation from the nearest airport, bus terminal, or train station.

Reservations

Reservations are advised during the high season (Oct.–March) in Bangkok and highly advised year-round at the beach resorts on Phuket and Ko Samui. Hotels

PRICES

HOTELS

An indication of the cost of a double room without breakfast is given by $ signs.

$$$$$	Over $200
$$$$	$150–$200
$$$	$100–$150
$$	$50–$100
$	Under $50

RESTAURANTS

An indication of the cost of a three-course dinner without drinks is given by $ signs.

$$$$$	Over $40
$$$$	$30–$40
$$$	$20–$30
$$	$10–$20
$	Under $10

elsewhere experience relatively low occupancy rates year-round, and visitors who do not have reservations on their arrival can usually find a room without trouble, aside from major holidays and over the Christmas vacation.

Reservations are best made through your local travel agent or with a reputable tour company that can also help with transportation around the country. Make reservations for major international chains with properties in Thailand by calling their toll-free number in the United States. Making an overseas phone call direct to hotels in Thailand is not recommended owing to the possibility of language difficulties and a lack of written evidence to provide the guarantee of a room.

Mid-price and luxury hotels have faxes, which provide a more efficient reservation service. Be sure to provide the date and time of your arrival, your e-mail address for subsequent contact, along with your length of stay and any special requirements.

E-mail is rapidly taking over as an effective route for direct reservations. Most hotels now have websites with photos. They may also provide maps and often give "Internet discounts" for room reservations made via their website—generally 25–35 percent. Be prepared to provide details and your credit card number for advance billing.

Prices
All hotels can provide rate sheets that show their "rack rates," including all applicable taxes and service charges. These additional charges are almost always included in the prices on the tariff sheet and generally add 25–35 percent to the total bill, depending on the regional location of the property.

Hotel prices fluctuate significantly year by year, depending on the popularity of the destination and recent construction trends, which create pockets of oversupply. At times, it can be challenging to find a room, especially during the high season. Bangkok has suffered from a hotel glut for several years and as a result most hotels are running at moderate occupancy rates.

Discounts are rarely given at beach resorts, but travelers with some bargaining skills can generally obtain a discount of 25–40 percent off the rack rate elsewhere.

Most hotels have two classes of rooms: superior and deluxe. Deluxe rooms are only slightly more expensive than superior rooms and are often larger and have better furnishings. The hotels in Bangkok often have special "executive rooms" on "executive floors" designed for traveling businessmen, who can enjoy complimentary breakfast and evening cocktails.

Expect to pay the same price for a room with a single queen or two twin beds. Small additional charges may be levied to bring in a third bed, although this surcharge may be dropped for families traveling with children. Hotels only enforce a two- or three-day minimum stay policy during major holidays such as Christmas and Chinese New Year. There is no

requirement to dine in the hotel café or restaurant. Budget hotels sometimes include a buffet breakfast in the room charge.

Credit cards
Most moderate and luxury hotels and resorts accept Visa (V) and Mastercard (MC), and to a lesser degree, American Express (AE). Diners Club is only accepted at a handful of superior hotels. Many hotels post credit-card stickers near their front door to inform potential guests which cards are acceptable at the front desk.

Hotel groups
U.S. contact numbers:
Accor Group, tel 800/221-4542
Best Western, tel 800/528-1234
Hilton, tel 800/445-8667
Dusit, tel 800/44-UTELL
Four Seasons, tel 800/332-3442
Holiday Inn, tel 800/HOLIDAY
Hyatt, tel 800/327-0200
Leading Hotels of the World, tel 800/223-6800
Mandarin Oriental, tel 800/526-6566
Marriott, tel 800/228-9290
Meridien, tel 800/543-4300
Pan Pacific, tel 800/538-4040
Radisson, tel 800/777-7800
Regent, tel 800/545-4000
Shangri-La, tel 800/942-5050
Westin, tel 800/228-3000

RESTAURANTS

Thailand has one of the world's most exotic cuisines, and dining out is likely to be a highlight of your visit. Typical Thai dining is often alfresco.

Types of restaurants
Luxury hotels invariably have a coffee shop, a Thai restaurant, an elaborate Chinese restaurant (aimed at wealthy Chinese guests), and some form of Western restaurant, whether an American steakhouse or fine French restaurant.

Moderately priced hotels usually provide a simple café or perhaps an informal restaurant serving a combination of Western, Chinese, and Thai

dishes at reasonable prices. In all the major tourist destinations you will also find large numbers of small, independent cafés and restaurants almost exclusively owned and operated by foreigners who have settled in the country. Some of these Dutch, German, Swiss, French, English, and American outlets are surprisingly good, providing a welcome alternative to pricey hotel fare.

Authentic Thai cafés are found in larger towns, but most Thais prefer to eat outdoors at the market or at street stalls, to enjoy the cool of the evening and the ambience of being around friends and family. Although the setting may appear somewhat primitive, the Thais are scrupulous about cleanliness, and dishes are invariably well cooked. Note that, since few Thais speak English, you will need to do the point-and-order routine to select prepared dishes from the aluminum pots.

Dining hours
Cafés and restaurants in most hotels follow familiar opening hours, with a buffet breakfast served from perhaps 6:30 to 10 a.m., lunch from 11:30 to 3 p.m., and dinner from 5:30 to about 10:30 p.m. Trendier independent restaurants in major tourist destinations often stay open nightly until midnight or later depending on demand and time of year. Outdoors, it's possible to find soups, noodle dishes, and fried rice at almost any time, especially in larger urban areas and beach resorts.

Meals
Meals served in Western-style cafés and restaurants follow the traditional order, starting with appetizers and then soup or salad before the main course. Thais rarely follow such a formal pattern but prefer to order all dishes at the same time, which are then distributed around the table and shared together as a common meal. Nobody seems

HOTELS & RESTAURANTS

to mind if the soup arrives after the main course and desserts are delivered midway through the entrée. If you want courses to be served in a specific order, make this clear to your server.

Paying & tipping

Servers in Thailand rarely bring the check without a specific request from the customer. A 15 percent service charge and any applicable taxes will be automatically added to your bill in all better cafés and restaurants. Small Thai cafés will not add this service charge, though it is considered polite to leave spare change on the table as a modest gratuity.

Restaurants in popular tourist destinations occasionally attempt to overcharge Western customers, so check your bill carefully before paying and inquire about any unknown charges. If you are brought a bowl of peanuts or other appetizers without request, you may want to check about any possible charges before consuming the item.

Important notes

The hotels and restaurants listed below have been grouped by region, then alphabetically within price categories.

As the bus service in Thailand is notoriously inefficient and confusing, all hotels should be reached by taxi, although in Bangkok some are easily accessible by Skytrain.

All of the following hotels have at least one café or restaurant, all rooms are air-conditioned, and all hotels have outdoor rather than indoor swimming pools. All multi-leveled (three floors or more) hotels and resorts have elevators.

All hotels offer both smoking and nonsmoking rooms, and all restaurants will have a non-smoking area. Finally, all of the following hotels accept major credit cards.
L = lunch D = dinner

BANGKOK

🏨 IMPERIAL QUEEN'S PARK
🍴 $$$$$
199 SUKHUMVIT SOI 22
TEL 02-261-9000
FAX 02-261-9530
The largest hotel in Bangkok looms over the mostly deserted Benjasiri Park in mid-Sukhumvit. This massive structure naturally has everything imaginable within its walls, including almost a dozen cafés, restaurants, and pubs for diversion, a pair of swimming pools, and conference facilities for up to 3,000. Rooms are large and well designed, while service standards remain high despite the size of the property.
🛏 1,300 + 35 suites
🚈 Skytrain: Asoke 🅿️ 🔃
🔃 🚊 🍽 🏧 All major cards

SOMETHING SPECIAL

🏨 ORIENTAL
One of the finest hotels in the world according to virtually every traveler's survey ever taken, the Oriental is the ultimate accommodation and dining experience in Bangkok. Rooms are supremely elegant and traditionally decorated, with a staggering range of facilities, and the personal service is outstanding. Enjoy the Sala Rim Nam restaurant on the opposite bank of the river (see p. 364), the China House in an elegantly restored colonial residence, and the Normandie, one of the finest French restaurants in the country. The hotel dates from 1876 and has served as temporary home for a slew of Hollywood movie stars and famous writers.
$$$$$
48 ORIENTAL AVE.
TEL 02-236-0400
FAX 02-236-1939
🛏 396 🅿️ 🔃 🔃 🚊
🍽 🏧 All major cards

🏨 THE REGENT
🍴 $$$$$
155 RATCHADAMRI RD.
TEL 02-251-6127
FAX 02-253-9195
Situated a few blocks from the shopping centers near Siam Square, this legendary hotel has a magnificent two-story lobby fixed with an overwhelming amount of teakwood, polished marble, and silk furnishing, hovered over by one of the most attentive staffs in the city. Among the dining options are a Western grill with entertainment most evenings, the Italian Biscotti (see p. 364), a mezzanine coffee shop, a tea lounge for an afternoon break from the heat, a sushi bar, and the main Spice Market restaurant. Rooms are stylish, large, and decorated in a restrained style that invites comfort and relaxation.
🛏 370 🚈 Skytrain: Rajadamri 🅿️ 🔃 🔃 🚊
🍽 🏧 All major cards

🏨 SHANGRI-LA
🍴 $$$$$
89 SOI WAT SUAN PHU, OFF CHAROEN KRUNG RD.
TEL 02-236-7777
FAX 02-236-8579
The Shangri-La makes the most of its superb riverside setting with an awesome glass wall in the lobby that provides stunning views over the river to Thon Buri. Dining options range from Thai (Salathip—see p. 364) and Japanese to the superb Italian restaurant Angelini. Rooms are fairly large and well furnished, and most have been renovated in recent years.
🛏 850 + 57 suites
🚈 Skytrain: Taksin Bridge
🅿️ 🔃 🔃 🚊 🍽
🏧 All major cards

🏨 SHERATON GRANDE SUKHUMVIT
🍴 $$$$$
250 SUKHUMVIT SOI 12
TEL 02-653-0333
FAX 02-653-0400

HOTELS & RESTAURANTS

This fine hotel attracts guests for its wide range of facilities, luxurious appointments, and handy location near the Times Square shopping center, boutiques, and entertainment venues. No expense has been spared on the lobby, business center, and rooms, which each have an additional dressing room and large marble bathroom. Among the hotel's half-dozen eating places is Riva's, which serves lunch and dinner and converts into a hot nightclub in the later evening hours.
ℹ 445 🚆 Skytrain: Asoke 🅿 🔁 🆑 🏊 🏋
🆑 All major cards

▥ THE SUKHOTHAI
$$$$$
13/3 S. SATHORN RD.
TEL 02-287-0222
FAX 02-287-4980
Perhaps the most restrained and Zenlike sanctuary in Bangkok, this soaring hotel is well removed from the traffic and noise that plagues most other districts in town. The design emphasis is on simplicity, and artistic motifs recall the glorious days of Sukhothai. Art objects of museum quality abound, while glass walls and enclosed carp ponds provide a feeling of perfect serenity. Dining options range from a Thai restaurant surrounded by lily ponds to an Italian outlet set on a lovely terrace. Rooms are spacious and neatly combine Thai styles with modern accents, along with antiques and fine arts.
ℹ 224 + 38 suites
🚆 Skytrain: Saladaeng 🅿
🔁 🆑 🏊 🏋 🆑 All major cards

▥ WESTIN BANYAN TREE
$$$$$
21/100 S. SATHORN RD.
TEL 02-679-1200
FAX 02-679-1199
This luxurious hotel caters to sophisticated travelers and

businessmen who demand only the finest. The 60-story building lacks personality, but the hotel rooms—primarily those on the upper floors of the gray tower—provide unequaled city vistas. Amenities include a very complete business center, large spa, a rooftop Chinese restaurant that will take your breath away, and the Rom Sai, which serves Thai, Chinese, and other Asian specialties. Rooms have desks, computer ports, and fax machines.
ℹ 216 suites 🅿 🔁 🆑
🏊 🏋 🆑 All major cards

▥ AMARI WATERGATE
$$$$–$$$$$
847 PETCHABURI RD.
TEL 02-653-9000
FAX 02-653-9045
Rising unobtrusively near the Pratunam Market, this hotel is known for its friendly personality and central location. The exterior is unremarkable, but the gaily decorated and very lively lobby makes a good first impression. Dining options include an American-style bar and grill and a fancy Italian café. Informality is the rule here, whether visiting the attached shopping center or just relaxing in one of the elegant and spacious rooms, which are among the largest in the city.
ℹ 576 + 12 suites 🅿 🔁
🆑 🏊 🏋 🆑 All major cards

▥ AMARI AIRPORT
$$$$
333 CHERT VIDTHAKAS RD.
TEL 02-566-1020
FAX 02-566-1941
The best hotel near Don Muang International Airport, the Amari is 20 miles (32 km) from downtown Bangkok and is connected directly with the airport via an enclosed walkway. Public spaces are in good condition, and rooms are well priced for their luxurious appointments. There

is a 24-hour coffee shop and a popular American bar and grill. This is a convenient option for those who arrive late at night or who must depart early from the airport.
ℹ 427 🅿 🔁 🆑 🏊
🏋 🆑 All major cards

▥ CROWNE PLAZA BANGKOK
$$$$
981 SILOM RD.
TEL 02-238-4300
FAX 02-283-5289
One of the premium line Holiday Inns, this hotel is well situated between the nightlife enclave of Patpong and the more luxurious properties on the river. Ensconced in the gleaming 27-story tower is a spacious lobby decorated with marble and silk, a cozy lounge for afternoon tea, and several restaurants including the Tandoori, one of the most popular Indian spots in town (see p. 364). Rooms are clean and new; the best are in the Crowne Tower.
ℹ 595 + 7 suites 🅿 🔁
🆑 🏊 🏋 🆑 All major cards

▥ DUSIT THANI HOTEL
🍴 $$$$
RAMA IV AT SILOM RD.
TEL 02-236-0450
FAX 02-236-6400
This venerable hotel overlooks Lumphini Park. Its impressive lobby interiors are kept under constant renovation and spacious rooms outfitted with every possible amenity. The richness and profuse use of wood, marble, and silk, plus famous service from a very experienced staff, make this hotel one of the best in town. Restaurants include Hamilton's (see p. 364) and a rooftop international restaurant with superb views.
ℹ 520 + 15 suites
🚆 Skytrain: Saladaeng 🅿
🔁 🆑 🏊 🏋 🆑 All major cards

HOTELS & RESTAURANTS

🏨 GRAND HYATT ERAWAN BANGKOK
$$$$
494 RATCHADAMRI RD.
TEL 02-254-1234
FAX 02-254-6308

One of the largest and finest hotels in the shopping district near Siam Square, this 21-story building has a soaring lobby and naturally styled rooms in pleasing timber tones. The five restaurants serve Thai, Chinese, and Continental food. There is a bakery, a garden bar, and a ballroom that has space for 1,500 guests.

🛏 380 + 18 suites 🚆 Skytrain: Chidlom 🅿 ⬆ 🍴 ♨ 📺 💳 All major cards

🏨 HILTON 🍴 INTERNATIONAL BANGKOK
$$$$$
2 WITTHAYU RD.
TEL 02-253-0123
FAX 02-253-6509

Tucked away on a relatively quiet street, this older property lacks the modernity or classic charm of other upscale hotels, but compensates with the largest gardens and hotel grounds in the city. The lobby and public halls are rather utilitarian, but Ma Maison café is among the better French restaurants in Bangkok (see p. 363). Rooms are spacious, if in need of some refurbishment.

🛏 338 + 12 suites 🚆 Skytrain: Phayathai 🅿 ⬆ 🍴 ♨ 📺 💳 All major cards

🏨 AMARI BOULEVARD
$$$
SUKHUMVIT SOI 5
TEL 02-255-2930
FAX 02-255-2950

This is a reasonably priced, fairly luxurious hotel in the middle of the Sukhumvit nightlife district, with a cozy, almost family feel. The pool is smaller than at more expensive hotels and only a coffee shop is found in the original wing, but service levels are high. Standard rooms are stylish yet basic, while deluxe rooms have private garden patios.

🛏 315 + 10 suites 🚆 Skytrain: Nana 🅿 ⬆ 🍴 ♨ 📺 💳 All major cards

🏨 BEST WESTERN BAIYOKE SUITE
$$$
130 RATCHAPRAROP RD.
TEL 02-255-0330
FAX 02-254-5553

Located in Thailand's second tallest building, this all-suite hotel is easily reached by taxi. You can't miss the distinctive rainbow-hued exterior. There are tremendous views from all of the upper rooms, which ascend the 43 floors to a rooftop observation deck and restaurant with equally remarkable vistas. Good value for families.

🛏 255 suites 🅿 ⬆ 🍴 ♨ 📺 💳 All major cards

🏨 GRAND PACIFIC
$$$
259 SUKHUMVIT RD. NEAR SOI ASOKE
TEL 02-651-1000
FAX 02-255-2441

Conveniently located opposite the Times Square shopping complex, this distinctive hotel (it has a blue exterior) is popular with group tours. Visitors are welcome in the seventh-floor lobby and can enjoy a gym, spa, and other facilities. Meals can be taken in the coffee shop, steakhouse, Chinese restaurant, or Japanese café. The most popular spot is Horizons Sky Lounge & Karaoke, with magnificent panoramic views. Rooms are modern and reasonably spacious, yet unspectacularly furnished.

🛏 387 🚆 Skytrain: Asoke 🅿 ⬆ 🍴 ♨ 📺 💳 All major cards

PRICES

HOTELS
An indication of the cost of a double room without breakfast is given by $ signs.

$$$$$	Over $200
$$$$	$150–$200
$$$	$100–$150
$$	$50–$100
$	Under $50

RESTAURANTS
An indication of the cost of a three-course dinner without drinks is given by $ signs.

$$$$$	Over $40
$$$$	$30–$40
$$$	$20–$30
$$	$10–$20
$	Under $10

🏨 IMPERIAL IMPALA
$$$
SUKHUMVIT SOI 24
TEL 02-259-0053
FAX 02-258-8747

A somewhat older hotel in a convenient location at mid-Sukhumvit, the Imperial Impala shares most facilities with its adjacent sister property, the Imperial Tara (see below). Among the shared amenities are a fitness center, shopping center, coffee shop, Thai café, and upscale Japanese restaurant. Rooms are basic but acceptable for a short stay.

🛏 165 🚆 Skytrain: Asoke 🅿 ⬆ 🍴 ♨ 📺 💳 All major cards

🏨 IMPERIAL TARA
$$$
SUKHUMVIT SOI 26
TEL 02-259-2900
FAX 02-259-2856

This smaller hotel on a quiet alley off Sukhumvit is conveniently linked to, and shares facilities with, the Imperial Impala (see above), both of which are popular with local and Japanese travelers. Facilities are good, and the rooms are acceptable, though perhaps not up to the standards of other similarly

---

priced properties in Bangkok. The location, however, is convenient for many visitors.

ⓘ 165 + 6 suites 🚇 Skytrain: Asoke 🅿 ⇄ 🅢 🚹 🔽 🅰 All major cards

🏨 INDRA REGENT
$$$
120 RATCHAPRAROP RD.
TEL 02-208-0022
FAX 02-208-0388
This venerable hotel has maintained good standards over the years. The dirty exterior may seem off-putting, but through the doors is a hotel with professional staff, reasonable facilities, several restaurants (including a highly regarded Thai option), and decent rooms that are all well appointed with comfortable furnishings.

ⓘ 439 + 12 suites 🅿 ⇄ 🅢 🚹 🔽 🅰 All major cards

🏨 LANDMARK
$$$
138 SUKHUMVIT SOI 4
TEL 02-254-0404
FAX 02-653-2694
This is one of the original luxury hotels in this central neighborhood, and years of constant refurbishing and renovation have kept it at the head of the pack, while providing a less expensive alternative to more recent hotels. Dining options include Thai, Japanese, Chinese, and Continental, and the rooftop restaurant, the Hibiscus, has outstanding views. Corner rooms are extra spacious. Service standards are some of the finest in town.

ⓘ 370 + 45 suites 🚇 Skytrain: Nana 🅿 ⇄ 🅢 🚹 🔽 🅰 All major cards

🏨 J.W. MARRIOTT
$$$
4 SUKHUMVIT SOI 2
TEL 02-656-7700
FAX 02-656-7711
This modern hotel is in an

excellent central location near the shopping complexes of Siam Square and Sukhumvit Road. The exterior shows little imagination, though the lobby is spacious and inviting, and the modest-size rooms are decorated in a cheery and stylishly modern design. Restaurants include a California-Asian café (J.W.'s California—see p. 366) and a more upscale Chinese restaurant.

ⓘ 435 rooms 🚇 Skytrain: Nana 🅿 ⇄ 🅢 🚹 🔽 🅰 All major cards

🏨 MONARCH LEE GARDENS
$$$
188 SILOM RD.
TEL 02-238-1991
FAX 02-238-1999
A 38-story high-rise hotel, this competes well beside the more recognized properties in the same neighborhood, and is within walking distance of Patpong and the shops on Silom Road. Facilities include a health club and business center, and restaurants include Japanese and French, along with a famous Chinese option on the rooftop. Good value for mid-level travelers.

ⓘ 454 + 32 suites 🚇 Skytrain: Saladaeng 🅿 ⇄ 🅢 🚹 🔽 🅰 All major cards

🏨 NOVOTEL SIAM SQUARE
$$$
SIAM SQUARE SOI 6
TEL 02-255-6888
FAX 02-255-1824
This popular hotel lies right in the middle of Siam Square and within a few minutes' walk of the World Trade Center and MBK shopping emporiums (see p. 382). Despite its size, it has a surprisingly intimate feel. Rooms are reasonably large and well appointed. As with most Novotel properties, it is a popular choice for European visitors.

ⓘ 427 + 5 suites 🚇 Skytrain: Siam Square 🅿 ⇄ 🅢 🚹 🔽 🅰 All major cards

🏨 PAN PACIFIC
$$$
952 RAMA IV RD.
TEL 02-632-9000
FAX 02-632-9001
Situated within walking distance of the Patpong nightlife area, this hotel is also unfortunately surrounded by expressways, mass transit schemes, and nonstop traffic jams—although the attentive staff does its best to greet guests and help them forget the world below. Most of the rooms are near the top of the building, with views over Lumphini Park. Dining choices include a Chinese restaurant, Hai Tien Lo, dressed up in black marble, and Keyaki for Japanese fare.

ⓘ 235 + 14 suites 🚇 Skytrain: Saladaeng 🅿 ⇄ 🅢 🚹 🔽 🅰 All major cards

🏨 PENINSULA
🍽 $$$
333 CHAROEN NAKORN RD.
THON BURI
TEL 02-861-1111
FAX 02-861-1112
One of Bangkok's newest luxury hotels, the Peninsula invites guests to escape the traffic and pollution of the city and relax in a tranquil yet reasonably central location. The soaring 39-story structure has seven restaurants (including the Mei Jiang—see p. 363), lovely gardens set with palms and other tropical foliage, a riverside swimming pool, tennis courts, and some of the most spacious rooms in town.

ⓘ 370 + 60 suites 🅿 ⇄ 🅢 🚹 🔽 🅰 All major cards

🏨 ROYAL MERIDIEN
🍴 BANGKOK
$$$
973 PHLOEN CHIT RD.
TEL 02-656-0444
FAX 02-656-0555

Located opposite the Erawan shrine on the grounds of the Grand Hyatt (see p. 360), this soaring white wonder has restored the reputation of the French chain after years inside the adjacent, older structure. The original Le Meridien remains open but now caters primarily to budget tour groups, while most North American visitors opt for the towering structure at the corner of Ratchadamri Road. Beyond the entrance lies a grand lobby lined with marble. The premier restaurants are the Espresso (see p. 366) and the Chinese Summer Palace. Rooms are fairly large and decorated in light earth tones. There are great views from the upper rooms.

🛈 375 + 44 suites 🚉 Skytrain: Ploenchit 🛗 🔌 🏊 🍸 🅰 All major cards

🏨 ROYAL ORCHID
🍴 SHERATON HOTEL & TOWERS
$$$
2 CAPTAIN BUSH LN.
TEL 02-266-0123
FAX 02-236-8320

Another famous hotel magnificently situated on the riverbank. Although this hotel is older than many other properties in Bangkok, its recently refurbished rooms now provide larger double beds and all modern facilities. Business suites are also available. The decor is predominantly Western. Restaurants include Giorgio's (see p. 364), a Thai restaurant, and a popular 24-hour coffee shop. Location, convenience, and expansive riverside gardens are the main draws.

🛈 756 + 75 suites 🅿️ 🛗 🔌 🏊 🍸 🅰 All major cards

🏨 BEL-AIRE PRINCESS
$$
SUKHUMVIT SOI 5
TEL 02-253-4300
FAX 02-255-8850

This consistently popular mid-level hotel, tucked away in a very quiet alley just a few minutes' walk from busy Sukhumvit Road, is a good choice for peace and quiet. Facilities include a California-style café, a popular Indian restaurant, a gym, and a business center. Rooms are decent, and the staff friendly and efficient.

🛈 150 🚉 Skytrain: Nana 🅿️ 🛗 🔌 🏊 🍸 🅰 All major cards

🏨 GRAND CHINA PRINCESS
$$
215 YAOWARAT RD.
TEL 02-224-9977
FAX 02-224-7999

The only decent hotel in Chinatown, this is the place for the adventurous traveler who wishes to explore this remarkable neighborhood. Simplicity is the key, but all public areas and rooms are kept clean and functional, as are the Chinese restaurant—the Siang Ping Loh—and the 24-hour coffee shop. Best bet for relaxation is the rooftop revolving bar, which guarantees great views over Chinatown and the river.

🛈 155 + 19 suites 🅿️ 🛗 🔌 🏊 🍸 🅰 All major cards

🏨 MARRIOTT ROYAL GARDEN RIVERSIDE
$$
257/1–3 CHAROEN NAKORN RD., THON BURI
TEL 02-476-0021
FAX 02-476-1120

Situated on the opposite side of the river and about 3 miles (2 km) south of the Oriental, this is a resort-within-the-city, the perfect place to visit Bangkok but enjoy the charms and character of a more rural Thailand. The hotel has extensive grounds and a series of buildings. Dining options include an elaborate Chinese restaurant and a branch of Trader Vic's. You can also enjoy Japanese-American steaks at Benihana's, Chinese delicacies at the Rice Mill, and seafood and views at the Market Restaurant. Rooms are spacious and airy, and many have tremendous views of the constant activity on the river—one of the wonders of Bangkok.

🛈 416 + 15 suites 🅿️ 🛗 🔌 🏊 🍸 🅰 All major cards

🏨 NARAI
$$
222 SILOM RD.
TEL 02-237-0100
FAX 02-236-7161

In an excellent location almost midway between Patpong and the river, this 15-story hotel provides a very reasonable alternative to the much more luxurious and expensive hotels in the neighborhood. There are several restaurants on the main floor, and the revolving option, La Rotonde Grill, on the 15th floor, is great fun. The hotel is basic but has all the standard facilities. Rooms are decorated in a pleasing, clean, modern style.

🛈 409 + 20 suites 🚉 Skytrain: Surasak 🛗 🔌 🏊 🍸 🅰 All major cards

🏨 ROYAL PRINCESS
$$
269 LAN LUANG RD.
TEL 02-281-3088
FAX 02-280-1314

This decent hotel is in an unusual location near the Royal Palace, Sanam Luang, and Banglamphu backpacker's district. Facilities include cafés and restaurants, a fitness room, and surprisingly large rooms that are kept clean and tidy.

🛈 166 + 5 suites 🅿️ 🛗 🔌 🏊 🍸 🅰 All major cards

SIAM INTER-CONTINENTAL BANGKOK
$$
967 RAMA I RD.
TEL 02-53-0355
FAX 02-254-5474

An older and architecturally distinctive hotel in the shopping district of Bangkok near the World Trade Center, the Siam Inter-Continental has an oddly swooping roof that is meant to resemble an ancient Siamese warrior's hat. Most of the rooms are behind this landmark, on the spacious grounds of the former Saprathum Palace. Rooms in the Garden wings are superior to those in the Tower wing for their views and easy access to the swimming pool.

🛏 389 + 16 suites
🚆 Skytrain: Phayathai 🅿
🔄 🔆 🏊 🏋 🅢 All major cards

SILOM CITY INN
$
SILOM SOI 22 AT 72 SOI PRACHUM
TEL 02-234-6923
FAX 02-237-1383

This simple hotel offers excellent value within a few blocks of the shops, boutiques, and nightclubs of the Silom-Surawong district. Often overlooked by Western visitors, this small gem has most of the necessary facilities and acceptable deluxe rooms with standard amenities. The interior is stylish, and the staff is exceptionally willing to help.

🛏 70 + 12 suites 🅿 🔄
🔆 🏊 🏋 🅢 All major cards

BEST BANGKOK RESTAURANTS

Bangkok has hundreds of restaurants serving virtually every form of food on the planet, and many of these restaurants change ownership, names, and cuisines with the seasons. The most accurate listing of current offerings can

be found in *Metro*, a monthly English-language magazine that divides Bangkok restaurants into categories based on nationality. *Metro* also sponsors a yearly contest that names the best restaurants in town. Based on their latest recommendations, here are some recent winners:

Best Thai Restaurant in a Hotel
Celadon (The Sukhothai)
Ruen Thai (Grand Hyatt Erawan)
Spice Market (The Regent)
Salathip (Shangri-La)

Best Chinese Restaurant in a Hotel
Mei Jiang (Peninsula)
Bai Yun (Westin Banyan Tree)
The Chinese Restaurant (Grand Hyatt Erawan)
Mayflower (Dusit Thani)

Best Brunch Buffet
Espresso (Royal Meridien)
The Captain's Table (Grand Pacific)
Colonnade (The Sukhothai)
The Dining Room (Grand Hyatt Erawan)
Trader Vic's (Marriott Royal Garden Riverside)

Best Restaurant with Thai Dance Performance
Baan Thai
Sala Rim Nam (Oriental)

CAFÉ SIAM
$$$$
4 SOI SRIAKSON
TEL 02-671-0031

Difficult to find, but worth the effort to dine in this classy art deco restaurant (phone them first so they can fax a map). The menu offers mostly French cuisine, although it also has a good selection of popular Thai curries, plus a reasonable list of wines and cocktails.

🍽 120 🚆 Skytrain: Saladaeng 🔆 🅿
🕐 Closed 2 p.m.–6 p.m. 🔆
🅢 All major cards

LOY NAVA DINNER CRUISES
$$$
37 CHAROEN NAKORN RD. KLONGSAN
TEL 02-437-4932

Five-star dining on the *Tahsaneeya Nava*, the only antique teakwood rice barge in Bangkok. This is a good chance to get away from the noise and traffic while seeing the historical landmarks—including the Grand Palace and Wat Arun—as you cruise along the Chao Phraya river. The menu offers a choice of Thai, vegetarian, and seafood dishes in set-menu style, and while the range is not fantastic the meals are authentic and the atmosphere pleasant.

🍽 55 🅿 🅢 All major cards

MA MAISON
$$$
HILTON INTERNATIONAL
2 WITTHAYU RD.
TEL 02-253-0123

A favorite of high society and local power brokers, Ma Maison, in the Hilton International (see p. 360), is known for its elegant yet unpretentious interior design, its extensive wine list, and its innovative French dishes.

🍽 65 🚆 Skytrain: Phayathai
🅿 🔆 🅢 All major cards

MEI JIANG
$$$
PENINSULA HOTEL,
333 CHAROEN NAKORN RD.
THON BURI
TEL 02-861-2888

Inside the Peninsula, one of Bangkok's finest hotels (see p. 361), is this esteemed Chinese restaurant, which has smartly avoided all the tired clichés in its decor and style of cuisine. The restaurant is like an elegant and under-stated club, and the food emphasizes lightness and health. Views across the Chao Phraya to Bangkok are outstanding, while service is up to lofty Peninsula standards.

HOTELS & RESTAURANTS

🏨 60 🚊 Ferry from the Oriental 🅿 💲 🚫 All major cards

🍴 SALA RIM NAM

This elegantly designed restaurant, across the river from (and owned by) the **Oriental** (see p. 358), is the best place to enjoy an evening of exceptionally fine Thai cuisine and impressive classical dance entertainment. Lunch is also served, though most visitors opt for the dinner, which is an outstanding fixed menu of Royal Thai cuisine. Reservations are recommended.

$$$
ORIENTAL HOTEL,
48 ORIENTAL AVE.
TEL 02-437-3080
🏨 75 🚊 Ferry from the Oriental 🅿 🕐 Closed national holidays 💲 🚫 All major cards

🍴 SALATHIP

$$$
SHANGRI-LA HOTEL
89 SOI WAT SUAN PHU
TEL 02-236-7777

While the dining can be enjoyed indoors in air-conditioned comfort at this romantically designed venue in the Shangri-La (see p. 358), the most memorable choice is to reserve a table on the outside veranda. Arrive early enough to take in the spectacular sunset over the Chao Phraya river.

🏨 95 🚊 Skytrain: Taksin Bridge 🅿 💲 🚫 All major cards

🍴 BUSSARACUM

$$$
425 SOI PHIPAT 2, SILOM RD.
TEL 02-266-6312

One of the original upscale Royal Thai restaurants, the Bussaracum is known for its quiet setting and its selection of fine and expensive dining venues. Rather than catering to the conservative tastes of foreigners, Bussaracum aims for authenticity in its dishes, which range from seafood and curries to spicy vegetarian options. It is essential to reserve a table in advance.

🏨 45 🅿 💲 🕐 Closed L Mon. 💲 🚫 All major cards

🍴 BISCOTTI

$$–$$$
REGENT HOTEL
155 RATCHADAMRI RD.
TEL 02-255-5443

Bangkok has been mad about Italian cuisine for decades, and the current favorite is this unpretentious venue in the upscale Regent (see p. 358). Meals are acclaimed as some of the finest Continental fare in town, and the decor is lively and fun. The place is filled with music and conversation, and it has an open kitchen where you can watch the chefs preparing the pasta and veal specialties.

🏨 70 🚊 Skytrain: Rajadamri 🅿 💲 🚫 All major cards

🍴 GIORGIO'S

$$–$$$
ROYAL ORCHID SHERATON
HOTEL, 2 CAPTAIN BUSH LN.
TEL 02-266-0123

The signature restaurant at the riverside Royal Orchid Sheraton (see p. 362) attracts diners for its lunchtime buffet and more sophisticated à la carte choices in the evening. Italian dishes and other Continental fare are prepared with great style. Reservations are recommended to ensure a table on the terrace with views over the river.

🏨 80 🅿 💲 🚫 All major cards

🍴 HAMILTON'S

$$–$$$
DUSIT THANI HOTEL
RAMA IV RD.
TEL 02-236-0450

This small but elegant room, in the upscale Dusit Thani (see p. 359), is named after the first U.S. ambassador to

Thailand, and is furnished in mid-19th century style. Western fare is the theme here, with excellent steaks, lobster, and regional dishes such as Cajun and Tex-Mex.

🏨 40 🚊 Skytrain: Saladaeng 🅿 🕐 Closed Sun. 💲 🚫 All major cards

🍴 TANDOORI

$$–$$$
CROWNE PLAZA HOTEL
981 SILOM RD.
TEL 02-238-4300

Bangkok's finest Indian cuisine can be enjoyed in this gracious restaurant, in the Crowne Plaza hotel (see p. 359) in the middle of the city's traditional Hindu district. The emphasis is on the flavors of northern India, including the tandoori style of preparation. The kitchen is led by a famous chef from New Delhi, who maintains excellence in both the vegetarian and nonvegetarian selections.

🏨 75 🅿 💲 🚫 All major cards

🍴 BAAN THAI

$$
7 SUKHUMVIT SOI 32
TEL 02-233-6912

A longtime favorite with

visitors, who can enjoy dinner followed by a performance of Thai classical dance nightly around 9 p.m. The food has been tamed down for sensitive palates, and the theater performance is inferior to that at the Sala Rim Nam (see p. 364). That said, the prices are reasonable, and this an acceptable introduction to traditional Thai food and dance.

🛏 140 🚈 Skytrain: Thong Lo 🅿 🆂 🆂 All major cards

SOMETHING SPECIAL

🍴 CABBAGES & CONDOMS

This world-famous restaurant, tucked away in an alley off busy Sukhumvit, is the brainchild of the former family planning director for Thailand, Khun Meechai, to raise funds for AIDS and birth control programs. Despite the odd name and unusual merchandise sold at the front desk (condom keychains and the like), the classic Thai dishes are excellent and the decor (almost exclusively condom-related) adds to the charm.

$$
10 SUKHUMVIT SOI 12
TEL 02-229-4633
🛏 50 🚈 Skytrain: Asoke 🅿 🆂 🆂 All major cards

🍴 CAFÉ BONGO
$$
44 CONVENT RD.
TEL 02-632-0920
This cozy café, bakery, wine bar, and restaurant off Silom Road is known for its innovative preparation of Western dishes along with a limited selection of local fare. Specialties include paella, tapas, and osso bocco. Keep walking down the street for similar operations popular with local trendsetters and office workers from the nearby financial district.
🛏 30 🕐 Closed Sun. 🆂 🆂 All major cards

🍴 CIRCLE
$$
20–27 RUAM RUDEE VILLAGE, SOI RUAM RUDEE
TEL 02-650-8047
Several trendy cafés and restaurants are situated on this street near the shopping centers at Siam Square. The Circle has California-fusion cuisine with a range of highly innovative dishes. Classic Thai dishes add to the eclectic mix.
🛏 55 🚈 Skytrain: Ploenchit 🅿 🕐 Closed L daily 🆂 🆂 All major cards

🍴 HARMONIQUE
$$
22 CHAROEN KRUNG RD. SOI 34
TEL 02-237-8175
Somewhat removed from the tourist scene, this popular Thai café is set in a lovely and very quiet courtyard among old terrace houses. Indulge yourself with the tasty Thai delicacies either on the outside patio or indoors, where you can enjoy the antiques that fill the cozy rooms.
🛏 45 🅿 🆂 🆂 All major cards

🍴 LOT 24
$$
93 SUKHUMVIT SOI 24
TEL 02-259-5170
This popular, trendy restaurant in the heart of the Sukhumvit district offers classic Thai dishes at reasonable prices. The environment is high-tech, in an attractive black-and-white theme. The *tom yam* soups, *gaeng* curries, and other staples attract large parties.
🛏 40 🚈 Skytrain: Phrom Pong 🆂 🆂 All major cards

🍴 THE MANGO TREE
$$
37 SOI TANTAWAN, SURAWONGSE RD.
TEL 02-236-2820
This restaurant, located in the heart of the Silom business district and beautifully laid out with plenty of greenery and foliage, is actually a classical

Thai house that is about a hundred years old. The owner, Khun Pitaya, has deliberately made few changes to the original house, which gives you a range of settings from which to choose—you can dine indoors, alfresco, or among the foliage of the garden. There is an excellent range of curries and food from all around Thailand, with such specialties as garlic and pepper duck and *tom yum ruam mit*, a traditional spicy soup. Feel free to let the cook know if you want any dish specially prepared.
🛏 200 🚈 Skytrain: Saladaeng 🆂 🅿 🆂 🆂 All major cards

🍴 RIVER CITY BBQ
$$
RIVER CITY COMPLEX YOTA RD.
TEL 02-237-0077
While there are also outlets of this famous self-service barbecue on Royal City Avenue and in the Tower wing of the Ambassador hotel on Sukhumvit Road, the best choice is the original location on the top floor of the River City Complex. Enjoy superb views over the river while cooking your own meal of meats, chicken, fish, and vegetables in a bubbling pot of spicy broth.
🛏 85 🕐 Closed L daily 🆂 🆂 All major cards

🍴 BOURBON STREET
$
29/4 WASHINGTON SQ. SUKHUMVIT SOI 22
TEL 02-259-0328
Local American expatriates often fill this restaurant and bar—in a low-key entertainment district known as Washington Square—lured by the American-style breakfasts and Louisiana Cajun dishes that dominate the dinner menu. Tex-Mex and other North American specialties are served on a rotating basis throughout the week.

HOTELS & RESTAURANTS

🛏 35 🚉 Skytrain: Phrom Pong 🅿 ⊘ All major cards

🍴 CHOKCHAI STEAKHOUSE
$
SUKHUMVIT SOI 23
TEL 02-259-9596
A member of one of Bangkok's famous chain of steakhouses, Chokchai's central location makes it a favorite of Western visitors. Choose from a variety of steaks, including T-bones and spicy pepper steaks.
🛏 50 🚉 Skytrain: Asoke
🅿 ⊘ All major cards

🍴 DUX BAR & GRILL
$
72/2 LANG SUAN SOI 5
TEL 02-252-5646
Located in an old renovated house in the middle of "restaurant row," this charming place is known for its various preparations of duck, with an interior decor to match the menu—dominated by duck motifs and wooden duck reproductions.
🛏 45 🅿 🕐 Closed L Sat. & L/D Sun. ⊘ ⊘ All major cards

SOMETHING SPECIAL

🍴 ESPRESSO
A classy buffet with outstanding food, Espresso's is in the Royal Meridien, one of the most elegant hotels in the neighborhood (see p. 362). A French chef oversees the cooking, with innovative Continental fare rarely found elsewhere in Bangkok. Reservations are recommended for the Sunday buffet.
$
ROYAL MERIDIEN BANGKOK
973 PHLOEN CHIT RD.
TEL 02-656-6430
🛏 65 🚉 Skytrain: Ploenchit
🅿 ⊘ ⊘ All major cards

🍴 HAI HUA TIAN
$
113 SONG SAWAT RD.
TEL 02-222-3029
Chinatown has dozens of excellent cafés for Cantonese specialties, including this small outlet chiefly known for its preparation of bird's-nest and shark's-fin soups. Goat and steamed prawns are also specialties. Crab claws and other seafood items are prepared in both sweet and pungent black bean sauces.
🛏 30 ⊘ No cards

🍴 HENDRIX 26
$
ATHAKAVEE SOI 1, SUKHUMVIT SOI 26
TEL 02-661-2544
This relatively new addition to the trendy café scene is owned by a former hotelier. Dishes are mostly Continental with an emphasis on Mediterranean fare, and there are also seafood items such as soft-shelled crab and sautéed prawns.
🛏 45 🚉 Skytrain: Phrom Pong 🅿 🕐 Closed Sun.
⊘ ⊘ All major cards

🍴 J.W.'S CALIFORNIA
$
J.W. MARRIOTT HOTEL
4 SUKUMVIT SOI 2
TEL 02-656-7700
While the J.W. Marriott hotel may not be the most innovative structure in the city (see p. 361), the food served in its principal café has become a hit with locals, who appreciate the freshness of the ingredients and live music in the evenings—which can range from salsa to flamenco.
🛏 70 🚉 Skytrain: Nana
🅿 ⊘ ⊘ All major cards

🍴 LANG SUAN BALCONY
$
2ND FLOOR, SOI LANG SUAN
TEL 02-251-9822
Thai and international cuisine with one of Bangkok's best wine selections. Depending on the kind of atmosphere you would prefer, you can choose between a table in the cozy dining room or on the balcony overlooking busy Soi

Lang Suan. *Gaeng keeyo wahn maprao orn* (green curry with coconut) is a favorite here, though there are many other authentic dishes from which to choose, as well as a good range of Western fare.
🛏 40 🚉 Skytrain: Chidlom
🅿 ⊘ ⊘ All major cards

🍴 NEW DHABA
$
1133 CHAROEN KRUNG RD.
TEL 02-254-2474
Bangkok's Indian community is largely located on the streets and alleys near the General Post Office, and many of the better Hindu cafés can also be found here. New Dhaba, just opposite the G.P.O., is typical, with its cozy comforts, southern Indian vegetarian dishes, and northern Indian specialties prepared by a trio of talented chefs. There is a full bar and wine list.
🛏 30 ⊘ No cards

🍴 PATPONG SEAFOOD
$
OPPOSITE PATPONG NIGHT BAZAAR, SILOM RD.
TEL 02-637-0508
A huge range of seafood dishes is on offer in this bustling open-air night-time spot, including lobster and the ever popular *ning manao*—steamed lemon fish with a mountain of herbs and spices piled on top. Order the food as you want it, and savor the freshness of the seafood, bought daily from the market.
🛏 150 🅿 ⊘ All major cards

🍴 PLANET HOLLYWOOD
$
GAYSORN PLAZA, 999 PHLOEN CHIT RD.
TEL 02-656-1358
Both Thais and resident expatriots patronize the famous chain outlet, where movie themes and huge portions of American fare make an impression on the very hungry. Live bands play most evenings from around 9:30 p.m.

🏢 80 🚉 Skytrain: Chidlom
🅿 ❄ 💳 All major cards

🍴 RATSSTUBE
$
GOETHE INSTITUT, 101 SOI
NGAM DUPHLI
TEL 02-286-4258
Some of the best German
cooking in town is found at
the café at the Goethe
Institut, where homemade
sausage, sauerkraut, and fried
potatoes characterize the
menu. The atmosphere is
often enhanced with German
language films, which attract a
surprising number of Thais
along with the local German-
speaking community.
🏢 55 🅿 ❄ 💳 All major
cards

🍴 SUN FAR MYANMAR FOOD CENTRE
$
107/1 PAN RD. OFF SILOM RD.
TEL 02-266-8787
This inexpensive Burmese
café, on the same street as
the Myanmar Embassy, serves
regional dishes such as the
famous tea-leaf salad.
🏢 25 💳 No cards

🍴 TAKIANG
$
62 CHOCKPADIPONG RD.
TEL 02-281-2837 OR 02-282-
4524
The cozy character of this
restaurant, popular with
locals, creates an intimacy
that would not be particularly
appropriate for large groups.
Lots of timber and a well
thought out design are the
main drawcards here, though
the food is also excellent
and authentic.
🏢 50 🅿 ❄ 💳 All major
cards

🍴 TONY ROMA'S
$
SUKHUMVIT SOI 3
TEL 02-254-2912
This longtime favorite almost
single-handedly introduced
American cowboy decor to
the city and claims its culinary

fame from its barbecued baby
back ribs, along with all the
other American staples. Salads
are enormous.
🏢 65 🚉 Skytrain: Nana ❄
💳 All major cards

🍴 VEGAS GRILL
$
TRINITY COMPLEX, SILOM SOI 3
TEL 02-231-5360
Popular with office workers
and the occasional tourist, this
restaurant offers seafood and
steak dishes at reasonable
prices. Selections include
imported Alaskan king crab
and both domestic and
imported steaks, all cooked
to perfection.
🏢 45 🚉 Skytrain: Saladaeng
❄ 💳 All major cards

AROUND BANGKOK

AYUTTHAYA

🏨 AYUTTHAYA GRAND
$
75/5 ROTCHANA RD.
TEL 035-335483
FAX 035-335492
This mid-level hotel, east of
town, attracts businessmen
and the occasional tourists
with decent if standard
rooms, a coffee shop for
breakfast, a utilitarian
restaurant with Thai and
Western dishes, and a
nightclub for evening
diversion.
🛏 145 🅿 ❄ 🌊 💳 All
major cards

🏨 KRUNGSRI RIVER
$
27/2 ROTCHANA RD.
TEL 035-242996
FAX 035-243777
Most visitors do Ayutthaya as
a day trip from Bangkok,
which is a pity since the ruins
are at their best near sunset
and sunrise. A half-dozen
guesthouses are located near
the market, and a few
moderately priced hotels are
near the river. None is world
class, but the Krungsri River

is decent and has clean, air-
conditioned rooms with
private baths. Request a
room with a river view and
be sure to explore the
market in the evening.
🛏 206 + 18 suites 🅿 ❄
🌊 💳 All major cards

KANCHANABURI

🏨 FELIX RIVER KWAI RESORT
$
9/1 MUY 3 THAMAKHAM
TEL 034-515061
FAX 034-515095
This hotel has a good
location just 100 yards from
the famous bridge and within
walking distance of all the
cafés and souvenir shops. The
resort has spacious and
relaxing grounds that have
been developed into some of
the most outstanding gardens
in this part of the country.
The lobby is comfortable, and
there are several decent
restaurants, a cocktail lounge,
a small but adequate fitness
center, and even a business
center. Rooms are well
stocked with amenities and
come brightly decorated in
pastel tones.
🛏 255 🅿 ❄ 🌊 🏋
💳

🏨 RIVER KHWAE HOTEL
$$
284/3–6 CHOOTO RD.
MUANG DISTRICT
TEL 034-511269
The River Khwae Hotel is set
back from the river, which is
not such a bad thing.
Although you have to
sacrifice the picturesque river
view, you won't have to suffer
the ear bashing of the late-
night floating discos. Deluxe
single bedrooms or double-
bed suites are available, as are
banquet and seminar rooms
and a swimming pool. Service
here is also very friendly and
of a high standard.
🛏 169 🅿 ❄ 🌊 💳 All
major cards

LOP BURI

🏨 LOPBURI INN
$
28/9 NARAI MAHARAT RD.
TEL 036-412300
FAX 036-412457
Lop Buri receives few overnight visitors, and the town's only hotel with air-conditioned rooms is the Lopburi Inn. Little more than a motel, it has clean rooms and hot showers, and is a step above the budget hotels around the old town.
🛏 136 🅿 📺 🗂All major cards

EAST COAST

PATTAYA

🏨 DUSIT RESORT
$$$$
240/2 BEACH RD.
TEL 038-425611
FAX 038-428239
Clinging to a small cliff at the northern end of the main beach is this outlet of Thailand's largest hotel chain. The grounds are lovely, and the four-story lobby atrium is the most impressive bit of architecture in Pattaya. Among the facilities, restaurants include a Chinese room and three cocktail lounges. water sports from windsurfing to sailing are available. Rooms are stylish and done up in chic Thai-Western motifs.
🛏 464 + 26 suites 🅿 📶 📺 📶 🍽 🗂 All major cards

🏨 ROYAL GARDEN RESORT PATTAYA
$$$
218 BEACH RD.
TEL 038-412120
FAX 038-429926
Visitors who seek a quality mid-level hotel within walking distance of the cabarets and nightclubs in south Pattaya stay here, a five-minute stroll from the so-called Walking Street. The lobby is surprisingly modest for such a large property and the restaurants are hardly spectacular, but many of the rooms directly facing the beach are absolutely wonderful. Adjacent to the resort is Pattaya's best shopping complex, a great place to dine and shop in air-conditioned comfort.
🛏 292 🅿 📶 📶 📺 🗂 All major cards

SOMETHING SPECIAL

🏨 ROYAL CLIFF BEACH RESORT
This series of cliffside towers midway between Pattaya and Jomtien is the finest hotel on the eastern seaboard and one of the best in the country. After a few years of shortcomings, it appears that this hotel-resort complex has returned to form with a renewed spirit among the staff and managers and major additions to the property such as the convention center. The complex has almost a dozen restaurants, cafés, cocktail lounges, and music venues. Rooms range from utilitarian to splendid—choose according to your budget and preference from the 24-story Royal Cliff Grand to the all-suite Royal Wing.
$$$$
ROYAL CLIFF BAY
TEL 038-250421
FAX 02-250500
🛏 921 + 110 suites 🅿 📶 📶 📶 📺 🗂All major cards

🍽 AMARI ORCHID RESORT
$$
BEACH RD.
TEL 038-428161
FAX 038-428165
The Amari Orchid occupies a large acreage a few hundred yards south of the Dusit. Perhaps the most striking aspects here are the spacious and elegantly manicured gardens that separate the hotel from the beach. The superb dining options range from the Italian La Gritta restaurant to the colorful colonial-style **Henry J. Bean's** (see p. 369), by the beach. Rooms vary in quality according to the building—the Loggia Suites are best.
🛏 236 🅿 📶 📶 📶 📺 🗂 All major cards

🏨 MONTIEN PATTAYA
$$
PATTAYA 2 RD.
TEL 038-428155
FAX 038-423155
Tucked away between Beach Road and Pattaya 2 Road, the Montien is an elegant and surprisingly sophisticated 15-story hotel. It is surrounded by delightful tropical gardens, which complement the refined furnishings of the public rooms. Restaurants are top-notch, as are the hotel facilities and rooms, which are kept immaculately.
🛏 300 + 12 suites 🅿 📶 📶 📶 📺 🗂 All major cards

🏨 BUDGET SAWATDEE SEA VIEW
$
SOI 10 PATTAYA RD.
TEL 038-428229

The rooms here are tidy and comfortable, with air-conditioning, TVs, and hot water. The rates are good, and the hotel is close to the beach.
🛏 30

🏨 SEAVIEW RESORT HOTEL
$
SOI 18 PATTAYA–NAKLUA RD.
TEL 038-429317
FAX 034 423668
Comfortable air-conditioned rooms with easy beach access. The Seaview is well located for trips into either Pattaya or Jomtien.
🛏 155 ⊟ 🌊 🔲 All major cards

🍽 BRUNO'S RESTAURANT & WINE BAR
$$
463/77 SRI NAKORN CENTRE
NORTH PATTAYA
TEL 038-361073
One of the more famous restaurants in Pattaya, Bruno's serves French and Swiss dishes under the direction of the former manager of the Royal Cliff Beach Resort. Thai and international food also feature on the menu. The upstairs wine "cellar" is considered the most extensive on the east coast.
🍴 45 🅿 🔲 🔲 All major cards

🍽 HENRY J. BEAN'S BAR & GRILL
$$
AMARI ORCHID RESORT
BEACH RD.
TEL 038-428161
Western and Thai dishes, a wide range of brews, and nightly entertainment in this romantically restored old house (part of the **Amari Orchid** hotel—see p. 368) make it one of Pattaya's most special evening venues.
🍴 65 🅿 🔲 🔲 All major cards

see p. 368

SOMETHING SPECIAL

🍽 HOPF BREW HOUSE
This immense operation has been the most successful new restaurant in recent years, consistently drawing the crowds for its excellent German and Italian food, variety of beers and spirits, and entertainment. The latter ranges from ragtime bands to jazz combos, and the family atmosphere makes this one of the best places in town for a good night out.
$$
219 BEACH RD.
SOUTH PATTAYA
TEL 038-710650
🍴 90 🅿 🔲 🔲 All major cards

🍽 LOBSTER POT
$$
228 BEACH RD.
SOUTH PATTAYA
TEL 038-426083
Overlooking the water at the extreme south end of town, on a section of road known as the Walking Street, this restaurant is typical of many in the area. Diners choose their particular fish or seafood from open displays and then have their selection cooked in any variety of ways, from steamed to fried with scallions and black bean sauce. The outdoor terrace is perfect for sunsets, but arrive early for the best seats.
🍴 90 🔲 🔲 All major cards

🍽 MAI KAI SUPPER CLUB
$$
BEACH RD., NORTH PATTAYA
TEL 038-428645
This Polynesian restaurant is near the Hotel Tropicana in the north end of town. Polynesian, Thai, Chinese, and Western dishes are served, and live entertainment is provided most evenings during the high season.
🍴 70 ⏰ Closed L daily 🔲 All major cards

🍽 PINNACLE REVOLVING RESTAURANT
$$
PATTAYA WATER PARK,
345 JOMTIEN BEACH RD.
TEL 038-251201
A few miles south of Pattaya, at Jomtien Beach, is an enormous tower topped with a revolving restaurant. While the food (Thai and Western dishes) is hardly spectacular, the views over the Gulf of Thailand are incredible.
🍴 95 🅿 🔲 🔲 All major cards

🍽 SUGAR HUT
$$
PATTAYA–JOMTIEN RD.
TEL 038-251686
Perhaps the most elegant Thai restaurant in Pattaya, this collection of teakwood pavilions is situated on the undulating road that leads south from Pattaya to Jomtien Beach. Specialties here include *sai krok* (Thai sausage) and *kar mu* (leg of pork). This place has superb atmosphere and is well worth the short taxi ride from central Pattaya.
🍴 85 🅿 🔲 🔲 All major cards

SOMETHING SPECIAL

🍽 NEW ORLEANS CAFÉ
Some consider this cozy café the best addition to the food scene in several years, especially for the high quality of its Western dishes, including the famous baby back ribs. There are also Thai dishes on offer, and the service is top notch.
$$
BEACH RD. SOI
PATTAYALAND 2
TEL 038-428662
🍴 40 🔲 🔲 All major cards

🍽 CAPTAIN'S CORNER STEAK HOUSE
$
PATTAYA–JOMTIEN RD.
TEL 038-364318
A few miles south of central

Pattaya on the road to Jomtien, this spacious garden restaurant is known for its all-you-can-eat Texas-style barbecues, which draw the crowds every night.
🍴 75 🅿 🕐 Closed L 💳 All major cards

🍴 MOON RIVER PUB
$
NORTH PATTAYA RD.
TEL 038-370614
This restaurant and nightclub is very popular with the local expatriate community. They have made this northern U.S.-style country and western spot near the Thai Garden Resort among the friendliest gathering places in town. The food includes Thai and Western dishes.
🍴 55 🅿 💳 All major cards

🍴 MOTTA MAHAL
$
323/26 SOI SAEN SAMRAN
SOUTH PATTAYA
TEL 038-429908
Pattaya has several standard Indian restaurants complete with exotic decor and sitar music on the stereo. The huge menu at the Motta Mahal runs the gamut from southern *thali* combinations to classic tandooris. Dishes tend to be mild but can be made more fiery on request.
🍴 35 🕐 Closed L daily 💳 All major cards

🍴 PIC KITCHEN
$
PATTAYA 2 RD. SOI 5
TEL 038-428374
This is a longtime favorite of many visitors, who come to enjoy superb Thai dishes in a romantic setting enhanced by jazz entertainment and classical dance several times a week. Dishes are prepared mild for foreign taste but can be spiced up on request.
🍴 65 🅿 💳 All major cards

🍴 RUEN THAI RESTAURANT
$$
485/3 SOI 2
SOUTH PATTAYA RD.
TEL 038-425911
The Ruen Thai is nicely set up amid a tropical garden, which could almost lead you to think you weren't in south Pattaya. Here they serve the usual Thai dishes (Western food is also available), though the main drawcard is classical dancing in the evenings.
🍴 400 💳 All major cards

🍴 THAI HOUSE
$
171 NORTH PATTAYA RD.
TEL 038-370579
This upscale Thai restaurant is one of the best in Pattaya, and classical Thai dance perfor-mances are given most nights starting around 8 p.m. A taxi is necessary to reach this isolated restaurant.
🍴 60 🅿 💳 All major cards

🍴 VIENTIANE
$
185 PATTAYA 2 RD.
TEL 038-411298
As the name implies, this restaurant serves Laotian and Issan dishes, along with a wide selection of Thai, Chinese, and Western standards. The atmosphere is somewhere between a rustic open-air café and a more formal restaurant.
🍴 50 💳 All major cards

🍴 YAMATO
$
219/51 SOI YAMATO
SOUTH PATTAYA
TEL 038-429685
This longtime favorite has been in place for so many years that locals now call its street Soi Yamato in its honor. An older establishment with rustic decor, it serves standard Japanese dishes.
🍴 35 🕐 Closed L daily 💳 All major cards

NORTHEAST THAILAND

KHON KAEN

🏨 SOFITEL RAJA ORCHID
$$
9/9 PRACHA SUMRAN RD.
TEL 043-322155
FAX 043-322150
This reasonably priced hotel is the best option in town. At 22 stories, the gleaming structure almost completely dominates Khon Kaen. Marble, potted flowers, and richly upholstered furniture characterize the lobby, which leads off to restaurants serving Thai, Chinese, Japanese, Western, and even Vietnamese cuisine. The hotel's biggest draw is the underground entertainment plaza, where cocktail lounges, nightclubs, and a German microbrewery attract local citizens. Rooms are immaculate and fitted with every possible gadget.
🛏 293 🅿 💳 All major cards

NAKHON RATCHASIMA (KHORAT)

🏨 ROYAL PRINCESS KHORAT
$
1/37 SURANARI RD.
TEL 044-256629
FAX 044-256601
Khorat has relatively new accommodations, one of which is this edifice located a few miles outside town but just a few minutes by taxi from the central market. Facilities are limited, but the Royal Princess has clean and brightly decorated rooms with television, minibars, and other modern conveniences.
🛏 188 🅿 💳 All major cards

🏨 SIMA THANI HOTEL
$
68 MITTRAPHAP RD.
TEL 044-213112
FAX 044-213121

Another 1990s addition to the Khorat hotel scene is this reasonably luxurious hotel also situated a few miles outside town. Although the public spaces and rooms have deteriorated somewhat, the hotel has decent restaurants and efficient staff with good English. The pool, health club, and nightclub make this the best choice in town.

144 P ⇄ S ⚓ ⛑ **All major cards**

NONG KHAI

MEKONG ROYAL
$
222 CHOMANEE RD.
TEL 042-420024
FAX 042-421280
Nong Khai is a sleepy town near the Friendship Bridge. While many guesthouses and budget hotels here have closed in recent years, this solitary semiluxurious hotel manages to stay in business. The client shortage has forced cutbacks in staff, but rooms remain in decent condition with all the modern facilities you would expect.

199 P ⇄ S ⚓ ⛑ **All major cards**

PHITSANULOK

PAILYN
$-$$
36 BOROMATRAILOKART RD.
TEL 055-252412
FAX 055-258185
One of the newer hotels, this is in a central location within walking distance of the riverside cafés. It has a coffee shop, a restaurant, a small convention center, and a nightclub that competes with the older venue at the Amarin Nakhon (see below). Rooms are in good condition, with basic decor, and the staff is the best in town.

134 P ⇄ S ⚓ **All major cards**

AMARIN NAKHON
$
3/1 CHAO PHRAYA RD.
TEL 055-219044
FAX 055-258945
This hotel is probably the best in town, but basic is the key word for all hotels in Phitsanulok. It is characterized by acceptable rooms, friendly staff, a popular coffee shop, and a nightclub that thumps along until the early hours.

146 P ⇄ S ⚓ **All major cards**

SUKHOTHAI

PAILYN SUKHOTHAI
$
1003 CHAROD VITHITHONG RD.
TEL 055-613310
FAX 055-613317
Most visitors find a budget hotel or guesthouse in old Sukhothai, but tour groups and upscale travelers sometimes select this large hotel 5 miles (8 km) east of town. It is an almost luxurious, if rather poorly planned, hotel, and it has several restaurants and a health club.

245 P ⇄ S ⚓ **All major cards**

CHIANG MAI

WESTIN CHIANGMAI
$$$$
318/1 CHIANG MAI–LAMPHUN RD.
TEL 053-275300
FAX 053-275299
Chiang Mai's largest and finest hotel provides the most comfortable rooms in town but suffers from an inconvenient location about 6 miles (10 km) south of the center. Acres of marble, European rather than Thai styling, and several upscale restaurants and boutiques give this hotel a decidedly intimidating feel, although the rooms compensate with space,

design, and sheer elegance.

526 + 12 suites P ⇄ S ⚓ ⛑ **All major cards**

REGENT RESORT CHIANG MAI
One of Thailand's most exclusive, stylish, and elegant resorts is magnificently situated about 12 miles (18 km) northwest of Chiang Mai, on a hillside overlooking rice fields, with soaring mountains in the distance. Regarded as without peer by many guests, this extraordinary resort has been fashioned in traditional northern Lanna style in its Pavilion Suites and private villas, of which a limited number are available to overnight guests. The levels of service speak volumes about the care and thought given to this resort. Many guests come solely for the world-class spa, while others enjoy any of the four nearby golf courses, or perhaps mountain-bike riding in the hills. If you can afford the tariff, this is one of the finest experiences in Thailand.

$$$$$
MAE RIM–SAMOENG OLD RD.
TEL 053-298181
FAX 053-298189
64 suites + 11 villas
🚕 Hotel taxi from Chiang Mai P S ⚓ ⛑ **All major cards**

AMARI RINCOME
$$$
1 NIMMANHAEMINDA RD.
TEL 053-221130
FAX 053-221915
This seven-story "garden hotel" is well maintained. It has a café and restaurant serving Thai and Western dishes, two pools, a tennis court, and a business center. Guest rooms are attractive and refurbished on a regular schedule, making this Chiang Mai's best-value hotel in the luxury category.

158 P ⇄ S ⚓ ⛑ **All major cards**

HOTELS & RESTAURANTS

🏨 AMITY GREEN HILLS CHIANG MAI
$$

24 SUPER HIGHWAY
TEL 053-220100
FAX 053-221602

This budget/mid-priced 14-story hotel is somewhat off the beaten track. Its attractive lobby is stuffed with local antiques and artifacts. Guest rooms are well maintained and provide fine views from the upper floors.

ⓘ 198 P 🔄 🔲 �.
📺 All major cards

🏨 CHIANG MAI ORCHID
$$

23 HUAY KAEW RD.
TEL 053-222099
FAX 053-221625

This modestly priced hotel, about 3 miles (5 km) from downtown Chiang Mai, is surprisingly stylish. There are three dining options: a café, a basic Chinese outlet, and a fancy French restaurant for a splurge. The hotel has a nightclub that hosts live bands. The guest rooms are clean and decorated in pastel shades.

ⓘ 267 P 🔄 🔲 �.
📺 All major cards

🏨 CHIANGMAI HILLS
$

18 HUAY KAEW RD.
TEL 053-210030
FAX 053-210035

An older hotel in the budget category that caters to large tour groups and local conventions. The public areas, Japanese café, and basic furnishings in the rooms should prove adequate to those on a budget.

ⓘ 249 P 🔄 🔲 �.
📺 All major cards

🏨 ROYAL PRINCESS CHIANG MAI
$

112 CHANG KLAN RD.
TEL 053-281033
FAX 053-281044

Conveniently located in the center of town, opposite the Night Market, this nine-story property is very good value and is popular year-round. The lobby decor and general ambience are basic but acceptable, and the hotel has three restaurants and a basement nightclub. Rooms are well maintained.

ⓘ 198 P 🔄 🔲 �.
📺 All major cards

SOMETHING SPECIAL

🍽 THE GALLERY

On the eastern bank of the Ping River, this combined art gallery and restaurant serves superb Thai food. The atmosphere is marvelous, especially in the early evening as the sun sets over the river and Doi Suthep. Romantic types will love the intimate alcoves and decks, which cling to the side of the river and provide a great deal of privacy.

$$

25 CHAROEN RAT RD.
TEL 053-248601

🔢 40 P All major cards

🍽 THE GOOD VIEW
$$

13 CHAROEN RAT RD.
TEL 053-241866

This restaurant is in a teak-wood mansion on the eastern bank of the river. It has a creative menu (specialties include *yum woon sen*, or jellied noodles, and *bo bria*, or spring rolls), a superb environment, and excellent views over the river. Arts, antiques, and home furnishings are also sold.

🔢 30 P All major cards

🍽 NANG NUAL SEAFOOD RESTAURANT
$$

27 KO KLANG RD.
TEL 053-281961

The largest restaurant in Chiang Mai, 5 miles (8 km) south of the city center, specializes in seafood and ostentatious decor at a wonderful location on the riverbank. Try the *pla raad prik* (fish grilled with chili).

🔢 240 P All major cards

🍽 OLD CHIANG MAI CULTURAL CENTER
$$

185 WULAI RD.
TEL 053-274093

The venerable cultural hall, south of town in a residential neighborhood, specializes in traditional *kun toke* (Northern-style) dinners. Food is served in a teakwood dining hall, and dance performances take place next door in a conventional amphitheater.

🔢 250 P Closed L daily All major cards

🍽 PICCOLA ROMA
$$

3/2 CHAROEN PRATHET RD.
TEL 053-271256

This is perhaps the best Italian restaurant in town, offering a wide choice of pastas, veal, and chicken dishes that are prepared by the resident owner/chef, who hails from northern Italy. Although the atmosphere

PRICES

HOTELS
An indication of the cost of a double room without breakfast is given by **$** signs.

$$$$$	Over $200
$$$$	$150–$200
$$$	$100–$150
$$	$50–$100
$	Under $50

RESTAURANTS
An indication of the cost of a three-course dinner without drinks is given by **$** signs.

$$$$$	Over $40
$$$$	$30–$40
$$$	$20–$30
$$	$10–$20
$	Under $10

is a little jaded, the food remains excellent.

🍴 40 🚭 🟦 All major cards

🍴 THE PUB
$$
88 HUAY KAEO RD.
TEL 053-211550
Decorated in an Olde English style, this establishment has been a focal point for the Chiang Mai expatriate community for over 20 years. The food emphasizes English and French cuisine, while the atmosphere shines with homey touches such as a roaring fire most evenings.

🍴 50 🅿 🚭 🟦 All major cards

🍴 THE RIVERSIDE BAR & RESTAURANT
Some of the most romantic restaurants in Chiang Mai are strung out along the east bank of the Ping River, between Nawarat and Ranca Bridges. The Riverside is one such restaurant, where virtually every table has a river view. It serves decent Thai and Western dishes (specialties include *yum woon sen*, or jellied noodles, and green chicken curry) but is especially recommended for its live entertainment, which starts about 9:30 p.m.

$$
9 CHAROEN RAT RD.
TEL 053-243239
🍴 65 🅿 🟦 No cards

🍴 WHOLE EARTH
$$
88 SRI DONCHAI RD.
TEL 053-282463
One of the oldest restaurants in town, this is also one of the most romantic, in a lovely teak house almost completely surrounded by gardens and lakes. The food is primarily Indian with an emphasis on vegetarian dishes, although a few seafood and meat items are included.

🍴 40 🚭 🟦 No cards

🍴 AROON RAI
$
45 KOTCHASAN RD.
TEL 053-276947
The atmosphere may be lacking, but this open-air café just south of Tha Phae Gate has been serving the finest Issan food in Chiang Mai for years. Among the regional specialties are pork curry, a spicy salsa called *nam prik*, sticky rice, fried bamboo shoots, and sausage stuffed with pork.

🍴 80 🟦 No cards

🍴 BACCO
$
158 THA PHAE RD.
TEL 053-251389
Italian dishes are prepared under the supervision of an Italian expatriate. Italian soccer matches are shown weekly on his television set, and the owner is always happy to make suggestions on dishes.

🍴 45 🟦 All major cards

🍴 BIERSTUBE
$
33 MOON MUANG RD.
TEL 053-278869
Although German food is the primary emphasis at this simple café in the center near Tha Phae Gate, it also prepares assorted Thai dishes. All are served by some of the friendliest waitresses in town.

🍴 30 🟦 No cards

🍴 DIAMOND RIVERSIDE HOTEL RESTAURANT
$
33 CHAROEN PRATHET RD.
TEL 053-270081
This is the most elegant place in town to enjoy a traditional *kun toke* (Northern-style) dinner followed by a short performance of Thai classical dance and theater. While more expensive than similar offerings at the **Old Chiang Mai Cultural Center** (see p. 372), the intimate setting ensures superior views, and the food is

a few notches above its rival.

🍴 80 🅿 🕐 Closed L daily 🚭 🟦 All major cards

🍴 GALAE
$
65 SUTHEP RD.
TEL 053-278655
Visitors with private transportation may enjoy a stop at this popular café, wonderfully situated a few miles west of town at the base of the road that leads up to Doi Suthep. Although the food is nothing special (dishes are Thai and Northern Thai—try the *kow pat nam*, or fried rice with spicy sausage), the views of the valley are superb.

🍴 45 🅿 🟦 No cards

🍴 GALARE FOOD COURT
$
NIGHT BAZAAR, CHANGKLAN RD.
TEL 053-272067
The Galare Food Court has an excellent range of inexpensive stalls serving up all different kinds of food from around Southeast Asia, India, and China. The lively atmosphere of the night bazaar is enhanced by the classical dancing and Northern Thai music, which are performed here every night free of charge.

🍴 200 🅿 🟦 No cards

🍴 J.J.'S
$
MONTRI HOTEL, MOON MUANG RD.
TEL 053-213088
This popular air-conditioned café near Tha Phae Gate attracts Thais, backpackers staying in the nearby guesthouses, and a fair number of tourists, who appreciate the comfortable modern surroundings along with well-prepared food. Specialties include a wide range of *jan deeyo* (single-plate) Thai dishes, along with Western baked goods such as sandwiches, rolls,

and pastries.

🏠 55 🅢 🅐 **All major cards**

CHIANG RAI

🏨 DUSIT ISLAND RESORT
$$–$$$
1129 KRAISORASIT RD.
TEL 053-715777
FAX 053-715801
This is a very impressive nine-story hotel just outside town on an island in the Mae Kok River. Visitors stay here for the immaculate marble-covered public areas, the three restaurants (including a wonderful rooftop option that serves Continental and Asian cuisines), and facilities that include tennis courts and an 18-hole golf course. Rooms are spacious; those on the upper floors have superb views over the mountains.
🛏 271 + 12 suites 🅿 🖿 🅢 🖾 🖽 🅐 **All major cards**

🏨 WIANG INN
$$
893 PHAHOLYOTHIN RD.
TEL 053-711543
FAX 053-711877
This basic mid-level hotel has been serving the needs of travelers for over 20 years. Although there is nothing fancy about the place, its central location and decent facilities make it the preferred choice for informed visitors.
🛏 258 🅿 🖿 🅢 🖾 🅐 **All major cards**

GOLDEN TRIANGLE

🏨 LE MERIDIEN BAAN BORAN RESORT
$$$–$$$$
CHIANG SAEN
TEL 053-784084
FAX 053-784090
One of the most unusual resorts in Northern Thailand, this luxurious place lies east of Chiang Saen, near the intersection of Thailand, Laos, and Myanmar. Remote, exclusive, and always struggling for

improved business, this wonderfully designed escape provides the perfect base to explore the region and retreat to sheer luxury each evening. Two restaurants and three levels of rooms make this an amazing destination in one of Thailand's remoter areas.
🛏 110 🅿 🖿 🅢 🖾 🖽 🅐 **All major cards**

MAE HONG SON

🏨 IMPERIAL TARA MAE HONG SON
$–$$
149 MU 8, MAIN HIGHWAY
TEL 053-611021
FAX 053-611252
Upscale tourists choose this semiluxurious hotel at the south end of town. Owned by one of the largest hotel chains, it provides excellent food and lodging at reasonable prices. Tropical design typifies the public areas, while Northern-Thai style carries through in the restaurant, which serves Thai, Chinese, and Western dishes. Rooms are simple and feature local materials such as bamboo and rattan.
🛏 104 🅿 🖿 🅢 🖾 🖽 🅐 **All major cards**

SOUTHERN THAILAND

HUA HIN & CHA-AM

🏨 CHIVA-SOM SPA & RESORT
$$$$$
73/4 PETCHKASEM RD.
HUA HIN
TEL 032-536536
FAX 032-511154
As with the rest of the world, Thailand has gone mad with "spa fever," and dedicated spa resorts are opening across the country. The Chiva-Som is widely considered the finest dedicated spa resort in Thailand. All the standard treatments are available with Asian-Thai twists, along with the requisite tranquil setting,

healthy meals, and cultural pursuits such as music. Guest rooms are available in the ocean-view building or in individual chalets surrounded by gardens and lakes.
🛏 295 rooms 🅿 🅢 🖾 🖽 🅐 **All major cards**

🏨 SOFITEL CENTRAL HUA HIN

Formerly the Railway Hotel, this grand old lady is one of the most historic hotels in Southeast Asia, with a legacy that rivals the Oriental in Bangkok and Raffles in Singapore. It was constructed in 1923 to host the royal family and other wealthy residents of Bangkok who fled the city and established Hua Hin as the original beach resort in Thailand. After years of neglect, the hotel was tastefully restored in 1986. The gardens are large and lovely, while the interior is decorated with oriental rugs, gleaming chandeliers, and polished marble floors. Royal Thai cuisine (using coconut cream, plenty of spices, and exotic ingredients such as shark's fin) is served in the acclaimed Salathai restaurant, while further refreshments are available in a beachside chalet and a café that resembles an old railway car. Rooms are superbly furnished with period accents. The history, setting, and refined service make this an outstanding resort.
$$$–$$$$
1 DAMNOEN KASEM RD.,
HUA HIN
TEL 032-512021
FAX 032-511014
🛏 218 + 38 villas 🅿 🖿 🅢 🖾 🖽 🅐 **All major cards**

🏨 DUSIT RESORT AND POLO CLUB
$$$
1349 PETCHKASEM RD.
CHA-AM
TEL 032-520009
FAX 032-520296
This exclusive resort is the

premium choice for the discriminating traveler. As the name implies, it is centered around the neighboring polo club, where visitors can indulge their love of the game and spend time in the various restaurants or multiplicity of cocktail lounges and bars. Those not inclined to riding horses while swatting at a ball can swim, play tennis, or enjoy golf. Rooms are available in four levels from standards to studio apartments.
🛈 302 🅿 ⇄ 🚭 🏊
🏋 🅰 All major cards

🏨 MELIA HUA HIN RESORT
$$$
33 NARESDAMRI RD., HUA HIN
TEL 032-512879
FAX 032-511135
The sleepy town of Hua Hin changed dramatically in the early 1990s with the construction of this 15-story hotel complex directly over the central part of the principal beach. Today, the Melia provides the most luxurious and conveniently placed accommodations around. Enjoy the extensive recreational facilities, and top-notch restaurants such as the Mediterranean Goya. Request a room facing the ocean.
🛈 295 + 10 suites 🅿 ⇄
🚭 🏊 🏋 🅰 All major cards

🏨 REGENT CHA-AM BEACH RESORT
$$$
849/21 REGENT CHA-AM BEACH
TEL 032-471480
FAX 032-471277
Set on a long stretch of white-sand beach, midway between Hua Hin and Cha-Am, this is the largest property in the region and a popular destination for families and groups. All possible forms of recreation are on offer, from volleyball and tennis to diving and sailing. There is a wide choice of restaurants and

bars. Rooms vary from tacky cubicles to deluxe chalets.
🛈 670 🅿 ⇄ 🚭 🏊
🏋 🅰 All major cards

🏨 ROYAL GARDEN RESORT
$$$
107/1 PETCHKASEM BEACH RD.
TEL 032-511811
FAX 032-512422
Three miles (5 km) north of Hua Hin, this popular resort is owned by one of Thailand's most respected chains and has excellent facilities, superb management, and wonderful rooms at reasonable prices. Restaurants include Thai, Italian, and even a Bavarian café. Facilities include a gym, children's playground, and golf on two nearby courses. Rooms are decorated with a tropical theme.
🛈 220 🅿 🚭 🏊 🏋
🅰 All major cards

🏨 ROYAL GARDEN VILLAGE
$$$
43/1 PHETKASEM BEACH RD.
TEL/FAX 032-520250
The more elegant sister to the Royal Garden Resort (see above), the Village creates its ambience with traditional Thai architecture, vast landscaped gardens filled with flowers and native shrubs, and an open-air Thai restaurant for evening repasts. Dining options also include a café facing the gardens and beach, and weekly barbecues by the pool. All the standard sports facilities are available. Rooms are elaborate but tastefully decorated.
🛈 162 🅿 🚭 🏊 🏋
🅰 All major cards

KO SAMUI

🏨 POPPIES SAMUI
$$$$$
28/1 MU 3, SOUTH CHAWENG BEACH
TEL 077-422419
FAX 077-422420
One of the most attractive

hotels, Poppies is an offshoot of the famed hotel on Kuta Beach in Bali. This tiny and immaculately designed escape is a delight, from the charming guest rooms to the tropical gardens. Fish ponds, Thai sculpture, and gurgling streams add to the tranquility. Amenities are limited to a small swimming pool, an open-air bar and lounge, and a regally decorated restaurant known for its Royal Thai cuisine. Guests are ensconced in luxurious cottages decorated with teak and silk.
🛈 24 🅿 🚭 🏊 🏋
🅰 All major cards

SOMETHING SPECIAL

🏨 ROYAL MERIDIEN BAAN TALING NGAM
The finest resort on Ko Samui is also one of the most elegant in Southeast Asia. More than just a pricey escape from the crowds, this oasis of tranquility transports you to another world. The resort is elevated on a mountainous outcrop that provides unforgettable views over the ocean, especially at sunset. Public rooms are sumptuously decorated, with good use of natural materials and open-air architecture designed to maximize the views in all directions. Along with a breezy dining venue and stylish cocktail lounge, the resort offers a bluff restaurant with Mediterranean fare, and a beachside café for seafood and Italian cuisine. All forms of water sports are available at the nearby beach. Rooms range from Deluxe Salas to Cliff Villas, resplendent with art and antiques.
$$$$$
295 MU 3, THALING NGAM
SOUTHWEST SAMUI
TEL 077-423019
FAX 077-423220
🛈 72 rooms 🅿 🚭 🏊
🏋 🅰 All major cards

SOMETHING SPECIAL

🏨 TONGSAI BAY COTTAGES & HOTEL

This fabulous resort between Chaweng and Bophut Beaches provides the best combination of luxury and location on the island, with friendly service thrown in. Tongsai is tucked away inside its own private cove with a beach, manicured gardens, and comfortable chalets arranged to provide views for all guests. The principal building is an open-air affair, with reception and lounges followed by the main restaurant. Below is an outstanding pool and beachside restaurant, where the atmosphere is relaxed and informal. Recreation is limited, although water sports can be arranged through the front desk. Individual chalets are in warm colors and set with rattan furniture.

$$$$$
84 MU 5, TONGSAI BAY
NORTHEAST SAMUI
TEL 077-425015
FAX 077-425462
🛈 72 units 🅿 🅢 🌊
📺 🃏 All major cards

🏨 SANTIBURI DUSIT RESORT

$$$$$
12/12 MU 1, MAENAM BAY
NORTH SAMUI
TEL 077-425031
FAX 077-425040

Santiburi is the second most exclusive property on Ko Samui, offering the widest range of water sports on the island. This is a highly polished and professional resort, well used to pampering its guests. The architecture lacks imagination and resembles a generic international style. That aside, this north shore escape boasts a fine Thai restaurant, as well as a Continental restaurant. Rooms are either in villas or suites, and adorned with silk, reproduction antiques, and

spacious baths. Service is impeccable, but the isolation may not suit all visitors.
🛈 73 🅿 🅢 🅢 🌊
📺 🃏 All major cards

🏨 AMARI PALM REEF RESORT

$$$$
14/3 MU 2, NORTH CHAWENG BEACH
TEL 077-422015
FAX 077-422394

This is the signature property of the major hotel chain. It has two sections: one next to the beach and the other across the road (be sure to request beachside accommodations). The resort is low-rise and done in Thai style, with a small lobby and several restaurants, including an informal Thai affair with an upstairs section where diners may sit on the floor. An open-air coffee shop and bar have wonderful views over the beach. Rooms vary from basic units without views to superior beachside villas.
🛈 104 🅿 🅢 🌊 📺
🃏 All major cards

🏨 CENTRAL SAMUI

$$$$
38/2 MU 3, CENTRAL CHAWENG BEACH
TEL 077-230500
FAX 077-422385

Visitors seeking luxury accommodations in the middle of the best beach on the island should head directly to this property on Chaweng Beach. The Central ensures a high level of comfort in an ideal location, tucked behind a formidable wall that blocks all street noise. A fortress of tranquility, it has vast manicured lawns and gardens, and a stunning beach. The building style is 19th-century British colonial, but Thai influence is seen in the dining outlets and in the attentive service. Dining options include an enormous main restaurant, a smaller Thai outlet, and a cocktail bar on the second floor with views over the

entire estate. Guest rooms are immaculate and range from standard outfits to more extravagant offerings.
🛈 208 🅿 🅢 🅢 🌊
📺 🃏 All major cards

🏨 BLUE LAGOON RESORT

$$$
99 MU 2, NORTH CHAWENG BEACH
TEL 077-422037
FAX 077-422401

Some of the best sand on Samui is found at the northern end of Chaweng just in front of this budget hotel. Motel-like buildings are set around manicured gardens and landscaped lawns that lead to the swimming pool and the beach. A rather ordinary restaurant serves Western and kow tom (rice soup) breakfasts and other Thai specialties, though most residents seem to prefer the cafés and pubs outside the hotel boundaries. Rooms are fairly large and adequately furnished. Some superior rooms face the beach, but most face the interior gardens and pool.
🛈 71 🅿 🅢 🌊 🃏 All major cards

IMPERIAL BOAT HOUSE
$$$
83 MU 5, CHOENG MON BEACH, NORTHEAST SAMUI
TEL 077-425041
FAX 077-425460
This unusual resort at the eastern end of Choeng Mon Beach is named after a collection of traditional fishing boats, which have been beached and converted into small chalets to complement the more usual guesthouses. Overall, the effect is rather odd. The regular section of the hotel comprises two wings behind the central lobby, while the converted boats are scattered along the path to the beach. At the time of writing the hotel was closed for renovation—call for details.
🛏 216 🚕 Taxi 🅿 🔄 🔲 🌊 🏥 🆑 All major cards

IMPERIAL SAMUI RESORT
$$$
86 MU 3, SOUTH CHAWENG BEACH
TEL 077-422020
FAX 077-422396
At the southern end of Chaweng, this Mediterranean-style resort has whitewashed walls, arched hallways, and roofs of glazed terra-cotta tiles. The location provides a degree of privacy, though rooms in the additional wing across the road lack ocean views or easy access to the pool. Facilities include two restaurants serving Thai and Western dishes, a saltwater and freshwater pool, limited shopping, and two bars. Guest rooms have tropical touches, with lots of bamboo.
🛏 155 🅿 🔄 🔲 🌊 🏥 🆑 All major cards

CORAL BAY RESORT
$$
YA NOI BAY
TEL 077-422223
FAX 077-422392
Two miles (3 km) north of Chaweng Bay, this unusual resort is in the middle of a coconut plantation. Curious rather than luxurious, it appeals to visitors wishing to retreat into the jungle. Facilities are basic but there's a rather moody lounge, a bar, a gift shop, and a restaurant serving reasonably priced Thai, Chinese, and Western fare. The best place to relax is on the elevated terrace. The beach can vary through the year from muddy shoals to sandy islets spotted with coral reefs. Guests are housed in individual bungalows on stilts with thatched roofs, which are well maintained but basic.
🛏 42 🅿 🔲 🌊 🏥 All major cards

THE FAR SOUTH

PHUKET

SOMETHING SPECIAL

🛏 🍴 AMANPURI
The Aman hotel chain is world famous, and this is where it all started. Set in tropical splendor over a near-private beach, this jewel has welcomed Hollywood stars and heads of state since its opening over 20 years ago. The resort has aged well. Amanpuri melds the best traditional architecture of Bali, Myanmar, and Thailand. Public areas are open-air, with lofty ceilings, while lounges and restaurants are constructed to maximize the views. Both restaurants—one Thai, one Italian—are first-class experiences. You can even cruise on the hotel's private yacht. Guest rooms are filled with antiques and interesting artifacts.
$$$$$
PANSEA BEACH
TEL 076-324333
FAX 076-324100
🛏 70 🅿 🔲 🌊 🏥 All major cards

BANYAN TREE
🍴 LAGUNA PHUKET
$$$$$
BANG TAO BAY
TEL 076-324374
FAX 076-324375
This is the new hyper-elegant kid on the block, Bolstered by accolades from around the world, it has made a serious challenge to the **Amanpuri** (see left). The resort is based on Zen minimalism, and lakes provide calm. It offers all forms of spa therapy, from herbal saunas to mud baths. Facilities include tennis courts, an 18-hole golf-course, a cocktail lounge, and several restaurants, including an Asian seafood option. Individual chalets are widely scattered, and golf carts shuttle guests.
🛏 110 🅿 🔲 🌊 🏥 🆑 All major cards

DUSIT LAGUNA RESORT
$$$$$
BANG TAO BAY
TEL 076-324320
FAX 076-324174
This medium-size resort is the principal hotel at the immense planned community at Bang Tao Bay. The surrounding landscaped hills form part of the resort's golf course. Everything is on grand scale: an enormous lobby, spacious restaurants, long corridors, big rooms and bathrooms, and acres of carpet and marble. The beach is only a short walk away, and recreational facilities include tennis courts and a giant chessboard. Six restaurants offer everything from Italian to an American grill. Rooms are in a modern style.
🛏 226 + 12 suites 🅿 🔄 🔲 🌊 🏥 🆑 All major cards

MERIDIEN PHUKET
$$$$$
RELAX BAY
TEL 076-340480
FAX 076-341583
This property is set on its

own private cove and is ideal for families, with a good range of activities for kids. The wonderful beach is reserved for hotel guests, and two enormous swimming pools cover almost the entire area between the hotel towers. Restaurant choices include Thai, Japanese, Italian, Continental, and French. Recreational facilities are outstanding and include all the standards plus a children's club, a dive shop, and a yacht that sponsors cruises out to nearby islands. Rooms are ordinary but functional.

ⓘ 477 🅿 🔄 📶 🏊
📺 All major cards

SOMETHING SPECIAL

🏨 ROYAL MERIDIEN PHUKET YACHT CLUB

This resort at the southwest corner of the island is perched on the side of a cliff, with fabulous views to Cape Promthep. The only sign of civilization is the eerie sight of a wind turbine. Most of the resort appears buried in the jungle, with only the balconies of the rooms and chalets peering out. Diners can linger in the open-air Mediterranean restaurant for breakfast or in the Regatta, which serves Italian fare. Rooms are enormous, adorned with beautiful wood, extravagant furniture, and bathrooms so large you might need a map.

$$$$$
NAI HARN BEACH
TEL 076-381156
FAX 076-381164
ⓘ 110 + 10 suites 🅿 🔄
📶 🏊 📺 All major cards

🏨 PHUKET CHEDI
$$$$$
PANSEA BEACH
TEL 076-324017
FAX 076-324252
The Phuket Chedi creates a close imitation of the Amanpuri (see p. 377), with its breezy and elegant

buildings, Continental restaurant, and outstanding sea views. Leisure facilities include a billiards room, two bars, a well-stocked library, and water sports (the core activity here). Guest cottages are elegant and comfortable, and the service is great.

ⓘ 110 🅿 🔄 📶 🏊 📺
🏊 All major cards

🏨 SHERATON GRANDE LAGUNA BEACH
$$$$$
BANG TAO BAY
TEL 076-324101
FAX 076-324108
This is Phuket's largest resort. Among the seven restaurants are a Thai outlet by the beach, a traditional steak and lobster grill, and a multileveled Chinese affair. You can visit the tennis courts, health center, entertainment room, or spa, or stroll down to the beach for water sports. Although the exterior of this hotel leaves much to be desired, the guest rooms are beautiful.

ⓘ 325 + 18 suites 🅿 🔄
🔄 📶 📺 All major cards

🏨 BOATHOUSE
$$$$
KATA BEACH
TEL 076-330557
FAX 076-330561
This old favorite has received rave reviews since it first opened its doors in the early 1980s. Much of its fame rests on its open-air restaurant, which attracts large numbers of diners who drop by for cocktails and seafood at sunset. The property is small, and the years have not been entirely kind: Renovation has been haphazard, and the two swimming pools have fallen into disuse. The restaurant is still a winner, however, and the chief reason to stay at this once great hotel.

ⓘ 36 🅿 🔄 📶 📺
🏊 All major cards

🏨 KATA THANI HOTEL & BEACH RESORT
$$$$
KATA NOI BEACH
TEL 076-330124
FAX 076-330426
Beach lovers will be thrilled with the quality of the sand here, and all can enjoy the spacious landscaped lawns and gardens. Several restaurants provide fine food at reasonable prices, including an American grill and a Thai restaurant with views of the garden and beach. The resort has a wide variety of accommodations, so check before accepting rooms across the road or facing the gardens rather than the beach.

ⓘ 465 🅿 🔄 🔄 📶
📺 🏊 All major cards

🏨 PEARL VILLAGE
$$$$
NAI YANG BEACH
TEL 076-327006
FAX 076-327338
To get completely off the beaten track, head to the northwest of the island and Nai Yang Beach. The beach itself is mediocre, but the near complete lack of human beings makes this an idyllic setting for those so inclined. Dining options range from a Thai restaurant to a simple thatched café. The resort scores points with its horses, which can be rented for rides along the beach. Pearl Village also has a center for sailing, diving, fishing, and excursions on its yacht. Select between rooms in the central complex or an individual bungalow.

ⓘ 226 🅿 🔄 📶 📺
🏊 All major cards

🏨 PHUKET ARCADIA HOTEL & RESORT
$$$$
KARON BEACH
TEL 076-396433
FAX 076-396136
Few hotels on Karon Beach come larger than this collection of circular towers. Popular with tour groups,

the hotel does an excellent job for its size. Restaurants range from noodle shops to refined Italian emporiums. Recreational needs are met by three swimming pools, squash and tennis courts, miniature golf, and a water sports center. Rooms are well maintained and surprisingly large.

🛈 680 ℗ ⇄ 🅢 ⚊ 🖤 🅢 All major cards

⊞ PHUKET CABANA RESORT
$$$$
PATONG BEACH
TEL 076-340138
FAX 076-340178
This is one of the few hotels located directly on Patong Beach, and convenience is the chief advantage to staying here. The hotel is rather old, and some rooms are in need of renovation. There's a simple restaurant and an attractive pool facing the ocean. Rooms should be inspected prior to acceptance as quality varies.

🛈 80 ℗ 🅢 ⚊ 🖤 🅢 All major cards

⊞ AMARI CORAL BEACH RESORT
$$$–$$$$
PATONG BEACH
TEL 076-340106
FAX 076-340115
This elegant yet informal hotel is a white stucco affair situated on the rocks at the southern end of Patong Beach. The cantilevered bungalows and resort buildings are reminiscent of the Greek islands, with panoramic views from most rooms. Restaurants include Thai and Italian outlets, but the café at the hotel pier is the place to gather at sunset. Recreation is amply provided by two pools, tennis courts, and a variety of water sports. Rooms are gaily decorated in Mediterranean colors.

🛈 202 + 8 suites ℗ 🅢 🖤 🅢 All major cards

⊞ CAPE PANWA
$$$
CAPE PANWA
TEL 076-391123
FAX 076-391177
This romantic hotel on the isolated southeast corner of the island is highly regarded: Leonardo DiCaprio stayed here during filming of *The Beach*. The hotel has a Mediterranean feel, with lovely chalets that tumble from the main building down an incline toward the ocean. Restaurants include Italian and French options, and a Thai restaurant in an old building known as the Panwa House—not only one of the most romantic restaurants on the island but also recommended for its fine cuisine. A nightclub occupies a converted lighthouse. Rooms are lovely and well maintained.

🛈 219 + 12 suites ℗ ⇄ 🅢 ⚊ 🖤 🅢 All major cards

⊞ KAMALA BAY TERRACE RESORT
$$$
KAMALA BAY
TEL 076-270801
FAX 076-270832
The resort is a collection of hillside cottages at the southern end of this slightly scruffy bay. Public areas are clean and attractive, and the breezy open-air café is an excellent place for breakfast. Guest rooms are constructed up the side of a mountain, and only the young and fit should take any room above mid-mountain level. Rooms are in great shape, and views over the bay are the norm.

🛈 122 ℗ 🅢 ⚊ 🖤 🅢 All major cards

⊞ KAMALA BEACH ESTATE
$$$
KAMALA BAY
TEL 076-270756
FAX 076-324115
Offering one of the best deals in the neighborhood, these private apartments are rented out by the day, week, or month. Guests not only get a decent bedroom but also a fully equipped kitchen and spacious living room.

🛈 29 ℗ 🅢 ⚊ 🖤 🅢 All major cards

⊞ MARINA COTTAGE
$$$
KARON BEACH
TEL 076-330625
FAX 076-330516
Set on top of the hill that separates Karon and Kata Beaches is this wonderful gem, an alluring collection of cottages set around spacious lawns and gardens above a private beach. The prices are steep considering the simplicity of the facilities and rooms, but otherwise this operation is a winner. A pair of casual restaurants provides sustenance, and there is a cocktail lounge with fine views over the ocean. Cottages are well spaced around the tropical gardens and priced according to view.

🛈 104 ℗ 🅢 ⚊ 🖤 🅢 All major cards

⊞ METROPOLE PHUKET
$$
1 SOI SURIN, MONTRI RD.
PHUKET TOWN
TEL 076-215050
FAX 076-215990
This hotel is truly luxurious and represents the best-value accommodation on Phuket. It is an international affair with marble, sculpture, and silk in the public rooms. Guest rooms are modern in style with a nod to Thai tastes in the artwork and carved wooden furniture. Few Western visitors stay here, but those in the know make this their home.

🛈 250 ℗ ⇄ 🅢 ⚊ 🖤 🅢 All major cards

⊞ ROYAL PARK BEACH RESORT
$$
BANG TAO BAY

HOTELS & RESTAURANTS

TEL 076-324021
FAX 076-324243
Travelers on a budget who wish to avoid the more touristy parts of Phuket can venture to the northwest side of the island, where this hotel is just south of the immense **Dusit Laguna Resort** (see p. 377). It resembles a simple American motel, with modest facilities and reasonable prices to match. Dining choices include a Thai restaurant, but most visitors wait for the nightly barbecue on the beach. Rooms are only average, but they are well maintained.
🏨 115 🅿 🔲 🔳 🔳
🔳 All major cards

🍴 BAAN RIM PA
$$
PATONG–KAMALA BEACH RD.
PATONG BEACH
TEL 076-340789
This upscale Thai restaurant is perched on the rocky cliff at the north end of Patong Beach. Dishes are imaginative if somewhat tame for the diner seeking adventure, but the views from the veranda are nothing short of amazing.
🔳 145 🔳 All major cards

🍴 OLD SIAM
$$
THAVORN PALM BEACH RESORT, KARON BEACH
TEL 076-396090
Perhaps the loveliest and most romantic dinner-dance show venue on the island, Old Siam has Thai dance and drama performances on Wednesday and Sunday evenings. You can dine *kun toke* (Northern Thai) style inside an air-conditioned pavilion, or outside on a second-floor terrace for fine views over the beach.
🔳 120 🔳 🔳 All major cards

🍴 SUANG SAWAN
$$
PATONG–KAMALA BEACH RD.
PATONG BEACH
TEL 076-344175
This upscale restaurant at the

northern end of Patong Beach is in a cliffside location with outstanding bay views. It is open daily from 11 a.m. until midnight; reservations are recommended at sunset.
🔳 45 🔳 🔳 All major cards

🍴 ROCK HARD CAFÉ
$
82/51 SOI BANGLA, PATONG BEACH
TEL 076-340409
Several years ago the popular Doolie's Diner was converted into this chain restaurant, which has no relationship to the similarly named U.S. operation. Diners can sit inside in air-conditioned comfort or opt for the veranda. The American and Mexican fare includes ribs, roast chicken, imported steaks, and burgers.
🔳 80 🕐 Closed L daily 🔳
🔳 All major cards

KO PHI PHI

🏨 PALM BEACH TRAVELODGE RESORT
$$$
54 MU 8, CAPE LAEM THONG
TEL 076-214654
FAX 076-215090
This resort is on a private beach on the northeastern tip of the island, so special transportation must be arranged with the hotel in advance. The themes are simplicity, traditional design, and plentiful water sports. Individual cottages are arranged around the central hall, which has an open-air lobby, a cozy cocktail lounge, and a restaurant that serves up varied dishes and sponsors weekend barbecues. Guest cottages are earthy but air-conditioned.
🏨 80 🔳 Boat 🔳 🔳
🔳 All major cards

🏨 P.P. INTERNATIONAL RESORT
$$
CAPE LAEM THONG

TEL 076-214272
FAX 076-214301
While there's not much that is "international" here, the central building has a cocktail lounge, a decent restaurant serving Thai seafood and Western dishes, and an entertainment room with pool and video games. A rental shop on the beach rents out snorkeling gear. Guests stay in individual cottages with teak floors.
🏨 70 units 🔳 Boat 🔳
🔳 🔳 All major cards

KRABI

SOMETHING SPECIAL

🏨 DUSIT RAYAVADEE RESORT
The prime real estate at the southern tip of the cape is almost completely taken up with the ultra-luxurious Dusit Rayavadee. This resort is set in a stunning natural environment of limestone pinnacles, azure sea, and perfect white sand. Among the facilities are a restaurant specializing in Royal Thai cuisine and a cozy lounge with evening entertainment. Guests are housed in chic two-story chalets. Service is impeccable, and most guests find it difficult to even consider leaving.
$$$$$
67 MU 5, SAI THAI–SUSAN HOY RD., PHRA NANG
TEL 075-620740
FAX 075-620630
🏨 100 🔳 Boat 🔳 🔳
🔳 🔳 All major cards

SHOPPING

Shopping is one of the delights of Thailand, and there is a staggering range of items from which to select: fine jewelry set with sparkling rubies and sapphires, carved Buddhist effigies, clothing made from Thai silk and fine cottons, silverwork bowls and utensils, brass cutlery, reproductions of classic European furniture, and, of course, all those carved elephants. You can also add to this list temptations such as authentic and "instant" antiques, precious art, delicate ceramics, leather coats, and 24-hour suits.

BARGAINING

Prices for most of these goods are surprisingly reasonable considering the time and craftsmanship that goes into their manufacture. Of course, bargaining is expected in many small shops and from individual artisans, especially in the tourist zones of Bangkok, Chiang Mai, and Phuket. The general rule is to offer half the price quoted by the merchant and then slowly move toward a middle price that reflects a discount of 25–33 percent. You might expect a discount of at least 50 percent from street merchants and tourist shops selling souvenirs. Prices are generally fixed in larger shopping centers.

CAUTIONS

Shoppers should exercise a degree of caution as rules are different here in Thailand. Generally, refunds are rarely given and once a product is purchased there will be no exchanges. Receipts are often provided upon request, but receipts do not guarantee exchange or refund privileges, so examine all items carefully before you hand over your cash or credit card. Deposits are nonrefundable.

You should also be wary of touts, who are paid generous commissions for bringing customers into stores. There is absolutely no reason to allow anyone to take you around town on a shopping expedition, no matter how great the promised savings—especially if it's a "special one-day jewelry sale."

Thailand produces very convincing counterfeits such as Rolex watches and Nike running shoes. Fake clothing items may not break the bank, but be aware that fake gems are rampant in Thailand, and only professionals should spend serious money on gems or jewelry here. Most of the so-called antiques sold in the country are also clever fakes. Note that authentic antiques require a special government license for legal export.

SHOPPING CENTERS

The best introduction to shopping in Thailand is to visit one of the huge shopping centers in Bangkok, most of which are located near the Siam Square–Ploenchit–Rama 1 neighborhood. By spending a few hours exploring stores such as Central City and Zen, you will soon understand the range of products and price ranges. Prices are fixed and clearly marked on all items here.

Most large department stores also have a floor with handicrafts and other items geared towards tourists. While you can probably find better quality and prices in a more authentic setting, this is a good way to gauge general price ranges for handicrafts. The best deals in the large shopping centers are found in the clothing departments, where prices are surprisingly reasonable.

Modern shopping centers are usually air-conditioned and provide a welcome relief from the heat and humidity. Food courts and small entertainment venues are often located on the top floor or in the basement.

MARKETS

Old-fashioned traditional markets still dominate the smaller towns. They may appear dark and dank, and smell like a medieval carnival, but they compensate for this with all the local color and vibrancy of authentic Thai life. Most towns have one central market that is open daily until around 4 p.m. and includes an indoor section for meats and other valuable food items, and an outdoor section for fruit and vegetables. If your stomach is not prepared for the often strange and odiferous world of the interior market, stick to the outdoor sections where you can watch the merchants in action.

SPECIALTIES

Thailand produces a large variety of handicrafts that are unique to the country, and certain products are best purchased near their area of origin. For example, Thai silk has traditionally been produced in the Northeast or Issan region, and those searching for shell or coconut items will be best rewarded in the South, around Phuket and Ko Samui. Ayutthaya has long been known for its sculpted stonework, which is sold in outdoor markets near the historic buildings of the ancient capital, while the ceramic industry is closely associated with the Sawankalok ceramic tradition near Sukhothai.

The greatest concentration of handicrafts is found in and around Chiang Mai. Wood-carving, silverwork, silk weaving, and furniture are produced in hundreds of small shops and factories around the city. In fact, if you are going to Thailand chiefly to shop, save most of your time and money for the bargains of Chiang Mai.

WHAT TO BUY

Products produced in Thailand will be cheaper than in the United States, while imported items such as Japanese electronics will be less expensive back home, as import duties in Thailand remain high. The most popular craft items are silk, precious stones, "instant" antiques, carved wooden images, hill-tribe handicrafts, bronzeware cutlery, nielloware, celadon pottery, and lacquerware.

Thai silk is perhaps the most famous national product, and can be 100 percent silk or interwoven with synthetic fibers to improve wearability and reduce the naturally rough texture of pure, raw silk. Beware of fake silk made entirely from rayon or of a composite of synthetics and cotton.

Most antiques sold in the country are actually modern reproductions cleverly made to appear old and sometimes sold under false pretenses. Unless you are an expert, it's best to assume that all antiques are modern fakes and negotiate prices accordingly.

It is illegal to export any authentic antique and also to export any image of the Buddha, unless you are Buddhist yourself. Most images that appear to be Buddhas are actually figures of kneeling monks or female deities, often modeled after Burmese prototypes.

PAYMENT

Major credit cards are accepted in all department stores and most shops that cater to visitors. Traveler's checks are closely inspected—Thailand has a long-running problem with stolen traveler's checks—but are usually accepted by larger merchants anxious to make a sale. Small shops and those that conduct little business with foreigners will most likely only accept Thai currency. Shops in tourist zones may also take U.S. dollars as payment.

VALUE ADDED TAX

Value added tax (VAT), set at 7 percent, is collected on all purchases in Thailand. Special arrangements allow travelers to obtain a VAT refund when all legal conditions are fulfilled. Visitors who depart Thailand by air from an international airport and have not been in the country more than 180 days in a calendar year qualify for a refund. VAT refunds apply only to goods taken out of the country within 60 days from the date of purchase, and all goods must be purchased from stores that display the "VAT Refund for Tourists" sticker. You must spend at least 2,000BHT in a single day, and the total amount of goods purchased must be not less than 5,000BHT. VAT refund forms are filled out in the store and then presented at the VAT refund counter in the departure lounge of the airport. Gems do not qualify for a VAT refund.

BANGKOK

Bangkok's major shopping centers are chiefly located in the Siam Square–Ploenchit–Rama 1 district, and along Sukhumvit Road between Sois 10 and 24. Small tourist shops are abundant along Silom Road and Sukhumvit Road near the inner *sois* from Soi 4 to Soi 12 (note that *soi* means "alley" and *thanon* "road").

While the range of products is fairly uniform across the city, Chinatown is distinctive for gold chains and photographic equipment, Silom Road for antiques and expensive clothing, Sukhumvit for made-to-order suits and leather products, Pratunam for inexpensive clothes and shoes, and Banglamphu for tribal handicrafts and silverwork. Computers, software, CD-ROMs, and MP3 discs are best purchased at Panthip Plaza.

SHOPPING CENTERS
CENTRAL BANGKOK
The World Trade Center
Rama 1 at Ratchadamri Rd., tel 02-255-9400. This is the largest shopping center in Bangkok, with six floors of shops, restaurants, grocery stores, Internet cafés, and an ice-skating rink, all anchored by the mid-priced **Zen Central** at one end and the upscale **Isetan** at the other. It's a great place to wander in air-conditioned comfort.

Mahboonkrong (MBK) Center Rama 1 at Phaya Thai Rd., tel 02-217-9119. An older but nevertheless impressive shopping center with less expensive and less exclusive offerings, just across the road from the World Trade Center. Popular with teenagers and budget shoppers, the immense eight-level complex has restaurants and cafés on the ground floor, several popular jazz nightclubs upstairs in the back, six cinemas, and hundreds of small shops selling everything from trinkets to designer jewelry.
Siam Square Rama 1 at Phaya Thai Rd. The oldest shopping center in Bangkok, constructed in an open-air style in the 1960s and now filled with inexpensive stationary stores, hardware shops, and other utilitarian outlets. The complex is also home to the Novotel Siam Square (see p. 361), with a Hard Rock Café in the back, and dozens of small restaurants.
Gaysorn Plaza Phloen Chit at Ratchadamri Rd., tel 02-656-1149. A small, upscale complex with pricey boutiques and quality handicraft shops on the second floor. Planet Hollywood (see p. 366) and the handicraft emporium Narayana Phand (see p. 383) complete the scene.
Siam Center Rama 1 Rd., tel 02-658-1000. A reasonably priced shopping center popular with local teenagers and well stocked with trendy clothing shops and other merchandise for the young.
Amarin Plaza Phloen Chit at Ratchadamri Rd., tel 02-207-0222. Another upscale shopping center for designer fashion, with some very slick restaurants. The primary anchor is the Japanese department store **Sogo**, while the most distinctive element is the extravagant Romanesque exterior architecture.
Peninsula Plaza Ratchadamri, just south of Phloen Chit Rd., tel 02-253-9762. Somewhat off the beaten track, but excellent for antique shops, boutiques, and a large Asia Books outlet.

Central Chidlom Phloen Chit at Chidlom Rd., tel 02-655-7777. Chidlom is the largest shopping chain in Thailand, and this is their newest branch, which specializes in moderately priced clothing and household goods. There's also an extensive collection of Thai handicrafts at lower prices than in most comparable stores.
Panthip Plaza Petchaburi Rd., near the Amari Watergate hotel (see p. 359), tel 02-254-9797. A few blocks east of the shopping centers listed above, this towering complex is known as the computer center of the country. Always jammed, it not only sells computers and accessories but also bootleg copies of CD-ROMs and MP3 discs.

SUKHUMVIT ROAD
Ploenchit Center Sukhumvit Soi 2, tel 02-656-8600. A fairly small yet attractive and well-stocked shopping center, beside the J.W. Marriott hotel (see p. 361). Moderately priced Asian restaurants occupy the second floor, and clothing sales are held regularly in the basement.
The Emporium Sukhumvit Soi 24, tel 02-664-8000. One of the newest shopping centers in the neighborhood, aimed squarely at the money crowd with its designer-name shops and pricey cafés in a monolithic building set with tons of marble and glass.

SILOM ROAD
Central Department Store Silom, near Pramuan Rd., tel 02-233-6930. The oldest shopping center in this neighborhood lacks trendy charm but offers reasonably priced clothing, household items, and other basics. On the upper floor is a selection of local handicrafts.
Oriental Place Oriental Ln., tel 02-266-0186. Linked with the Oriental hotel (see p. 358), this upscale emporium has top-drawer clothing boutiques and exclusive antiques. The building is also striking, with a handsome facade and elegant interiors.
Silom Village Silom, near Pramuan Rd., tel 02-234-4448. A

small shopping complex with a good selection of shops catering almost exclusively to visitors.

STREET MARKETS
Chatuchat Weekend Market Off Paholyothin Rd., tel 02-272-4631. Thailand's largest flea market takes place every weekend in the eastern part of town and is now reachable in record time with the Skytrain. It spreads over 35 acres (14 ha) and is loosely organized according to the type of goods on sale. It's a baffling wonderland of stalls and shops, with everything from antiques and fine clothing to old magazines and pure junk. For a quick tour, explore the side of the market along Sois 1–4, where you find amulets and religious articles, handicrafts and antiques, textiles both old and new, souvenirs, stamps and coins, and ethnic crafts from the hill tribes. Chatuchak also has outdoor cafés, a post office and small tourist information center, and several banks.
Pratunam Market Petchaburi and Ratchaprarop Rds. Just two blocks west of the World Trade Center is Thailand's largest clothing emporium, a confusing but fascinating rabbit warren of tiny shops selling all types of clothing at bargain basement prices. The quality may leave something to desire, but the range of goods and authentic atmosphere of the market make this a great experience.
Pak Khlong Market Memorial Bridge at the Chao Phraya river. A huge vegetable-and-fruit market inside an old warehouse, where hundreds of merchants sell to thousands of daily shoppers. The smell can be overwhelming, but the color and cacophony are thrilling.
Sampeng Lane Chinatown. This narrow, crowded alley in Chinatown near the Chao Phraya, is just a crazy place, with great atmosphere, hordes of people, and great bargains in clothing and household goods.

OTHER OUTLETS

ANTIQUES
River City Shopping Complex Sri Phaya Rd., tel 02-237-0077. Thailand's largest and most famous collection of antique stores spreads over several floors, alongside less expensive shops for imitation antiques. Antiques auctions are held monthly in this gargantuan building, next door to the Royal Orchid Sheraton Hotel (see p. 362).
Ma Peng Seng 942 Rama IV Rd., tel 02-234-1285. A highly respected antiques dealer with top-quality items—at prices to match.
Elephant House 67/12 Soi Pra Phinit, tel 02-286-2780. An old antique shop in an odd location off Sathorn Tai Road in the Silom district, known for its decorative artwork and carved wooden artifacts, including genuine Burmese antiques and modern reproductions.
Rasi Sayam Sukhumvit Soi 23, tel 02-286-5592. One of many small, intriguing shops that generally sell "instant" antiques, with a scattering of authentic items thrown in for good measure. This particular shop offers higher quality than most.

HANDICRAFTS
Narayana Phand 295/2 Ratchaprarop Rd., tel 02-252-4670. A privately owned handicraft center under the patronage of the royal family. A high proportion of its proceeds go directly to the artisans, often impoverished hill-tribe people. The place is huge and stocks every handicraft sold in Thailand, at fixed and reasonable prices.
Chitralada Another handicraft center that enjoys royal support and pledges to distribute most profits back to the artisans, often handicapped Thais, rather than middlemen. Chitralada has shops at the Oriental Plaza, Grand Palace, Vimanmek, Thaniya Plaza, Amari Watergate Hotel, and Marriott Royal Garden Riverside Hotel.

SILK

Jim Thompson Silk 9 Surawong Rd., tel 02-234-4900. The most famous name in silk has outlets on Surawong Road near Rama IV Road, in the Oriental hotel (see p. 358), in Isetan at the World Trade Center (see p. 382), and at the Grand Hyatt Erawan hotel (see p. 360). Quality is the highest in the country, with prices to match.
Shinawatra Silk Thailand's second most famous silk merchant has shops on South Sathorn Road in the Silom district and at Sukhumvit Soi 23, tel 02-234-4900.
Kanitha 768 Silom Rd., tel 02-252-7761. A small but highly respected interior-design boutique, with top-quality silks and stylish modern furnishings.
Design Thai 304 Silom Rd., tel 02-235-1553. Another small interior-design boutique with superb silks and contemporary furnishings.

CHIANG MAI

Chiang Mai has the greatest array of handicrafts in the country. Most of the shops are just east of town along the road leading to the village of San Kamphaeng. The sheer number of shops and factories along this route precludes detailed descriptions, but among the more famous and respected outlets are Jolie Femme Silk, Thai Shop, Chiang Mai Silver, Iyara Art, Borisoothi Antiques, Shinawatra Thai Silk, Nakorn Ping Leather, Chiang Mai Treasure, Arts and Crafts, the umbrella village of Borsang, San Kamphaeng Kilns, and another Shinawatra Silk Factory just before Highway 1006 splits into two directions.

SHOPPING CENTERS

Kaed Sua Kaew (KSK) Huay Kaew Rd., tel 053-224444. The largest modern, air-conditioned shopping center in town, with five floors of shops, fast-food outlets, and several cinemas.
Tantrapan An older but serviceable shopping center with branches on Tha Phae Road, at the airport, and near Chang Puak Gate. Prices tend to be lower than at KSK.

OTHER OUTLETS

HILL-TRIBE HANDICRAFTS

Hill-tribe crafts are best purchased from the following nonprofit organizations, which return most of the funds they make to the craftsperson rather than it going to the shop owner or middleman.
Hill Tribes Product Foundation 21/17 Suthep Rd., near Wat Suan Dok, tel 053-277743.
Thai Tribal Crafts 208 Bumrungrat Rd., near McCormick Hospital, tel 053-241043.

ANTIQUES

Antiques Corner Chiang Mai Night Bazaar, Chang Klan Rd., 2nd floor. A group of antique shops tucked away on the second floor of the shopping complex beside the Chiang Inn. They include Yonok Treasure, The Lost Heavens, Oriental Spirit, Chilli Antiques & Arts, Lanna Antiques, and Pusaka.
Chiang Saen Art Souvenirs 68–70 Rat Chiang Saen Rd., tel 053-273176. Antiques and modern reproductions in bronze, stone, silver, and wood, with a special emphasis on Buddhist amulets.

CERAMICS

Mengrai Kilns 79/2 Arak Rd. Soi Samlarm 6, tel 053-272063. An outstanding range, including their famous celadons fashioned after prototypes discovered at Sawankalok near Sukhothai. Their retail shop is conveniently located in the southwest corner of the historic walled town.
Ban Phor Liang Muen 36 Phra Pok Klao Rd., tel 053-278187. An unusual ceramic and terra-cotta factory set around a lovely old teak house and expansive gardens, producing kitschy but fun items for the casual collector. Also situated in the southwest corner of old Chiang Mai.

SILVERWORK

Silverwork was first produced here in small shops along Wualai Road, on the southern edge of town. The city sprawl has since completely enveloped the silversmiths.
Siam Silverware 5 Wualai Rd., tel 053-274736. For over 50 years this shop has been producing some of the best silverwork in Thailand, still superior to that in the shops east of town.
Sipsong Panna Nantawan Arcade, 95/19 Nimanhemin Rd., tel 053-216096. Another established favorite with an excellent reputation, now in this arts and crafts shopping arcade.

TEXTILES

Naenna Textile Studio 138 Soi Chang Kian, tel 053-226042. Quality textiles designed by the owner, Patricia Cheesman Naenna. She is an expert on Thai textiles and the author of several books on the subject.
The Loom 27 Ratchamankha Rd., tel 053-278892. Another quality store with fabrics from all regions of Thailand, plus samples imported from Cambodia, Laos, and Myanmar—all displayed in a lovely old teak house a few blocks south of Tha Phae Gate.
Duangjitt House Nantawan Arcade, 95/10 Nimanhemin Rd., tel 053-215167. Both antiques and fine textiles are sold in this long-running shop, which also maintains an outlet on the third floor of the Chiang Inn Plaza on Chang Klan Road.

ENTERTAINMENT & ACTIVITIES

Bars and nightclubs in the major urban areas are a familiar scene, but Thailand also has a number of cultural venues where visitors can learn about the traditional performance arts of dance and drama. For an authentic experience, you may find it more rewarding to attend any of the annual festivals described below. Details of the main sporting activities—water sports and golf—are also listed below.

PERFORMING ARTS

Bangkok has the only formal performing halls in the country. In addition, some restaurants sponsor dinner-dance performances almost every night.

National Theater Chao Fa Rd., tel 02-224-1342. Bangkok's original cultural hall puts on lavish dance spectacles several times yearly, plus weekly shows on Sunday afternoons.

Thailand Cultural Centre Ratchadphisek Rd., tel 02-247-0028. This all-purpose hall sponsors events from classical music to traditional Thai dramas.

Chalern Krung Royal Theatre 66 Charoen Krung Rd., tel 02-221-6239. Thailand's newest venue for performing arts, including the *khon* and *lakhon*, is this renovated cinema just four blocks from the Grand Palace.

Erawan Hotel Shrine Phloen Chit at Ratchadamri Rd. Free outdoor dance performances can be seen daily at this famous shrine on the grounds of the Grand Hyatt Erawan hotel (see p. 360).

MAJOR FESTIVALS

Thailand has many festivals; the following highlights often include a spectacular parade, followed by evening performances of classical dance and drama.

January

Don Chedi Memorial Fair Suphanburi. Week-long festival; celebrates the defeat of the Burmese by Prince Naresuan. *(Late Jan.)*

Nakhon Phanom Prathat Phanom Festival Nakhon Phanom. A week-long fair held at the most honored stupa in the Northeast. *(Late Jan.)*

King Mengrai Festival Chiang Rai. Northern festival to honor King Mengrai, founder of the Lanna Kingdom, with parade and sound-and-light show. *(Late Jan.)*

February

Makha Puja Nationwide. Important Buddhist festival with candlelight processions around major temples. *(Feb. full moon)*

Chiang Mai Flower Festival Chiang Mai. The northern city honors its chief product with processions, floats, and beauty contests. *(Early Feb.)*

Chainat Giant Straw Birds Chainat. A southern event that features giant models of birds constructed with dried rice stalks. *(Early Feb.)*

Chinese New Year Nationwide. Asia's most important festival for the Chinese community is best observed in predominantly Chinese towns such as Nakhon Sawan, a few hours north of Bangkok. *(Late Jan.–mid-Feb.)*

March

Wat Phra Buddhaphat Fair Saraburi. Thousands of pilgrims flood this small town to honor a giant imprint of the foot of Buddha. *(Early March)*

Singing Dove Festival Yala. Southern festival with bird displays and bird-singing contests. *(Mid-March)*

Thao Suranari Fair Nakhon Ratchasima. The female military hero is honored for her spirited resistance against Lao forces during a siege from Vientiane. *(Late March)*

April

Pattaya Festival Pattaya. Major week-long festival at Thailand's original beach resort, three hours from the capital, with both cultural and hedonistic offerings. *(Early April)*

Songkran Nationwide. The Thai New Year is also known as the "water festival," when everyone is drenched by friends, family, and strangers—a welcome respite from the heat. *(Mid-April)*

Si Satchanalai Ordinations Si Satchanalai. Dozens of young monks are ordained into the Buddhist priesthood after a very colorful and photogenic parade. *(Late April)*

May

Visaka Puja Nationwide. A major Buddhist holiday that commemorates the birth, death, and enlightenment of the Buddha with candlelight processions around the temples. *(Early May)*

Royal Ploughing Ceremony Bangkok. Hindu ceremony held annually at Sanam Luang to ensure good fortune for the nation's farmers. *(Early May)*

Rocket Festival Northeast Thailand. Rockets are fired into the air to bring rain, a specialty of the Northeast and at its most spectacular in the town of Yasothan. *(Mid-May)*

July

Khao Phansa Nationwide. A popular day for young men to enter the Buddhist priesthood at the beginning of the "rains retreat." *(Mid-July)*

Candle Festival Ubon Ratchathani. Major parade with over 100 lavishly decorated floats, dance performances, traditional Issan music, and other cultural shows. *(Mid-July)*

Asanha Puja Nationwide. Buddha's first sermon is celebrated in temples throughout Thailand. *(July full moon)*

September

Phichit Boat Races Phichit. Long-tail boat races are held around the country at the height of the rainy season. The most famous venues are Nan, Phimai, Nakhon Phanom, and Phichit. *(Early Sept.)*

Narathiwat Fair Narathiwat. A week-long Muslim fair with boat races, singing-dove competitions, and demonstrations of traditional martial arts. *(Late Sept.)*

October
Phuket Vegetarian Festival Phuket Town. Major Chinese festival with a parade, Chinese cultural performances, and men who pierce their body with needles, knives, and sharpened steel blades. *(Late Sept.–early Oct.)*
Sakhon Nakhon Wax Candle Festival Sakhon Nakhon. The end of Buddhist Lent and the rains retreat is marked with boat races and an elaborate parade of floats, giant candles, and beauty queens. *(Mid-Oct.)*
Ok Phansa Nationwide. End of the three-month Lenten season, when Buddhists present new robes to monks. *(Mid–late Oct.)*

November
Loy Krathong Nationwide. Delightful festival with day-long parades, beauty contests, and evening water events to honor the ancient water spirit of Mae Kong Ka. *(Mid-Nov.)*
Wat Saket Fair Bangkok. The city's largest temple fair, with folk dance and drama, modern entertainment, and a candlelight procession around the Golden Mount of Wat Saket. *(Mid-Nov.)*
Surin Elephant Roundup Surin. Thailand's most famous animal and national symbol is honored with staged elephant hunts, rodeos, and elephant polo to the amusement of thousands of visitors. *(Late Nov.)*
River Kwai Historical Week Kanchanaburi. A week-long festival to remember the events of World War II, with exhibitions, memorial services, and a sound-and-light show over the famous bridge. *(Late Nov.)*

December
King's Birthday Bangkok. King Bhumibol Adulyadej is honored with a parade down Rachadamoen Klang Avenue. *(Dec. 5)*

Chiang Mai Winter Fair Chiang Mai. Major cool-season festival with cultural activities, beauty contests, and a grand parade. *(Late Dec.)*

ACTIVITIES

As Thailand opens up more and more to tourist demands, so too do the options for tourist activities increase. Around Pattaya, Phuket, and the other popular islands, the range of water sports is usually as large as at any developed coastal resort in the world. Activities include all forms of watercraft, paragliding, and, for snorkeling and diving enthusiasts, some of the best underwater viewing that nature has to offer.

Rockclimbing has also taken off in recent years, especially in Krabi, where the limestone formations of the coast and islands provide steep walls and overhangs to give even the more experienced climbers a challenge worth scaling. For full details, contact the local tourist office in Krabi (see p. 338).

If you are heading north to Chiang Mai, Chiang Rai, or Mae Hong Son, you will find plenty of opportunities to get out into the mountains and away from the busy atmosphere of the cities and popular seaside resorts. There are several options to help you decide just how you'd like to get away from it all.

Wherever you are in Thailand, packages for every activity available locally can be organized direct through your guesthouse or hotel tour desk—simply tell them what you want to do, and they'll set it up for you. Shopfront travel agents are found in large numbers in all tourist centers and offer similar services. In general, their tours are well organized and excellent value. Never accept tour offers from street touts or from *tuk tuk* or taxi drivers.

SCUBA DIVING
Scuba diving used to be limited to a handful of dive shops in

Pattaya, but today there are professional dive facilities in many locations, from Phuket in the South to Ko Si Chang near the Cambodian border. With some 1,355 miles (2,170 km) of coastline on the Gulf of Thailand and the Andaman Sea, Thailand offers a wide variety of dive possibilities among some of the world's richest marine fauna.

This is a tropical country with warm waters, and a wet suit is not required to explore the exceptionally clear waters on either side of the Thai peninsula. The relatively high water temperature also encourages the growth of marine life and sustains coral beds, which have largely escaped the environmental destruction so common elsewhere in Southeast Asia. From major dive destinations such as Phuket, you can do quick offshore dives, conduct full-day dive excursions to nearby islands and reefs, or join live-aboard dive boats for longer expeditions to dive destinations such as the Surin and Similan Islands.

Thailand offers something for every level of diver. Novices can earn PADI or NAUI certification from accredited dive schools located at all major dive destinations, while more seasoned divers can explore wrecks and coral canyons or sign up for advance classes to further their dive education.

Dive seasons
Ideal dive conditions exist throughout the year at various beaches and islands, depending on their location in relation to the annual monsoons. Phuket and other islands on the west side of the peninsula are subject to storms and rainfall during the summer monsoons from June to November, but generally enjoy dry and clear weather for the remainder of the year. Across the peninsula are the dive destinations of Ko Samui, Ko Tao, and Chumphon, which are dry and clear from June to November, but receive modest rainfall during the milder

northeast monsoons from November to May. So to escape the rain, just move to the other side of the peninsula. East coast dive spots such as Pattaya and Ko Si Chang rarely witness monsoons, and so diving is possible here all year.

Even at the peak of the rainy season in Phuket, there will be periods of sunshine when divers can make day excursions to nearby islands and reefs to enjoy calm seas and decent visibility. Dive operators survey weather conditions daily and make decisions based on longer forecasts.

Southwest Thailand dive destinations

Phuket is the dive capital of Thailand in terms of number of dive companies and variety of dive opportunities. Pattaya continues to sell more individual dives owing to its location—it is just two hours from Bangkok. Serious divers tend to head directly to Phuket or perhaps across the peninsula to Ko Samui, from where they continue north up to Ko Tao.

Phuket Thailand's largest island has dive opportunities ranging from easy day trips to longer multi-day excursions to the Similan and Surin Islands. Several dive companies also offer escorted dive trips beyond the Surin Islands into Myanmar waters around the so-called Burmese Banks. Phuket has over 20 dive operators, who rent equipment and provide professional instruction for a variety of PADI certifications.

Ko Phi Phi and Phangnga Bay Islands south of Phuket are often limestone karsts that drop sharply into the sea and provide unique underwater vistas for divers. Ko Phi Phi Don and Ko Bida Nok are the favored dive sites, along with the islands in Phangnga Bay, which are generally reached with a dive boat from Phuket.

Similan Islands This nine-island archipelago is one of the premier dive sites in Southeast Asia for its varied bottom topography and rich sea life. As the Similans are about four hours from Phuket, they are best visited with a live-aboard vessel.

Surin Islands North of the Similans and 94 miles (150 km) from Phuket is the final dive archipelago before you enter Myanmar waters. The Surin Islands are chiefly known for their superb corals, inhabited by sailfish and large pelagics.

Ko Lanta and Trang South of Phuket and Krabi, several islands and beach towns with promising dive sites are just making their impact on the scuba scene. Dive companies on Phuket can help with details.

Southeast Thailand dive destinations

Ko Samui & Ko Tao
Samui may be the second most popular resort in the country, but divers head four hours north to the tiny island of Ko Tao, which has the best diving in the Gulf of Thailand. Dive shops on Samui organize multi-day dive excursions.

Chumphon Bustling Chumphon marks the point where corals and fringe reefs make their appearance in Thailand, and is popular with local divers and more intrepid visitors.

East Coast dive destinations

Pattaya Thailand's oldest beach resort continues to draw thousands of divers annually to its offshore islands, which may not be as spectacular as those in the Andaman Sea or near Samui, but are conveniently reached from Bangkok in just a few hours. Pattaya has about a dozen dive shops.

Ko Si Chang The marine national park near the Cambodian border includes many small islands with superb corals, and calm dive conditions prevail throughout most of the year. Skin- and scuba-diving shops are located at White Beach.

OTHER WATER SPORTS

Sea kayaking A relatively new addition to the adventure travel scene, sea kayaking uses hardshell or inflatable kayaks, mostly around Phuket and Phangnga Bay. Several companies in Phuket now offer kayak excursions, from short day trips to multi-day voyages through the islands and partially submerged caves around Phangnga Bay. Prices and levels of experience vary widely between companies, so compare carefully before selecting an outfitter.

Windsurfing Wind conditions and equipment rentals are best at Pattaya and Jomtien Beach, which has been the country's windsurfing capital for many years. Breezes blow strongest during the northeast monsoon season from February to May. Phuket gets decent wind during the summer months.

Surfing This activity has never taken off in Thailand owing to the lack of dependable waves on the beaches and islands. Surf boards can be rented in Pattaya and Phuket, but most surfers prefer to head straight for the Philippines or Indonesia.

GOLF

Thailand has become a popular golfing destination over the last few years, and there are now approximately 260 golf courses in the kingdom, many to international standards. Thailand has played host to many international tournaments, and golf's image has also received a boost with the rise to fame of Tiger Woods (born to a Thai mother, he was awarded honorary citizenship despite never having lived in Thailand). While golf still remains the domain of the more wealthy, the green fees and equipment rental in Thailand are among the cheapest in the world. The most popular areas for golfing tours include Kanchanaburi, Hua Hin, and Phuket. Many golfing operators are now established in the kingdom, and the range of options to suit your preference and time frame are unlimited—though be sure to avoid the rainy seasons.

TREKKING

There are dozens of tour companies in Chiang Mai, Chiang Rai, and Mae Hong Son districts that offer trekking (hiking) tours in the mountains of the North. A typical trek lasts two to three days (though shorter or longer treks can be arranged) and will include overnight accommodation at a hill-tribe village, where you can experience local traditions and food and drink. You may or may not get to sleep on a soft mattress, though after a tough day's trek you probably won't notice the hardness of a bamboo floor anyway. Trekking tours can vary widely in terms of standard, so be sure to deal with a licenced operator as recommended by your hotel or by the local TAT office.

ELEPHANT SAFARIS

Symbolically, the elephant is Thailand's national animal. Elephants play a large part in traditional culture and are also a popular drawcard at shows and festivals. While the introduction of modern technology has seen a decline in the use of elephants for logging, some operations do still use elephants that have been trained at specialized camps (parng chang). There are several such camps around the northern provinces that can be visited, where you can see elephants and their riders (mahouts) showing off their skills and versatility, after which you can take an elephant ride yourself. Most camps or trekking companies will gladly arrange for longer safaris, or you may wish to include an elephant ride with a trekking tour (see above).

CYCLING/MOUNTAIN-BIKING TOURS

With a good bike, a fair degree of fitness, and a recommended guide there is a lot of fun to be had out there. If you just want to get away from Chiang Mai city on a day trip then you can always pick up a bike and a map of Doi Suthep, and rent a pickup

(songthaew) to take you to the summit, just 30 minutes' drive from the center. From here you can spend the day exploring the trails, waterfalls, and hill-tribe villages dotted around the mountain as you wind your way back down to Chiang Mai.

RAFTING

There are two types of rafting on offer, both available in the North. Whitewater rafting is centered on Pai, in Mae Hong Son, and is available from the onset of the wet season (July–Feb.). The more placid form—bamboo rafting—can be found along the Thai–Laos border (on the Mekong River), departing from Chiang Rai (on the Mae Kok), or west of Bangkok in Kanchanaburi province. All-inclusive tours lasting up to three days (depending on location and time of year) can be arranged with tour companies, which provide large "house rafts" for you to sleep on. Again, for reasons of safety it is recommended you ask at the tourist office for a reputable company.

ADVENTURE SPORTS

Thailand provides a wide range of adventure sports, though the base centers for these may often be located far apart.

Bungee jumping

Tarzan's Jungle Bungee Jump in the village of Kata, Phuket, is set in beautiful natural surroundings. The jump is a 160-foot (50 m) drop from a man-made tower suspended above a lake that used to be an open gem mine.

Sea canoeing

This activity has become very popular around the limestone outcrops of Phuket and Krabi, and many operators are now in the business of leading tourists into the hawngs, or rooms, found around the coastline. Paddling tours also venture into mangrove channels where

you can get a closer look at estuarine wildlife. Sea Canoe Thailand, tel 076-212172, the original operator of these eco-tours and winner of many tourism awards, is still regarded as the best.

Microlighting

You can go up in a microlight at Chiang Mai, on the road to Doi Saket. The immediate scenery here is nothing spectacular, but if you are looking for a bird's-eye view of water buffaloes working the rice paddies and of Thai village life then this is the best way to do it. Rates start at 1,200BHT for 15 minutes, although this should be negotiable. Call Discovery Adventure International Co. Ltd., tel 053-868460.

LANGUAGE GUIDE

Thais really appreciate it when visitors to their country make an effort to speak their language. Learning even just a few basic greetings and how to say "thank you" usually makes a big difference to how locals react to you, and using a bit of Thai when bargaining in the market often helps to bring the price down. As you travel farther off the tourist path you will find it more necessary to speak Thai, though most younger Thais have a rudimentary knowledge of basic English.

For men, the pronoun *pom* is used for "I," and the word *krup* is added at the end of a sentence to make the phrase politer, or to show respect. For women, the first person pronoun *dichan* is used, while the word *kar* is added in the place of *krup*. For example, man: *Khun sabai dee mai krup?* (You are fine, no?); woman: *Dichan sabai dee, kawb khun kar* (I'm fine, thank you). (Note: Adults generally don't use the terms *krup* or *kar* when speaking to children.)

Above all else, if words fail you and there seems to be a breakdown in communication, smile and try to laugh about it—a common Thai response.

Note that the Thai words/phrases below have been transliterated to give as clear a guide to pronounciation as possible. Words may be spelled differently on signs, menus, maps, etc.

GENERAL CONVERSATION
Hello *sawadee krap* (used by men), *sawadee ka* (used by women)
How are you? *pen yangai?*
I'm fine *sa bai dee*
May I have... *kor...*
Thank you *kawp khun*
Excuse me *khaw thawt*
What is your name *khun cheu arrai?*
My name is *pom cheu* (spoken by male)
My name is *dichan cheu* (spoken by female)
I come from *phom maa jaak* (spoken by male)
I come from *dichan maa jaak* (spoken by female)
America/Canada/Australia *Ameriga/Kanada/ Australia*
I'm just traveling about *pai teeyo*
I had/am having a great time *sanuk dee*

LANGUAGE DIFFICULTIES
I speak little Thai *puut pasa Thai nitnoy*
I don't understand *mai kow jai*
Do you understand? *kow jai mai?*
It doesn't matter *mai pen rai*

GENERAL QUESTIONS & ANSWERS
yes *chai*
no *mai*
okay *oh-kay*
don't want *mai ao*
don't have *mai mee*

sorry *kor towt*
I want *pom tong karn* (spoken by male)
I want *dichan tong karn* (spoken by female)
I don't know *mai loo*
no good *mai dee*
What's this called in Thai? *nee pasa Thai riak waa arrai?*
where is? *yoo tee nai?*
when? *meua rai?*
how much? *tai rai?*

DIRECTIONS
I'm going to *pai*
Where can I get a map? *seu pantee dai tee nai?*
How far is it to? *pai taorai?*

TRANSPORTATION
air-conditioned bus *rot tooa*
ordinary bus *rot tammada*
bus station *sattani rot may*
minibus *rot dtoo*
ticket *tua*
timetable *talang waylar*
railway station *sattani rot fai*
train *rot fai*
express *duan*
sleeper *rot nawn*
seat *tee nung*
airport *sanam bin*
airline office *tee tam ngan saai kam bin*
plane *krueng bin*
boat *rua*
boat dock *tah rua*
longtail boat *rua harng yao*
ferry *rua doy sarn*
ferry pier *tha*
taxi *teksi*
bicycle *rot jakrayan*
motorcycle *rot motorsai*

GEOGRAPHY & PLACES
tourist office *samnakngan karn tong tiao*
embassy *sathan toot*
post office *praisinee*
bank *tanakarn*
market *talaat*
museum *pipitapun*
police station *sattani tamruat*
beach *hart*
island *ko*
archipelago *mu ko*
village *ban*

Temple architecture
wat temple complex
bot rectangular meeting hall
chedi bell-shaped structure housing Buddha relic
wihan secondary meeting hall
prang decoratively carved tower
prasat sanctuary tower
sala open-sided building used as community hall

HOTELS & RESTAURANTS
hotel *rong raem*
guesthouse *guest how*
men's toilet *hong naam chai*
women's toilet *hong naam ying*
restaurant *raan aahaan*
café *raan garfay*
night market *talaat toh rung*
Please bring me the menu *kor doo menu*
May I have? *kor?*
The food is delicious *ahan arroi*
The bill please *kor check bin*

SHOPPING
How much is this? *nee taorai?*
Do you have…? *mee…mai?*
too big *yai kern pai*
too small *lek kern pai*
too expensive *paeng pai*

EMERGENCIES
I need a doctor *tong haa mor*
I need a dentist *tong haa mor fun*
please help *chuay duay*
emergency *chook chern*
hospital *rong payabarn*

TIME
What is the time? *gee mong laew?*
today *wan nee*
yesterday *meaua wan nee*
tomorrow *prung nee*
morning *ton chao*
afternoon *bai*
evening *yen*

DAYS OF THE WEEK
Sunday *wan aathit*
Monday *wan jun*
Tuesday *wan ungkarn*
Wednesday *wan poot*
Thursday *wan pryhart*
Friday *wan sook*
Saturday *wan sao*

NUMBERS
1 *neung*
2 *song*
3 *saam*
4 *sii*
5 *haa*
6 *hok*
7 *jet*
8 *bpat*
9 *gow*
10 *sip*
15 *sip-haa*
20 *yeesip*
25 *yeesip-haa*
100 *neung loi*
1,000 *neung pun*

MENU READER

GLOSSARY OF POPULAR THAI DISHES
(See also pp. 20–23)
kow pud fried rice
pad-thai Thai-style fried noodles
pad see yoo Chinese-style noodles in soya sauce
tom yum gung sour and spicy prawn soup
kow soi gai spicy northern chicken curry
panang red Thai curry
tom kar gai sour and spicy chicken
yum woon sen jellied noodles with sour sauce
kwe-teeyo noodles in soup
som tan papaya salad (an Issan dish)
kun toke classic meal of the North

GENERAL FOOD TERMS
to eat *kin*
to drink *duem*
salt *gleua*
sugar *narm tan*
egg *kai*
bread *kanom pung*
liquid, as in curry or soup *gaeng*
dry, without soup *haeng*
spicy, pungent, peppery *pet*
not hot *mai pet*

MEATS & SEAFOOD
chicken *gai*
spiced ground beef *larb*
meatball *luke chin neaua*
pork *mu*
spicy sausages *nam*
beef *neaa*
duck *pet*
fish *pla*
crab *pu*
shellfish *hoi*
prawn *gung*
dried fish *pla hang*

FRUITS
banana *kluay*
coconut *maprow*
durian *toorian*
guava *farlung*
jackfruit *kanoon*
lime *manao*
mango *mamuang*
mangosteen *mangkut*
papaya *malakor*
pineapple *sap-parot*
rambutan *ngaw*

DRINKS
drinking water *naam deum*
purified bottled water; *naam deum kuat*
milk *nom*
tea *naam cha*